CONTENTS

VOLUME 14
ART AND LITERATURE

CONTENTS

THE PENGUIN FREUD LIBRARY
VOLUME 14

•

ART AND LITERATURE

JENSEN'S *GRADIVA*,
LEONARDO DA VINCI
AND OTHER WORKS

Sigmund Freud

•

*Translated from the German
under the general editorship of James Strachey*

*The present volume
edited by Albert Dickson*

PENGUIN BOOKS

PENGUIN BOOKS

Published by the Penguin Group
Penguin Books Ltd, 27 Wrights Lane, London W8 5TZ, England
Penguin Putnam Inc., 375 Hudson Street, New York, New York 10014, USA
Penguin Books Australia Ltd, Ringwood, Victoria, Australia
Penguin Books Canada Ltd, 10 Alcorn Avenue, Toronto, Ontario, Canada M4V 3B2
Penguin Books India (P) Ltd, 11, Community Centre, Panchsheel Park, New Delhi – 110 017, India
Penguin Books (NZ) Ltd, Private Bag 102902, NSMC, Auckland, New Zealand
Penguin Books (South Africa) (Pty) Ltd, 5 Watkins Street, Denver Ext 4, Johannesburg 2094, South Africa

Penguin Books Ltd, Registered Offices: Harmondsworth, Middlesex, England

Art and Literature:
Jensen's 'Gradiva',
Leonardo da Vinci
and other works

Present English translations first published in *The Standard Edition of the Complete
Psychological Works of Sigmund Freud* by the Hogarth Press and the Institute of
Psycho-Analysis, London, as follows:

Delusions and Dreams in Jensen's 'Gradiva', 'Creative Writers and Day-Dreaming',
Volume IX (1959); 'Psychopathic Characters on the Stage', Volume VII (1953);
Leonardo da Vinci and a Memory of his Childhood, Volume IX (1957); 'The Theme of
the Three Caskets', Volume XII (1958); 'The Moses of Michaelangelo', 'Postscript
to "The Moses of Michaelangelo"', Volume XIII (1955); 'On Transience', 'Some
Character-Types Met with in Psychoanalytic Work', Volume XIV (1957); 'A
Childhood Recollection from *Dichtung und Wahrheit*', 'The "Uncanny"', Volume
XVII (1955); 'A Seventeenth-Century Demonological Neurosis', Volume XIX (1961);
'Humour', 'Dostoevsky and Parricide', 'The Goethe Prize', Volume XXI (1961).

'Sigmund Freud: A Sketch of His Life and Ideas' first published in *Two Short Accounts
of Psycho-Analysis* in Pelican Books 1962

This collection, *Art and Literature*, first published in Pelican Books 1985
Reprinted in Penguin Books 1990
7

Printed and bound in Great Britain by Antony Rowe Ltd.,
Chippenham, Wiltshire
Filmset in Monophoto Bembo

INTRODUCTION TO THE PENGUIN FREUD LIBRARY

The Penguin Freud Library (formerly *The Pelican Freud Library*) is intended to meet the needs of the general reader by providing all Freud's major writings in translation together with an appropriate linking commentary. It is the first time that such an edition has been produced in paperback in the English language. It does not supplant *The Standard Edition of the Complete Psychological Works of Sigmund Freud*, translated from the German under the general editorship of James Strachey in collaboration with Anna Freud, assisted by Alix Strachey and Alan Tyson, editorial assistant Angela Richards (Hogarth Press, 24 volumes, 1953–74). The *Standard Edition* remains the fullest and most authoritative collection published in any language. It does, however, provide a large enough selection to meet the requirements of all but the most specialist reader – in particular it aims to cater for students of sociology, anthropology, criminology, medicine, aesthetics and education, all of them fields in which Freud's ideas have established their relevance.

The texts are reprinted unabridged, with corrections, from the *Standard Edition*. The editorial commentary – introductions, footnotes, internal cross-references, bibliographies and indexes – is also based upon the *Standard Edition*, but it has been abridged and where necessary adapted to suit the less specialized scope and purposes of the *Penguin Freud Library*. Some corrections have been made and some new material added.

Selection of Material

This is not a complete edition of Freud's psychological works – still less of his works as a whole, which included important

7

contributions to neurology and neuropathology dating from the early part of his professional life. Of the psychological writings, virtually all the major works have been included. The arrangement is by subject-matter, so that the main contributions to any particular theme will be found in one volume. Within each volume the works are, for the main part, in chronological sequence. The aim has been to cover the whole field of Freud's observations and his theory of psychoanalysis: that is to say, in the first place, the structure and dynamics of human mental activity; secondly, psychopathology and the mechanism of mental disorder; and thirdly, the application of psychoanalytic theory to wider spheres than the disorders of individuals which Freud originally, and indeed for the greater part of his life, investigated – to the psychology of groups, to social institutions and to religion, art and literature.

In his 'Sigmund Freud: A Sketch of his Life and Ideas' (p. 11 ff. below), James Strachey includes an account of Freud's discoveries as well as defining his principal theories and tracing their development.

Writings excluded from the Edition

The works that have been excluded are: (1) The neurological writings and most of those very early works from the period before the idea of psychoanalysis had taken form. (2) Writings on the actual technique of treatment. These were written specifically for practitioners of psychoanalysis and for analysts in training and their interest is correspondingly specialized. Freud never in fact produced a complete text on psychoanalytic treatment and the papers on technique only deal with selected points of difficulty or theoretical interest. (3) Writings which cover the same ground as other major works which have been included; for example, since the *Library* includes the *Introductory Lectures on Psychoanalysis* and the *New Lectures*, it was decided to leave out several of the shorter expository works in which Freud surveys the whole subject. Similarly, because the *Interpretation of Dreams* is included, the shorter writings on this topic have been omitted. (4) Freud's private correspondence, much of which has now been published in translation.[1] This is not to imply that such letters are without interest or importance though they have not yet received full critical treatment. (5) The numerous short writings such as reviews of books, prefaces to other authors' works, obituary notices and little *pièces d'occasion* – all of which lose interest to a large extent when separated from the books or occasions to which they refer and which would often demand long editorial explanations to make them comprehensible.

All of these excluded writings (with the exception of the works on neurology and the private letters) can be found in the *Standard Edition*.

Editorial Commentary

The bibliographical information, included at the beginning of the Editor's Note or Introduction to each work, gives the title of the German (or other) original, the date and place of its first publication and the position, where applicable, of the work in Freud's *Gesammelte Werke*, the most complete edition at present available of the works in German (published by S. Fischer Verlag, Frankfurt am Main). Details of the first translation of each work into English are also included, together with the *Standard Edition* reference. Other editions are listed only if they contain significant changes. (Full details of all German editions published in Freud's lifetime and of all English editions prior to the *Standard Edition* are included in the *Standard Edition*.)

The date of original publication of each work has been added to the half-title page, with the date of composition included in square brackets wherever it is different from the former date.

Further background information is given in introductory notes and in footnotes to the text. Apart from dealing with the time and circumstances of composition, these notes aim

1. [See the list, p. 23 *n*. below, and the details in the Bibliography, p. 473 ff.]

to make it possible to follow the inception and development of important psychoanalytic concepts by means of systematic cross-references. Most of these references are to other works included in the *Penguin Freud Library*. A secondary purpose is to date additions and alterations made by Freud in successive revisions of the text and in certain cases to provide the earlier versions. No attempt has been made to do this as comprehensively as in the *Standard Edition*, but variants are given whenever they indicate a definite change of view. Square brackets are used throughout to distinguish editorial additions from Freud's text and his own footnotes.

It will be clear from this account that an overwhelming debt is due to the late James Strachey, the general editor and chief translator of the *Standard Edition*. He indeed was mainly responsible for the idea of a *Pelican Freud Library*, and for the original plan of contents. Miss Anna Freud and Mrs Alix Strachey, both now deceased, gave advice of the greatest value. The late Mr Ernst Freud and the Publications Committee of the Institute of Psycho-Analysis also helped in the preparations for this edition.

ANGELA RICHARDS

SIGMUND FREUD

A SKETCH OF HIS LIFE AND IDEAS

SIGMUND FREUD was born on 6 May 1856 in Freiberg, a small town in Moravia, which was at that time a part of Austria-Hungary. In an external sense the eighty-three years of his life were on the whole uneventful and call for no lengthy history.

He came of a middle-class Jewish family and was the eldest child of his father's second wife. His position in the family was a little unusual, for there were already two grown-up sons by his father's first wife. These were more than twenty years older than he was and one of them was already married, with a little boy; so that Freud was in fact born an uncle. This nephew played at least as important a part in his very earliest years as his own younger brothers and sisters, of whom seven were born after him.

His father was a wool-merchant and soon after Freud's birth found himself in increasing commercial difficulties. He therefore decided, when Freud was just three years old, to leave Freiberg, and a year later the whole family settled in Vienna, with the exception of the two elder half-brothers and their children, who established themselves instead in Manchester. At more than one stage in his life Freud played with the idea of joining them in England, but nothing was to come of this for nearly eighty years.

In Vienna during the whole of Freud's childhood the family lived in the most straitened conditions; but it is much to his father's credit that he gave invariable priority to the charge of Freud's education, for the boy was obviously intelligent and was a hard worker as well. The result was that he won a place in the 'Gymnasium' at the early age of nine, and for the last six of the eight years he spent at the school he was regularly top of his class. When at the age of seventeen he passed out of school his career was still undecided; his education so far had been of the most general kind, and, though he seemed in any case destined for the University, several faculties lay open to him.

Freud insisted more than once that at no time in his life did he feel 'any particular predilection for the career of a doctor. I was moved, rather,' he says, 'by a sort of curiosity, which was, however, directed more towards human concerns than towards natural objects.'[1] Elsewhere he writes: 'I have no knowledge of having had any craving in my early childhood to help suffering humanity ... In my youth I felt an over-powering need to understand something of the riddles of the world in which we live and perhaps even to contribute something to their solution.'[2] And in yet another passage in which he was discussing the sociological studies of his last years: 'My interest, after making a lifelong *détour* through the natural sciences, medicine, and psychotherapy, returned to the cultural problems which had fascinated me long before, when I was a youth scarcely old enough for thinking.'[3]

What immediately determined Freud's choice of a scientific career was, so he tells us, being present just when he was leaving school at a public reading of an extremely flowery essay on 'Nature', attributed (wrongly, it seems) to Goethe. But if it was to be science, practical considerations narrowed the choice to medicine. And it was as a medical student that Freud enrolled himself at the University in the autumn of 1873 at the age of seventeen. Even so, however, he was in no hurry to obtain a medical degree. For his first year or two he attended lectures on a variety of subjects, but gradually concentrated first on biology and then on physiology. His very first piece of research was in his third year at the University, when he was deputed by the Professor of Comparative Anatomy to investigate a detail in the anatomy of the eel, which involved the dissection

1. [*An Autobiographical Study* (1925d), near the opening of the work.]
2. ['Postscript to *The Question of Lay Analysis*' (1927a).]
3. ['Postscript (1935) to *An Autobiographical Study*' (1935a).]

of some four hundred specimens. Soon afterwards he entered the Physiological Laboratory under Brücke, and worked there happily for six years. It was no doubt from him that he acquired the main outlines of his attitude to physical science in general. During these years Freud worked chiefly on the anatomy of the central nervous system and was already beginning to produce publications. But it was becoming obvious that no livelihood which would be sufficient to meet the needs of the large family at home was to be picked up from these laboratory studies. So at last, in 1881, he decided to take his medical degree, and a year later, most unwillingly, gave up his position under Brücke and began work in the Vienna General Hospital.

What finally determined this change in his life was something more urgent than family considerations: in June 1882 he became engaged to be married, and thenceforward all his efforts were directed towards making marriage possible. His fiancée, Martha Bernays, came of a well-known Jewish family in Hamburg, and though for the moment she was living in Vienna she was very soon obliged to return to her remote North-German home. During the four years that followed, it was only for brief visits that he could have glimpses of her, and the two lovers had to content themselves with an almost daily interchange of letters. Freud now set himself to establishing a position and a reputation in the medical world. He worked in various departments of the hospital, but soon came to concentrate on neuroanatomy and neuropathology. During this period, too, he published the first inquiry into the possible medical uses of cocaine; and it was this that suggested to Koller the drug's employment as a local anaesthetic. He soon formed two immediate plans: one of these was to obtain an appointment as *Privatdozent*, a post not unlike that of a university lecturer in England, the other was to gain a travelling bursary which would enable him to spend some time in Paris, where the reigning figure was the great Charcot. Both of these aims, if they were realized, would, he felt, bring him real advantages, and in 1885, after a hard struggle, he achieved them both.

The months which Freud spent under Charcot at the Salpêtrière (the famous Paris hospital for nervous diseases) brought another change in the course of his life and this time a revolutionary one. So far his work had been concerned entirely with physical science and he was still carrying out histological studies on the brain while he was in Paris. Charcot's interests were at that period concentrated mainly on hysteria and hypnotism. In the world from which Freud came these subjects were regarded as barely respectable, but he became absorbed in them, and, though Charcot himself looked at them purely as branches of neuropathology, for Freud they meant the first beginnings of the investigation of the mind.

On his return to Vienna in the spring of 1886 Freud set up in private practice as a consultant in nervous diseases, and his long-delayed marriage followed soon afterwards. He did not, however, at once abandon all his neuropathological work: for several more years he studied in particular the cerebral palsies of children, on which he became a leading authority. At this period, too, he produced an important monograph on aphasia. But he was becoming more and more engaged in the treatment of the neuroses. After experimenting in vain with electrotherapy, he turned to hypnotic suggestion, and in 1888 visited Nancy to learn the technique used with such apparent success there by Liébeault and Bernheim. This still proved unsatisfactory and he was driven to yet another line of approach. He knew that a friend of his, Dr Josef Breuer, a Vienna consultant considerably his senior, had some ten years earlier cured a girl suffering from hysteria by a quite new procedure. He now persuaded Breuer to take up the method once more, and he himself applied it to several fresh cases with promising results. The method was based on the assumption that hysteria was the product of a psychical trauma which had been forgotten by the patient; and the treatment consisted in inducing her in a hypnotic state to recall the forgotten trauma to the accompaniment of appropriate emotions. Before very long Freud began to make changes both in the procedure and in the underlying theory; this led eventually to a breach with Breuer, and to the ultimate development by Freud of the whole system of ideas to which he soon gave the name of psychoanalysis.

From this moment onwards – from 1895, perhaps – to the very end of his life, the whole of Freud's intellectual existence revolved around this development, its far-reaching implications, and its theoretical and practical repercussions. It would, of course, be impossible to give in a few sentences any consecutive account of Freud's discoveries and ideas, but an attempt will be made presently to indicate in a disconnected fashion some of the main changes he has brought about in our habits of thought. Meanwhile we may continue to follow the course of his external life.

His domestic existence in Vienna was essentially devoid of episode: his home and his consulting rooms were in the same house from 1891 till his departure for London forty-seven years later. His happy marriage and his growing family – three sons and three daughters – provided a solid counterweight to the difficulties which, to begin with at least, surrounded his professional career. It was not only the nature of his discoveries that created prejudice against him in medical circles; just as great, perhaps, was the effect of the intense anti-semitic feeling which dominated the official world of Vienna: his appointment to a university professorship was constantly held back by political influence.

One particular feature of these early years calls for mention on account of its consequences. This was Freud's friendship with Wilhelm Fliess, a brilliant but unbalanced Berlin physician, who specialized in the ear and throat, but whose wider interests extended over human biology and the effects of periodic phenomena in vital processes. For fifteen years, from 1887 to 1902, Freud corresponded with him regularly, reported the development of his ideas, forwarded him long drafts outlining his future writings, and, most important of all, sent him an essay of some forty thousand words which has been given the name of a 'Project for a Scientific Psychology'. This essay was composed in 1895, at what might be described as the watershed of Freud's career, when he was reluctantly moving from physiology to psychology; it is an attempt to state the facts of psychology in purely neurological terms. This paper and all the rest of Freud's communications to Fliess have, by a lucky chance, survived: they throw a fascinating light on the development of Freud's ideas and show how much of the later findings of psychoanalysis were already present in his mind at this early stage.

Apart from his relations with Fliess, Freud had little outside support to begin with. He gradually gathered a few pupils round him in Vienna, but it was only after some ten years, in about 1906, that a change was inaugurated by the adhesion of a number of Swiss psychiatrists to his views. Chief among these were Bleuler, the head of the Zürich mental hospital, and his assistant Jung. This proved to be the beginning of the first spread of psychoanalysis. An international meeting of psychoanalysts gathered at Salzburg in 1908, and in 1909 Freud and Jung were invited to give a number of lectures in the United States. Freud's writing began to be translated into many languages, and groups of practising analysts sprang up all over the world. But the progress of psychoanalysis was not without its set-backs: the currents which its subject-matter stirred up in the mind ran too deep for its easy acceptance. In 1911 one of Freud's prominent Viennese supporters, Alfred Adler, broke away from him, and two or three years later Jung's differences from Freud led to their separation. Almost immediately after this came the First World War and an interruption of the international spread of psychoanalysis. Soon afterwards, too, came the gravest personal tragedies – the death of a daughter and of a favourite grandchild, and the onset of the malignant illness which was to pursue him relentlessly for the last sixteen years of his life. None of these troubles, however, brought any interruption to the development of Freud's observations and inferences. The structure of his ideas continued to expand and to find ever wider applications – particularly in the sociological field. By now he had become generally recognized as a figure of world celebrity, and no honour pleased him more than his election in 1936, the year of his eightieth birthday, as a Corresponding Member of the Royal Society. It was no doubt this fame, supported by the efforts of influential admirers, including, it is said, President Roosevelt, that protected him from the worst excesses of the National Socialists when Hitler invaded Austria in 1938, though they seized and destroyed his publications. Freud's departure from Vienna was nevertheless essential, and in June of that year, accompanied by some of his family, he made the journey to London, and it was there, a year later, on 23 September 1939, that he died.

It has become a journalistic cliché to speak of Freud as one of the revolutionary founders of modern thought and to couple his name with that of Einstein. Most people would, however, find it almost as hard to summarize the changes introduced by the one as by the other.

Freud's discoveries may be grouped under three headings – an instrument of research, the findings produced by the instrument, and the theoretical hypotheses inferred from the findings – though the three groups were of course mutually interrelated. Behind all of Freud's work, however, we should posit his belief in the universal validity of the law of determinism. As regards physical phenomena this belief was perhaps derived from his experience in Brücke's laboratory and so, ultimately, from the school of Helmholtz; but Freud extended the belief uncompromisingly to the field of mental phenomena, and here he may have been influenced by his teacher, the psychiatrist Meynert, and indirectly by the philosophy of Herbart.

First and foremost, Freud was the discoverer of the first instrument for the scientific examination of the human mind. Creative writers of genius had had fragmentary insight into mental processes, but no systematic method of investigation existed before Freud. It was only gradually that he perfected the instrument, since it was only gradually that the difficulties in the way of such an investigation became apparent. The forgotten trauma in Breuer's explanation of hysteria provided the earliest problem and perhaps the most fundamental of all, for it showed conclusively that there were active parts of the mind not immediately open to inspection either by an onlooker or by the subject himself. These parts of the mind were described by Freud, without regard for metaphysical or terminological disputes, as the unconscious. Their existence was equally demonstrated by the fact of post-hypnotic suggestion, where a person in a fully waking state performs an action which had been suggested to him some time earlier, though he had totally forgotten the suggestion itself. No examination of the mind could thus be considered complete unless it included this unconscious part of it in its scope. How was this to be accomplished? The obvious answer seemed to be: by means of hypnotic suggestion; and this was the instrument used by Breuer and, to begin with, by Freud. But it soon turned out to be an imperfect one, acting irregularly and uncertainly and sometimes not at all. Little by little, accordingly, Freud abandoned the use of suggestion and replaced it by an entirely fresh instrument, which was later known as 'free association'. He adopted the unheard-of plan of simply asking the person whose mind he was investigating to say whatever came into his head. This crucial decision led at once to the most startling results; even in this primitive form Freud's instrument produced fresh insight. For, though things went along swimmingly for a while, sooner or later the flow of associations dried up: the subject would not or could not think of anything more to say. There thus came to light the fact of 'resistance', of a force, separate from the subject's conscious will, which was refusing to collaborate with the investigation. Here was one basis for a very fundamental piece of theory, for a hypothesis of the mind as something dynamic, as consisting in a number of mental forces, some conscious and some unconscious, operating now in harmony now in opposition with one another.

Though these phenomena eventually turned out to be of universal occurrence, they were first observed and studied in neurotic patients, and the earlier years of Freud's work were largely concerned with discovering means by which the 're-sistance' of these patients could be overcome and what lay behind it could be brought to light. The solution was only made possible by an extraordinary piece of self-observation on Freud's part – what we should now describe as his self-analysis. We are fortunate in having a contemporary first-hand description of this event in his letters to Fliess which have already been mentioned. This analysis enabled him to discover the nature of the unconscious processes at work in the mind and to understand why there is such a strong resistance to their becoming conscious; it enabled him to devise techniques for overcoming or evading the resistance in his patients; and, most important of all, it enabled him to realize the very great difference between the mode of functioning of these unconscious processes and that of our familiar conscious ones. A word may be said on each of these three points, for in fact they constitute the core of Freud's contributions to our knowledge of the mind.

The unconscious contents of the mind were found to consist wholly in the activity of conative trends – desires or wishes – which derive their energy directly from the primary physical instincts. They function quite regardless of any consideration other than that of obtaining immediate satisfaction, and are thus liable to be out of step with those more conscious elements in the mind which are concerned with adaptation to reality and the avoidance of external dangers. Since, moreover, these primitive trends are to a greater extent of a sexual or of a destructive nature, they are bound to come in conflict with the more social and civilized mental forces. Investigations along this path were what led Freud to his discoveries of the long-disguised secrets of the sexual life of children and of the Oedipus complex.

In the second place, his self-analysis led him to an inquiry into the nature of dreams. These turned out to be, like neurotic symptoms, the product of a conflict and a compromise between the primary unconscious impulses and the secondary conscious ones. By analysing them into their elements it was therefore possible to infer their hidden unconscious contents; and, since dreams are common phenomena of almost universal occurrence, their interpretation turned out to be one of the most useful technical contrivances for penetrating the resistances of neurotic patients.

Finally, the painstaking examination of dreams enabled Freud to classify the remarkable differences between what he termed the primary and secondary processes of thought, between events in the unconscious and conscious regions of the mind. In the unconscious, it was found, there is no sort of organization or coordination: each separate impulse seeks satisfaction independently of all the rest; they proceed uninfluenced by one another; contradictions are completely inoperative, and the most opposite impulses flourish side by side. So, too, in the unconscious, associations of ideas proceed along lines without any regard to logic: similarities are treated as identities, negatives are equated with positives. Again, the objects to which the conative trends are attached in the unconscious are extraordinarily changeable – one may be replaced by another along a whole chain of associations that have no rational basis. Freud perceived that the intrusion into conscious thinking of mechanisms that belong properly to the primary process accounts for the oddity not only of dreams but of many other normal and pathological mental events.

It is not much of an exaggeration to say that all the later part of Freud's work lay in an immense extension and elaboration of these early ideas. They were applied to an elucidation of the mechanisms, not only of the psychoneuroses and psychoses but also of such normal processes as slips of the tongue, making jokes, artistic creation, political institutions, and religions; they played a part in throwing fresh light on many applied sciences – archaeology, anthropology, criminology, education; they also served to account for the effectiveness of psychoanalytic therapy. Lastly, too, Freud erected on the basis of these elementary observations a theoretical superstructure, what he named a 'metapsychology', of more general concepts. These, however, fascinating as many people will find them, he always insisted were in the nature of provisional hypotheses. Quite late in his life, indeed, influenced by the ambiguity of the term 'unconscious' and its many conflicting uses, he proposed a new structural account of the mind in which the uncoordinated instinctual trends were called the 'id', the organized realistic part the 'ego', and the critical and moralizing function the 'super-ego' – a new account which has certainly made for a clarification of many issues.

This, then, will have given the reader an outline of the external events of Freud's life and some notion of the scope of his discoveries. Is it legitimate to ask for more? to try to penetrate a little further and to inquire what sort of person Freud was? Possibly not. But human curiosity about great men is insatiable, and if it is not gratified with true accounts it will inevitably clutch at mythological ones. In two of Freud's early books (*The Interpretation of Dreams* and *The Psychopathology of Everyday Life*) the presentation of his thesis had forced on him the necessity of bringing up an unusual amount of personal material. Nevertheless, or perhaps for that very reason, he intensely objected to any intrusion into his private life, and he was correspondingly the subject of a wealth of myths. According to the first and most naïve rumours, for instance, he was an abandoned profligate, devoted to the corruption of public morals. Later fantasies have tended in the opposite direction: he has been represented as a harsh moralist, a ruthless disciplinarian, an autocrat, egocentric and unsmiling, and an essentially unhappy man. To anyone who was acquainted with him, even slightly, both these pictures must seem equally preposterous. The second of them was no doubt partly derived from a knowledge of his physical sufferings during his last years; but partly too it may have been due to the unfortunate impression produced by some of his most widespread portraits. He disliked being photographed, at least by professional photographers, and his features on occasion expressed the fact; artists too seem always to have been overwhelmed by the necessity for representing the inventor of psychoanalysis as a ferocious and terrifying figure. Fortunately, however, alternative versions exist of a more amiable and truer kind – snapshots, for instance, taken on a holiday or with his children, such as will be found in his eldest son's memoir of his father (*Glory Reflected*, by Martin Freud [1957]). In many ways, indeed, this delightful and amusing book serves to redress the balance from more official biographies, invaluable as they are, and reveals something of Freud as he was in ordinary life. Some of these portraits show us that in his earlier days he had well-filled features, but in later life, at any rate after the First World War and even before his illness, this was no longer so, and his features, as well as his whole figure (which was of medium height), were chiefly remarkable for the impression they gave of tense energy and alert observation. He was serious but kindly and considerate in his more formal manners, but in other circumstances could be an entertaining talker with a pleasantly ironical sense of humour. It was easy to discover his devoted fondness for his family and to recognize a man who would inspire affection. He had many miscellaneous interests – he was fond of travelling abroad, of country holidays, of mountain walks – and there were other, more engrossing subjects, art, archaeology, literature. Freud was a very well read man in many languages, not only in German. He read English and French fluently, besides having a fair knowledge of Spanish and Italian. It must be remembered, too, that though the later phases of his education were chiefly scientific (it is true that at the University he studied philosophy for a short time) at school he had learnt the classics and never lost his affection for them. We happen to have a letter written by him at the age of seventeen to a school friend.[1] In it he describes his varying success in the different papers of his school-leaving examination: in Latin a passage from Virgil, and in Greek thirty-three lines from, of all things, *Oedipus Rex*.

In short, we might regard Freud as what in England we should consider the best kind of product of a Victorian up-bringing. His tastes in literature and art would obviously differ from ours, his views on ethics, though decidedly liberal, would

1. [Emil Fluss. The letter is included in the volume of Freud's correspondence (1960a).]

not belong to the post-Freudian age. But we should see in him a man who lived a life of full emotion and of much suffering without embitterment. Complete honesty and directness were qualities that stood out in him, and so too did his intellectual readiness to take in and consider any fact, however new or extraordinary, that was presented to him. It was perhaps an inevitable corollary and extension of these qualities, combined with a general benevolence which a surface misanthropy failed to disguise, that led to some features of a surprising kind. In spite of his subtlety of mind he was essentially unsophisticated, and there were sometimes unexpected lapses in his critical faculty — a failure, for instance, to perceive an untrustworthy authority in some subject that was off his own beat such as Egyptology or philology, and, strangest of all in someone whose powers of perception had to be experienced to be believed, an occasional blindness to defects in his acquaintances. But though it may flatter our vanity to declare that Freud was a human being of a kind like our own, that satisfaction can easily be carried too far. There must in fact have been something very extraordinary in the man who was first able to recognize a whole field of mental facts which had hitherto been excluded from normal consciousness, the man who first interpreted dreams, who first accepted the facts of infantile sexuality, who first made the distinction between the primary and secondary processes of thinking — the man who first made the unconscious mind real to us.

JAMES STRACHEY

[Those in search of further information will find it in the three-volume biography of Freud by Ernest Jones, an abridged version of which was published in Pelican in 1964 (reissued 1974), in the important volume of Freud's letters edited by his son and daughter-in-law, Ernst and Lucie Freud (1960a), in several further volumes of his correspondence, with Wilhelm Fliess (1950a), Karl Abraham (1965a), C. G. Jung (1974a), Oskar Pfister (1963a), Lou Andreas-Salomé (1966a), Edoardo Weiss (1970a) and Arnold Zweig (1968a), and above all in the many volumes of Freud's own works.]

CHRONOLOGICAL TABLE

This table traces very roughly some of the main turning-points in Freud's intellectual development and opinions. A few of the chief events in his external life are also included in it.

1856. 6 May. Birth at Freiberg in Moravia.

1860. Family settles in Vienna.

1865. Enters Gymnasium (secondary school).

1873. Enters Vienna University as medical student.

1876–82. Works under Brücke at the Institute of Physiology in Vienna.

1877. First publications: papers on anatomy and physiology.

1881. Graduates as Doctor of Medicine.

1882. Engagement to Martha Bernays.

1882–5. Works in Vienna General Hospital, concentrating on cerebral anatomy: numerous publications.

1884–7. Researches into the clinical uses of cocaine.

1885. Appointed *Privatdozent* (University Lecturer) in Neuropathology.

1885 (October)–1886 (February). Studies under Charcot at the Salpêtrière (hospital for nervous diseases) in Paris. Interest first turns to hysteria and hypnosis.

1886. Marriage to Martha Bernays. Sets up private practice in nervous diseases in Vienna.

1886–93. Continues work on neurology, especially on the cerebral palsies of children at the Kassowitz Institute in Vienna, with numerous publications. Gradual shift of interest from neurology to psychopathology.

1887. Birth of eldest child (Mathilde).

1887–1902. Friendship and correspondence with Wilhelm Fliess in Berlin. Freud's letters to him during this period, published posthumously in 1950, throw much light on the development of his views.

1887. Begins the use of hypnotic suggestion in his practice.

c. 1888. Begins to follow Breuer in using hypnosis for cathartic treatment of hysteria. Gradually drops hypnosis and substitutes free association.

1889. Visits Bernheim at Nancy to study his suggestion technique.

1889. Birth of eldest son (Martin).

1891. Monograph on Aphasia.
Birth of second son (Oliver).

1892. Birth of youngest son (Ernst).

1893. Publication of Breuer and Freud 'Preliminary Communication': exposition of trauma theory of hysteria and of cathartic treatment.
Birth of second daughter (Sophie).

1893–8. Researches and short papers on hysteria, obsessions, and anxiety.

1895. Jointly with Breuer, *Studies on Hysteria*: case histories and description by Freud of his technique, including first account of transference.

1893–6. Gradual divergence of views between Freud and Breuer. Freud introduces concepts of defence and repression and of neurosis being a result of a conflict between the ego and the libido.

1895. *Project for a Scientific Psychology*: included in Freud's letters to Fliess and first published in 1950. An abortive attempt to state psychology in neurological terms; but foreshadows much of Freud's later theories.
Birth of youngest child (Anna).

1896. Introduces the term 'psychoanalysis'.
Death of father (aged eighty).

1897. Freud's self-analysis, leading to the abandonment of the trauma theory and the recognition of infantile sexuality and the Oedipus complex.

1900. *The Interpretation of Dreams*, with final chapter giving first full account of Freud's dynamic view of mental processes, of the unconscious, and of the dominance of the 'pleasure principle'.

1901. *The Psychopathology of Everyday Life*. This, together with the book on dreams, made it plain that Freud's theories applied not only to pathological states but also to normal mental life.

1902. Appointed Professor Extraordinarius.

1905. *Three Essays on the Theory of Sexuality*: tracing for the first time the course of development of the sexual instinct in human beings from infancy to maturity.

c. 1906. Jung becomes an adherent of psychoanalysis.

1908. First international meeting of psychoanalysts (at Salzburg).

1909. Freud and Jung invited to the USA to lecture.
Case history of the first analysis of a child (Little Hans, aged five): confirming inferences previously made from adult analyses, especially as to infantile sexuality and the Oedipus and castration complexes.

c. 1910. First emergence of the theory of 'narcissism'.

1911–15. Papers on the technique of psychoanalysis.

1911. Secession of Adler.
Application of psychoanalytic theories to a psychotic case: the autobiography of Dr Schreber.

1912–13. *Totem and Taboo*: application of psychoanalysis to anthropological material.

1914. Secession of Jung.
'On the History of the Psycho-Analytic Movement'. Includes a polemical section on Adler and Jung.

Writes his last major case history, of the 'Wolf Man' (not published till 1918).

1915. Writes a series of twelve 'metapsychological' papers on basic theoretical questions, of which only five have survived.

1915–17. *Introductory Lectures*: giving an extensive general account of the state of Freud's views up to the time of the First World War.

1919. Application of the theory of narcissism to the war neuroses.

1920. Death of second daughter.

Beyond the Pleasure Principle: the first explicit introduction of the concept of the 'compulsion to repeat' and of the theory of the 'death instinct'.

1921. *Group Psychology*. Beginnings of a systematic analytic study of the ego.

1923. *The Ego and the Id*. Largely revised account of the structure and functioning of the mind with the division into an id, an ego, and a super-ego.

1923. First onset of cancer.

1925. Revised views on the sexual development of women.

1926. *Inhibitions, Symptoms, and Anxiety*. Revised views on the problem of anxiety.

1927. *The Future of an Illusion*. A discussion of religion: the first of a number of sociological works to which Freud devoted most of his remaining years.

1930. *Civilization and its Discontents*. This includes Freud's first extensive study of the destructive instinct (regarded as a manifestation of the 'death instinct').

Freud awarded the Goethe Prize by the City of Frankfurt.

Death of mother (aged ninety-five).

1933. Hitler seizes power in Germany: Freud's books publicly burned in Berlin.

1934–8. *Moses and Monotheism*: the last of Freud's works to appear during his lifetime.

1936. Eightieth birthday. Election as Corresponding Member of Royal Society.

1938. Hitler's invasion of Austria. Freud leaves Vienna for London.

An Outline of Psycho-Analysis. A final, unfinished, but profound exposition of psychoanalysis.

1939. 23 September. Death in London.

JAMES STRACHEY

DELUSIONS AND DREAMS IN JENSEN'S *GRADIVA*
(1907 [1906])

EDITOR'S NOTE

DER WAHN UND DIE TRÄUME IN
W. JENSENS *GRADIVA*

(A) GERMAN EDITIONS:

1907   Leipzig and Vienna: Heller. (Reissued in 1908 by
        Deuticke. 1912, 2nd ed., with 'Postscript'; 1924, 3rd
        ed.)
1941   *Gesammelte Werke*, **7**, 31–125.

(B) ENGLISH TRANSLATIONS:
Delusion and Dream

1917   New York: Moffat, Yard. (Tr. H. M. Downey.)
        (With an introduction by G. Stanley Hall. Omits
        Freud's 'Postscript'. Includes translation of Jensen's
        story.)
1921   London: George Allen & Unwin. (Reprint of above.)
1959   *Standard Edition*, **9**, 1–95. (Tr. James Strachey.)

The present edition is a corrected reprint of the *Standard
Edition* version, with a few editorial changes.

This was Freud's first published analysis of a work of literature,
apart, of course, from his comments on *Oedipus Rex* and *Hamlet*
in *The Interpretation of Dreams* (1900*a*), *P.F.L.*, **4**, 363–8. At an
earlier date, however, he had written a short analysis of Conrad
Ferdinand Meyer's story, 'Die Richterin' ['The Woman
Judge'], and had sent it to Fliess, enclosed in a letter dated 20
June 1898 (Freud, 1950*a*, Letter 91).

It was Jung, as we learn from Ernest Jones (1955, 382), who

brought Jensen's[1] book to Freud's notice, and Freud is reported to have written the present work especially to please Jung. This was in the summer of 1906, several months before the two men had met each other, and the episode was thus the herald of their five or six years of cordial relations. Freud's study was published in May 1907 and soon afterwards he sent a copy of it to Jensen. A short correspondence followed, which is referred to in the 'Postscript' below; Jensen's side of this correspondence (three shortish letters, dated 13 May, 25 May and 14 December 1907) has since been published in the *Psycho-analytische Bewegung*, **1** (1929), 207–11. The letters are most friendly in tone and give the impression that Jensen was flattered by Freud's analysis of his story. He appears even to have accepted the main lines of the interpretation. In particular, he declares that he has no recollection of having replied 'somewhat brusquely' when, as reported below, he was asked (apparently by Jung) whether he knew anything of Freud's theories.

Apart from the deeper significance which Freud saw in Jensen's work, there is no doubt that he must have been specially attracted by the scene in which it was laid. His interest in Pompeii was an old-established one, which appears more than once in his correspondence with Fliess (1950*a*), but it was several years before he actually visited Pompeii, in September 1902. Above all, Freud was fascinated by the analogy between the historical fate of Pompeii (its burial and subsequent excavation) and the mental events with which he was so familiar – burial by repression and excavation by analysis. Something of this analogy was suggested by Jensen himself (p. 76), and Freud enjoyed elaborating it here as well as in later contexts.

In reading Freud's study, it is worth bearing in mind its chronological place in his writings as one of his earliest psycho-analytic works. It was written only a year after the first publication of the 'Dora' case history (1905*e*) and the *Three*

1. Wilhelm Jensen (1837–1911) was a North German playwright and novelist, respected but not regarded as of very great distinction. In his *Auto-biographical Study* (1925*d*), *P.F.L.*, **15**, Freud spoke a little contemptuously of *Gradiva* as a work 'which has no particular merit in itself'.

Essays on Sexuality (1905*d*). Embedded in the discussion of *Gradiva*, indeed, there lies not only a summary of Freud's explanation of dreams but also what is perhaps the first of his semi-popular accounts of his theory of the neuroses and of the therapeutic action of psychoanalysis. It is impossible not to admire the almost prestidigital skill with which he extracts this wealth of material from what is at first sight no more than an ingenious anecdote. But it would be wrong to minimize the part played in the outcome, however unconsciously, by Jensen himself.

DELUSIONS AND DREAMS IN JENSEN'S *GRADIVA*

I

A GROUP of men who regarded it as a settled fact that the essential riddles of dreaming have been solved by the efforts of the author of the present work[1] found their curiosity aroused one day by the question of the class of dreams that have never been dreamt at all – dreams created by imaginative writers and ascribed to invented characters in the course of a story. The notion of submitting this class of dreams to an investigation might seem a waste of energy and a strange thing to undertake; but from one point of view it could be considered justifiable. It is far from being generally believed that dreams have a meaning and can be interpreted. Science and the majority of educated people smile if they are set the task of interpreting a dream. Only the common people, who cling to superstitions and who on this point are carrying on the convictions of antiquity, continue to insist that dreams can be interpreted. The author of *The Interpretation of Dreams* has ventured, in the face of the reproaches of strict science, to become a partisan of antiquity and superstition. He is, it is true, far from believing that dreams foretell the future, for the unveiling of which men have vainly striven from time immemorial by every forbidden means. But even he has not been able entirely to reject the relation of dreams to the future. For the dream, when the laborious work of translating it had been accomplished, revealed itself to him as a wish of the dreamer's represented as fulfilled; and who could deny that wishes are predominantly turned towards the future?

1. See Freud, *The Interpretation of Dreams* (1900*a*). [*P.F.L.*, **4**.]

33

I have just said that dreams are fulfilled wishes. Anyone who is not afraid of making his way through an abstruse book, and who does not insist on a complicated problem being represented to him as easy and simple in order to save him trouble and at the cost of honesty and truth, may find the detailed proof of this thesis in the work I have mentioned. Meanwhile, he may set on one side the objections which will undoubtedly occur to him against equating dreams and wish-fulfilments.

But we have gone a long way ahead. It is not a question yet of establishing whether the meaning of a dream can always be rendered by a fulfilled wish, or whether it may not just as often stand for an anxious expectation, an intention, a reflection, and so on. On the contrary, the question that first arises is whether dreams have a meaning at all, whether they ought to be assessed as mental events. Science answers 'no': it explains dreaming as a purely physiological process, behind which, accordingly, there is no need to look for sense, meaning or purpose. Somatic stimuli, so it says, play upon the mental instrument during sleep and thus bring to consciousness now one idea and now another, robbed of all mental content: dreams are comparable only to twitchings, not to expressive movements, of the mind.

Now in this dispute as to the estimation in which dreams should be held, imaginative writers seem to be on the same side as the ancients, as the superstitious public and as the author of *The Interpretation of Dreams*. For when an author makes the characters constructed by his imagination dream, he follows the everyday experience that people's thoughts and feelings are continued in sleep and he aims at nothing else than to depict his heroes' states of mind by their dreams. But creative writers are valuable allies and their evidence is to be prized highly, for they are apt to know a whole host of things between heaven and earth of which our philosophy has not yet let us dream. In their knowledge of the mind they are far in advance of us everyday people, for they draw upon sources which we have not yet opened up for science. If only this support given by writers in favour of dreams having a meaning were less ambiguous! A strictly critical eye might object that writers take their stand neither for nor against particular dreams having a psychical meaning; they are content to show how the sleeping mind twitches under the excitations which have remained active in it as off-shoots of waking life.

But even this sobering thought does not damp our interest in the fashion in which writers make use of dreams. Even if this inquiry should teach us nothing new about the nature of dreams, it may perhaps enable us from this angle to gain some small insight into the nature of creative writing. Real dreams were already regarded as unrestrained and unregulated structures – and now we are confronted by unfetered imitations of these dreams! There is far less freedom and arbitrariness in mental life, however, than we are inclined to assume – there may even be none at all. What we call chance in the world outside can, as is well known, be resolved into laws. So, too, what we call arbitrariness in the mind rests upon laws, which we are only now beginning dimly to suspect. Let us, then, see what we find!

There are two methods that we might adopt for this inquiry. One would be to enter deeply into a particular case, into the dream creations of one author in one of his works. The other would be to bring together and contrast all the examples that could be found of the use of dreams in the works of different authors. The second method would seem to be far the more effective and perhaps the only justifiable one, for it frees us at once from the difficulties involved in adopting the artificial concept of 'writers' as a class. On investigation this class falls apart into individual writers of the most various worth – among them some whom we are accustomed to honour as the deepest observers of the human mind. In spite of this, however, these pages will be devoted to an inquiry of the first sort. It happened that in the group of men among whom the notion first arose there was one[1] who recalled that in the work of fiction that had last caught his fancy there were several dreams which had, as it were, looked at him with familiar faces and invited

1. [This was Jung. See the Editor's Note above, pp. 29–30.]

him to attempt to apply to them the method of *The Interpretation of Dreams*. He confessed that the subject-matter of the little work and the scene in which it was laid may no doubt have played the chief part in creating his enjoyment. For the story was set in the frame of Pompeii and dealt with a young archaeologist who had surrendered his interest in life in exchange for an interest in the remains of classical antiquity and who was now brought back to real life by a roundabout path which was strange but perfectly logical. During the treatment of this genuinely poetic material the reader had been stirred by all kinds of thoughts akin to it and in harmony with it. The work was a short tale by Wilhelm Jensen – *Gradiva* – which its author himself described as a 'Pompeian phantasy'. [Jensen, 1903.]

And now I ought properly to ask all my readers to put aside this little essay and instead to spend some time in acquainting themselves with *Gradiva* (which first appeared in the bookshops in 1903), so that what I refer to in the following pages may be familiar to them. But for the benefit of those who have already read *Gradiva* I will recall the substance of the story in a brief summary; and I shall count upon their memory to restore to it all the charm of which this treatment will deprive it.

A young archaeologist, Norbert Hanold, had discovered in a museum of antiquities in Rome a relief which had so immensely attracted him that he was greatly pleased at obtaining an excellent plaster cast of it which he could hang in his study in a German university town and gaze at with interest. The sculpture represented a fully-grown girl stepping along, with her flowing dress a little pulled up so as to reveal her sandalled feet. One foot rested squarely on the ground; the other, lifted from the ground in the act of following after, touched it only with the tips of the toes, while the sole and heel rose almost perpendicularly. [See Plate 1.] It was probably the unusual and peculiarly charming gait thus presented that attracted the sculptor's notice and that still, after so many centuries, riveted the eyes of its archaeological admirer.

The interest taken by the hero of the story in this relief is the basic psychological fact in the narrative. It was not immediately explicable. 'Dr Norbert Hanold, Lecturer in Archaeology, did not in fact find in the relief anything calling for special notice from the point of view of his branch of science.' (3.)[1] 'He could not explain to himself what there was in it that had provoked his attention. He only knew that he had been attracted by something and that the effect had continued unchanged ever since.' But his imagination was occupied with the sculpture without ceasing. He found something 'of to-day' about it, as though the artist had had a glimpse in the street and captured it 'from the life'. He gave the girl thus pictured as she stepped along the name of 'Gradiva' – 'the girl who steps along'.[2] He made up a story that she was no doubt the daughter of an aristocratic family, perhaps 'of a patrician aedile,[3] who carried out his office in the service of Ceres', and that she was on her way to the goddess's temple. Then he found it hard to fit her quiet, calm nature into the busy life of a capital city. He convinced himself, rather, that she must be transported to Pompeii, and that somewhere there she was stepping across the curious stepping-stones which have been dug up and which made it possible to cross dry-foot from one side of the street to the other in rainy weather, though allowing carriage-wheels to pass between them as well. Her features struck him as having a *Greek* look and he had no doubt that she was of Hellenic origin. Little by little he brought the whole of his archaeological learning into the service of these and other phantasies relating to the original who had been the model for the relief.

But now he found himself confronted by an ostensibly scientific problem which called for a solution. It was a question of his arriving at the critical judgement as to 'whether Gradiva's gait as she stepped along had been reproduced by the sculptor in a life-like manner'. He found that he himself was not capable

1. [Plain numbers in brackets in the present translation are page references to Jensen, *Gradiva*, 1903.]
2. [The derivation of the name is further explained below, on p. 75.]
3. [A magistrate in charge of public buildings.]

JENSEN'S *GRADIVA*

of imitating it, and in his quest for the 'reality' of this gait he was led 'to make observations of his own from the life in order to clear the matter up'. (9.) This, however, forced him into a course of behaviour that was quite foreign to him. 'Hitherto, the female sex had been to him no more than the concept of something made of marble or bronze, and he had never paid the slightest attention to its contemporary representatives.' Social duties had always seemed to him an unavoidable nuisance; he saw and heard young ladies whom he came across in society so little that when he next met them he would pass them by without a sign; and this, of course, made no favourable impression on them. Now, however, the scientific task which he had taken on compelled him, in dry, but more especially in wet, weather, to look eagerly in the street at women's and girls' feet as they came into view – an activity which brought him some angry, and some encouraging, glances from those who came under his observation; 'but he was aware of neither the one nor the other.' (10.) As an outcome of these careful studies he was forced to the conclusion that Gradiva's gait was not discoverable in reality; and this filled him with regret and vexation.

Soon afterwards he had a terrifying dream, in which he found himself in ancient Pompeii on the day of the eruption of Vesuvius and witnessed the city's destruction. 'As he was standing at the edge of the forum beside the Temple of Jupiter, he suddenly saw Gradiva at no great distance from him. Till then he had had no thought of her presence, but now it occurred to him all at once and as though it was something natural that, since she was a Pompeian, she was living in her native town, and, *without his having suspected it, living as his contemporary.*' (12.) Fear of the fate that lay before her provoked him to utter a warning cry, whereupon the figure, as she calmly stepped along, turned her face towards him. But she then proceeded on her way untroubled, till she reached the portico of the temple [of Apollo]; there she took her seat on one of the steps and slowly laid her head down on it, while her face grew paler and paler, as though it were turning into marble. When he hurried after her, he found her stretched out on the broad step

38

with a peaceful expression, like someone asleep, till the rain of ashes buried her form.

When he awoke, the confused shouts of the inhabitants of Pompeii calling for help still seemed to echo in his ears, and the dull muttering of the breakers in the agitated sea. But even after his returning reflection recognized the sounds as the awakening signs of noisy life in a great city, he retained his belief for a long time in the reality of what he had dreamt. When at length he had freed himself of the notion that he himself had been present at the destruction of Pompeii almost two thousand years earlier, he was nevertheless left with what seemed a true conviction that Gradiva had lived in Pompeii and been buried there with the others in the year 79 A.D. The dream had as its result that now for the first time in his phantasies about Gradiva he mourned for her as someone who was lost.

While he was leaning out of the window, absorbed in these thoughts, his attention was caught by a canary warbling its song from a cage in the open window of the house opposite. Suddenly something passed with a start through the mind of the young man, who seems not yet to have fully woken from his dream. He thought he saw in the street a form like his Gradiva, and thought he even recognized her characteristic gait. Without thinking, he hurried into the street so as to catch up with her; and it was only the laughter and jeers of the passers-by at his early-morning attire that quickly drove him back into his house. When he was in his room again, the singing of the canary in its cage once more caught his attention and suggested a comparison with himself. He too, so it seemed to him, was like someone sitting in a cage, though it was easier for him to escape from it. As though as a further aftermath of his dream, and perhaps, too, under the influence of the mild air of spring, a resolve took shape in him to make a spring-time journey to Italy. A scientific excuse for it soon presented itself, even though 'the impulse to make this journey had arisen from a feeling he could not name'. (24.)

Let us pause for a moment at this journey, planned for such

remarkably uncogent reasons, and take a closer look at our hero's personality and behaviour. He still appears to us as incomprehensible and foolish; we have no idea how his peculiar folly will be linked to human feeling and so arouse our sympathy. It is an author's privilege to be allowed to leave us in such uncertainty. The charm of his language and the ingenuity of his ideas offer us a provisional reward for the reliance we place in him and for the still unearned sympathy which we are ready to feel for his hero. Of this hero we are further told that he was pre-ordained by family tradition to become an archaeologist, that in his later isolation and independence he was wholly absorbed in his studies and had turned completely away from life and its pleasures. Marble and bronze alone were truly alive for him; they alone expressed the purpose and value of human life. But nature, perhaps with benevolent intent, had infused into his blood a corrective of an entirely unscientific sort – an extremely lively imagination, which could show itself not only in his dreams but often in his waking life as well. This division between imagination and intellect destined him to become an artist or a neurotic; he was one of those whose kingdom is not of this world. Thus it was that it could come about that his interest was attached to a relief representing a girl stepping along in a peculiar fashion, that he wove his phantasies around her, imagined a name and origin for her, placed the figure he had created in the setting of the Pompeii that was buried more than eighteen hundred years before, and finally, after a strange anxiety-dream, magnified his phantasy of the existence and death of this girl named Gradiva into a delusion, which gained an influence over his actions. Such products of the imagination would seem to us astonishing and inexplicable if we met them in someone in real life. Since our hero, Norbert Hanold, is a fictitious person, we may perhaps put a timid question to his author, and ask whether his imagination was determined by forces other than its own arbitrary choice.

We had left our hero at the moment when he was apparently

being led by the song of a canary to decide on a journey to
Italy, the purpose of which was evidently not clear to him.
We learn further that he had no fixed plan or goal for his
journey. An inner restlessness and dissatisfaction drove him
from Rome to Naples and from thence further still. He found
himself among the swarm of honeymooners and was forced
to notice the loving couples of 'Edwins' and 'Angelinas',[1] but
was quite unable to understand their goings-on. He came to
the conclusion that of all the follies of mankind 'getting married
takes first place, as the greatest and most incomprehensible, and
the senseless honeymoon trips to Italy are, in a way, the
crowning touch of this idiocy'. (27.) Having been disturbed
in his sleep by the proximity of a loving couple in Rome, he
hurriedly fled to Naples, only to find other 'Edwins' and
'Angelinas' there. Having gathered from their conversation that
the majority of these pairs of birds had no intention of nesting
among the ruins of Pompeii, but were flying towards Capri,
he determined to do what they did not, and only a few days
after his departure found himself 'contrary to his expectation
and intentions' in Pompeii.

But without finding there the repose he was in search of.
The part which had so far been played by the honeymoon
couples, who had troubled his spirits and harassed his thoughts,
was now taken over by the house-flies, which he was inclined
to regard as the incarnation of all that is absolutely evil and
unnecessary. The two sorts of tormenting spirits melted into
a unity: some of the pairs of flies reminded him of the honeymooners, and he suspected that they too were addressing each
other in their language as 'dearest Edwin' and 'darling
Angelina'. Eventually, he could not but realize that 'his dissatisfaction was not caused only by his surroundings but that
its source was in part derived from within himself'. (42.) He
felt that 'he was discontented because he lacked something,
though it was not clear to him what'.

1. ['August' and 'Grete' in the original. The names recur frequently in
the course of the story and it has seemed best to replace them by those con-
ventionally applied to English honeymoon couples of the late Victorian age.]

Next morning he passed through the '*Ingresso*' into Pompeii, and, after getting rid of the guide, strolled aimlessly through the town, without, strangely enough, remembering that only a short time before he had been present in his dream at its burial. When later on, at the 'hot and holy'[1] mid-day hour, which the ancients regarded as the hour of ghosts, the other visitors had taken flight and the heaps of ruins lay before him desolate and bathed in sunlight, he found that he was able to carry himself back into the life that had been buried – but not by the help of science. 'What it taught was a lifeless, archaeological way of looking at things, and what came from its mouth was a dead, philological language. These were of no help to an understanding through the spirit, the feelings, the heart – put it as you please. Whoever had a longing for that must stand here alone, the only living creature, in the hot silence of mid-day, among the relics of the past, and look, but not with bodily eyes, and listen, but not with physical ears. And then ... the dead wakened and Pompeii began to live once more.' (55.)

While he was thus animating the past with his imagination, he suddenly saw the unmistakable Gradiva of his relief come out of a house and step trippingly over the lava stepping-stones to the other side of the street, just as he had seen her do in his dream the other night, when she had lain down as though to sleep, on the steps of the Temple of Apollo. 'And together with his memory something else came into his consciousness for the first time: without being aware himself of the impulse within him, he had come to Italy and had travelled on to Pompeii, without stopping in Rome or Naples, in order to see whether he could find any traces of her. And "traces" literally; for with her peculiar gait she must have left behind an imprint of her toes in the ashes distinct from all the rest.' (58.)

At this point the tension in which the author has hitherto held us grows for a moment into a painful sense of bewilderment. It is not only our hero who has evidently lost his balance; we too have lost our bearings in the face of the apparition of

1. [*Gradiva*, 51.]

Gradiva, who was first a marble figure and then an imaginary one. Is she a hallucination of our hero, led astray by his delusions? Is she a 'real' ghost? or a living person? Not that we need believe in ghosts when we draw up this list. The author, who has called his story a 'phantasy', has found no occasion so far for informing us whether he intends to leave us in our world, decried for being prosaic and governed by the laws of science, or whether he wishes to transport us into another and imaginary world, in which spirits and ghosts are given reality. As we know from the examples of *Hamlet* and *Macbeth*, we are prepared to follow him there without hesitation. If so, the imaginative archaeologist's delusion would have to be measured by another standard. Indeed, when we consider how improbable it must be that a real person could exist who bore an exact resemblance to the antique sculpture, our list of alternatives shrinks to two: a hallucination or a mid-day ghost. A small detail in the account soon cancels the first possibility. A large lizard was lying motionless, stretched out in the sun-shine, but fled at the approach of Gradiva's foot and darted away across the lava paving-stones. So it was no hallucination, but something outside our dreamer's mind. But could the reality of a *rediviva* startle a lizard?

Gradiva disappeared in front of the House of Meleager. We shall not be surprised to hear that Norbert Hanold pursued his delusion that Pompeii had come to life around him at the mid-day hour of ghosts and supposed that Gradiva too had come to life again and had entered the house in which she had lived before the fatal August day in 79 A.D. Ingenious speculations upon the personality of its owner (after whom the house was probably named), and upon Gradiva's relationship to him, shot through his head, and proved that his science was now completely in the service of his imagination. He entered the house, and suddenly found the apparition once more, sitting on some low steps between two yellow columns. 'There was something white stretched out across her knees; he could not clearly discern what it was; it seemed to be a sheet of papyrus . . .'

On the basis of his latest theories of her origin he addressed her in Greek, and waited with trepidation to learn whether, in her phantom presence she possessed the power of speech. Since she made no reply, he addressed her instead in Latin. Then, with a smile on her lips: 'If you want to speak to me', she said, 'you must do it in German.'

What a humiliation for us readers! So the author has been making fun of us, and, with the help, as it were, of a reflection of the Pompeian sunshine, has inveigled *us* into a delusion on a small scale, so that we may be forced to pass a milder judgement on the poor wretch on whom the mid-day sun was really shining. Now, however, that we have been cured of our brief confusion, we know that Gradiva was a German girl of flesh and blood – a solution which we were inclined to reject as the most improbable one. And now, with a quiet sense of superiority, we may wait to learn what the relation was between the girl and her marble image, and how our young archaeologist arrived at the phantasies which pointed towards her real personality.

But our hero was not torn from his delusion as quickly as we have been, for, as the author tells us, 'though his belief made him happy, he had to take the acceptance of quite a considerable number of mysteries into the bargain'. (140.) Moreover, this delusion probably had internal roots in him of which we know nothing and which do not exist in ourselves. In his case, no doubt, energetic treatment would seem necessary before he could be brought back to reality. Meanwhile all he could do was to fit his delusion into the wonderful experience he had just had. Gradiva, who had perished with the rest in the destruction of Pompeii, could be nothing other than a mid-day ghost who had returned to life for the brief ghostly hour. But why was it that, after hearing her reply delivered in German, he exclaimed 'I knew your voice sounded like that'? Not only we, but the girl herself was bound to ask the question, and Hanold had to admit that he had never heard it, though he had expected to in his dream, when he called to her as she

44

lay down to sleep on the temple steps. He begged her to do the same thing again as she had then; but now she rose, gave him a strange look, and in a few paces disappeared between the columns of the court. A pretty butterfly had shortly before fluttered round her for a while; and he interpreted it as a messenger from Hades reminding the dead girl that she must return, since the mid-day hour of ghosts was at an end. Hanold still had time to call after the girl as she vanished: 'Will you return here to-morrow at the mid-day hour?' To us, however, who can now venture upon more sober interpretations, it looks as though the young lady had seen something improper in the remark addressed to her by Hanold and had left him with a sense of having been insulted; for after all she could have known nothing of his dream. May not her sensibility have detected the erotic nature of his request, whose motive in Hanold's eyes lay in its relation to his dream?

After Gradiva's disappearance our hero had a careful look at all the guests congregated for their mid-day meal at the Hotel Diomède and went on to do the same at the Hotel Suisse, and he was then able to feel assured that in neither of the only two hotels known to him in Pompeii was there anyone bearing the remotest resemblance to Gradiva. He would of course have rejected as nonsensical the idea that he might actually meet Gradiva in one of the two inns. And presently the wine pressed from the hot soil of Vesuvius helped to intensify the whirl of feeling in which he spent the day.

For the following day one thing only was fixed: that Hanold must once more be in the House of Meleager at mid-day; and, in expectation of that moment, he made his way into Pompeii by an irregular route – over the ancient city wall. A sprig of asphodel, hung about with its white bell-shaped blossoms, seemed to him significant enough, as the flower of the under-world, for him to pluck it and carry it with him. But as he waited, the whole science of archaeology seemed to him the most pointless and indifferent thing in the world, for another interest had taken possession of him: the problem of 'what could be the nature of the bodily apparition of a being like Gradiva, who was at once dead and, even though only at the mid-day hour, alive'. (80.) He was fearful, too, that he might not meet her that day, for perhaps her return could be permitted only at long intervals; and when he perceived her once again between the columns, he thought her apparition was only a trick of his imagination, and in his pain exclaimed: 'Oh! if only you still existed and lived!' This time, however, he had evidently been too critical, for the apparition possessed a voice, which asked him if he was meaning to bring her the white flower, and engaged him, disconcerted once again, in a long conversation.

To his readers, however, to whom Gradiva has already grown of interest as a living person, the author explains that the displeased and repelling look which she had given him the day before had yielded to an expression of searching interest and curiosity. And indeed she now proceeded to question him, asked for an explanation of his remark on the previous day and inquired when it was that he had stood beside her as she lay down to sleep. In this way she learnt of his dream, in which she had perished along with her native city, and then of the marble relief and the posture of the foot which had so much attracted the archaeologist. And now she showed herself ready to demonstrate her gait, and this proved that the only divergence from the original portrait of Gradiva was that her sandals were replaced by light sand-coloured shoes of fine leather – which she explained as being an adaptation to the present day. She was evidently entering into his delusion, the whole compass of which she elicited from him, without ever contradicting it. Only once did she seem to be distracted from the part she was playing, by an emotion of her own; and this was when, with his thoughts on the relief, he declared that he had recognized her at the first glance. Since at this stage of their conversation she still knew nothing about the relief, it was natural for her to misunderstand Hanold's words; but she quickly recovered herself, and it is only to us that some of her remarks sound as though they had a double sense, as though besides their meaning in the context of the delusion they also meant something real and present-day – for instance, when she regretted that he had not succeeded in confirming the Gradiva gait in his experiments in the streets: 'What a pity! perhaps you would not have had to make the long journey here!' (89.) She also learned that he had given her portrait on the relief the name of 'Gradiva', and told him her real name, 'Zoe'. 'The name suits you beautifully, but it sounds to me like a bitter mockery, for Zoe means life.' 'One must bow to the inevitable', was her reply, 'and I have long grown used to being dead.' Promising to be at the same place again at the mid-day hour next day, she bade him farewell after once more asking him for the sprig of asphodel: 'to those who are more fortunate people give roses in the spring; but to me it is right that you should give the flower of forgetfulness.' (90.) No doubt melancholy suited someone who had been so long dead and had returned to life again for a few short hours.

We are beginning to understand now, and to feel some hope. If the young lady in whose form Gradiva had come to life again accepted Hanold's delusion so fully, she was probably doing so in order to set him free from it. There was no other way of doing so; to contradict it would have put an end to any such possibility. Even the serious treatment of a real case of illness of the kind could proceed in no other way than to begin by taking up the same ground as the delusional structure and then investigating it as completely as possible. If Zoe was the right person for the job, we shall soon learn, no doubt, how to cure a delusion like our hero's. We should also be glad to know how such delusions arise. It would be a strange coincidence – but, nevertheless, not without an example or parallel – if the treatment of the delusion were to coincide with its investigation and if the explanation of its origin were to be revealed precisely while it was being dissected. We may suspect, of course, that, if so, our case of illness might end up as a 'commonplace' love-story. But the healing power of love against a delusion is not to be despised – and was not our hero's infatuation for his Gradiva sculpture a complete instance of being in love with something past and lifeless?

*

After Gradiva's disappearance, there was only a distant sound, like the laughing call of a bird flying over the ruined city. The young man, now by himself, picked up a white object that had been left behind by Gradiva: not a sheet of papyrus, but a sketch-book with pencil drawings of various scenes in Pompeii. We should be inclined to regard her having forgotten the book there as a pledge of her return, for it is our belief that no one forgets anything without some secret reason or hidden motive.

The remainder of the day brought Hanold all manner of strange discoveries and confirmations, which he failed to synthesize into a whole. He perceived to-day in the wall of the portico where Gradiva had vanished a narrow gap, which was wide enough, however, to allow someone unusually slim to pass through it. He recognized that Zoe-Gradiva need not have sunk into the earth here – an idea which now seemed to him so unreasonable that he felt ashamed of having once believed in it; she might well have used the gap as a way of reaching her grave. A slight shadow seemed to melt away at the end of the Street of the Tombs in front of what is known as the Villa of Diomedes.

In the same whirl of feeling as on the previous day, and deep in the same problems, he now strolled round the environs of Pompeii. What, he wondered, might be the bodily nature of Zoe-Gradiva? Would one feel anything if one touched her hand? A strange urge drove him to a determination to put this experiment to the test. Yet an equally strong reluctance held him back even from the very idea.

On a sun-bathed slope he met an elderly gentleman who, from his accoutrements, must be a zoologist or botanist and who seemed to be engaged in a hunt. This individual turned towards him and said: 'Are you interested in *faraglionensis* as well? I should hardly have suspected it, but it seems to be quite probable that it occurs not only on the Faraglioni Islands off Capri, but has established itself on the mainland too. The method prescribed by our colleague Eimer[1] is a really good

1. [A well-known zoologist of the second half of the nineteenth century.]

one; I have made use of it many times already with excellent results. Please keep quite still ...' (96.) Here the speaker broke off and placed a snare made of a long blade of grass in front of a crack in the rocks out of which the small iridescent blue head of a lizard was peering. Hanold left the lizard-hunter with a critical feeling that it was scarcely credible what foolish and strange purposes could lead people to make the long journey to Pompeii – without, needless to say, including in his criticism himself and his intention of searching in the ashes of Pompeii for Gradiva's footprints. Moreover, the gentleman's face seemed familiar, as though he had had a glimpse of it in one of the two hotels; his manner of address, too, had been as though he were speaking to an acquaintance.

In the course of his further walk, he arrived by a side-road at a house which he had not yet discovered and which turned out to be a third hotel, the 'Albergo del Sole'.[1] The landlord, with nothing else to do, took the opportunity of showing off his house and the excavated treasures it contained to their best advantage. He asserted that he had been present when the pair of young lovers had been found in the neighbourhood of the Forum, who, in the knowledge of their inevitable doom, had awaited death closely embraced in each other's arms. Hanold had heard of this before, and had shrugged his shoulders over it as a fabulous tale invented by some imaginative story-teller; but to-day the landlord's words aroused his belief and this was increased when a metal clasp was produced, covered with a green patina, which was said to have been retrieved from the ashes beside the girl's remains. He purchased this clasp without any further critical doubts, and when, as he left the *albergo*, he saw in an open window a nodding sprig of asphodel covered with white blossoms, the sight of the funeral flowers came over him as a confirmation of the genuineness of his new possession.

But with the clasp a new delusion took possession of him, or rather the old one had a small piece added to it – no very good augury, it would seem, for the treatment that had been

1. [The 'Hotel of the Sun'.]

begun. A pair of young lovers in an embrace had been dug out not far from the Forum, and it was in that very neighbourhood, by the Temple of Apollo, that in his dream he had seen Gradiva lie down to sleep. Was it not possible that in fact she had gone further along from the Forum and had met someone and that they had then died together? A tormenting feeling, which we might perhaps liken to jealousy, arose out of this suspicion. He appeased it by reflecting on the uncertainty of the construction, and brought himself to his senses far enough to be able to take his evening meal at the Hotel Diomède. There his attention was drawn by two newly-arrived visitors, a He and a She, whom he was obliged to regard as a brother and sister on account of a certain resemblance between them – in spite of the difference in the colour of their hair. They were the first people he had met on his journey who made a sympathetic impression on him. A red Sorrento rose worn by the girl aroused some kind of memory in him, but he could not think what. At last he went to bed and had a dream. It was a remarkably senseless affair, but was obviously hashed up from his day's experiences. 'Somewhere in the sun Gradiva was sitting, making a snare out of a blade of grass to catch a lizard in, and said: "Please keep quite still. Our lady colleague is right; the method is a really good one and she has made use of it with excellent results."' He fended off this dream while he was still asleep, with the critical thought that it was utter madness, and he succeeded in freeing himself from it with the help of an invisible bird which uttered a short laughing call and carried off the lizard in its beak.

In spite of all this turmoil, he woke up in a rather clearer and steadier frame of mind. A branch of a rose-tree bearing flowers of the sort he had seen the day before on the young lady's breast reminded him that during the night someone had said that people give roses in the spring. Without thinking, he picked a few of the roses, and there must have been something connected with them that had a relaxing effect on his mind. He felt relieved of his unsociable feelings, and went by the usual way to Pompeii, burdened with the roses, the metal clasp and the sketch-book, and occupied with a number of problems concerning Gradiva. The old delusion had begun to show cracks: he was beginning to wonder whether she might be in Pompeii, not at the mid-day hour only, but at other times as well. The stress had shifted, however, to the latest addition, and the jealousy attaching to it tormented him in all sorts of disguises. He could almost have wished that the apparition might remain visible to his eyes alone, and elude the perception of others: then, in spite of everything, he could look on her as his own exclusive property. While he was strolling about, waiting for the mid-day hour, he had an unexpected encounter. In the *Casa del Fauno* he came upon two figures in a corner in which they must have thought themselves out of sight, for they were embraced in each other's arms and their lips were pressed together. He was astonished to recognize in them the sympathetic couple from the previous evening. But their behaviour now did not seem to fit a brother and sister: their embrace and their kiss seemed to him to last too long. So after all they were a pair of lovers, presumably a young honeymoon couple – yet another Edwin and Angelina. Curiously enough, however, this time the sight of them caused him only satisfaction; and with a sense of awe, as though he had interrupted some secret act of devotion, he withdrew unobserved. An attitude of respectfulness, which he had long been without, had returned to him.

When he reached the House of Meleager, he was once more overcome by such a violent dread of finding Gradiva in someone else's company that when she appeared the only words he found to greet her with were: 'Are you alone?' It was with difficulty that he allowed her to bring him to realize that he had picked the roses for her. He confessed his latest delusion to her – that she was the girl who had been found in the Forum in a lover's embrace and who had owned the green clasp. She inquired, not without a touch of mockery, whether he had found the thing in the sun perhaps: the sun (and she used the [Italian] word '*sole*') produced all kinds of things like that. He admitted that he was feeling dizzy in his head, and she suggested as a cure that he should share her small picnic meal with her. She offered him half of a roll wrapped up in tissue paper and ate the other half herself with an obviously good appetite. At the same time her perfect teeth flashed between her lips and made a slight crunching sound as they bit through the crust. 'I feel as though we had shared a meal like this once before, two thousand years ago', she said; 'can't you remember?' (118.) He could think of no reply, but the improvement in his head brought about by the food, and the many indications she gave of her actual presence, were not without their effect on him. Reason began to rise in him and to throw doubt on the whole delusion of Gradiva's being no more than a mid-day ghost – though no doubt it might be argued on the other hand that she herself had just said that she had shared a meal with him two thousand years ago. As a means of settling the conflict an experiment suggested itself: and this he carried out craftily and with regained courage. Her left hand, with its delicate fingers, was resting on her knees, and one of the house-flies whose impertinence and uselessness had so much roused his indignation alighted on it. Suddenly Hanold's hand was raised in the air and descended with a vigorous slap on the fly and Gradiva's hand.

This bold experiment had two results: first, a joyful conviction that he had without any doubt touched a real, living, warm human hand, but afterwards a reproof that made him jump up in a fright from his seat on the steps. For, from Gradiva's lips, when she had recovered from her astonishment, there rang out these words: 'There's no doubt you're out of your mind, Norbert Hanold!' As everyone knows, the best method of waking a sleeper or a sleep-walker is to call him by his own name. But unluckily there was no chance of observing the effects produced on Norbert Hanold by Gradiva's calling him by his name (which he had told no one in Pompeii). For at this critical moment the sympathetic pair of lovers from the *Casa del Fauno* appeared, and the young lady exclaimed in a tone of joyful surprise: 'Zoe! Are you here too? And on your honeymoon like us? You never wrote me a word about it!' In face of this new evidence of Gradiva's living reality, Hanold took flight.

Nor was Zoe-Gradiva very agreeably surprised by this unexpected visit, which interrupted her in what was apparently an important task. But she quickly pulled herself together and made a fluent reply to the question, in which she explained the situation to her friend — and even more to us — and which enabled her to get rid of the young couple. She congratulated them; but she was not on her honeymoon. 'The young man who's just gone off is labouring, like you, under a remarkable aberration. He seems to think there's a fly buzzing in his head. Well, I expect everyone has some sort of insect there. It's my duty to know something about entomology, so I can help a little in cases like that. My father and I are staying at the Sole. Something got into *his* head too, and the brilliant idea occurred to him besides of bringing me here with him on condition that I amused myself on my own at Pompeii and made no demands of any kind on him. I told myself I should dig out something interesting here even by myself. Of course I hadn't counted on making the find that I have — I mean my luck in meeting you, Gisa.' (124.) But now, she added, she must hurry off, so as to be company for her father at his lunch in the 'Sun'. And she departed, after having introduced herself to us as the daughter of the zoologist and lizard-catcher and after having, by all kinds of ambiguous remarks, admitted her therapeutic intention and other secret designs as well.

The direction she took, however, was not towards the Hotel of the Sun, where her father was waiting for her. But it seemed to her too as though a shadowy form was seeking its grave near the Villa of Diomedes, and was vanishing beneath one of the monuments. And for that reason she directed her steps towards the Street of the Tombs, with her foot lifted almost perpendicularly at each step. It was to this same place that Hanold had fled in his shame and confusion. He wandered ceaselessly up and down in the portico of the garden, engaged in the task of disposing of the remains of his problem by an intellectual effort. One thing had become undeniably clear to him: that he had been totally without sense or reason in believing that he had been associating with a young Pompeian woman who had come to life again in a more or less physical shape. It could not be disputed that this clear insight into his delusion was an essential step forward on his road back to a sound understanding. But, on the other hand, this living woman, with whom the other people communicated as though she were as physically real as themselves, was Gradiva, and she knew his name; and his scarcely awakened reason was not strong enough to solve this riddle. He was hardly calm enough emotionally, either, to show himself capable of facing so hard a task, for he would have preferred to have been buried along with the rest two thousand years before in the Villa of Diomedes, so as to be quite certain of not meeting Zoe-Gradiva again.

Nevertheless, a violent desire to see her again struggled against what was left of the inclination to flight still lingering in him.

As he turned one of the four corners of the colonnade, he suddenly recoiled. On a broken fragment of masonry was sitting one of the girls who had perished here in the Villa of Diomedes. This, however, was a last attempt, quickly rejected, at taking flight into the realm of delusion. No, it was Gradiva, who had evidently come to give him the final portion of her treatment. She quite correctly interpreted his first instinctive movement as an attempt to leave the building, and showed him that it was impossible for him to run away, for a terrific downpour of rain had begun outside. She was ruthless, and began her examination by asking him what he had been trying to do with the fly on her hand. He had not the courage to make use of a particular pronoun,[1] but he did have the courage

1. [The pronoun of the second person singular. The point of some of what follows is necessarily lost in English. In all his remarks to Gradiva hitherto, Hanold had used the second person singular, partly, no doubt, because that would be the classical usage. Now, however, that he was beginning to realize that he was talking to a modern German girl, he felt that the second person singular was far too familiar and affectionate. Gradiva, on the other hand, has used the second person singular throughout in speaking to him.]

for something more important – for asking her the decisive question:

'As someone said, I was rather confused in my head, and I must apologize for treating the hand ... I can't understand how I could be so senseless ... but I can't understand either how its owner could point out my ... my unreasonableness to me by my own name.' (134.)

'So your understanding has got as far as that, Norbert Hanold. But I can't say I'm surprised at it, you've accustomed me to it so long. I needn't have come to Pompeii to discover it again, and you could have confirmed it a good hundred miles nearer home.

'A hundred miles nearer', she explained, as he still failed to understand, 'diagonally across the street from where you live – in the house at the corner. There's a cage in my window with a canary in it.'

These last words, as he heard them, affected him like a distant memory: that must have been the same bird whose song had given him the idea of his journey to Italy.

'My father lives in that house: the Professor of Zoology, Richard Bertgang.'

So, since she was his neighbour, she knew him by sight and by name. We feel a sense of disillusionment: the solution falls flat and seems unworthy of our expectations.

Norbert Hanold showed that he had not yet regained his independence of thought when he replied: 'So you[1] ... you are Fräulein Zoe Bertgang? But she looked quite different ...'

Fräulein Bertgang's answer shows us that all the same there had been other relations between the two of them besides their simply being neighbours. She could argue in favour of the familiar '*du*', which he had used naturally to the mid-day ghost but had drawn back from in speaking to the live girl, but on behalf of which she claimed ancient rights: 'If you find this

1. ['*Sie*', the German pronoun of the third person plural, which is always used in formal speech instead of the '*du*' of the second person singular.]

formal mode of address more suitable, I can use it too. But I find the other comes to my lips more naturally. I don't know if I looked different in the early days when we used to run about together in a friendly way or sometimes, by way of a change, used to bump and thump each other. But if you[1] had even once looked at me attentively in recent years, it might have dawned on you that I've looked like this for quite a time.'

So there had been a childhood friendship between them – perhaps a childhood love – which justified the '*du*'. This solution, it may be, falls just as flat as the one we first suspected. We are brought to a much deeper level, however, when we realize that this childhood relationship unexpectedly explains a number of details in what had happened in their contemporary contact. Consider, for instance, the slapping of Zoe-Gradiva's hand. Norbert Hanold found a most convincing reason for it in the necessity for reaching an experimental answer to the problem of the apparition's physical reality. But was it not at the same time remarkably like a revival of the impulse for the 'bumping and thumping' whose dominance in their childhood was shown by Zoe's words? And think, again, of how Gradiva asked the archaeologist whether it did not seem to him that they had shared a meal like this two thousand years before. This unintelligible question suddenly seems to have a sense, if we once more replace the historical past by the personal one – childhood – of which the girl still had lively memories but which the young man appeared to have forgotten. And now the discovery dawns upon us that the young archaeologist's phantasies about his Gradiva may have been an echo of his forgotten childhood memories. If so, they were not capricious products of his imagination, but determined, without his knowing it, by the store of childhood impressions which he had forgotten, but which were still at work in him. It should be possible for us to show the origin of the phantasies in detail, even though we can only guess at them. He imagined, for instance, that Gradiva

1. [From this point to the middle of her next speech, when, as will be seen, she finally rebels, Zoe makes a valiant attempt to use the formal '*Sie*'.]

must be of *Greek* origin and that she was the daughter of a respected personage – a priest of Ceres, perhaps. This seems to fit in pretty well with his knowing that she bore the Greek name of Zoe and that she belonged to the family of a professor of zoology. But if Hanold's phantasies were transformed memories, we may expect to find an indication of the source of those phantasies in the information given us by Zoe Bertgang. Let us listen to what she has to say. She has told us of their intimate friendship in their childhood, and we shall now hear of the further course taken by this childhood relationship.

'At that time, as a matter of fact, up to about the age when, I don't know why, people begin to call us *"Backfisch"*,[1] I had got accustomed to being remarkably dependent on you and believed I could never in the world find a more agreeable friend. I had no mother or sister or brother, my father found a slow-worm in spirits considerably more interesting than me; and everyone (and I include girls) must have *something* to occupy their thoughts and whatever goes along with them. That was what you were then. But when archaeology took hold of you I discovered – you must forgive me, but really your polite innovation sounds to me *too* ridiculous and, besides, it doesn't fit in with what I want to express – as I was saying, it turned out that you'd[2] become an unbearable person who (at any rate so far as I was concerned) no longer had any eyes in his head or tongue in his mouth, or any memory, where my memory had stuck, of our friendship when we were children. No doubt that was why I looked different from before. For when from time to time I met you in society – it happ⌐₋₋₋d once as recently as last winter – you didn't see me, still less did I hear you say a word. Not that there was any distinction for me in that, for you treated everyone else alike. I was thin air for you, and you – with your tuft of fair hair that I'd rumpled for you often enough in the past – you were as dull, as dried-up, and as

1. [Literally 'fish for frying'. The common German slang term equivalent to 'flapper' or 'teenager'.]

2. [From this point onwards she finally reverts to '*du*'.]

tongue-tied as a stuffed cockatoo, and at the same time as grandiose as an — *archaeopteryx* — yes, that's right, that's what they call the antediluvian bird monstrosity they've dug up. Only there was one thing I hadn't suspected: that there was an equally grandiose phantasy lodged in your head of looking on me too, here in Pompeii, as something that had been dug up and come to life again. And when all at once there you were standing in front of me quite unexpectedly, it took me quite a lot of trouble at first to make out what an incredible cobweb your imagination had spun in your brain. After that, it amused me and quite pleased me in spite of its lunacy. For, as I told you, I hadn't suspected it of you.'

Thus she tells us plainly enough what with the years had become of their childhood friendship. In her it grew until she was thoroughly in love, for a girl must have something to which she can give her heart. Fräulein Zoe, the embodiment of cleverness and clarity, makes her own mind quite transparent to us. While it is in any case the general rule for a normally constituted girl to turn her affection towards her father in the first instance, Zoe, who had no one in her family but her father, was especially ready to do so. But her father had nothing left over for her: all his interest was engrossed by the objects of his science. So she was obliged to cast her eyes around upon other people, and became especially attached to her young playmate. When he too ceased to have any eyes for her, her love was not shaken by it but rather increased, for he had become like her father, was, like him, absorbed by science and held apart by it from life and from Zoe. Thus it was made possible for her to remain faithful in her unfaithfulness — to find her father once more in her loved one, to include both of them with the same emotion, or, as we may say, to identify both of them in her feeling. What is our justification for this piece of psychological analysis, which might well seem arbitrary? The author has presented us with it in a single, but highly characteristic, detail. When Zoe described the transformation in her former playmate which had so greatly disturbed her, she abused him by comparing him to an archaeopteryx, the bird-like monstrosity which belongs to the archaeology of zoology. In that way she found a single concrete expression of the identity of the two figures. Her complaint applies with the same word to the man she loved and to her father. The archaeopteryx is, we might say, a compromise idea or an intermediate idea[1] in which her thought about the folly of the man she loved coincided with the analogous thought about her father.

With the young man, things had taken a different turn. Archaeology took hold of him and left him with an interest only in women of marble and bronze. His childhood friendship, instead of being strengthened into a passion, was dissolved, and his memories of it passed into such profound forgetfulness that he did not recognize or notice his early playmate when he met her in society. It is true that when we look further we may doubt whether 'forgetfulness' is the correct psychological description of the fate of these memories in our young archaeologist. There is a kind of forgetting which is distinguished by the difficulty with which the memory is awakened even by a powerful external summons, as though some internal resistance were struggling against its revival. A forgetting of this kind has been given the name of 'repression' in psychopathology; and the case which our author has put before us seems to be an example of this repression. Now we do not know in general whether the forgetting of an impression is linked with the dissolution of its memory-trace in the mind; but we can assert quite definitely of 'repression' that it does not coincide with the dissolution or extinction of the memory. What is repressed cannot, it is true, as a rule make its way into memory without more ado; but it retains a capacity for effective action, and, under the influence of some external event, it may one day bring about psychical consequences which can be regarded as products of a modification of the forgotten memory and as derivatives of it and which remain

1. [Ideas of this kind play an important part in dreams and, indeed, wherever the primary psychical process is dominant. See *The Interpretation of Dreams* (1900*a*), *P.F.L.*, **4**, 755.]

unintelligible unless we take this view of them. We have already seemed to recognize in Norbert Hanold's phantasies about Gradiva derivatives of his repressed memories of his childhood friendship with Zoe Bertgang. A return like this of what has been repressed is to be expected with particular regularity when a person's erotic feelings are attached to the repressed impressions – when his erotic life has been attacked by repression. In such cases the old Latin saying holds true, though it may have been coined first to apply to expulsion by external influences and not to internal conflicts: 'Naturam expelles furca, tamen usque recurret.'[1] But it does not tell us everything. It only informs us of the fact of the return of the piece of nature that has been repressed; it does not describe the highly remarkable manner of that return, which is accomplished by what seems like a piece of malicious treachery. It is precisely what was chosen as the instrument of repression – like the '*furca*' of the Latin saying – that becomes the vehicle for the return: in and behind the repressing force, what is repressed proves itself victor in the end. This fact, which has been so little noticed and deserves so much consideration, is illustrated – more impressively than it could be by many examples – in a well-known etching by Félicien Rops; and it is illustrated in the typical case of repression in the life of saints and penitents. An ascetic monk has fled, no doubt from the temptations of the world, to the image of the crucified Saviour. And now the cross sinks down like a shadow, and in its place, radiant, there rises instead the image of a voluptuous, naked woman, in the same crucified attitude. Other artists with less psychological insight have, in similar representations of temptation, shown Sin, insolent and triumphant, in some position alongside of the Saviour on the cross. Only Rops has placed Sin in the very place of the Saviour on the cross. He seems to have known that, when what has been repressed returns, it emerges from the repressing force itself.

1. ['You may drive out Nature with a pitchfork, but she will always return.' This is actually a line of Horace (*Epistles*, I, 10, 24). It is misquoted in the German editions.]

It is worth while pausing in order to convince oneself from pathological cases how sensitive a human mind becomes in states of repression to any approach by what has been repressed, and how even trivial similarities suffice for the repressed to emerge behind the repressing force and take effect by means of it. I once had under medical treatment a young man – he was still almost a boy – who, after he had first unwillingly become acquainted with the process of sex, had taken flight from every sexual desire that arose in him. For that purpose he made use of various methods of repression: he intensified his zeal in learning, exaggerated his dependence on his mother, and in general assumed a childish character. I will not here enter into the manner in which his repressed sexuality broke through once more precisely in his relation to his mother; but I will describe a rarer and stranger instance of how another of his bulwarks collapsed on an occasion which could scarcely be regarded as sufficient. Mathematics enjoys the greatest reputation as a diversion from sexuality. This had been the very advice to which Jean-Jacques Rousseau was obliged to listen from a lady who was dissatisfied with him: 'Lascia le donne e studia la matematica!'[1] So too our fugitive threw himself with special eagerness into the mathematics and geometry which he was taught at school, till suddenly one day his powers of comprehension were paralysed in the face of some apparently innocent problems. It was possible to establish two of these problems: 'Two bodies come together, one with a speed of . . . etc.' and 'On a cylinder, the diameter of whose surface is m, describe a cone . . . etc.' Other people would certainly not have regarded these as very striking allusions to sexual events; but he felt that he had been betrayed by mathematics as well, and took flight from it too.

If Norbert Hanold were someone in real life who had in this way banished love and his childhood friendship with the help of archaeology, it would have been logical and according to rule that what revived in him the forgotten memory of the

1. ['Give up women and study mathematics!']

girl he had loved in his childhood should be precisely an antique sculpture. It would have been his well-deserved fate to fall in love with the marble portrait of Gradiva, behind which, owing to an unexplained similarity, the living Zoe whom he had neglected made her influence felt.

Fräulein Zoe seems herself to have shared our view of the young archaeologist's delusion, for the satisfaction she expressed at the end of her 'frank, detailed and instructive speech of castigation' could scarcely have been based on anything but a recognition that from the very first his interest in Gradiva had related to herself. It was *this* which she had not expected of him, but which, in spite of all its delusional disguise, she saw for what it was. The psychical treatment she had carried out, however, had now accomplished its beneficent effect on him. He felt free, for his delusion had now been replaced by the thing of which it could only have been a distorted and inadequate copy. Nor did he any longer hesitate to remember her and to recognize her as the kind, cheerful, clever playmate who in essentials was not in any way changed. But he found something else very strange –

'You mean', said the girl, 'the fact of someone having to die so as to come alive; but no doubt that must be so for archaeologists.' (141.) Evidently she had not forgiven him yet for the roundabout path by way of archaeology which he had followed from their childhood friendship to the new relation that was forming.

'No, I mean your name ... Because "Bertgang" means the same as "Gradiva" and describes someone "who steps along brilliantly".'[1] (142.)

We ourselves were unprepared for this. Our hero was beginning to cast off his humility and to play an active part. Evidently he was completely cured of his delusion and had risen above it; and he proved this by himself tearing the last threads of the cobweb of his delusion. This, too, is just how

1. [The German root *'bert'* or *'brecht'* is akin to the English 'bright'; similarly *'gang'* is akin to 'go' (in Scotland 'gang').]

patients behave when one has loosened the compulsion of their delusional thoughts by revealing the repressed material lying behind them. Once they have understood, they themselves bring forward the solutions of the final and most important riddles of their strange condition in a number of ideas that suddenly occur to them. We had already guessed that the Greek origin of the imaginary Gradiva was an obscure result of the Greek name 'Zoe'; but we had not ventured to approach the name 'Gradiva' itself, and had let it pass as the untrammelled creation of Norbert Hanold's imagination. But, lo and behold! that very name now turns out to have been a derivative – indeed a translation – of the repressed surname of the girl he had loved in the childhood which he was supposed to have forgotten.

The tracing back of the delusion and its resolution were now complete. What the author now adds is no doubt designed to serve as a harmonious end to his story. We cannot but feel reassured about the future when we hear that the young man, who had earlier been obliged to play the pitiable part of a person in urgent need of treatment, advanced still further on the road to recovery and succeeded in arousing in her some of the feelings under which he himself had suffered before. Thus it was that he made her jealous by mentioning the sympathetic young lady who had previously interrupted their tête-à-tête in the House of Meleager, and by confessing that she had been the first woman for whom he had felt a very great liking. Whereupon Zoe prepared to take a chilly leave of him, remarking that everything had now returned to reason – she herself not least; he could look up Gisa Hartleben (or whatever she was now called) again and give her some scientific assistance over the purpose of her visit to Pompeii; she herself, however, must go back to the Albergo del Sole where her father was expecting her for lunch; perhaps they would meet again some time at a party in Germany or in the moon. But once more he was able to make the troublesome fly an excuse for taking possession first of her cheek and then of her lips, and to set in motion the aggressiveness which is a man's inevitable duty in love-making. Once only a shadow seemed to fall on their happiness, when Zoe declared that now she really must go back to her father or he will starve at the Sole. 'Your father? ... what will happen? ...' (147.) But the clever girl was able swiftly to quiet his concern. 'Probably nothing will happen. I'm not an indispensable part of his zoological collection. If I had been, perhaps I shouldn't have been so foolish as to give my heart to you.' In the exceptional event, however, of her father taking a different view from hers, there was a safe expedient. Hanold need only cross to Capri, catch a *Lacerta faraglionensis* there (he could practise the technique on her little finger), set the creature free over here, catch it again before the zoologist's eyes, and let him choose between a *faraglionensis* on the mainland and his daughter. The scheme, it is easy to see, was one in which the mockery was tinged with bitterness; it was a warning, as it were, to her fiancé not to keep too closely to the model on which she had chosen him. Here again Norbert Hanold reassures us, by showing by all sorts of apparently small signs the great transformation that had taken place in him. He proposed that he and his Zoe should come for their honeymoon to Italy and Pompeii, just as though he had never been indignant with the honeymooning Edwins and Angelinas. He had completely lost from his memory all his feelings against those happy pairs, who had so unnecessarily travelled more than a hundred miles from their German home. The author is certainly right in bringing forward a loss of memory like this as the most trustworthy sign of a change of attitude. Zoe's reply to the plan for the scene of their honeymoon suggested by 'her childhood friend who had also in a sense been dug out of the ruins again' (150) was that she did not feel quite alive enough yet to make a geographical decision of that sort.

The delusion had now been conquered by a beautiful reality; but before the two lovers left Pompeii it was still to be honoured once again. When they reached the Herculanean Gate, where, at the entrance to the Via Consolare, the street is crossed by some ancient stepping-stones, Norbert Hanold paused and asked the girl to go ahead of him. She understood him 'and, pulling up her dress a little with her left hand, Zoe Bertgang, Gradiva rediviva, walked past, held in his eyes, which seemed to gaze as though in a dream; so, with her quietly tripping gait, she stepped through the sunlight over the stepping-stones to the other side of the street.' With the triumph of love, what was beautiful and precious in the delusion found recognition as well.

In his last simile, however – of the 'childhood friend who had been dug out of the ruins' – the author has presented us with the key to the symbolism of which the hero's delusion made use in disguising his repressed memory. There is, in fact, no better analogy for repression, by which something in the mind is at once made inaccessible and preserved, than burial of the sort to which Pompeii fell a victim and from which it could emerge once more through the work of spades. Thus it was that the young archaeologist was obliged in his phantasy to transport to Pompeii the original of the relief which reminded him of the object of his youthful love. The author was well justified, indeed, in lingering over the valuable similarity which his delicate sense had perceived between a particular mental process in the individual and an isolated historical event in the history of mankind.[1]

1. [Freud himself adopted the fate of Pompeii as a simile for repression in more than one later passage. See, for instance, the 'Rat Man' case history (1909*d*), written not long after the present work; *P.F.L.*, **9**, 57.]

II

BUT after all, what we really intended to do originally was only to investigate two or three dreams that are to be found here and there in *Gradiva* with the help of certain analytic methods. How has it come about, then, that we have been led into dissecting the whole story and examining the mental processes in the two chief characters? This has not in fact been an unnecessary piece of work; it was an essential preliminary. It is equally the case that when we try to understand the real dreams of a real person we have to concern ourselves intensively with his character and his career, and we must get to know not only his experiences shortly before the dream but also those dating far back into the past. It is even my view that we are still not free to turn to our proper task, but that we must linger a little more over the story itself and carry out some further preliminary work.

My readers will no doubt have been puzzled to notice that so far I have treated Norbert Hanold and Zoe Bertgang, in all their mental manifestations and activities, as though they were real people and not the author's creations, as though the author's mind were an absolutely transparent medium and not a refractive or obscuring one. And my procedure must seem all the more puzzling since the author has expressly renounced the portrayal of reality by calling his story a 'phantasy'. We have found, however, that all his descriptions are so faithfully copied from reality that we should not object if *Gradiva* were described not as a phantasy but as a psychiatric study. Only at two points has the author availed himself of the licence open to him of laying down premisses which do not seem to have their roots in the laws of reality. The first time is where he makes the young archaeologist come upon what is undoubtedly an ancient relief but which so closely resembles a person living long afterwards, not only in the peculiarity of the posture of the foot as it steps along but in every detail of facial structure and bodily attitude, that the young man is able to take the physical appearance of that person to be the sculpture come to life. And the second time is where he makes the young man meet the living woman precisely in Pompeii; for the dead woman had been placed there only by his imagination, and the journey to Pompeii had in fact carried him away from the living woman, whom he had just seen in the street of the town in which he lived. This second provision of the author's, however, involves no violent departure from actual possibility; it merely makes use of chance, which unquestionably plays a part in many human histories; and furthermore he uses it to good purpose, for this chance reflects the fatal truth that has laid it down that flight is precisely an instrument that delivers one over to what one is fleeing from. The first premiss seems to lean more towards phantasy and to spring entirely from the author's arbitrary decision – the premiss on which all that follows depends, the far-reaching resemblance between the sculpture and the live girl, which a more sober choice might have restricted to the single feature of the posture of the foot as it steps along. We might be tempted here to allow the play of our own phantasy to forge a link with reality. The name of 'Bertgang' might point to the fact that the women of that family had already been distinguished in ancient days by the peculiarity of their graceful gait; and we might suppose that the Germanic Bertgangs were descended from a Roman family one member of which was the woman who had led the artist to perpetuate the peculiarity of her gait in the sculpture. Since, however, the different variations of the human form are not independent of one another, and since in fact even among ourselves the ancient types reappear again and again (as we can see in art collections), it would not be totally impossible that a modern Bertgang might reproduce the shape of her ancient ancestress in all the other features of her bodily structure as well. But it would no doubt be wiser, instead of such speculations, to inquire from the author himself what were the sources from which this part of his creation was derived; we should then have a good prospect of showing once again how what was ostensibly an arbitrary decision rested in fact upon law. But since access to the sources in the author's mind is not open to us,[1] we will leave him with an undiminished right to construct a development that is wholly true to life upon an improbable premiss – a right of which Shakespeare, for instance, availed himself in *King Lear*.[2]

Apart from this, it must be repeated, the author has presented us with a perfectly correct psychiatric study, on which we may measure our understanding of the workings of the mind – a case history and the history of a cure which might have been designed to emphasize certain fundamental theories of medical psychology. It is strange enough that the author should have done this. But how if, on being questioned, he were completely to deny any such purpose? It is so easy to draw analogies and to read meanings into things. Is it not rather we who have slipped into this charming poetic story a secret meaning very far from its author's intentions? Possibly. We shall come back to the question later. For the moment, however, we have tried to save ourselves from making any such tendentious interpretation by giving the story almost entirely in the author's own words. Anyone who compares our reproduction with the actual text of *Gradiva* will have to concede us that much.

Perhaps, too, in most people's eyes we are doing our author a poor service in declaring his work to be a psychiatric study. An author, we hear them say, should keep out of the way of any contact with psychiatry and should leave the description of pathological mental states to the doctors. The truth is that no truly creative writer has ever obeyed this injunction. The description of the human mind is indeed the domain which is most his own; he has from time immemorial been the precursor of science, and so too of scientific psychology. But the frontier between states of mind described as normal and pathological is in part a conventional one and in part so

1. [Cf. the 'Postscript' to this work, p. 117 below.]
2. [Some further comment on the 'improbable premiss' to *King Lear* will be found at the end of Freud's paper on 'The Theme of the Three Caskets' (1913*f*), p. 246 below.]

fluctuating that each of us probably crosses it many times in the course of a day. On the other hand, psychiatry would be doing wrong if it tried to restrict itself permanently to the study of the severe and gloomy illnesses that arise from gross injuries to the delicate apparatus of the mind. Deviations from health which are slighter and capable of correction, and which to-day we can trace back no further than to disturbances in the inter-play of mental forces, arouse its interest no less. Indeed, only through the medium of these can it understand either normal states or the phenomena of severe illness. Thus the creative writer cannot evade the psychiatrist nor the psychiatrist the creative writer, and the poetic treatment of a psychiatric theme can turn out to be correct without any sacrifice of its beauty.[1]

And it is really correct — this imaginative picture of the history of a case and its treatment. Now that we have finished telling the story and satisfied our own suspense, we can get a better view of it, and we shall now reproduce it with the technical terminology of our science, and in doing so we shall not feel disconcerted at the necessity for repeating what we have said before.

Norbert Hanold's condition is often spoken of by the author as a 'delusion', and we have no reason to reject that designation. We can state two chief characteristics of a 'delusion', which do not, it is true, describe it exhaustively, but which distinguish it recognizably from other disorders. In the first place it is one of the group of pathological states which do not produce a direct effect upon the body but are manifested only by mental indications. And secondly it is characterized by the fact that in it 'phantasies' have gained the upper hand — that is, have obtained belief and have acquired an influence on action. If we recall Hanold's journey to Pompeii in order to look for Gradiva's peculiarly formed footprints in the ashes, we shall have a fine example of an action under the dominance of a

1. [Another discussion by Freud of the use of psychopathological material by creative writers will be found in a posthumously published essay, 'Psycho-pathic Characters on the Stage' (1942a), p. 119 ff. below.]

delusion. A psychiatrist would perhaps place Norbert Hanold's delusion in the great group of 'paranoia' and possibly describe it as 'fetishistic erotomania', because the most striking thing about it was his being in love with the piece of sculpture and because in the psychiatrist's view, with its tendency to coarsen everything, the young archaeologist's interest in feet and the postures of feet would be bound to suggest 'fetishism'. Nevertheless all such systems of nomenclature and classification of the different kinds of delusion according to their subject-matter have something precarious and barren about them.[1]

Furthermore, since our hero was a person capable of developing a delusion on the basis of such a strange preference, a strict psychiatrist would at once stamp him as a *dégénéré* and would investigate the heredity which had remorselessly driven him to this fate. But here the author does not follow the psychiatrist, and with good reason. He wishes to bring the hero closer to us so as to make 'empathy' easier; the diagnosis of '*dégénéré*', whether it is right or wrong, at once puts the young archaeologist at a distance from us, for we readers are the normal people and the standard of humanity. Nor is the author greatly concerned with the hereditary and constitutional pre-conditions of the state, but on the other hand he plunges deep into the personal mental make-up which can give rise to such a delusion.

In one important respect Norbert Hanold behaved quite differently from an ordinary human being. He took no interest in living women; the science of which he was the servant had taken that interest away from him and displaced it on to women of marble or bronze. This is not to be regarded as a trivial peculiarity; on the contrary, it was the basic precondition of the events to be described. For one day it came about that one particular sculpture of that kind laid claim to the whole of the interest which is ordinarily directed only to a living woman, and with that his delusion was there. We then see unrolled

1. In point of fact, the case of N.H. would have to be described as a hysterical delusion, not a paranoic one. The indications of paranoia are absent from it.

before our eyes the manner in which his delusion is cured through a happy turn of events, and his interest displaced back from the marble to a living woman. The author does not let us follow the influences which led our hero to turn away from women; he only informs us that his attitude was not explained by his innate disposition, which, on the contrary, included some amount of imaginative (and, we might add, erotic) needs. And, as we learn later in the story, he did not avoid other children in his childhood: he had a friendship at that age with a little girl, was her inseparable companion, shared his little meals with her, used to thump her too and let her rumple his hair. It is in attachments such as this, in combinations like this of affection and aggressiveness, that the immature erotism of childhood finds its expression; its consequences only emerge later, but then they are irresistible, and during childhood itself it is as a rule recognized as erotism only by doctors and creative writers. Our own writer shows us clearly that he too is of the same opinion; for he makes his hero suddenly develop a lively interest in women's feet and their way of placing them. This interest was bound to bring him a bad reputation both among scientists and among the women of the town he lived in, a reputation of being a foot-fetishist; but *we* cannot avoid tracing the interest back to the memory of his childhood playmate. For there can be no doubt that even in her childhood the girl showed the same peculiarity of a graceful gait, with her toes almost perpendicularly raised as she stepped along; and it was because it represented that same gait that an ancient marble relief acquired such great importance for Norbert Hanold. Incidentally we may add that in his derivation of the remarkable phenomenon of fetishism the author is in complete agreement with science. Ever since Binet [1888] we have in fact tried to trace fetishism back to erotic impressions in childhood.[1]

The state of permanently turning away from women

---

1. [Binet's views on fetishism were described in Freud's *Three Essays on the Theory of Sexuality* (1905*d*), to which however he added a footnote in 1920 casting doubts on their adequacy. (*P.F.L.*, **7**, 67 and *n*. 1.) See also Freud's paper on fetishism (1927*e*), ibid., **7**, 345.]

produces a personal susceptibility, or, as we are accustomed to say, a 'disposition' to the formation of a delusion. The development of the mental disorder sets in at the moment when a chance impression arouses the childhood experiences which have been forgotten and which have traces, at least, of an erotic colouring. 'Arouses', however, is certainly not the right description, if we take into account what follows. We must repeat the author's accurate account in correct psychological technical terms. When Norbert Hanold saw the relief, he did not remember that he had already seen a similar posture of the foot in his childhood friend; he remembered nothing at all, but all the effects brought about by the relief originated from this link that was made with the impression of his childhood. Thus the childhood impression was stirred up, it became active, so that it began to produce effects, but it did not come into consciousness – it remained 'unconscious', to use a term which has to-day become unavoidable in psychopathology. We are anxious that this unconscious shall not be involved in any of the disputes of philosophers and natural philosophers, which have often no more than an etymological importance. For the time being we possess no better name for psychical processes which behave actively but nevertheless do not reach the consciousness of the person concerned, and that is all we mean by our 'unconsciousness'. When some thinkers try to dispute the existence of an unconscious of this kind, on the ground that it is nonsensical, we can only suppose that they have never had to do with the corresponding mental phenomena, that they are under the spell of the regular experience that everything mental that becomes active and intense becomes at the same time conscious as well, and that they have still to learn (what our author knows very well) that there are most certainly mental processes which, in spite of being intense and producing effects, none the less remain apart from consciousness.

We said a little earlier that Norbert Hanold's memories of his childhood relations with Zoe were in a state of 'repression'; and here we have called them 'unconscious' memories. So we must now pay a little attention to the relation between these two technical terms, which, indeed, appear to coincide in their meaning. It is not difficult to make the matter plain. 'Unconscious' is the wider concept; 'repressed' is the narrower one. Everything that is repressed is unconscious; but we cannot assert that everything unconscious is repressed. If when Hanold saw the relief he had remembered his Zoe's gait, what had earlier been an unconscious memory of his would have become simultaneously active and conscious, and this would have shown that it had not earlier been repressed. 'Unconscious' is a purely descriptive term, one that is indefinite in some respects and, as we might say, static. 'Repressed' is a dynamic expression, which takes account of the interplay of mental forces; it implies that there is a force present which is seeking to bring about all kinds of psychical effects, including that of becoming conscious, but that there is also an opposing force which is able to obstruct some of these psychical effects, once more including that of becoming conscious. The mark of something repressed is precisely that in spite of its intensity it is unable to enter consciousness. In Hanold's case, therefore, from the moment of the appearance of the relief onwards, we are concerned with something unconscious that is repressed, or, more briefly, with something repressed.

Norbert Hanold's memories of his childhood relations with the girl with the graceful gait were repressed; but this is not yet the correct view of the psychological situation. We remain on the surface so long as we are dealing only with memories and ideas. What is alone of value in mental life is rather the feelings. No mental forces are significant unless they possess the characteristic of arousing feelings. Ideas are only repressed because they are associated with the release of feelings which ought not to occur. It would be more correct to say that repression acts upon feelings, but we can only be aware of these in their association with ideas.[1] So that it was Norbert Hanold's

1. [Some of this would need to be expressed differently in order to fit in with Freud's later and more elaborate discussions of repression, which are to be found, for instance, in Sections III and IV of his paper on 'The Unconscious' (1915*e*), *P.F.L.*, 11, 179–89.]

erotic feelings that were repressed; and since his erotism knew and had known no other object than Zoe Bertgang in his childhood, his memories of her were forgotten. The ancient relief aroused the slumbering erotism in him, and made his childhood memories active. On account of a resistance to erotism that was present in him, these memories could only become operative as unconscious ones. What now took place in him was a struggle between the power of erotism and that of the forces that were repressing it; the manifestation of this struggle was a delusion.

Our author has omitted to give the reasons which led to the repression of the erotic life of his hero; for of course Hanold's concern with science was only the instrument which the repression employed. A doctor would have to dig deeper here, but perhaps without hitting upon the reason in this case. But, as we have insisted with admiration, the author has not failed to show us how the arousing of the repressed erotism came precisely from the field of the instruments that served to bring about the repression. It was right that an antique, the marble sculpture of a woman, should have been what tore our archaeologist away from his retreat from love and warned him to pay off the debt to life with which we are burdened from our birth.

The first manifestations of the process that had been set going in Hanold by the relief were phantasies, which played around the figure represented in it. The figure seemed to him to have something 'of to-day' about her, in the best sense of the words, and it was as though the artist had captured her 'from the life' stepping along the street. He gave the girl in the ancient relief the name of 'Gradiva', which he constructed on the model of an epithet of the war-god striding into battle – 'Mars Gradivus'. He endowed her personality with more and more characteristics. She may have been the daughter of a respected personage, of a patrician, perhaps, who was connected with the temple service of a deity. He thought he could trace a Greek origin in her features; and finally he felt compelled to remove her from the busy life of a capital and to transport her to the

more peaceful Pompeii, and there he made her step across the
lava stepping-stones which made it possible to cross from one
side of the street to the other. These products of his phantasy
seem arbitrary enough, but at the same time innocently un-
suspicious. And, indeed, even when for the first time they gave
rise to an incitement to action – when the archaeologist,
obsessed by the problem of whether this posture of the feet
corresponded to reality, began to make observations from life
in order to examine the feet of contemporary women and girls
– even this action was screened by conscious scientific motives,
as though all his interest in the sculpture of Gradiva had sprung
from the soil of his professional concern with archaeology. The
women and girls in the street, whom he chose as the subjects
of his investigation, must, of course, have taken another,
crudely erotic view of his behaviour, and we cannot but think
them right. We ourselves can be in no doubt that Hanold was
as much in ignorance of the motives of his researches as he
was of the origin of his phantasies about Gradiva. These, as
we learned later, were echoes of his memories of his youthful love, derivatives of those memories, transformations and
distortions of them, after they had failed to make their way
into his consciousness in an unmodified form. The ostensibly
aesthetic judgement that the sculpture had something 'of to-
day' about it took the place of his knowledge that a gait of
that kind belonged to a girl whom he knew and who stepped
across the street *at the present time*. Behind the impression of
the sculpture being 'from the life' and the phantasy of its subject
being Greek lay his memory of the name Zoe, which means
'life' in Greek. 'Gradiva', as we learn from our hero himself
at the end of the story, after he has been cured of his delusion,
is a good translation of the surname 'Bertgang' which means
something like 'someone who steps along brilliantly or
splendidly'. The details about Gradiva's father originated from
Hanold's knowledge that Zoe Bertgang was the daughter of
a respected teacher at the university, which can well be translated into classical terms as 'temple service'. Finally, his phantasy
transported her to Pompeii, not 'because her quiet, calm nature

seemed to demand it', but because no other or better analogy could be found in his science for his remarkable state, in which he became aware of his memories of his childhood friendship through obscure channels of information. Once he had made his own childhood coincide with the classical past (which it was so easy for him to do), there was a perfect similarity between the burial of Pompeii – the disappearance of the past combined with its preservation – and repression, of which he possessed a knowledge through what might be described as 'endopsychic' perception.[1] In this he was employing the same symbolism that the author makes the girl use consciously towards the conclusion of the story: 'I told myself I should be able to dig out something interesting here even by myself. Of course I hadn't counted on making the find that I have ...' (124.) And at the very end she replied to Hanold's plan for their honeymoon with a reference to 'her childhood friend who had also in a sense been dug out of the ruins again'. (150.)

Thus in the very first products of Hanold's delusional phantasies and actions we already find a double set of determinants, a derivation from two different sources. One of these is the one that was manifest to Hanold himself, the other is the one which is revealed to us when we examine his mental processes. One of them, looked at from Hanold's point of view, was conscious to him, the other was completely unconscious to him. One of them was derived wholly from the circle of ideas of the science of archaeology, the other arose from the repressed childhood memories that had become active in him and from the emotional instincts attached to them. One might be described as lying on the surface and covering the other, which was, as it were, concealed behind it. The scientific motivation might be said to serve as a pretext for the unconscious erotic one, and science had put itself completely at the service of the delusion. It should not be forgotten, however, that the unconscious determinants could not effect anything that did not simultaneously satisfy the conscious, scientific ones.

1. [Cf. *The Psychopathology of Everyday Life* (1901*b*), *P.F.L.*, **5**, 321, and the 'Rat Man' case history (1909*d*), ibid., **9**, 111 f.]

The symptoms of a delusion – phantasies and actions alike –
are in fact the products of compromise between the two mental
currents, and in a compromise account is taken of the demands
of each of the two parties to it; but each side must also renounce
a part of what it wanted to achieve. Where a compromise comes
about it must have been preceded by a struggle – in this case
it was the conflict we have assumed between suppressed erotism
and the forces that were keeping it in repression. In the
formation of a delusion this struggle is in fact unending. Assault
and resistance are renewed after the construction of each
compromise, which is never, so to speak, entirely satisfying.
Our author too is aware of this, and that is why he makes
a peculiar unrest dominate this stage of his hero's disorder, as
a precursor and guarantee of further developments.

These significant peculiarities – the double motivation of
phantasies and decisions, and the construction of conscious pretexts for actions to whose motivation the repressed has made
the major contribution – will meet us often, and perhaps more
clearly, in the further course of the story. And this is just as
it should be, for the author has thus grasped and represented
the unfailing chief characteristic of pathological mental
processes.

The development of Norbert Hanold's delusion proceeded
with a dream which, since it was not occasioned by any new
event, seems to have arisen entirely out of his mind, filled as
it was by a conflict. But let us pause before we inquire whether,
in the construction of his dreams, too, the author meets our
expectation that he possesses a deep understanding. Let us ask
first what psychiatric science has to say to his hypotheses about
the origin of a delusion and what attitude it takes to the part
played by repression and the unconscious, to conflict and to
the formation of compromises. In short, let us ask whether
this imaginative representation of the genesis of a delusion can
hold its own before the judgement of science.

And here we must give what will perhaps be an unexpected
answer. In fact the situation is quite the reverse: it is science

that cannot hold its own before the achievement of the author. Science allows a gulf to yawn between the hereditary and constitutional preconditions of a delusion and its creations, which seem to emerge ready-made – a gulf which we find that our author has filled. Science does not as yet suspect the importance of repression, it does not recognize that in order to explain the world of psychopathological phenomena the unconscious is absolutely essential, it does not look for the basis of delusions in a psychical conflict, and it does not regard their symptoms as compromises. Does our author stand alone, then, in the face of united science? No, that is not the case (if, that is, I may count my own works as part of science), since for a number of years – and, until recently, more or less alone[1] – I myself have supported all the views that I have here extracted from Jensen's *Gradiva* and stated in technical terms. I indicated, in most detail in connection with the states known as hysteria and obsessions, that the individual determinant[2] of these psychical disorders is the suppression of a part of instinctual life and the repression of the ideas by which the suppressed instinct is represented, and soon afterwards I repeated the same views in relation to some forms of delusion.[3] The question whether the instincts concerned in this causation are always components of the sexual instinct or may be of another kind as well is a problem which may be regarded as a matter of indifference in the particular case of the analysis of *Gradiva*; for in the instance chosen by our author what was at issue was quite certainly nothing other than the suppression of erotic feelings. The validity of the hypotheses of psychical conflict and of the formation of symptoms by means of compromises

1. See Bleuler's important work, *Affektivität, Suggestibilität, Paranoia* and C. G. Jung's *Diagnostische Assoziationsstudien*, both published in Zürich in 1906. – [*Added* 1912:] To-day, in 1912, I am able to retract what is said above as being no longer true. Since it was written, the 'psychoanalytic movement' started by me has become widely extended, and it is constantly growing.

2. [As contrasted, presumably, with a more general, inherited factor.]

3. See the author's *Sammlung kleiner Schriften zur Neurosenlehre*, 1906 [in particular, the second paper on 'The Neuro-Psychoses of Defence' (1896*b*), *Standard Ed.*, **3**, 159].

between the two mental currents struggling against each other has been demonstrated by me in the case of patients observed and medically treated in real life, just as I have been able to in the imaginary case of Norbert Hanold.[1] Even before me, Pierre Janet, a pupil of the great Charcot, and Josef Breuer, in collaboration with me, had traced back the products of neurotic, and especially of hysterical, illness to the power of unconscious thoughts.[2]

When, from the year 1893 onwards, I plunged into investigations such as these of the origin of mental disturbances, it would certainly never have occurred to me to look for a confirmation of my findings in imaginative writings. I was thus more than a little surprised to find that the author of *Gradiva*, which was published in 1903, had taken as the basis of its creation the very thing that I believed myself to have freshly discovered from the sources of my medical experience. How was it that the author arrived at the same knowledge as the doctor – or at least behaved as though he possessed the same knowledge?

Norbert Hanold's delusion, as I was saying, was carried a step further by a dream which occurred in the middle of his efforts to discover a gait like Gradiva's in the streets of the town where he lived. It is easy to give the content of this dream in brief. The dreamer found himself in Pompeii on the day on which that unhappy city was destroyed, and experienced its horrors without being in danger himself; he suddenly saw Gradiva stepping along there, and understood all at once, as though it was something quite natural, that since she was a Pompeian, she was living in her native town, and 'without his having suspected it, living as his contemporary'. He was seized with fear on her account and gave a warning cry, whereupon she turned her face towards him for a moment. But she proceeded on her way without paying any attention to him,

1. Cf. 'Fragment of an Analysis of a Case of Hysteria' (1905e) [*P.F.L.*, 8, 29].

2. Cf. *Studies on Hysteria* (Freud, 1895d, with Breuer) [ibid., 3].

lay down on the steps of the Temple of Apollo, and was buried in the rain of ashes after her face had lost its colour, as though it were turning into white marble, until it had become just like a piece of sculpture. As he was waking up, he interpreted the noises of a big city penetrating into his bedroom as the cries for help of the despairing inhabitants of Pompeii and the thunder of the wildly agitated sea. The feeling that what he had dreamt had really happened to him would not leave him for some time after he had awoken, and a conviction that Gradiva had lived in Pompeii and had perished there on the fatal day was left over with him by the dream as a fresh starting-point for his delusion.

It is not so easy for us to say what the author intended with this dream and what caused him to link the development of the delusion precisely to a dream. Zealous investigators, it is true, have collected plenty of examples of the way in which mental disturbances are linked to dreams and arise out of dreams.[1] It appears, too, that in the lives of a few eminent men impulses to important actions and decisions have originated from dreams. But these analogies are not of much help to our understanding; so let us keep to our present case, our author's imaginary case of Norbert Hanold the archaeologist. By which end are we to take hold of a dream like this so as to fit it into the whole context, if it is not to remain no more than an unnecessary decoration of the story?

I can well imagine that at this point a reader may exclaim: 'The dream is quite easily explained – it is a simple anxiety-dream, occasioned by the noises of the city, which were misinterpreted into the destruction of Pompeii by the archaeologist, whose mind was occupied with his Pompeian girl.' In view of the low opinion generally prevailing of the performances of dreams, all that is usually asked from an explanation of one is that some external stimulus shall be found that more or less coincides with a piece of the dream's content. This external stimulus to dreaming would be supplied by the

1. Sante de Sanctis (1899). [Cf. *The Interpretation of Dreams* (1900a), *P.F.L.*, 4, 160 ff.]

noise which woke the sleeper; and with this, interest in the dream would be exhausted. If only we had some reason for supposing that the town was noisier than usual that morning! If only, for instance, the author had not omitted to tell us that Hanold, against his usual practice, had slept that night with his windows open! What a pity the author did not take the trouble to do that! And if only anxiety-dreams were as simple as that! But no, interest in the dream is not so easily exhausted.

There is nothing essential for the construction of a dream in a link with an external sensory stimulus. A sleeper can disregard a stimulus of this kind from the external world, or he can allow himself to be awakened by it without constructing a dream, or, as happened here, he can weave it into his dream if that suits him for some other reason; and there are numerous dreams of which it is impossible to show that their content was determined in this way by a stimulus impinging on the sleeper's senses.[1] No, we must try another path.

We may perhaps find a starting-point in the after-effects left by the dream in Hanold's waking life. Up to then he had had a phantasy that Gradiva had been a Pompeian. This hypothesis now became a certainty for him, and a second certainty followed – that she was buried along with the rest in the year 79 A.D.[2] Melancholy feelings accompanied this extension of the delusional structure, like an echo of the anxiety which had filled the dream. This fresh pain about Gradiva does not seem very intelligible to us; Gradiva would have been dead for many centuries even if she had been saved from destruction in the year 79 A.D. Or ought we not to argue in this kind of way either with Norbert Hanold or with the author himself? Here again there seems no path to an understanding. Nevertheless it is worth remarking that the increment which the delusion acquired from this dream was accompanied by a feeling with a highly painful colouring.

Apart from that, however, we are as much at a loss as before. This dream is not self-explanatory, and we must resolve to

1. [Cf. *The Interpretation of Dreams* (1900a), *P.F.L.*, **4**, 318–19.]
2. See the text of *Gradiva* (15).

borrow from my *Interpretation of Dreams* and apply to the present example a few of the rules to be found in it for the solution of dreams.

One of these rules is to the effect that a dream is invariably related to the events of the day before the dream.[1] Our author seems to be wishing to show that he has followed this rule, for he attaches the dream immediately to Hanold's 'pedestrian researches'. Now these had no meaning other than a search for Gradiva, whose characteristic gait he was trying to recognize. So the dream ought to have contained an indication of where Gradiva was to be found. And it does so, by showing her in Pompeii; but that is no novelty to us.

Another rule tells us that, if a belief in the reality of the dream-images persists unusually long, so that one cannot tear oneself out of the dream, this is not a mistaken judgement provoked by the vividness of the dream-images, but is a psychical act on its own: it is an assurance, relating to the content of the dream, that something in it is really as one has dreamt it;[2] and it is right to have faith in this assurance. If we keep to these two rules, we must conclude that the dream gave some information as to the whereabouts of the Gradiva he was in search of, and that that information tallied with the real state of things. We know Hanold's dream: does the application of these two rules to it yield any reasonable sense?

Strange to say, it does. The sense is merely disguised in a particular way so that it is not immediately recognizable. Hanold learned in the dream that the girl he was looking for was living in a town and contemporaneously with him. Now this was true of Zoe Bertgang; only in the dream the town was not the German university town but Pompeii, and the time was not the present but the year 79 A.D. It is, as it were, a distortion by displacement: what we have is not Gradiva in the present but the dreamer transported into the past. Nevertheless, in this manner, the essential and new fact is stated: *he*

---

1. [*The Interpretation of Dreams* (1900*a*), P.F.L., **4**, 249 ff.]

2. [Ibid., **4**, 276, 491–2. Freud insisted upon this point again in his comments on the 'Wolf Man' dream (1918*b*), ibid., **9**, 264.]

is in the same place and time as the girl he is looking for. But whence come this displacement and disguise which were bound to deceive both us and the dreamer over the true meaning and content of the dream? Well, we already have the means at our disposal for giving a satisfactory answer to that question.

Let us recall all that we have heard about the nature and origin of the phantasies which are the precursors of delusions [p. 69 ff.]. They are substitutes for and derivatives of repressed memories which a resistance will not allow to enter consciousness unaltered, but which can purchase the possibility of becoming conscious by taking account, by means of changes and distortions, of the resistance's censorship. When this compromise has been accomplished, the memories have turned into phantasies, which can easily be misunderstood by the conscious personality – that is, understood so as to fit in with the dominant psychical current. Now let us suppose that dream-images are what might be described as the creations of people's physiological [i.e. non-pathological] delusions – the products of the compromise in the struggle between what is repressed and what is dominant which is probably present in every human being, including those who in the day-time are perfectly sound in mind. We shall then understand that dream-images have to be regarded as something distorted, behind which something else must be looked for, something *not* distorted, but in some sense objectionable, like Hanold's repressed memories behind his phantasies. We can give expression to the contrast which we have thus recognized, by distinguishing what the dreamer remembers when he wakes up as the *manifest content of the dream* from what constituted the basis of the dream before the distortion imposed by the censorship – namely, the *latent dream-thoughts*. Thus, interpreting a dream consists in translating the manifest content of the dream into the latent dream-thoughts, in undoing the distortion which the dream-thoughts have had to submit to from the censorship of the resistance. If we apply these notions to the dream we are concerned with, we shall find that its latent dream-thoughts can only have been: 'the girl you are looking for with the graceful gait is really living in this town with you.' But in that form the thought could not become conscious. It was obstructed by the fact that a phantasy had laid it down, as the result of an earlier compromise, that Gradiva was a Pompeian; consequently, if the real fact that she was living in the same place and at the same time was to be affirmed, there was no choice but to adopt the distortion: 'You are living at Pompeii at the time of Gradiva.' This then was the idea which was realized by the manifest content of the dream, and was represented as a present event actually being experienced.

It is only rarely that a dream represents, or, as we might say, 'stages', a single thought: there are usually a number of them, a tissue of thoughts. Another component of the content of Hanold's dream can be detached, the distortion of which can easily be got rid of, so that the latent idea represented by it can be detected. This is a piece of the dream to which once again it is possible to extend the assurance of reality with which the dream ended. In the dream Gradiva as she steps along is transformed into a marble sculpture. This is no more than an ingenious and poetical representation of the real event. Hanold had in fact transferred his interest from the living girl to the sculpture: the girl he loved had been transformed for him into a marble relief. The latent dream-thoughts, which were bound to remain unconscious, sought to change the sculpture back into the living girl; what they were saying to him accordingly was something like: 'After all, you're only interested in the statue of Gradiva because it reminds you of Zoe, who is living here and now.' But if this discovery could have become conscious, it would have meant the end of the delusion.

Are we perhaps under an obligation to replace in this way each separate piece of the manifest content of the dream by unconscious thoughts? Strictly speaking, yes; if we were interpreting a dream that had really been dreamt, we could not avoid that duty. But in that case, too, the dreamer would have to give us the most copious explanations. Clearly we cannot carry out this requirement in the case of the author's creation; nevertheless, we shall not overlook the fact that we have not yet submitted the main content of the dream to the process of interpretation or translation.

For Hanold's dream was an anxiety-dream. Its content was frightening, the dreamer felt anxiety while he slept and he was left with painful feelings afterwards. Now this is far from convenient for our attempt at an explanation; and we must once again borrow heavily from the theory of dream-interpretation. We are warned by that theory not to fall into the error of tracing the anxiety that may be felt in a dream to the content of the dream, and not to treat the content of the dream as though it were the content of an idea occurring in waking life. It points out to us how often we dream the most ghastly things without feeling a trace of anxiety. The true situation, we learn, is quite a different one, which cannot be easily guessed, but which can be proved with certainty. The anxiety in anxiety-dreams, like neurotic anxiety in general, corresponds to a sexual affect, a libidinal feeling, and arises out of libido by the process of repression.[1] When we interpret a dream, therefore, we must replace anxiety by sexual excitement. The anxiety that originates in this way has – not invariably, but frequently – a selective influence on the content of the dream and introduces into it ideational elements which seem, when the dream is looked at from a conscious and mistaken point of view, to be appropriate to the affect of anxiety. As I have said, this is not invariably so, for there are plenty of anxiety-dreams in which the content is not in the least frightening and where it is therefore impossible to give an explanation on conscious lines of the anxiety that is felt.

I am aware that this explanation of anxiety in dreams sounds very strange and is not easy to credit; but I can only advise the reader to come to terms with it. Moreover it would be a very remarkable thing if Norbert Hanold's dream could be reconciled with this view of anxiety and could be explained

1. Cf. my first paper on the anxiety neurosis (1895*b*) and *The Interpretation of Dreams*. [*P.F.L.*, **10**, 31 ff., and ibid., **4**, 245–6, 739 ff. – Freud put forward an amended view of the origin of anxiety in *Inhibitions, Symptoms and Anxiety* (1926*d*), ibid., **10**, 320 ff.]

in that way. On that basis, we should say that the dreamer's erotic longings were stirred up during the night and made a powerful effort to make conscious his memory of the girl he loved and so to tear him out of his delusion, but that those longings met with a fresh repudiation and were transformed into anxiety, which in its turn introduced into the content of the dream the terrifying pictures from the memories of his schooldays. In this manner the true unconscious content of the dream, his passionate longing for the Zoe he had once known, became transformed into its manifest content of the destruction of Pompeii and the loss of Gradiva.

So far, I think, it sounds plausible. But it might justly be insisted that, if erotic wishes constitute the undistorted content of the dream, it ought also to be possible to point at least to some recognizable residue of those wishes concealed somewhere in the transformed dream. Well, even that may be possible, with the help of a hint from a later part of the story. When Hanold had his first meeting with the supposed Gradiva, he recollected the dream and begged the apparition to lie down again as he had seen her do then.[1] Thereupon, however, the young lady rose indignantly and left her strange companion, for she had detected the improper erotic wish behind what he had said under the domination of his delusion. We must, I think, accept Gradiva's interpretation; even in a real dream we cannot always expect to find a more definite expression of an erotic wish.

The application of a few of the rules of dream-interpretation to Hanold's first dream has thus resulted in making it intelligible to us in its main features and in inserting it into the nexus of the story. Surely, then, the author must have observed these rules in creating it? We might ask another question, too: why did the author introduce a dream at all to bring about the further development of the delusion? In my opinion it was an ingenious

1. 'No, I didn't hear you speak. But I called to you when you lay down to sleep, and I stood beside you then – your face was as peaceful and beautiful as marble. May I beg of you – lie down once more on the step as you did then.' (70.)

notion and once again true to reality. We have already heard that in real illnesses a delusion very often arises in connection with a dream, and, after what we have learnt about the nature of dreams, there is no need to see a fresh riddle in this fact. Dreams and delusions arise from the same source – from what is repressed. Dreams are, as one might say, the physiological delusions of normal people. Before what is repressed has become strong enough to break through into waking life as a delusion, it may easily have achieved a first success, under the more favourable conditions of the state of sleep, in the form of a dream with persisting effects. For during sleep, along with a general lowering of mental activity, there is a relaxation in the strength of the resistance with which the dominant psychical forces oppose what is repressed. It is this relaxation that makes the formation of dreams possible, and that is why dreams give us our best access to a knowledge of the unconscious part of the mind – except that, as a rule, with the re-establishment of the psychical cathexes of waking life, the dream once more takes to flight and the ground that had been won by the unconscious is evacuated once again.

III

In the further course of the story there is yet another dream, which may perhaps tempt us even more than the first to try to translate it and insert it into the train of events in the hero's mind. But we should save very little by diverging from the author's account and hurrying on immediately to this second dream; for no one who wishes to analyse someone else's dream can avoid turning his attention in the greatest detail to all the dreamer's experiences, both external and internal. It will probably be best, therefore, to keep close to the thread of the story and to intersperse it with our glosses as we proceed.

The construction of the fresh delusion about Gradiva's death during the destruction of Pompeii in the year 79 A.D. was not the only result of the first dream, which we have already analysed. Immediately after it Hanold decided on his journey to Italy, which eventually brought him to Pompeii. But, before that, something else happened to him. As he was leaning out of the window, he thought he saw a figure in the street with the bearing and gait of his Gradiva. In spite of being insufficiently dressed, he hurried after her, but failed to overtake her, and was driven back into the house by the jeers of the passersby. When he was in his room once more, the song of a canary from its cage in the window of a house opposite stirred up in him a mood in which he too seemed to be a prisoner longing for freedom; and his spring-time journey was no sooner decided on than it was carried out.

The author has thrown a particularly clear light on this journey of Hanold's and has allowed him to have a partial insight into his own internal processes. Hanold of course found himself a scientific pretext for his journey, but this did not last long. After all, he was in fact aware that 'the impulse to make this journey had arisen from a feeling he could not name'. A strange restlessness made him dissatisfied with everything he came across, and drove him from Rome to Naples and from there to Pompeii; but even at this last halting-place he was still uneasy in his mood. He was annoyed at the folly of the honeymooners, and enraged at the impertinence of the house-flies which inhabit Pompeii's hotels. But at last he could no longer disguise from himself 'that his dissatisfaction could not be caused solely by what was around him but that there was something that sprang from himself as well'. He thought he was over-excited, felt 'that he was discontented because he lacked something, but he had no idea what. And this ill-humour followed him about everywhere.' In this frame of mind he was even furious with his mistress – with science. When in the heat of the mid-day sun he wandered for the first time through Pompeii, 'the whole of his science had not merely abandoned him, but had left him without the slightest desire to find her again. He remembered her only as something in the far distance, and he felt that she had been an old, dried-up, tedious aunt, the dullest and most unwanted creature in the world.' (55.)

And then, while he was in this disagreeable and confused state of feeling, one of the problems attaching to his journey was solved for him – at the moment when he first saw Gradiva stepping through Pompeii. Something 'came into his consciousness for the first time: without being aware himself of the impulse within him, he had come to Italy and had travelled on to Pompeii, without stopping in Rome or Naples, in order to see whether he could find any traces of her. And "traces" literally; for with her peculiar gait she must have left behind an imprint of her toes in the ashes distinct from all the rest.' (58.)

Since the author has taken so much trouble over describing the journey, it must be worth while too to discuss its relation to Hanold's delusion and its position in the chain of events. The journey was undertaken for reasons which its subject did not recognize at first and only admitted to himself later on, reasons which the author describes in so many words as 'unconscious'. This is certainly taken from the life. One does not need to be suffering from a delusion in order to behave like this. On the contrary, it is an event of daily occurrence for a person – even a healthy person – to deceive himself over the motives for an action and to become conscious of them only after the event, provided only that a conflict between several currents of feeling furnishes the necessary condition for such a confusion. Accordingly, Hanold's journey was from the first calculated to serve the delusion, and was intended to take him to Pompeii, where he could proceed further with his search for Gradiva. It will be recalled that his mind was occupied with that search both before and immediately after the dream, and that the dream itself was simply an answer which was stifled by his consciousness. Some power which we do not recognize was, however, also inhibiting him to begin with from becoming aware of his delusional intention; so that, for the conscious reasons for his journey, he was left only with insufficient pretexts which had to be renewed from place to place. The author presents us with a further puzzle by making the dream, the discovery of the supposed Gradiva in the street, and the decision to undertake the journey as a result of the singing canary succeed one another as a series of chance events without any internal connection with one another.

This obscure region of the story is made intelligible to us by some explanations which we derive from the later remarks of Zoe Bertgang. It was in fact the original of Gradiva, Fräulein Zoe herself, whom Hanold saw out of his window walking past in the street (89) and whom he nearly overtook. If this had happened, the information given him by the dream – that she was in fact living at the same time and in the same town as he was – would by a lucky chance have received an irresistible confirmation, which would have brought about the collapse of his internal struggle. But the canary, whose singing sent Hanold off on his distant journey, belonged to Zoe, and its cage stood in her window diagonally across the street from Hanold's house. (135.) Hanold, who, according to the girl's accusation, had the gift of 'negative hallucination', who possessed the art of not seeing and not recognizing people who were actually present, must from the first have had an unconscious knowledge of what we only learned later. The indications of Zoe's proximity (her appearance in the street and her bird's singing so near his window) intensified the effect of the dream, and in this position, so perilous for his resistance to his erotic feelings, he took to flight. His journey was a result of his resistance gathering new strength after the surge forward of his erotic desires in the dream; it was an attempt at flight from the physical presence of the girl he loved. In a practical sense it meant a victory for repression, just as his earlier activity, his 'pedestrian researches' upon women and girls, had meant a victory for erotism. But everywhere in these oscillations in the struggle the compromise character of the outcome was preserved: the journey to Pompeii, which was supposed to lead him away from the living Zoe, led him at least to her surrogate, to Gradiva. The journey, which was undertaken in defiance of the latent dream-thoughts, was nevertheless following the path to Pompeii that was pointed out by the manifest content of the dream. Thus at every fresh struggle between erotism and resistance we find the delusion triumphant.

This view of Hanold's journey as a flight from his awakening erotic longing for the girl whom he loved and who was so close to him is the only one which will fit in with the description of his emotional states during his stay in Italy. The repudiation of erotism which dominated him was expressed there in his disgust at the honeymooners. A short dream which he had in his *albergo* in Rome, and which was occasioned by the proximity of a German loving couple, 'Edwin and Angelina', whose evening conversation he could not help hearing through the thin partition-wall, throws a retrospective light, as it were, on the erotic drift of his first major dream. In the new dream he was once again in Pompeii and Vesuvius was once again erupting, and it was thus linked to the earlier dream whose effects persisted during the journey. This time, however, among the people imperilled were – not, as on the former occasion, himself and Gradiva but – the Apollo Belvedere and the Capitoline Venus, no doubt by way of an ironical exaltation of the couple in the next room. Apollo lifted Venus up, carried her out, and laid her down on some object in the dark which seemed to be a carriage or cart, since it emitted 'a creaking noise'. Apart from this, the interpretation of the dream calls for no special skill. (31.)

Our author, who, as we have long since realized, never introduces a single idle or unintentional feature into his story, has given us another piece of evidence of the asexual current which dominated Hanold during his journey. As he roamed about for hours in Pompeii, 'strangely enough it never once recurred to his memory that a short time before he had dreamt of being present at the burial of Pompeii in the eruption of 79 A.D.' (47.) It was only when he caught sight of Gradiva that he suddenly remembered the dream and became conscious at the same time of the delusional reason for his puzzling journey. How could this forgetting of the dream, this barrier of repression between the dream and his mental state during the journey, be explained, except by supposing that the journey was undertaken not at the direct inspiration of the dream but as a revolt against it, as an emanation of a mental power that refused to know anything of the secret meaning of the dream?

But on the other hand Hanold did not enjoy this victory over his erotism. The suppressed mental impulse remained powerful enough to revenge itself on the suppressing one with discontent and inhibition. His longings turned into restlessness and dissatisfaction, which made his journey seem pointless to him. His insight into his reasons for the journey at the bidding of the delusion was inhibited and his relations with his science, which in such a spot should have stirred all his interest, were interfered with. So the author shows us his hero after his flight from love in a kind of crisis, in a state of complete confusion and distraction, in a turmoil such as we usually find at the climax of an illness, when neither of the two conflicting powers has any longer a sufficiently superior strength over the other for the margin between them to make it possible to establish a vigorous mental régime. But here the author intervenes help-fully, and smoothes things out by making Gradiva apppear at this juncture and undertake the cure of the delusion. By the power he possesses of guiding the people of his creation towards a happy destiny, in spite of all the laws of necessity which he makes them obey, he arranges that the girl, to avoid whom Hanold had fled to Pompeii, shall be transported to that very place. In this way he corrects the folly to which the young man was led by his delusion – the folly of exchanging the home of the living girl whom he loved for the burial-place of her imaginary substitute.

With the appearance of Zoe Bertgang as Gradiva, which marks the climax of tension in the story, our interest, too, soon takes a new direction. So far we have been present at the development of a delusion; now we are to witness its cure. And we may ask whether the author has given a purely fanciful account of the course of this cure or whether he has constructed it in accordance with possibilities actually present. Zoe's own words during her conversation with her newly-married friend give us a definite right to ascribe to her an intention to bring about the cure. (124 [p. 53].) But how did she set about it? When she had got over the indignation aroused in her by his suggestion that she should lie down to sleep again as she had 'then', she returned next day at the same mid-day hour to the same spot, and proceeded to entice out of Hanold all the secret knowledge her ignorance of which had prevented her from understanding his behaviour the day before. She learnt about his dream, about the sculpture of Gradiva, and about the peculiarity of gait which she herself shared with it. She accepted the role of the ghost awakened to life for a brief hour, a role for which, as she perceived, his delusion had cast her, and, by accepting the flowers of the dead which he had brought without conscious purpose, and by expressing a regret that he had not given her roses, she gently hinted in ambiguous words at the possibility of his taking up a new position. (90 [p. 47].)

This unusually clever girl, then, was determined to win her childhood's friend for her husband, after she had recognized that the young man's love for her was the motive force behind the delusion. Our interest in her behaviour, however, will probably yield for the moment to the surprise which we may feel at the delusion itself. The last form taken by it was that Gradiva, who had been buried in 79 A.D., was now able, as a mid-day ghost, to exchange words with him for an hour, at the end of which she must sink into the ground or seek her grave once more. This mental cobweb, which was not brushed away either by his perceiving that the apparition was wearing modern shoes or by her ignorance of the ancient languages and her command of German, which was not in existence in her day, certainly seems to justify the author's description of his story as a 'Pompeian phantasy', but it seems also to exclude any possibility of measuring it by the standards of clinical reality.

Nevertheless, on closer consideration this delusion of Hanold's seems to me to lose the greater part of its improbability. The author, indeed, has made himself responsible for one part of it by basing his story on the premiss that Zoe was in every detail a duplicate of the relief. We must therefore avoid shifting the improbability of this premiss on to its consequence – that Hanold took the girl for Gradiva come to life. Greater value is given to the delusional explanation by the fact that the author has put no rational one at our disposal. Moreover the author has adduced contributory and mitigating circumstances on behalf of his hero's excesses in the shape of the glare of the *campagna* sunlight and the intoxicating magic of the wine grown on the slopes of Vesuvius. But the most important of all the explanatory and exculpatory factors remains the ease with which our intellect is prepared to accept something absurd provided it satisfies powerful emotional impulses. It is an astonishing fact, and one that is too generally overlooked, how readily and frequently under these psychological conditions people of even the most powerful intelligence react as though they were feeble-minded; and anyone who is not too conceited may see this happening in himself as often as he pleases. And this is far more so if some of the mental processes concerned are linked with unconscious or repressed motives. In this connection I am happy to quote the words of a philosopher, who writes to me: 'I have been noting down the instances I myself experience of striking mistakes and unthinking actions, for which one finds motives afterwards (in a most unreasonable way). It is an alarming thing, but typical, to find how much folly this brings to light.' It must be remembered, too, that the belief in spirits and ghosts and the return of the dead, which finds so much support in the religions to which we have all been attached, at least in our childhood, is far from having disappeared among educated people, and that many who are sensible in other respects find it possible to combine spiritualism with reason. A man who has grown rational and sceptical, even, may be ashamed to discover how easily he may for a moment return to a belief in spirits under the combined impact of strong emotion and perplexity. I know of a doctor who had once lost one of his women patients suffering from Graves' disease [exophthalmic goitre], and who could not get rid of a faint suspicion that he might have contributed to the unhappy outcome by a thoughtless prescription. One day, several years later, a girl entered his consulting-room, who, in spite of all his efforts, he could not help recognizing as the dead one. He could frame only a single thought: 'So after all it's true that the dead can come back to life.' His dread did not give way to shame till the girl introduced herself as the sister of the one who had died of the same disease as she herself was suffering from. The victims of Graves' disease, as has often been observed, have a marked facial resemblance to one another; and in this case this typical likeness was reinforced by a family one. The doctor to whom this occurred was, however, none other than myself; so I have a personal reason for not disputing the clinical possibility of Norbert Hanold's temporary delusion that Gradiva had come back to life. The fact, finally, is familiar to every psychiatrist that in severe cases of chronic delusions (in paranoia) the most extreme examples occur of ingeniously elaborated and well-supported absurdities.

After his first meeting with Gradiva, Norbert Hanold had drunk his wine first in one and then in the other of the two restaurants that he knew in Pompeii, while the other visitors were engaged in eating the main meal of the day. 'Of course

it never came into his head to think of the nonsensical idea'
that he was doing it in order to discover in which of the hotels
Gradiva was living and taking her meals. But it is difficult to
say what other sense his actions could have had. On the day
after their second meeting in the House of Meleager, he had
all kinds of strange and apparently unconnected experiences.
He found a narrow gap in the wall of the portico, at the point
where Gradiva had disappeared. He met a foolish lizard–catcher
who addressed him as though he were an acquaintance. He
discovered a third hotel, in an out–of–the–way situation, the
'Albergo del Sole', whose proprietor palmed off on him a metal
clasp with a green patina as a find from beside the remains
of a Pompeian girl. And, lastly, in his own hotel he noticed
a newly-arrived young couple whom he diagnosed as a brother
and sister and whom he found sympathetic. All these
impressions were afterwards woven together into a 'remarkably
senseless' dream, which ran as follows:

'Somewhere in the sun Gradiva was sitting, making a snare
out of a blade of grass to catch a lizard in, and said: "Please
keep quite still. Our lady colleague is right; the method is a
really good one and she has made use of it with excellent
results."'

He fended off this dream while he was still asleep, with the
critical thought that it was utter madness, and cast around in
all directions to get free from it. He succeeded in doing so
with the help of an invisible bird, which uttered a short laughing
call and carried off the lizard in its beak.

Are we to venture on an attempt at interpreting this dream
too – that is, at replacing it by the latent thoughts from whose
distortion it must have arisen? It is as senseless as only a dream
can be expected to be; and this absurdity of dreams is the main-
stay of the view which refuses to characterize dreams as
completely valid psychical acts and maintains that they arise
out of a purposeless excitation of the elements of the mind.

We are able to apply to this dream the technique which may
be described as the regular procedure for interpreting dreams.

It consists in paying no attention to the apparent connections in the manifest dream but in fixing our eyes upon each portion of its content independently, and in looking for its origin in the dreamer's impressions, memories, and free associations. Since, however, we cannot question Hanold, we shall have to content ourselves with referring to his impressions, and we may very tentatively put our own associations in place of his.

'Somewhere in the sun Gradiva was sitting, catching lizards and speaking.' What impression of the previous day finds an echo in this part of the dream? Undoubtedly the encounter with the elderly gentleman, the lizard–catcher, who was thus replaced in the dream by Gradiva. He sat or lay 'on a sun-bathed slope' and he, too, spoke to Hanold. Furthermore, Gradiva's remarks in the dream were copied from this man's remarks: viz. 'The method prescribed by our colleague Eimer is a really good one; I have made use of it many times already with excellent results. Please keep quite still.' Gradiva used much the same words in the dream, except that 'our colleague Eimer' was replaced by an unnamed 'lady colleague'; moreover, the 'many times' in the zoologist's speech was omitted in the dream and the order of the sentences was somewhat altered. It seems, therefore, that this experience of the previous day was transformed into the dream with the help of a few changes and distortions. Why this particular experience? And what is the meaning of the changes – the replacement of the elderly gentleman by Gradiva and the introduction of the enigmatic 'lady colleague'?

There is a rule in interpreting dreams which runs as follows: 'A speech heard in a dream is always derived from one that has been heard or made by the dreamer in waking life.'[1] This rule seems to have been observed here: Gradiva's speech is only a modification of the old zoologist's speech which Hanold had heard the day before. Another rule in dream-interpretation would tell us that when one person is replaced by another or when two people are mixed up together (for instance, by one

---

1. [Cf. *The Interpretation of Dreams*, P.F.L., **4**, 545 ff.]

of them being shown in a situation that is characteristic of the other), it means that the two people are being equated, that there is a similarity between them.[1] If we venture to apply this rule too to our dream, we should arrive at this translation: 'Gradiva catches lizards just like the old man; she is skilled in lizard-catching just as he is.' This result cannot exactly be said to be intelligible as yet; but we have yet another puzzle to solve. To what impression of the previous day are we to relate the 'lady colleague' who in the dream replaces the famous zoologist Eimer? Fortunately we have very little choice here. A 'lady colleague' can only mean another girl – that is to say, the sympathetic young lady whom Hanold had taken for a sister travelling with her brother. 'She was wearing a red Sorrento rose in her dress, the sight of which reminded him of something as he looked across from his corner of the dining-room, but he could not think what.' This remark of the author's gives us a right to regard her as the 'lady colleague' in the dream. What Hanold could not recall were, it cannot be doubted, the words spoken by the supposed Gradiva, who had told him, as she asked him for the white flowers of the dead, that in the spring people give happier girls roses. But behind those words there had lain a hint of wooing. So what sort of lizard-catching was it that the happier 'lady colleague' had carried out so successfully?

Next day Hanold came upon the supposed brother and sister in an affectionate embrace, and was thus able to correct his earlier mistake. They were in fact a pair of lovers, and moreover on their honeymoon, as we discovered later when they so unexpectedly interrupted Hanold's third interview with Zoe. If now we are willing to assume that Hanold, though consciously taking them for a brother and sister, had immediately recognized their true relationship (which was unambiguously betrayed next day) in his unconscious, Gradiva's speech in the dream acquires a clear meaning. The red rose had become the symbol of a love-relation. Hanold understood that the couple were already what he and Gradiva had yet to become; the

1. [Ibid., **4**, 431 ff.]

lizard-catching had come to signify man-catching; and Gradiva's speech meant something like: 'Only let me alone: I know how to win a man just as well as the other girl does.'

But why was it necessary for this penetration of Zoe's intentions to appear in the dream in the form of the old zoologist's speech? Why was Zoe's skill in man-catching represented by the old gentleman's skill in lizard-catching? Well, we can have no difficulty in answering that question. We guessed long ago that the lizard-catcher was none other than Bertgang, the professor of zoology and Zoe's father, who, incidentally, must have known Hanold too — which explains how he came to address him as an acquaintance. Let us assume, once again, that in his unconscious Hanold at once recognized the professor. 'He had a vague notion that he had already had a passing glimpse of the lizard-hunter's face, probably in one of the two hotels.' This, then, is the explanation of the strange disguise under which the intention attributed to Zoe made its appearance: she was the lizard-catcher's daughter and had acquired her skill from him.

The replacement of the lizard-catcher by Gradiva in the content of the dream is accordingly a representation of the relation between the two figures which was known to Hanold in his unconscious; the introduction of the 'lady colleague' instead of 'our colleague Eimer' allowed the dream to express Hanold's realization that she was wooing a man. So far the dream welded together ('condensed', as we say) two experiences of the previous day into one situation, in order to bring to expression (in a very obscure way, it is true) two discoveries which were not allowed to become conscious. But we can go further, we can diminish the strangeness of the dream still more and we can demonstrate the influence of his other experiences of the previous day on the form taken by the manifest dream.

We may declare ourselves dissatisfied with the explanation that has hitherto been given of why it was that precisely the scene of the lizard-catching was made into the nucleus of the dream, and we may suspect that still other elements of the dream-thoughts were bringing their influence to bear in the emphasis that was laid on the 'lizard' in the manifest dream. Indeed, it may easily have been so. It will be recalled that Hanold had discovered a gap in the wall at the point where Gradiva had seemed to vanish – a gap 'which was nevertheless wide enough to allow a form that was unusually slim' to slip through. This observation led him in daytime to make an alteration in his delusion – an alteration to the effect that when Gradiva disappeared from his sight she did not sink into the earth but used the gap as a way of reaching her grave. In his unconscious thoughts he may have told himself that he had now discovered the natural explanation of the girl's surprising disappearance. But must not the idea of slipping through narrow gaps and disappearing in them have recalled the behaviour of lizards? Was not Gradiva herself in this way behaving like an agile little lizard? In our view, then, the discovery of the gap in the wall contributed to determining the choice of the element 'lizard' in the manifest content of the dream. The lizard situation in the dream represented this impression of the previous day as well as the encounter with Zoe's father, the zoologist.

And what if now, growing bold, we were to try to find a representation in the content of the dream of the one experience of the previous day which has not yet been exploited – the discovery of the third inn, the Albergo del Sole? The author has treated this episode at such length and has linked so many things to it that it would surprise us if it alone had made no contribution to the construction of the dream. Hanold went into this inn, which, owing to its out-of-the-way situation and its distance from the railway station, had remained unknown to him, to purchase a bottle of soda-water to cool his heated blood. The landlord took the opportunity of displaying his antiquities, and showed him a clasp which he pretended had belonged to the Pompeian girl who had been found in the neighbourhood of the Forum closely embraced by her lover. Hanold, who had never hitherto believed this often-repeated tale, was now compelled by a power unknown to him to believe in the truth of this moving story and in the genuineness of the find; he purchased the brooch and left the inn with his acquisition. As he was going out, he saw, standing in a glass of water in a window, a nodding sprig of asphodel covered with white blossoms, and took the sight of it as a confirmation of the genuineness of his new possession. He now felt a positive conviction that the green clasp had belonged to Gradiva and that she had been the girl who had died in her lover's arms. He quieted the jealousy which thereupon seized him, by deciding that next day he would show the clasp to Gradiva herself and arrive at certainty about his suspicion. It cannot be denied that this was a curious new piece of delusion; yet are we to suppose that no trace of it was to be found in his dream of the same night?

It will certainly be worth while to explain the origin of this addition to the delusion and to look for the fresh piece of unconscious discovery which was replaced by the fresh piece of delusion. The delusion appeared under the influence of the landlord of the 'Sun Hotel' to whom Hanold behaved in such a remarkably credulous fashion that it was almost as though he had been given a hypnotic suggestion by him. The landlord showed him a metal clasp for a garment, represented it as genuine and as having belonged to the girl who had been found buried in the arms of her lover; and Hanold, who was capable of being sufficiently critical to doubt both the truth of the story and the genuineness of the clasp, was at once taken in, and purchased the highly dubious antique. Why he should have behaved in this way is quite incomprehensible, and there is nothing to suggest that the landlord's personality might offer us a solution. But there is yet another riddle about the incident, and two riddles often solve each other. As he was leaving the *albergo* he saw a sprig of asphodel standing in a glass in a window and took it as a confirmation of the genuineness of the metal clasp. How could that have come about? But fortunately this last point is easy to solve. The white flower was no doubt the one which he had given to Gradiva at midday, and it is perfectly true that something was confirmed by the sight of it in the window of the inn. Not, it is true, the genuineness of the clasp, but something else that had already become clear to him when he discovered this *albergo* after having previously overlooked it. Already on the day before he had behaved as though he was searching in the two Pompeii hotels to find the person who appeared to him as Gradiva. And now, since he had so unexpectedly come upon a third one, he must have said to himself in his unconscious: 'So *this* is where she is staying!' And added, as he was going out: 'Yes, that's right! There's the asphodel that I gave her! So that's her window!' This then was the new discovery which was replaced by the delusion, and which could not become conscious because its underlying postulate that Gradiva was a living person whom he had once known could not become conscious.

But how did the replacement of the new discovery by the delusion take place? What happened, I think, was that the sense of conviction attaching to the discovery was able to persist and was retained, while the discovery itself, which was inadmissible to consciousness, was replaced by another ideational content connected with it by associations of thought. Thus the sense of conviction became attached to a content which was in fact foreign to it and this, in the form of a delusion, won a recognition which did not apply to it. Hanold transferred his conviction that Gradiva lived in the house to other impressions which he had received in the house; this led to his credulity in regard to the landlord's remarks, the genuineness of the metal clasp and the truth of the anecdote about the discovery of the embracing lovers – but only through his linking what he heard in the house with Gradiva. The jealousy which was already latent in him seized upon this material and the consequence was the delusion (though it contradicted his first dream) that Gradiva was the girl who had died in her lover's arms and that the clasp he had bought had belonged to her.

It will be observed that his conversation with Gradiva and her hint at wooing him (her 'saying it with flowers') had already brought about important changes in Hanold. Traits of masculine desire – components of the libido – had awakened in him, though it is true that they could not yet dispense with the disguise of conscious pretexts. But the problem of the 'bodily nature' of Gradiva, which pursued him all that day [pp. 45 and 48], cannot disavow its origin in a young man's erotic curiosity about a woman's body, even if it is involved in a scientific question by the conscious insistence on Gradiva's peculiar oscillation between death and life. His jealousy was a further sign of the increasingly active aspect of Hanold's love; he expressed this jealousy at the beginning of their conversation the next day and with the help of a fresh pretext proceeded to touch the girl's body and, as he used to do in the far-off past, to hit her.

But it is now time to ask ourselves whether the method of constructing a delusion which we have inferred from our author's account is one that is known from other sources, or whether, indeed, it is possible at all. From our medical knowledge we can only reply that it is certainly the correct method, and perhaps the sole method, by which a delusion acquires the unshakable conviction which is one of its clinical characteristics. If a patient believes in his delusion so firmly, this is not because his faculty of judgement has been overturned and does not arise from what is false in the delusion. On the contrary, there is a grain of truth concealed in every delusion,[1] there is something in it that really deserves belief, and this is the source of the patient's conviction, which is therefore to that extent justified. This true element, however, has long been repressed. If eventually it is able to penetrate into consciousness, this time in a distorted form, the sense of conviction attaching to it is over-intensified as though by way of compensation and is now attached to the distorted substitute of the repressed truth, and protects it from any critical attacks. The conviction is displaced, as it were, from the unconscious truth on to the conscious error that is linked to it, and remains fixated there precisely as a result of this displacement. The instance of the formation

1. [Freud expressed this view at many points throughout his writings. See, for instance, *The Psychopathology of Everyday Life* (1901*b*), P.F.L., **5**, 318, and *Moses and Monotheism* (1939*a*), ibid., **13**, 378–9, 379 *n*. 1.]

of a delusion which arose from Hanold's first dream is no more than a similar, though not identical, example of such a displacement. Indeed, the method described here by which conviction arises in the case of a delusion does not differ fundamentally from the method by which a conviction is formed in normal cases, where repression does not come into the picture. We all attach our conviction to thought-contents in which truth is combined with error, and let it extend from the former over the latter. It becomes diffused, as it were, from the truth over the error associated with it and protects the latter, though not so unalterably as in the case of a delusion, against deserved criticism. In normal psychology, too, being well-connected – 'having influence', so to speak – can take the place of true worth.

I will now return to the dream and bring out a small but not uninteresting feature in it, which forms a connection between two of its provoking causes. Gradiva had drawn a kind of contrast between the white asphodel blossoms and the red rose. Seeing the asphodel again in the window of the Albergo del Sole became an important piece of evidence in support of Hanold's unconscious discovery, which was expressed in the new delusion; and alongside this was the fact that the red rose in the dress of the sympathetic girl helped Hanold in his unconscious to a correct view of her relation to her companion, so that he was able to make her appear in the dream as the 'lady colleague'.

But where in the manifest content of the dream, it will be asked, do we find anything to indicate and replace the discovery for which, as we have seen, Hanold's new delusion was a substitute – the discovery that Gradiva was staying with her father in the third, concealed Pompeii hotel, the Albergo del Sole? Nevertheless it is all there in the dream, and not even very much distorted, and I merely hesitate to point to it because I know that even those of my readers who have followed me patiently so far will begin to rebel strongly against my attempts at interpretation. Hanold's discovery, I repeat, is fully announced in the dream, but so cleverly concealed that it is bound to be overlooked. It is hidden behind a play upon words, an ambiguity. 'Somewhere in the sun Gradiva was sitting.' We have quite correctly related this to the spot where Hanold met her father, the zoologist. But could it not also mean in the 'Sun' – that is, Gradiva is staying in the Albergo del Sole, the Sun Hotel? And was not the 'somewhere', which had no bearing on the encounter with her father, made to sound so hypocritically indefinite precisely because it introduced a definite piece of information about the place where Gradiva was staying? From my experience elsewhere of real dreams, I myself am perfectly certain that this is how the ambiguity is to be understood. But I should not in fact have ventured to present this piece of interpretative work to my readers, if the author had not at this point lent me his powerful assistance. He puts the very same play upon words into the girl's mouth when next day she saw the metal clasp: 'Did you find it in the Sun, perhaps, which produces things of this kind?' And since Hanold failed to understand what she had said, she explained that she meant the Sun Hotel, which they call 'Sole' here, and where she had already seen the purported antique.

And now let us make a bold attempt at replacing Hanold's 'remarkably senseless' dream by the unconscious thoughts that lay behind it and were as unlike it as possible. They ran, perhaps, as follows: 'She is staying in the "Sun" with her father. Why is she playing this game with me? Does she want to make fun of me? Or can it possibly be that she loves me and wants to have me as her husband?' – And no doubt while he was still asleep there came an answer dismissing this last possibility as 'the merest madness', a comment which was ostensibly directed against the whole manifest dream.

Critical readers will now justly inquire about the origin of the interpolation (for which I have so far given no grounds) of the reference to being ridiculed by Gradiva. The answer to this is given in *The Interpretation of Dreams*, which explains that if ridicule, derision, or embittered contradiction occurs in the dream-thoughts, this is expressed by the manifest dream being given a senseless form, by absurdity in the dream.[1] This absurdity does not mean, therefore, that there is any paralysis of psychical activity: it is a method of representation employed by the dream-work. As always happens at specially difficult points, the author once more comes to our help here. The senseless dream had a short epilogue, in which a bird uttered a laughing call and carried the lizard away in its beak. But Hanold had heard a similar laughing call after Gradiva's disappearance. It had in fact come from Zoe, who with this laugh was shaking off the gloomy seriousness of her underworld role. Gradiva had really laughed at him. But the dream-image of the bird carrying off the lizard may have been a recollection of the earlier dream, in which the Apollo Belvedere carried off the Capitoline Venus.

There may still be some readers who feel that the translation of the situation of lizard-catching by the idea of wooing has not been sufficiently well established. Some further support for it may be afforded by the consideration that Zoe in her conversation with her newly-married friend admitted precisely what Hanold's thoughts about her suspected – when she told her she had felt sure that she would 'dig out' something interesting in Pompeii. Here she was trespassing into the field of archaeology, just as he had trespassed, with his simile of lizard-catching, into the field of zoology; it was as though they were struggling towards each other and each were trying to assume the other's character.

Here then we seem to have finished off the interpretation of this second dream as well. Both of them have been made intelligible to us on the presupposition that a dreamer knows in his unconscious thoughts all that he has forgotten in his conscious ones, and that in the former he judges correctly what in the latter he misunderstands in a delusion. In the course of our arguments we have no doubt been obliged to make some assertions which have seemed strange to the reader because of their unfamiliarity; and we have probably often roused a

1. [*The Interpretation of Dreams*, P.F.L., **4**, 576.]

suspicion that what we pretended was the author's meaning was in fact only our own. I am anxious to do all I can to dissipate this suspicion, and for that reason I will gladly enter into more detail over one of the most delicate points – I mean the use of ambiguous words and phrases, such as: 'Somewhere in the Sun Gradiva was sitting.'

Anyone who reads *Gradiva* must be struck by the frequency with which the author puts ambiguous remarks into the mouths of his two principal characters. In Hanold's case these remarks are intended by him unambiguously and it is only the heroine, Gradiva, who is struck by their second meaning. Thus, for instance, when in reply to her first answer he exclaimed 'I knew your voice sounded like that', Zoe, who was still in ignorance, could not but ask how that could be, since he had not heard her speak before. In their second conversation the girl was for a moment thrown into doubt about his delusion, when he told her that he had recognized her at once. She could not help taking these words in the sense (correct so far as his unconscious was concerned) of being a recognition that their acquaintance went back to their childhood; whereas he, of course, knew nothing of this implication of his remark and explained it only by reference to his dominant delusion. On the other hand, the remarks made by the girl, whose personality shows the most lucid clarity of mind in contrast to Hanold's delusion, exhibit an *intentional* ambiguity. One of their meanings chimes in with Hanold's delusion, so as to be able to penetrate into his conscious understanding, but the other rises above the delusion and gives us as a rule its translation into the unconscious truth for which it stands. It is a triumph of ingenuity and wit to be able to express the delusion and the truth in the same turn of words.

Zoe's speech, in which she explains the situation to her friend and at the same time succeeds in getting rid of the interrupter, is full of ambiguities of this kind. It is in reality a speech made by the author and aimed more at the reader than at Zoe's newly-married 'colleague'. In her conversations with Hanold the ambiguity is usually effected by Zoe's using the same symbolism that we found in Hanold's first dream – the equation of repression and burial, and of Pompeii and childhood. Thus she is able in her speeches on the one hand to remain in the role for which Hanold's delusion has cast her, and on the other hand to make contact with the real circumstances and awaken an understanding of them in Hanold's unconscious.

'I have long grown used to being dead.' (90.) 'To me it is right that you should give the flower of forgetfulness.' (90.) In these sentences there was a faint foretaste of the reproaches which broke out clearly enough later on in her final lecture to him, in which she compared him to an archaeopteryx. 'The fact of someone having to die so as to come alive; but no doubt that must be so for archaeologists.' (141.) She made this last remark after the delusion had been cleared up, as though to give a key to her ambiguous speeches. But she made her neatest use of her symbolism when she asked: 'I feel as though we had shared a meal like this once before, two thousand years ago; can't you remember?' (118.) Here the substitution of the historical past for childhood and the effort to awaken the memory of the latter are quite unmistakable.

But whence comes this striking preference for ambiguous speeches in *Gradiva*? It is no chance event, so it seems to us, but a necessary consequence of the premises of the story. It is nothing other than a counterpart to the twofold determination of symptoms, in so far as speeches are themselves symptoms and, like them, arise from compromises between the conscious and the unconscious. It is simply that this double origin is more easily noticed in speeches than, for instance, in actions. And when, as is often made possible by the malleable nature of the material of speech, each of the two intentions lying behind the speech can be successfully expressed in the same turn of words, we have before us what we call an 'ambiguity'.

In the course of the psychotherapeutic treatment of a delusion or of an analogous disorder, ambiguous speeches of this kind are often produced by the patient as new symptoms of the briefest duration; and it can happen that the doctor finds himself too in the position of making use of them. In that way it not infrequently happens that with the meaning that is intended for the patient's conscious he stirs up an understanding of the meaning that applies to his unconscious. I know from experience that the part thus played by ambiguity is apt to raise the greatest objection in the uninitiated and to give rise to the greatest misunderstandings. But in any case our author was right in giving a place in his creation to a picture of this characteristic feature of what takes place in the formation of dreams and delusions.

IV

THE emergence of Zoe as a physician, as I have already remarked, arouses a new interest in us. We shall be anxious to learn whether a cure of the kind she performed upon Hanold is conceivable or even possible, and whether the author has taken as correct a view of the conditions for the disappearance of a delusion as he has of those for its genesis.

We shall unquestionably be met at this point by an opinion which denies that the case presented by the author possesses any such general interest and disputes the existence of any problem requiring solution. Hanold, it will be said, had no alternative but to abandon his delusion, after its subject, the supposed 'Gradiva' herself, had shown him that all his hypotheses were incorrect and after she had given him the most natural explanations of everything puzzling – for instance, of how it was that she had known his name. This would be the logical end of the matter; but since the girl had incidentally revealed her love to him, the author, no doubt to the satisfaction of his female readers, arranged that his story, a not uninteresting one otherwise, should have the usual happy ending in marriage. It would have been more consistent and equally possible, the argument will proceed, if the young scientist, after his error had been pointed out, had taken his leave of the lady with polite thanks and given as the reason for refusing her love the fact that he was able to feel an intense interest in antique women made of bronze or marble, and in their originals if they were accessible to contact, but that he did not know what to do with contemporary girls of flesh and blood. The author, in short, had quite arbitrarily tacked a love story on to his archaeological phantasy.

In rejecting this view as an impossible one, we observe in the first place that the beginnings of a change in Hanold were not shown only in his abandoning his delusion. Simultaneously, and indeed before his delusion was cleared up, an unmistakable craving for love awakened in him, which found its outcome, naturally as it were, in his courting the girl who had freed him from his delusion. We have already laid emphasis on the pretexts and disguises under which his curiosity about her 'bodily nature', his jealousy, and his brutal masculine instinct for mastery were expressed in the midst of his delusion, after his repressed erotic desire had led to his first dream. As further evidence of this we may recall that on the evening after his second interview with Gradiva a live woman for the first time struck him as sympathetic, though he still made a concession to his earlier horror of honeymooning couples by not recognizing her as being newly-married. Next morning, however, he was a chance witness of an exchange of endearments between the girl and her supposed brother, and he withdrew with a sense of awe as though he had interrupted some sacred act. His derision of 'Edwin and Angelina' was forgotten, and he had acquired a sense of respect for the erotic side of life.

Thus the author has drawn the closest link between the clearing up of the delusion and the outbreak of a craving for love, and he has paved the way for the inevitable outcome in a courtship. He knows the essential nature of the delusion better than his critics: he knows that a component of loving desire had combined with a component of resistance to it in bringing about the delusion, and he makes the girl who undertakes the cure sensitive to the element in Hanold's delusion which is agreeable to her. It was only this knowledge which could decide her to devote herself to the treatment; it was only the certainty of being loved by him that could induce her to admit her love to him. The treatment consisted in giving him back from outside the repressed memories which he could not set free from inside; but it would have had no effect if in the course of it the therapist had not taken his feelings into account and if her ultimate translation of the delusion had not been: 'Look, all this only means that you love me.'

The procedure which the author makes his Zoe adopt for curing her childhood friend's delusion shows a far-reaching similarity – no, a complete agreement in its essence – with a therapeutic method which was introduced into medical practice in 1895 by Dr Josef Breuer and myself, and to the perfecting of which I have since then devoted myself. This method of treatment, to which Breuer first gave the name of 'cathartic' but which I prefer to describe as 'psychoanalytic', consists, as applied to patients suffering from disorders analogous to Hanold's delusion, in bringing to their consciousness, to some extent forcibly, the unconscious whose repression led to their falling ill – exactly as Gradiva did with the repressed memories of their childhood relations. Gradiva, it is true, could carry out this task more easily than a doctor: in several respects she was in what may be described as an ideal position for it. The doctor, who has no pre-existing knowledge of his patient and possesses no conscious memory of what is unconsciously at work in him, must call a complicated technique to his help in order to make up for this disadvantage. He must learn how to infer with great certainty from the conscious associations and communications of the patient what is repressed in him, how to discover his unconscious as it betrays itself behind his conscious words and acts. He then brings about something like what Norbert Hanold grasped at the end of the story when he translated back the name 'Gradiva' into 'Bertgang'. The disorder vanishes while being traced back to its origin; analysis, too, brings simultaneous cure.

But the similarity between Gradiva's procedure and the analytic method of psychotherapy is not limited to these two points – the making conscious of what has been repressed and the coinciding of explanation with cure. It also extends to what turns out to be the essence of the whole change – to the awakening of feelings. Every disorder analogous to Hanold's delusion, what in scientific terms we are in the habit of calling 'psychoneuroses', has as its precondition the repression of a portion of instinctual life, or, as we can safely say, of the sexual instinct. At every attempt to introduce the unconscious and repressed causes of the illness into consciousness, the instinctual component concerned is necessarily aroused to a renewed struggle with the repressing powers, only to come to terms with them in the final outcome, often to the accompaniment of violent manifestations of reaction. The process of cure is accomplished in a relapse into love, if we combine all the many components of the sexual instinct under the term 'love'; and such a relapse is indispensable, for the symptoms on account of which the treatment has been undertaken are nothing other than precipitates of earlier struggles connected with repression or the return of the repressed, and they can only be resolved and washed away by a fresh high tide of the same passions. Every psychoanalytic treatment is an attempt at liberating repressed love which has found a meagre outlet in the compromise of a symptom. Indeed, the agreement between such treatments and the process of cure described by the author of *Gradiva* reaches its climax in the further fact that in analytic psychotherapy too the reawakened passion, whether it is love or hate, invariably chooses as its object the figure of the doctor.

It is here that the differences begin, which made the case of Gradiva an ideal one which medical technique cannot attain. Gradiva was able to return the love which was making its way from the unconscious into consciousness, but the doctor cannot. Gradiva had herself been the object of the earlier, repressed love; her figure at once offered the liberated current of love a desirable aim. The doctor has been a stranger, and must endeavour to become a stranger once more after the cure; he is often at a loss what advice to give the patients he has cured as to how in real life they can use their recovered capacity to love. To indicate the expedients and substitutes of which the doctor therefore makes use to help him to approximate with more or less success to the model of a cure by love which has been shown us by our author – all this would take us much too far away from the task before us.

And now for the final question, whose answer we have already evaded more than once. [Cf. pp. 68 and 79.] Our views on repression, on the genesis of delusions and allied disorders, on the formation and solution of dreams, on the part played by erotic life, and on the method by which such disorders are cured, are far from being the common property of science, let alone the assured possession of educated people. If the insight which has enabled the author to construct his 'phantasy' in such a way that we have been able to dissect it like a real case history is in the nature of knowledge, we should be curious to learn what were the sources of that knowledge. One of our circle – the one who, as I said at the beginning, was interested in the dreams in *Gradiva* and their possible interpretation [cf. foot-note, p. 35] – approached the author with the direct question whether he knew anything of such scientific theories as these. The author replied, as was to be expected, in the negative, and, indeed, somewhat brusquely.[1] His imagination, he said, had inspired *Gradiva*, and he had enjoyed it; if there was anyone whom it did not please, let him simply leave it alone. He had no suspicion of how greatly it had in fact pleased his readers.

It is quite possible that the author's disavowal does not stop at this. He may perhaps altogether deny any knowledge of the rules which we have shown that he has followed, and he may repudiate all the purposes we have recognized in his work. I do not regard this as improbable; but if it is so, there are only two possible explanations. It may be that we have produced a complete caricature of an interpretation by intro-ducing into an innocent work of art purposes of which its creator had no notion, and by so doing have shown once more how easy it is to find what one is looking for and what is occupying one's own mind – a possibility of which the strangest examples are to be found in the history of literature. Let every reader now make up his mind whether he is able to accept this explanation. We ourselves, of course, hold to the other view, the remaining alternative. Our opinion is that the author need have known nothing of these rules and purposes, so that he could disavow them in good faith, but that nevertheless we have not discovered anything in his work that is not already in it. We probably draw from the same source and work upon the same object, each of us by another method. And the agree-ment of our results seems to guarantee that we have both

1. [See, however, the Editor's Note, pp. 29–30.]

worked correctly. Our procedure consists in the conscious observation of abnormal mental processes in other people so as to be able to elicit and announce their laws. The author no doubt proceeds differently. He directs his attention to the unconscious in his own mind, he listens to its possible developments and lends them artistic expression instead of suppressing them by conscious criticism. Thus he experiences from himself what we learn from others – the laws which the activities of this unconscious must obey. But he need not state these laws, nor even be clearly aware of them; as a result of the tolerance of his intelligence, they are incorporated within his creations. We discover these laws by analysing his writings just as we find them from cases of real illness; but the conclusion seems inescapable that either both of us, the writer and the doctor, have misunderstood the unconscious in the same way, or we have both understood it correctly. This conclusion is of great value to us, and it is on its account that it has been worth while to investigate by the methods of medical psychoanalysis the way in which the formation and the cure of the delusions as well as the dreams are represented in Jensen's *Gradiva*.

We would seem to have reached the end. But an attentive reader might remind us that at the beginning we threw out an assertion that dreams are wishes represented as fulfilled and that we gave no proof of this. Well, we reply, what we have described in these pages might show how little justification there is for trying to cover the explanations we have to give of dreams with the single formula that dreams are wish-fulfilments. Nevertheless the assertion stands and can easily be proved too for the dreams in *Gradiva*. The latent dream-thoughts – we know what is meant by them – may be of the most various kinds; in *Gradiva* they are 'days' residues', thoughts that have been left over unnoticed and undealt-with from the mental activities of waking life. But in order for a dream to develop out of them, the co-operation of a wish (usually an unconscious one) is required; this contributes the motive force for constructing the dream, while the day's residues provide the material. In Norbert Hanold's first dream two wishes competed with each other in making the dream; one of them was actually admissible to consciousness, while the other belonged to the unconscious and operated from out of repression. The first was a wish, understandable in any archaeologist, to have been present as an eyewitness at the catastrophe in the year 79 A.D. What sacrifice would an archaeologist think too great if this wish could be realized in any way other than in a dream! The other wish, the other constructor of the dream, was of an erotic nature: it might be crudely and also incompletely stated as a wish to be there when the girl he loved lay down to sleep. This was the wish the rejection of which caused the dream to become an anxiety-dream. The wishes that were the motive forces of the second dream are perhaps less conspicuous; but if we recall its translation we shall not hesitate to describe them too as erotic. The wish to be taken captive by the girl he loved, to fall in with her wishes and to be subjected to her – for so we may construe the wish behind the situation of the lizard-catching – was in fact of a passive, masochistic character. Next day the dreamer hit the girl, as though he was dominated by the contrary erotic current ... But we must stop here, or we may really forget that Hanold and Gradiva are only creatures of their author's mind.

POSTSCRIPT TO THE SECOND EDITION
(1912)

IN the five years that have passed since this study was completed, psychoanalytic research has summoned up the courage to approach the creations of imaginative writers with yet another purpose in view. It no longer merely seeks in them for confirmations of the findings it has made from unpoetic, neurotic human beings; it also demands to know the material of impressions and memories from which the author has built the work, and the methods and processes by which he has converted this material into a work of art. It has turned out that these questions can be most easily answered in the case of writers who (like our Wilhelm Jensen, who died in 1911) were in the habit of giving themselves over to their imagination in a simple-minded joy in creating. Soon after the publication of my analytic examination of *Gradiva* I attempted to interest the elderly author in these new tasks of psychoanalytic research. But he refused his co-operation.

A friend of mine has since then drawn my attention to two other of the author's short stories, which might stand in a genetic relation to *Gradiva*, as preliminary studies or earlier attempts at a satisfactory poetical solution of the same problem in the psychology of love. The first of these stories, 'Der rote Schirm' ['The Red Parasol'], recalls *Gradiva* by the recurrence in it of a number of small *motifs*, such as white flowers of the dead, a forgotten object (Gradiva's sketch-book), and a significant small animal (the butterfly and the lizard in *Gradiva*), but more especially by the repetition of the main situation – the apparition in the mid-day glare of a summer's day of a girl who had died (or was believed to have died). In 'Der rote Schirm' the scene of the apparition is a ruined castle, just as are the ruins of the excavated Pompeii in *Gradiva*. The other story, 'Im gotischen Hause' ['In the Gothic House'], shows no such resemblances either to *Gradiva* or to 'Der rote Schirm' in its manifest content. But the fact that it was given an external unity with the latter story by being published with it under a common title[1] points unmistakably to their having a closely related latent meaning. It is easy to see that all three stories treat of the same theme: the development of a love (in 'Der rote Schirm' the inhibition of a love) as an after-effect of an intimate association in childhood of a brother-and-sister kind. I gather further from a review by Eva, Countess Baudissin (in the Vienna daily paper *Die Zeit* of 11 February 1912), that Jensen's last novel, *Fremdlinge unter den Menschen*,[2] which contains much material from the author's own childhood, describes the history of a man who 'sees a sister in the woman he loves'. In neither of the two earlier stories is there a trace of the main *motif* of *Gradiva*: the girl's peculiarly charming gait with the nearly perpendicular posture of her foot.

The relief of the girl who steps along in this way, which Jensen describes as being Roman, and to which he gives the name of 'Gradiva', is in fact derived from the zenith of Greek art. It is in the Museo Chiaramonti in the Vatican (No. 644), and has been restored and interpreted by Hauser [1903]. By the combination of 'Gradiva' and some other fragments, in Florence and Munich, two reliefs were obtained, each representing three figures, who seem to be identified as the Horae, the goddesses of vegetation, and the deities of the fertilizing dew who are allied to them.[3]

1. *Übermächte* [*Superior Powers*]. Two short stories by Wilhelm Jensen, Berlin, Emil Felber, 1892.

2. [*Strangers among Men*, Dresden, C. Reissner, 1911.]

3. [Hauser (loc. cit.) regards them as Roman copies of Greek originals of the latter part of the fourth century B.C. The 'Gradiva' relief is now in Section VII/2 of the Museo Chiaramonti and is numbered 1284.]

PSYCHOPATHIC CHARACTERS
ON THE STAGE
(1942 [1905–6])

PSYCHOPATHISCHE PERSONEN AUF DER BÜHNE

(A) GERMAN EDITIONS:

1962   *Neue Rundschau*, **73**, 53–7.
1969   *Studienausgabe*, **10**, 161–8.

(B) ENGLISH TRANSLATIONS:

'Psychopathic Characters on the Stage'

1942   *Psychoanalytic Quarterly*, **11** (4), 459–64. (Tr. H. A.
        Bunker. Incomplete.)
1953   *Standard Edition*, **7**, 303–10. (Tr. James Strachey.)

The present edition is a reprint of the *Standard Edition* version, with slight editorial modification.

Dr Max Graf, in an article in the *Psychoanalytic Quarterly*, **11** (1942), 465, relates that this paper was written by Freud in 1904 and presented to him by its author. It was never published by Freud himself. There must be some mistake about this date (the MS. itself is undated), for Hermann Bahr's play, *Die Andere*, which is discussed on p. 127, was first produced (in Munich and Leipzig) at the beginning of November 1905, and had its first Vienna performance on the 25th of the same month. It was not published in book form till 1906. The probability is, therefore, that the present paper was written late in 1905 or early in 1906. Our thanks are due to Dr Raymond Gosselin, editor of the *Psychoanalytic Quarterly*, for supplying us with a photostat of Freud's original manuscript. The handwriting is in places difficult to decipher, which accounts for a few divergences between the two English translations.

PSYCHOPATHIC CHARACTERS
ON THE STAGE

IF, as has been assumed since the time of Aristotle, the purpose
of drama is to arouse 'terror and pity'[1] and so 'to purge the
emotions', we can describe that purpose in rather more detail
by saying that it is a question of opening up sources of pleasure
or enjoyment in our emotional life, just as, in the case of
intellectual activity, joking or fun open up similar sources,
many of which that activity had made inaccessible. In this
connection the prime factor is unquestionably the process of
getting rid of one's own emotions by 'blowing off steam'; and
the consequent enjoyment corresponds on the one hand to the
relief produced by a thorough discharge and on the other hand,
no doubt, to an accompanying sexual excitation; for the latter,
as we may suppose, appears as a by-product whenever an affect
is aroused, and gives people the sense, which they so much
desire, of a raising of the potential of their psychical state. Being
present as an interested spectator at a spectacle or play[2] does
for adults what play does for children, whose hesitant hopes
of being able to do what grown-up people do are in that way
gratified. The spectator is a person who experiences too little,
who feels that he is a 'poor wretch to whom nothing of importance can happen', who has long been obliged to damp

1. [The German 'Mitleid' has the meaning of 'sympathetic suffering'.]
2. ['Schauspiel' is the ordinary German word for a dramatic performance.
Freud writes it here with a hyphen 'Schau-spiel' to bring out the word's
two components: 'Schau', 'spectacle', and 'Spiel', 'play' or 'game'. Freud
returned to this topic in his subsequent paper on 'Creative Writers and Day-
Dreaming' (1908e), p. 129 ff. below, and in Chapter II of Beyond the Pleasure
Principle (1920g), P.F.L., 11, 287.]

down, or rather displace, his ambition to stand in his own person at the hub of world affairs; he longs to feel and to act and to arrange things according to his desires – in short, to be a hero. And the playwright and actor enable him to do this by allowing him *to identify himself* with a hero. They spare him something, too. For the spectator knows quite well that actual heroic conduct such as this would be impossible for him without pains and sufferings and acute fears, which would almost cancel out the enjoyment. He knows, moreover, that he has only *one* life and that he might perhaps perish even in a *single* such struggle against adversity. Accordingly, his enjoyment is based on an illusion; that is to say, his suffering is mitigated by the certainty that, firstly, it is someone other than himself who is acting and suffering on the stage, and, secondly, that after all it is only a game, which can threaten no damage to his personal security. In these circumstances he can allow himself to enjoy being a 'great man', to give way without a qualm to such suppressed impulses as a craving for freedom in religious, political, social and sexual matters, and to 'blow off steam' in every direction in the various grand scenes that form part of the life represented on the stage.

Several other forms of creative writing, however, are equally subject to these same preconditions for enjoyment. Lyric poetry serves the purpose, more than anything, of giving vent to intense feelings of many sorts – just as was at one time the case with dancing. Epic poetry aims chiefly at making it possible to feel the enjoyment of a great heroic character in his hour of triumph. But drama seeks to explore emotional possibilities more deeply and to give an enjoyable shape even to forebodings of misfortune; for this reason it depicts the hero in his struggles, or rather (with masochistic satisfaction) in defeat. This relation to suffering and misfortune might be taken as characteristic of drama, whether, as happens in serious plays, it is only *concern* that is aroused, and afterwards allayed, or whether, as happens in tragedies, the suffering is actually realized. The fact that drama originated out of sacrificial rites (cf. the goat and the scapegoat) in the cult of the gods cannot be unrelated to this meaning of drama.[1] It appeases, as it were, a rising rebellion against the divine regulation of the universe, which is responsible for the existence of suffering. Heroes are first and foremost rebels against God or against something divine; and pleasure is derived, as it seems, from the affliction of a weaker being in the face of divine might – a pleasure due to masochistic satisfaction as well as to direct enjoyment of a character whose greatness is insisted upon in spite of everything. Here we have a mood like that of Prometheus, but alloyed with a paltry readiness to let oneself be soothed for the moment by a temporary satisfaction.

Suffering of every kind is thus the subject-matter of drama, and from this suffering it promises to give the audience pleasure. Thus we arrive at a first precondition of this form of art: that it should not cause suffering to the audience, that it should know how to compensate, by means of the possible satisfactions involved, for the sympathetic suffering which is aroused. (Modern writers have particularly often failed to obey this rule.) But the suffering represented is soon restricted to *mental* suffering; for no one wants *physical* suffering who knows how quickly all mental enjoyment is brought to an end by the changes in somatic feeling that physical suffering brings about. If we are sick we have one wish only: to be well again and to be quit of our present state. We call for the doctor and medicine, and for the removal of the inhibition on the play of phantasy which has pampered us into deriving enjoyment even from our own sufferings. If a spectator puts himself in the place of someone who is physically ill he finds himself without any capacity for enjoyment or psychical activity. Consequently a person who is physically ill can only figure on the stage as a piece of stage-property and not as a hero, unless, indeed, some peculiar physical aspects of his illness make psychical activity possible – such, for instance, as the sick man's forlorn state in the *Philoctetes* or the hopelessness of the sufferers in the class of plays that centre round consumptives.

1. [The subject of the hero in Greek tragedy is discussed in *Totem and Taboo* (1912–13), *P.F.L.*, **13**, 218–19.]

People are acquainted with mental suffering principally in connection with the circumstances in which it is acquired; accordingly, dramas dealing with it require some event out of which the illness shall arise and they open with an exposition of this event. It is only an apparent exception that some plays, such as the *Ajax* and the *Philoctetes*, introduce the mental illness as already fully established; for in Greek tragedies, owing to the familiarity of the material, the curtain rises, as one might say, in the middle of the play. It is easy to give an exhaustive account of the preconditions governing an event of the kind that is here in question. It must be an event involving conflict and it must include an effort of will together with resistance. This precondition found its first and grandest fulfilment in a struggle against divinity. I have already said that a tragedy of this kind is one of rebellion, in which the dramatist and the audience take the side of the rebel. The less belief there comes to be in divinity, the more important becomes the *human* regulation of affairs; and it is this which, with increasing insight, comes to be held responsible for suffering. Thus the hero's next struggle is against human society, and here we have the class of *social* tragedies. Yet another fulfilment of the necessary precondition is to be found in a struggle between individual men. Such are tragedies of *character*, which exhibit all the excitement of an 'agon' [ἀγών, conflict], and which are best played out between outstanding characters who have freed themselves from the bond of human institutions – which, in fact, must have *two* heroes. Fusions between these two last classes, with a hero struggling against institutions embodied in powerful characters, are of course admissible without question. Pure tragedies of character lack the rebellious source of enjoyment, but this emerges once again no less forcibly in social dramas (in Ibsen, for instance) than it did in the historical plays of the Greek classical tragedians.

When *religious* drama, *social* drama and drama of *character* differ essentially in the terrain where the action leading to the suffering is fought out, we can follow the course of drama on to yet another terrain, where it becomes *psychological* drama. Here the struggle that causes the suffering is fought out in the hero's mind itself — a struggle between different impulses, and one which must have its end in the extinction, not of the hero, but of one of his impulses; it must end, that is to say, in a renunciation. Combinations of any kind between this pre-condition and the earlier types are, of course, possible; thus institutions, for instance, can themselves be the cause of internal conflicts. And this is where we have tragedies of love; for the suppression of love by social culture, by human conventions, or the struggle between 'love and duty', which is so familiar to us in opera, are the starting-point of almost endless varieties of situations of conflict: just as endless, in fact, as the erotic day-dreams of men.

But the series of possibilities grows wider; and psychological drama turns into psychopathological drama when the source of the suffering in which we take part and from which we are meant to derive pleasure is no longer a conflict between two almost equally conscious impulses but between a conscious impulse and a repressed one. Here the precondition of enjoyment is that the spectator should himself be a neurotic, for it is only such people who can derive pleasure instead of simple aversion from the revelation and the more or less conscious recognition of a repressed impulse. In anyone who is not neurotic this recognition will meet only with aversion and will call up a readiness to repeat the act of repression which has earlier been successfully brought to bear on the impulse: for in such people a single expenditure of repression has been enough to hold the repressed impulse completely in check. But in neurotics the repression is on the brink of failing; it is unstable and needs a constant renewal of expenditure, and this expenditure is spared if recognition of the impulse is brought about. Thus it is only in neurotics that a struggle can occur of a kind which can be made the subject of a drama; but even in them the dramatist will provoke not merely an *enjoyment* of the liberation but a *resistance* to it as well.

The first of these modern dramas is *Hamlet*.[1] It has as its subject the way in which a man who has so far been normal becomes neurotic owing to the peculiar nature of the task by which he is faced, a man, that is, in whom an impulse that has hitherto been successfully repressed endeavours to make its way into action. *Hamlet* is distinguished by three characteristics which seem important in connection with our present discussion. (1) The hero is not psychopathic, but only becomes psychopathic in the course of the action of the play. (2) The repressed impulse is one of those which are similarly repressed in all of us, and the repression of which is part and parcel of the foundations of our personal evolution. It is this repression which is shaken up by the situation in the play. As a result of these two characteristics it is easy for us to recognize ourselves in the hero: we are susceptible to the same conflict as he is, since 'a person who does not lose his reason under certain conditions can have no reason to lose'.[2] (3) It appears as a necessary precondition of this form of art that the impulse that is struggling into consciousness, however clearly it is recognizable, is never given a definite name; so that in the spectator too the process is carried through with his attention averted, and he is in the grip of his emotions instead of taking stock of what is happening. A certain amount of resistance is no doubt saved in this way, just as, in an analytic treatment, we find derivatives of the repressed material reaching consciousness, owing to a lower resistance, while the repressed material itself is unable to do so. After all, the conflict in *Hamlet* is so effectively concealed that it was left to me to unearth it.

It may be in consequence of disregarding these three preconditions that so many other psychopathic characters are as unserviceable on the stage as they are in real life. For the victim of a neurosis is someone into whose conflict we can gain no insight if we first meet it in a fully established state. But, *per contra*, if we recognize the conflict, we forget that he is a sick

1. [Freud's first published discussion of *Hamlet* was in *The Interpretation of Dreams* (1900a), P.F.L., **4**, 366–8.]
2. [Lessing, *Emilia Galotti*, Act IV, Scene 7.]

man, just as, if he himself recognizes it, he ceases to be ill. It would seem to be the dramatist's business to induce the same illness in us; and this can best be achieved if we are made to follow the development of the illness along with the sufferer. This will be especially necessary where the repression does not already exist in us but has first to be set up; and this represents a step further than *Hamlet* in the use of neurosis on the stage. If we are faced by an unfamiliar and fully established neurosis, we shall be inclined to send for the doctor (just as we do in real life) and pronounce the character inadmissible to the stage.

This last mistake seems to occur in Bahr's *Die Andere*,[1] apart from a second one which is implicit in the problem presented in the play – namely, that it is impossible for us to put ourselves with conviction into the position of believing that one particular person has a prescriptive right to give the girl complete satisfaction. So that her case cannot become ours. Moreover, there remains a third mistake: namely that there is nothing left for us to discover and that our entire resistance is mobilized against this predetermined condition of love which is so unacceptable to us. Of the three formal preconditions that I have been discussing, the most important seems to be that of the diversion of attention.

In general, it may perhaps be said that the neurotic instability of the public and the dramatist's skill in avoiding resistances and offering fore-pleasures[2] can alone determine the limits set upon the employment of abnormal characters on the stage.

1. [This play by Hermann Bahr, the Austrian novelist and playwright (1863–1934), was first produced at the end of 1905. Its plot turns upon the dual personality of its heroine, who is unable, in spite of every effort, to escape from an attachment (based on her physical feelings) to a man who has her in his power. – This paragraph was omitted from the 1942 translation.]

2. [Cf. p. 141 and *n*. 1 below.]

CREATIVE WRITERS AND
DAY-DREAMING
(1908 [1907])

DER DICHTER UND DAS PHANTASIEREN

(A) GERMAN EDITIONS:

1908   *Neue Revue*, **1** (10) [March], 716–24.
1909   *S.K.S.N.*, **2**, 197–206. (1912, 2nd ed.; 1921, 3rd ed.)
1924   *Dichtung und Kunst*, 3–14.
1941   *Gesammelte Werke*, **7**, 213–23.

(B) ENGLISH TRANSLATIONS:

'The Relation of the Poet to Day-Dreaming'

1925   *Collected Papers*, **4**, 172–83. (Tr. I. F. Grant Duff.)
1959   *Standard Edition*, **9**, 141–53. (Modified version, with an
        altered title, of the 1925 translation.)

The present edition is a reprint of the *Standard Edition* version,
with a few editorial changes.

This was originally delivered as a lecture on 6 December 1907,
before an audience of ninety, in the rooms of the Viennese publisher and bookseller Hugo Heller, who was himself a member of
the Vienna Psycho-Analytical Society. A very accurate summary of the lecture appeared next day in the Viennese daily *Die
Zeit*; but Freud's full version was first published early in 1908
in a newly established Berlin literary periodical.

Some of the problems of creative writing had been touched
on shortly before in Freud's study on *Gradiva* (e.g., p. 115
above); and a year or two earlier he had approached the question
in an essay on 'Psychopathic Characters on the Stage' (1942a),
p. 119 ff. above. The centre of interest in the present paper,
however, lies in its discussion of phantasy – a topic which is
also discussed in the *Gradiva* study (p. 76 ff. above). See also
Freud's paper on 'Hysterical Phantasies' (1908a), *P.F.L.*, **10**, 83 ff.

CREATIVE WRITERS AND
DAY-DREAMING

WE laymen have always been intensely curious to know – like
the Cardinal who put a similar question to Ariosto[1] – from
what sources that strange being, the creative writer, draws his
material, and how he manages to make such an impression
on us with it and to arouse in us emotions of which, perhaps,
we had not even thought ourselves capable. Our interest is
only heightened the more by the fact that, if we ask him, the
writer himself gives us no explanation, or none that is satisfactory; and it is not at all weakened by our knowledge that
not even the clearest insight into the determinants of his choice
of material and into the nature of the art of creating imaginative
form will ever help to make creative writers of us.

If we could at least discover in ourselves or in people like
ourselves an activity which was in some way akin to creative
writing! An examination of it would then give us a hope of
obtaining the beginnings of an explanation of the creative work
of writers. And, indeed, there is some prospect of this being
possible. After all, creative writers themselves like to lessen
the distance between their kind and the common run of
humanity; they so often assure us that every man is a poet at
heart and that the last poet will not perish till the last man
does.

Should we not look for the first traces of imaginative activity
as early as in childhood? The child's best-loved and most intense
occupation is with his play or games. Might we not say that
every child at play behaves like a creative writer, in that he

1. [Cardinal Ippolito d'Este was Ariosto's first patron, to whom he
dedicated the *Orlando Furioso*. The poet's only reward was the question:
'Where did you find so many stories, Lodovico?']

creates a world of his own, or, rather, rearranges the things of his world in a new way which pleases him? It would be wrong to think he does not take that world seriously; on the contrary, he takes his play very seriously and he expends large amounts of emotion on it. The opposite of play is not what is serious but what is real. In spite of all the emotion with which he cathects his world of play, the child distinguishes it quite well from reality; and he likes to link his imagined objects and situations to the tangible and visible things of the real world. This linking is all that differentiates the child's 'play' from 'phantasying'.

The creative writer does the same as the child at play. He creates a world of phantasy which he takes very seriously – that is, which he invests with large amounts of emotion – while separating it sharply from reality. Language has preserved this relationship between children's play and poetic creation. It gives the name of *'Spiel'* ['play'] to those forms of imaginative writing which require to be linked to tangible objects and which are capable of representation. It speaks of a *'Lustspiel'* or *'Trauerspiel'* ['comedy' or 'tragedy': literally, 'pleasure play' or 'mourning play'] and describes those who carry out the representation as *'Schauspieler'* ['players': literally 'show-players']. The unreality of the writer's imaginative world, however, has very important consequences for the technique of his art; for many things which, if they were real, could give no enjoyment, can do so in the play of phantasy, and many excitements which, in themselves, are actually distressing, can become a source of pleasure for the hearers and spectators at the performance of a writer's work.

There is another consideration for the sake of which we will dwell a moment longer on this contrast between reality and play. When the child has grown up and has ceased to play, and after he has been labouring for decades to envisage the realities of life with proper seriousness, he may one day find himself in a mental situation which once more undoes the contrast between play and reality. As an adult he can look back on the intense seriousness with which he once carried on his games in childhood; and, by equating his ostensibly serious occupations of to-day with his childhood games, he can throw off the too heavy burden imposed on him by life and win the high yield of pleasure afforded by *humour*.[1]

As people grow up, then, they cease to play, and they seem to give up the yield of pleasure which they gained from playing. But whoever understands the human mind knows that hardly anything is harder for a man than to give up a pleasure which he has once experienced. Actually, we can never give anything up; we only exchange one thing for another. What appears to be a renunciation is really the formation of a substitute or surrogate. In the same way, the growing child, when he stops playing, gives up nothing but the link with real objects; instead of *playing*, he now *phantasies*. He builds castles in the air and creates what are called *day-dreams*. I believe that most people construct phantasies at times in their lives. This is a fact which has long been overlooked and whose importance has therefore not been sufficiently appreciated.

People's phantasies are less easy to observe than the play of children. The child, it is true, plays by himself or forms a closed psychical system with other children for the purposes of a game; but even though he may not play his game in front of the grown-ups, he does not, on the other hand, conceal it from them. The adult, on the contrary, is ashamed of his phantasies and hides them from other people. He cherishes his phantasies as his most intimate possessions, and as a rule he would rather confess his misdeeds than tell anyone his phantasies. It may come about that for that reason he believes he is the only person who invents such phantasies and has no idea that creations of this kind are widespread among other people. This difference in the behaviour of a person who plays and a person who phantasies is accounted for by the motives of these two activities, which are nevertheless adjuncts to each other.

A child's play is determined by wishes: in point of fact by a single wish – one that helps in his upbringing – the wish to be big and grown up. He is always playing at being 'grown

1. [See Chapter VII (7) of Freud's book on jokes (1905c), *P.F.L.*, **6**, 293 ff.]

up', and in his games he imitates what he knows about the lives of his elders. He has no reason to conceal this wish. With the adult, the case is different. On the one hand, he knows that he is expected not to go on playing or phantasying any longer, but to act in the real world; on the other hand, some of the wishes which give rise to his phantasies are of a kind which it is essential to conceal. Thus he is ashamed of his phantasies as being childish and as being unpermissible.

But, you will ask, if people make such a mystery of their phantasying, how is it that we know such a lot about it? Well, there is a class of human beings upon whom, not a god, indeed, but a stern goddess – Necessity – has allotted the task of telling what they suffer and what things give them happiness.[1] These are the victims of nervous illness, who are obliged to tell their phantasies, among other things, to the doctor by whom they expect to be cured by mental treatment. This is our best source of knowledge, and we have since found good reason to suppose that our patients tell us nothing that we might not also hear from healthy people.

Let us now make ourselves acquainted with a few of the characteristics of phantasying. We may lay it down that a happy person never phantasies, only an unsatisfied one. The motive forces of phantasies are unsatisfied wishes, and every single phantasy is the fulfilment of a wish, a correction of unsatisfying reality. These motivating wishes vary according to the sex, character and circumstances of the person who is having the phantasy; but they fall naturally into two main groups. They are either ambitious wishes, which serve to elevate the subject's personality; or they are erotic ones. In young women the erotic wishes predominate almost exclusively, for their ambition is as a rule absorbed by erotic trends. In young men egoistic and

1. [This is an allusion to some well-known lines spoken by the poet-hero in the final scene of Goethe's *Torquato Tasso*:
    'Und wenn der Mensch in seiner Qual verstummt,
    Gab mir ein Gott, zu sagen, wie ich leide.'
'And when mankind is dumb in its torment, a god granted me to tell how I suffer.']

ambitious wishes come to the fore clearly enough alongside
of erotic ones. But we will not lay stress on the opposition
between the two trends; we would rather emphasize the fact
that they are often united. Just as, in many altar-pieces, the
portrait of the donor is to be seen in a corner of the picture,
so, in the majority of ambitious phantasies, we can discover
in some corner or other the lady for whom the creator of the
phantasy performs all his heroic deeds and at whose feet all
his triumphs are laid. Here, as you see, there are strong enough
motives for concealment; the well-brought-up young woman
is only allowed a minimum of erotic desire, and the young
man has to learn to suppress the excess of self-regard which
he brings with him from the spoilt days of his childhood, so
that he may find his place in a society which is full of other
individuals making equally strong demands.

We must not suppose that the products of this imaginative
activity – the various phantasies, castles in the air and day-
dreams – are stereotyped or unalterable. On the contrary, they
fit themselves in to the subject's shifting impressions of life,
change with every change in his situation, and receive from
every fresh active impression what might be called a 'date-
mark'. The relation of a phantasy to time is in general very
important. We may say that it hovers, as it were, between three
times – the three moments of time which our ideation involves.
Mental work is linked to some current impression, some
provoking occasion in the present which has been able to arouse
one of the subject's major wishes. From there it harks back
to a memory of an earlier experience (usually an infantile one)
in which this wish was fulfilled; and it now creates a situation
relating to the future which represents a fulfilment of the wish.
What it thus creates is a day-dream or phantasy, which carries
about it traces of its origin from the occasion which provoked
it and from the memory. Thus past, present and future are
strung together, as it were, on the thread of the wish that runs
through them.

A very ordinary example may serve to make what I have
said clear. Let us take the case of a poor orphan boy to whom

you have given the address of some employer where he may perhaps find a job. On his way there he may indulge in a day-dream appropriate to the situation from which it arises. The content of his phantasy will perhaps be something like this. He is given a job, finds favour with his new employer, makes himself indispensable in the business, is taken into his employer's family, marries the charming young daughter of the house, and then himself becomes a director of the business, first as his employer's partner and then as his successor. In this phantasy, the dreamer has regained what he possessed in his happy childhood – the protecting house, the loving parents and the first objects of his affectionate feelings. You will see from this example the way in which the wish makes use of an occasion in the present to construct, on the pattern of the past, a picture of the future.

There is a great deal more that could be said about phantasies; but I will only allude as briefly as possible to certain points. If phantasies become over-luxuriant and over-powerful, the conditions are laid for an onset of neurosis or psychosis. Phantasies, moreover, are the immediate mental precursors of the distressing symptoms complained of by our patients. Here a broad by-path branches off into pathology.

I cannot pass over the relation of phantasies to dreams. Our dreams at night are nothing else than phantasies like these, as we can demonstrate from the interpretation of dreams.[1] Language, in its unrivalled wisdom, long ago decided the question of the essential nature of dreams by giving the name of *'day-dreams'* to the airy creations of phantasy. If the meaning of our dreams usually remains obscure to us in spite of this pointer, it is because of the circumstance that at night there also arise in us wishes of which we are ashamed; these we must conceal from ourselves, and they have consequently been repressed, pushed into the unconscious. Repressed wishes of this sort and their derivatives are only allowed to come to expression in a very distorted form. When scientific work had succeeded in elucidating this factor of *dream distortion*, it was no longer difficult to recognize that

1. Cf. Freud, *The Interpretation of Dreams* (1900a). [*P.F.L.*, **4**, 631–40.]

night dreams are wish-fulfilments in just the same way as day-dreams – the phantasies which we all know so well.

So much for phantasies. And now for the creative writer. May we really attempt to compare the imaginative writer with the 'dreamer in broad daylight',[1] and his creations with day-dreams? Here we must begin by making an initial distinction. We must separate writers who, like the ancient authors of epics and tragedies, take over their material ready-made, from writers who seem to originate their own material. We will keep to the latter kind, and, for the purposes of our comparison, we will choose not the writers most highly esteemed by the critics, but the less pretentious authors of novels, romances and short stories, who nevertheless have the widest and most eager circle of readers of both sexes. One feature above all cannot fail to strike us about the creations of these story-writers: each of them has a hero who is the centre of interest, for whom the writer tries to win our sympathy by every possible means and whom he seems to place under the protection of a special Providence. If, at the end of one chapter of my story, I leave the hero unconscious and bleeding from severe wounds, I am sure to find him at the beginning of the next being carefully nursed and on the way to recovery; and if the first volume closes with the ship he is in going down in a storm at sea, I am certain, at the opening of the second volume, to read of his miraculous rescue – a rescue without which the story could not proceed. The feeling of security with which I follow the hero through his perilous adventures is the same as the feeling with which a hero in real life throws himself into the water to save a drowning man or exposes himself to the enemy's fire in order to storm a battery. It is the true heroic feeling, which one of our best writers has expressed in an inimitable phrase: 'Nothing can happen to *me*!'[2] It seems to

1. ['*Der Träumer am hellichten Tag*.']
2. ['Es kann dir nix g'schehen!' This phrase, from a comedy by the Viennese dramatist Ludwig Anzengruber (1839–89), was a favourite one of Freud's. Cf. his 'Thoughts for the Times on War and Death' (1915*b*), *P.F.L.*, **12**, 86 and *n*. 1.]

me, however, that through this revealing characteristic of invulnerability we can immediately recognize His Majesty the Ego, the hero alike of every day-dream and every story.[1]

Other typical features of these egocentric stories point to the same kinship. The fact that all the women in the novel invariably fall in love with the hero can hardly be looked on as a portrayal of reality, but it is easily understood as a necessary constituent of a day-dream. The same is true of the fact that the other characters in the story are sharply divided into good and bad, in defiance of the variety of human characters that are to be observed in real life. The 'good' ones are the helpers, while the 'bad' ones are the enemies and rivals, of the ego which has become the hero of the story.

We are perfectly aware that very many imaginative writings are far removed from the model of the naïve day-dream; and yet I cannot suppress the suspicion that even the most extreme deviations from that model could be linked with it through an uninterrupted series of transitional cases. It has struck me that in many of what are known as 'psychological' novels only one person – once again the hero – is described from within. The author sits inside his mind, as it were, and looks at the other characters from outside. The psychological novel in general no doubt owes its special nature to the inclination of the modern writer to split up his ego, by self-observation, into many part-egos, and, in consequence, to personify the conflicting currents of his own mental life in several heroes. Certain novels, which might be described as 'eccentric', seem to stand in quite special contrast to the type of the day-dream. In these, the person who is introduced as the hero plays only a very small active part; he sees the actions and sufferings of other people pass before him like a spectator. Many of Zola's later works belong to this category. But I must point out that the psychological analysis of individuals who are not creative writers, and who diverge in some respects from the so-called norm, has shown us analogous variations of the day-dream, in which the ego contents itself with the role of spectator.

1. [Cf. 'On Narcissism' (1914c), ibid., II, 85 and n. 1.]

If our comparison of the imaginative writer with the day-dreamer, and of poetical creation with the day-dream, is to be of any value, it must, above all, show itself in some way or other fruitful. Let us, for instance, try to apply to these authors' works the thesis we laid down earlier concerning the relation between phantasy and the three periods of time and the wish which runs through them; and, with its help, let us try to study the connections that exist between the life of the writer and his works. No one has known, as a rule, what expectations to frame in approaching this problem; and often the connection has been thought of in much too simple terms. In the light of the insight we have gained from phantasies, we ought to expect the following state of affairs. A strong experience in the present awakens in the creative writer a memory of an earlier experience (usually belonging to his child-hood) from which there now proceeds a wish which finds its fulfilment in the creative work. The work itself exhibits elements of the recent provoking occasion as well as of the old memory.[1]

Do not be alarmed at the complexity of this formula. I suspect that in fact it will prove to be too exiguous a pattern. Nevertheless, it may contain a first approach to the true state of affairs; and, from some experiments I have made, I am inclined to think that this way of looking at creative writings may turn out not unfruitful. You will not forget that the stress it lays on childhood memories in the writer's life – a stress which may perhaps seem puzzling – is ultimately derived from the assumption that a piece of creative writing, like a day-dream, is a continuation of, and a substitute for, what was once the play of childhood.

We must not neglect, however, to go back to the kind of imaginative works which we have to recognize, not as original creations, but as the re-fashioning of ready-made and familiar material [p. 137]. Even here, the writer keeps a certain amount

1. [A similar view had already been suggested by Freud in a letter to Fliess of 7 July 1898, on the subject of one of C. F. Meyer's short stories (Freud, 1950a, Letter 92).]

of independence, which can express itself in the choice of material and in changes in it which are often quite extensive. In so far as the material is already at hand, however, it is derived from the popular treasure-house of myths, legends and fairy tales. The study of constructions of folk psychology such as these is far from being complete, but it is extremely probable that myths, for instance, are distorted vestiges of the wishful phantasies of whole nations, the *secular dreams* of youthful humanity.

You will say that, although I have put the creative writer first in the title of my paper, I have told you far less about him than about phantasies. I am aware of that, and I must try to excuse it by pointing to the present state of our knowledge. All I have been able to do is to throw out some encouragements and suggestions which, starting from the study of phantasies, lead on to the problem of the writer's choice of his literary material. As for the other problem – by what means the creative writer achieves the emotional effects in us that are aroused by his creations – we have as yet not touched on it at all. But I should like at least to point out to you the path that leads from our discussion of phantasies to the problems of poetical effects.

You will remember how I have said that the day-dreamer carefully conceals his phantasies from other people because he feels he has reasons for being ashamed of them. I should now add that even if he were to communicate them to us he could give us no pleasure by his disclosures. Such phantasies, when we learn them, repel us or at least leave us cold. But when a creative writer presents his plays to us or tells us what we are inclined to take to be his personal day-dreams, we experience a great pleasure, and one which probably arises from the confluence of many sources. How the writer accomplishes this is his innermost secret; the essential *ars poetica* lies in the technique of overcoming the feeling of repulsion in us which is undoubtedly connected with the barriers that rise between each single ego and the others. We can guess two of the methods used by this technique. The writer softens the character of his egoistic day-dreams by altering and disguising it, and he bribes us by the purely formal — that is, aesthetic — yield of pleasure which he offers us in the presentation of his phantasies. We give the name *incentive bonus* or *fore-pleasure*[1] to a yield of pleasure such as this, which is offered to us so as to make possible the release of still greater pleasure arising from deeper psychical sources. In my opinion, all the aesthetic pleasure which a creative writer affords us has the character of a fore-pleasure of this kind, and our actual enjoyment of an imaginative work proceeds from a liberation of tensions in our minds. It may even be that not a little of this effect is due to the writer's enabling us thenceforward to enjoy our own day-dreams without self-reproach or shame. This brings us to the threshold of new, interesting and complicated inquiries; but also, at least for the moment, to the end of our discussion.

1. [Freud applied his theory of 'fore-pleasure' and 'incentive bonus' to jokes in his book on that subject (1905*c*), *P.F.L.*, **6**, 187–9, and discussed it, in connection with the creative process, in Chapter VI of his *Autobiographical Study* (1925*d*), ibid., **15**. Cf. also his *Three Essays* (1905*d*), ibid., **7**, 130–33, and 'Psychopathic Characters on the Stage' (1942*a*), p. 127 above.]

LEONARDO DA VINCI AND A MEMORY OF HIS CHILDHOOD
(1910)

EDITOR'S NOTE

EINE KINDHEITSERINNERUNG DES LEONARDO DA VINCI

(A) GERMAN EDITIONS:

1910   Leipzig and Vienna: Deuticke. (1919, 2nd ed.; 1923, 3rd ed.)

1943   *Gesammelte Werke*, **8**, 128–211.

(B) ENGLISH TRANSLATIONS:

Leonardo da Vinci

1916   New York: Moffat, Yard. (Tr. A. A. Brill.)

1922   London: Kegan Paul. (Same translator, with a preface by Ernest Jones.)

1957   *Standard Edition*, **11**, 57–137. (Tr. Alan Tyson; with new title.)

The present edition is a corrected reprint of the *Standard Edition* version, with some editorial modifications.

That Freud's interest in Leonardo was of long standing is shown by a sentence in a letter to Fliess of 9 October 1898 (Freud, 1950*a*, Letter 98), in which he remarked that 'perhaps the most famous left-handed individual was Leonardo, who is not known to have had any love-affairs'.[1] This interest, furthermore, was not a passing one, for we find in Freud's reply to a 'questionnaire' on his favourite books (1906*f*) that he mentions among

---

1. A connection between bilaterality and bisexuality had been asserted by Fliess but questioned by Freud. An indirect reference to this controversy (which was one of the occasions for their estrangement) will be found on p. 230 below.

them Merezhkovsky's study of Leonardo (1903). But the immediate stimulus to writing the present work appears to have come in the autumn of 1909 from one of his patients who, as he remarked in a letter to Jung on 17 October, seemed to have the same constitution as Leonardo without his genius. He added that he was obtaining a book on Leonardo's youth from Italy; this was the monograph by Scognamiglio (1900). After reading this and other books on Leonardo, he spoke on the subject to the Vienna Psycho-Analytical Society on 1 December, but it was not until April 1910 that he finished writing his study. It was published at the end of May. Freud made a number of corrections and additions in the later issues of the book. Among these may be specially mentioned the short footnote on circumcision (p. 187 *n.* 1), the excerpt from Reitler (p. 159 *n.* 2), and the long quotation from Pfister (p. 208 *n.*), all of them added in 1919, and the discussion of the London cartoon (p. 207 *n.*), added in 1923.

This work of Freud's was not the first application of the methods of clinical psychoanalysis to the lives of historical figures. Experiments in this direction had already been made by others, notably by Sadger, who had published studies on Conrad Ferdinand Meyer (1908), Lenau (1909*a*) and Kleist (1909*b*).[1] Freud himself had never before embarked on a full-length biographical study of his kind, though he had previously made a few fragmentary analyses of writers, based on episodes in their works. Long before this, he had sent Fliess a study of C. F. Meyer's story, 'Die Richterin' ('The Woman Judge'), which threw light on its author's early life (Freud, 1950*a*, Letter 91). But his monograph on Leonardo was not only the first but the last of Freud's large-scale excursions into the field of biography. The book seems to have been greeted with more than the usual amount of disapproval, and Freud was evidently justified in defending himself in advance with the reflections

1. Freud made some remarks on the subject of psychoanalytic biography at a meeting of the Vienna Psycho-Analytical Society on 11 December 1907. (Cf. Jones, 1955, 383.)

at the beginning of Chapter VI – reflections which have a general application even to-day to the authors and critics of biographies.

It is a strange fact, however, that until very recently none of the critics of the present work seem to have lighted upon what is no doubt its weakest point. A prominent part is played by Leonardo's memory or phantasy of being visited in his cradle by a bird of prey. The name applied to this bird in his notebooks is 'nibio', which (in the modern form of 'nibbio') is the ordinary Italian word for 'kite'. Freud, however, throughout his study translates the word by the German 'Geier', for which the English can only be 'vulture'.[1]

Freud's mistake seems to have originated from some of the German translations which he used. Thus Marie Herzfeld (1906) uses the word 'Geier' in one of her versions of the cradle phantasy instead of 'Milan', the normal German word for 'kite'. But probably the most important influence was the German translation of Merezhkovsky's Leonardo book which, as may be seen from the marked copy in Freud's library, was the source of a very great deal of his information about Leonardo and in which he probably came across the story for the first time. Here too the German word used in the cradle phantasy is 'Geier', though Merezhkovsky himself correctly used 'korshun', the Russian word for 'kite'.

In the face of this mistake, some readers may feel an impulse to dismiss the whole study as worthless. It will, however, be a good plan to examine the situation more coolly and consider in detail the exact respects in which Freud's arguments and conclusions are invalidated.

In the first place the 'hidden bird' in Leonardo's picture (p. 208 n.) must be abandoned. If it is a bird at all, it is a vulture; it bears no resemblance to a kite. This 'discovery', however, was not made by Freud but by Pfister. It was not introduced

---

1. This was pointed out by Irma Richter in a footnote to her selection from Leonardo's notebooks (1952, 286). Like Pfister (p. 209 n. below), she refers to Leonardo's childhood memory as a 'dream'.

until the second edition of the work, and Freud received it with considerable reserve.

Next, and more important, comes the Egyptian connection. The hieroglyph for the Egyptian word for 'mother' ('*mut*') quite certainly represents a vulture and not a kite. Gardiner in his authoritative *Egyptian Grammar* (2nd ed., 1950, 469) identifies the creature as '*Gyps fulvus*', the griffon vulture. It follows from this that Freud's theory that the bird of Leonardo's phantasy stood for his mother cannot claim direct support from the Egyptian myth, and that the question of his acquaintance with that myth ceases to be relevant.[1] The phantasy and the myth seem to have no immediate connection with each other. Nevertheless each of them, taken independently, raises an interesting problem. How was it that the ancient Egyptians came to link up the ideas of 'vulture' and 'mother'? Does the Egyptologists' explanation that it is merely a matter of a chance phonetic coincidence meet the question? If not, Freud's discussion of androgynous mother-goddesses must have a value of its own, irrespective of its connection with the case of Leonardo. So too Leonardo's phantasy of the bird visiting him in his cradle and putting its tail into his mouth continues to cry out for an explanation even if the bird was not a vulture. And Freud's psychological analysis of the phantasy is not contradicted by this correction but merely deprived of one piece of corroborative support.

Apart, then, from the consequent irrelevance of the Egyptian discussion – though this nevertheless retains much of its independent value – the main body of Freud's study is unaffected by his mistake: the detailed construction of Leonardo's emotional life from his earliest years, the account of the conflict between his artistic and his scientific impulses, the deep analysis of his psychosexual history. And, in addition to this main topic, the study presents us with a number of not less important side-

1. Nor can the story of the virginal impregnation of vultures serve as evidence of Leonardo's having had an exclusive bond with his mother in his infancy – though the existence of that bond is not contradicted by the failure of this particular evidence.

themes: a more general discussion of the nature and workings of the mind of the creative artist, an outline of the genesis of one particular type of homosexuality, and – of special interest to the history of psychoanalytic theory – the first full emergence of the concept of narcissism.

LEONARDO DA VINCI AND A MEMORY OF HIS CHILDHOOD

I

WHEN psychiatric research, normally content to draw on frailer men for its material, approaches one who is among the greatest of the human race, it is not doing so for the reasons so frequently ascribed to it by laymen. 'To blacken the radiant and drag the sublime into the dust' is no part of its purpose,[1] and there is no satisfaction for it in narrowing the gulf which separates the perfection of the great from the inadequacy of the objects that are its usual concern. But it cannot help finding worthy of understanding everything that can be recognized in those illustrious models, and it believes there is no one so great as to be disgraced by being subject to the laws which govern both normal and pathological activity with equal cogency.

Leonardo da Vinci (1452–1519) was admired even by his contemporaries as one of the greatest men of the Italian Renaissance; yet in their time he had already begun to seem an enigma, just as he does to us to-day. He was a universal genius 'whose outlines can only be surmised – never defined'.[2] In his own time his most decisive influence was in painting, and it was left to us to recognize the greatness of the natural scientist (and engineer)[3] that was combined in him with the artist. Though

1.   [Es liebt die Welt, das Strahlende zu schwärzen
                Und das Erhabene in den Staub zu ziehn.

(The world loves to blacken the radiant and drag the sublime into the dust.)

From a poem by Schiller, 'Das Mädchen von Orleans', inserted as an extra prologue to the 1801 edition of his play *Die Jungfrau von Orleans*.]

2. The words are Jacob Burckhardt's, quoted by Konstantinowa (1907 [51]).

3. [The words in parentheses were added in 1923.]

he left behind him masterpieces of painting, while his scientific discoveries remained unpublished and unused, the investigator in him never in the course of his development left the artist entirely free, but often made severe encroachments on him and perhaps in the end suppressed him. In the last hour of his life, according to the words that Vasari gives him, he reproached himself with having offended God and man by his failure to do his duty in his art.[1] And even if this story of Vasari's has neither external nor much internal probability but belongs to the legend which began to be woven around the mysterious Master even before his death, it is still of incontestable value as evidence of what men believed at the time.

What was it that prevented Leonardo's personality from being understood by his contemporaries? The cause of this was certainly not the versatility of his talents and the range of his knowledge, which enabled him to introduce himself to the court of the Duke of Milan, Lodovico Sforza, called Il Moro, as a performer on a kind of lute of his own invention, or allowed him to write the remarkable letter to the same duke in which he boasted of his achievements as architect and military engineer. For the days of the Renaissance were quite familiar with such a combination of wide and diverse abilities in a single individual – though we must allow that Leonardo himself was one of the most brilliant examples of this. Nor did he belong to the type of genius who has received a niggardly outward endowment from Nature, and who in his turn places no value on the outward forms of life, but in a spirit of painful gloom flies from all dealings with mankind. On the contrary, he was tall and well-proportioned; his features were of consummate beauty and his physical strength unusual; he was charming in

1. 'Egli per reverenza, rizzatosi a sedere sul letto, contando il mal suo e gli accidenti di quello, mostrava tuttavia, quanto aveva offeso Dio e gli uomini del mondo, non avendo operato nell' arte come si conveniva.' ['He having raised himself out of reverence so as to sit on the bed, and giving an account of his illness and its circumstances, yet showed how much he had offended God and mankind in not having worked at his art as he should have done.'] Vasari [ed. Poggi, 1919, 43].

his manner, supremely eloquent, and cheerful and amiable to everyone. He loved beauty in the things that surrounded him; he was fond of magnificent clothing and valued every refinement of living. In a passage from the treatise on painting, which reveals his lively capacity for enjoyment, he compares painting with its sister arts and describes the hardships that await the sculptor: 'For his face is smeared and dusted all over with marble powder so that he looks like a baker, and he is completely covered with little chips of marble, so that it seems as if his back had been snowed on; and his house is full of splinters of stone and dust. In the case of the painter it is quite different ... for the painter sits in front of his work in perfect comfort. He is well-dressed and handles the lightest of brushes which he dips in pleasant colours. He wears the clothes he likes; and his house is full of delightful paintings, and is spotlessly clean. He is often accompanied by music or by men who read from a variety of beautiful works, and he can listen to these with great pleasure and without the din of hammers and other noises.'[1]

It is indeed quite possible that the idea of a radiantly happy and pleasure-loving Leonardo is only applicable to the first and longer period of the artist's life. Afterwards, when the downfall of Lodovico Moro's rule forced him to leave Milan, the city that was the centre of his activity and where his position was assured, and to pursue a life lacking in security and not rich in external successes, until he found his last asylum in France, the sparkle of his temperament may have grown dim and some strange sides of his nature may have been thrown into prominence. Moreover, the turning of his interests from his art to science, which increased as time went on, must have played its part in widening the gulf between himself and his contemporaries. All the efforts in which in their opinion he frittered away his time when he could have been industriously painting to order and becoming rich (as, for example, his former fellow-student Perugino did) seemed to them to be

1. *Trattato della Pittura* [Ludwig (1909, 36); also I. A. Richter (1952, 330 f.)].

LEONARDO DA VINCI

merely capricious trifling or even caused him to be suspected
of being in the service of the 'black art'. We are in a position
to understand him better, for we know from his notes what
were the arts that he practised. In an age which was beginning
to replace the authority of the Church by that of antiquity
and which was not yet familiar with any form of research not
based on presuppositions, Leonardo – the forerunner and by
no means unworthy rival of Bacon and Copernicus – was
necessarily isolated. In his dissection of the dead bodies of horses
and human beings, in his construction of flying machines, and
in his studies on the nutrition of plants and their reactions to
poisons, he certainly departed widely from the commentators
on Aristotle, and came close to the despised alchemists, in whose
laboratories experimental research had found some refuge at
least in those unfavourable times.

The effect that this had on his painting was that he took
up his brush with reluctance, painted less and less, left what
he had begun for the most part unfinished and cared little about
the ultimate fate of his works. And this was what he was blamed
for by his contemporaries: to them his attitude towards his art
remained a riddle.

Several of Leonardo's later admirers have made attempts to
acquit his character of the flaw of instability. In his defence
they claim that he is blamed for what is a general feature of
great artists: even the energetic Michelangelo, a man entirely
given up to his labours, left many of his works incomplete,
and it was no more his fault than it was Leonardo's in the parallel
instance. Moreover, in the case of some of the pictures, they
urge, it is not so much a question of their being unfinished
as of his declaring them to be so. What appears to the layman
as a masterpiece is never for the creator of the work of art
more than an unsatisfactory embodiment of what he intended;
he has some dim notion of a perfection, whose likeness time
and again he despairs of reproducing. Least of all, they claim,
is it right to make the artist responsible for the ultimate fate
of his works.

Valid as some of these excuses may be, they still do not cover the whole state of affairs that confronts us in Leonardo. The same distressing struggle with a work, the final flight from it and the indifference to its future fate may recur in many other artists, but there is no doubt that this behaviour is shown in Leonardo in an extreme degree. Solmi (1910, 12) quotes the remark of one of his pupils: 'Pareva, che ad ogni ora tremasse, quando si poneva a dipingere, e però non diede mai fine ad alcuna cosa cominciata, considerando la grandezza dell'arte, tal che egli scorgeva errori in quelle cose, che ad altri parevano miracoli.'[1] His last pictures, he goes on, the Leda, the Madonna di Sant' Onofrio, Bacchus, and the young St John the Baptist, remained unfinished 'come quasi intervenne di tutte le cose sue . . .'[2] Lomazzo, who made a copy of the Last Supper, refers in a sonnet to Leonardo's notorious inability to finish his works:

> Protogen che il pennel di sue pitture
> Non levava, agguaglio il Vinci Divo,
> Di cui opra non è finita pure.[3]

The slowness with which Leonardo worked was proverbial. He painted at the Last Supper in the Convent of Santa Maria delle Grazie in Milan, after the most thorough preparatory studies, for three whole years. One of his contemporaries, Matteo Bandelli, the story-writer, who at the time was a young monk in the convent, tells how Leonardo often used to climb up the scaffolding early in the morning and remain there till twilight never once laying his brush aside, and with no thought of eating or drinking. Then days would pass without his putting his hand to it. Sometimes he would remain for hours in front

1. ['He appeared to tremble the whole time when he set himself to paint, and yet he never completed any work he had begun, having so high a regard for the greatness of art that he discovered faults in things that to others seemed miracles.']

2. ['As happened more or less to all his works.']

3. ['Protogenes, who never lifted his brush from his work, was the equal of the divine Vinci, who never finished anything at all.'] Quoted by Scognamiglio (1900 [112]).

of the painting, merely examining it in his mind. At other times
he would come straight to the convent from the court in the
castle at Milan, where he was making the model of the equestrian statue for Francesco Sforza, in order to add a few strokes of
the brush to a figure, and then immediately break off.[1]
According to Vasari he spent four years in painting the portrait
of Mona Lisa, the wife of the Florentine Francesco del
Giocondo, without being able to bring it to final completion.
This circumstance may also account for the fact that the picture
was never delivered to the man who commissioned it, but
instead remained with Leonardo and was taken to France by
him.[2] It was bought by King Francis I, and to-day forms one
of the greatest treasures of the Louvre.

If these reports of the way in which Leonardo worked are
compared with the evidence of the extraordinarily numerous
sketches and studies which he left behind him and which exhibit
every *motif* appearing in his paintings in a great variety of forms,
we are bound totally to reject the idea that traits of hastiness and unsteadiness acquired the slightest influence over
Leonardo's relation to his art. On the contrary, it is possible
to observe a quite extraordinary profundity, a wealth of possibilities between which a decision can only be reached with
hesitation, demands which can hardly be satisfied, and an inhibition in the actual execution which is not in fact to be
explained even by the artist inevitably falling short of his ideal.
The slowness which had all along been conspicuous in Leonardo's work is seen to be a symptom of this inhibition and
to be the forerunner of his subsequent withdrawal from
painting.[3] It was this too which determined the fate of the Last
Supper – a fate that was not undeserved. Leonardo could not
become reconciled to fresco painting, which demands rapid
work while the ground is still moist, and this was the reason

1. Von Seidlitz (1909, **1**, 203).
2. Von Seidlitz (1909, **2**, 48).
3. Pater [1873, 100]: 'But it is certain that at one period of his life he
had almost ceased to be an artist.'

why he chose oil colours, the drying of which permitted him to protract the completion of the painting to suit his mood and leisure. These pigments, however, detached themselves from the ground on which they were applied and which separated them from the wall. Added to this, the defects in the wall, and the later fortunes of the building itself, determined what seems to be the inevitable ruin of the picture.[1]

The miscarriage of a similar technical experiment appears to have caused the destruction of the Battle of Anghiari, the painting which, in competition with Michelangelo, he began to paint some time afterwards on a wall of the Sala del Consiglio in Florence, and which he also abandoned in an unfinished condition. Here it seems as if an alien interest – in experimentation – at first reinforced the artistic one, only to damage the work later on.

The character of Leonardo the man showed some other unusual traits and apparent contradictions. A certain inactivity and indifference seemed obvious in him. At a time when everyone was trying to gain the widest scope for his activity – a goal unattainable without the development of energetic aggressiveness towards other people – Leonardo was notable for his quiet peaceableness and his avoidance of all antagonism and controversy. He was gentle and kindly to everyone; he declined, it is said, to eat meat, since he did not think it justifiable to deprive animals of their lives; and he took particular pleasure in buying birds in the market and setting them free.[2] He condemned war and bloodshed and described man as not so much the king of the animal world but rather the worst of the wild beasts.[3] But this feminine delicacy of feeling did not deter him from accompanying condemned criminals on their way to

1. See von Seidlitz (1909, **1** [205 ff.]) for the history of the attempts to restore and preserve the picture.
2. Müntz (1899, 18). A letter of a contemporary from India to one of the Medici alludes to this characteristic behaviour of Leonardo. (See J. P. Richter [1939, **2**, 103–4 *n*.].)
3. Bottazzi (1910, 186).

execution in order to study their features distorted by fear and to sketch them in his notebook. Nor did it stop him from devising the cruellest offensive weapons and from entering the service of Cesare Borgia as chief military engineer. He often gave the appearance of being indifferent to good and evil, or he insisted on measurement by a special standard. He accompanied Cesare in a position of authority during the campaign that brought the Romagna into the possession of that most ruthless and faithless of adversaries. There is not a line in Leonardo's notebooks which reveals any criticism of the events of those days, or any concern in them. A comparison suggests itself here with Goethe during the French campaign.

If a biographical study is really intended to arrive at an understanding of its hero's mental life it must not — as happens in the majority of biographies as a result of discretion or prudishness — silently pass over its subject's sexual activity or sexual individuality. What is known of Leonardo in this respect is little: but that little is full of significance. In an age which saw a struggle between sensuality without restraint and gloomy asceticism, Leonardo represented the cool repudiation of sexuality — a thing that would scarcely be expected of an artist and a portrayer of feminine beauty. Solmi quotes the following sentence of his which is evidence of his frigidity: 'The act of procreation and everything connected with it is so disgusting that mankind would soon die out if it were not an old-established custom and if there were not pretty faces and sensuous natures.'[1] His posthumous writings, which not only deal with the greatest scientific problems but also contain trivialities that strike us as scarcely worthy of so great a mind (an allegorical natural history, animal fables, jokes, prophecies),[2] are chaste — one might say even abstinent — to a degree that would cause surprise in a work of *belles lettres* even to-day. So resolutely do they shun everything sexual that it would seem as if Eros alone, the preserver of all living things, was not worthy

1. Solmi (1908 [24]).
2. Herzfeld (1906).

material for the investigator in his pursuit of knowledge.[1] It is well known how frequently great artists take pleasure in giving vent to their phantasies in erotic and even crudely obscene pictures. In Leonardo's case on the contrary we have only some anatomical sketches of the internal female genitals, the position of the embryo in the womb and so on.[2]

1. An exception to this (though an unimportant one) is perhaps to be found in his collected witticisms – *belle facezie* – which have not been translated. See Herzfeld (1906, 151). – [This reference to Eros as 'the preserver of all living things' seems to anticipate Freud's introduction of the name ten years later, in almost exactly the same phrase, as a general term for the sexual as opposed to the death instincts. See, for instance, *Beyond the Pleasure Principle* (1920*g*), *P.F.L.*, **11**, 323, 325.]

2. [*Footnote added* 1919:] Some remarkable errors are visible in a drawing made by Leonardo of the sexual act seen in anatomical sagittal section, which certainly cannot be called obscene [Fig. 1]. They were discovered by Reitler (1917) and discussed by him in the light of the account which I have given here of Leonardo's character:

'It is precisely in the process of portraying the act of procreation that this excessive instinct for research has totally failed – obviously only as a result of his even greater sexual repression. The man's body is drawn in full, the woman's only in part. If the drawing reproduced in Fig. 1 is shown to an unprejudiced onlooker with the head visible but all the lower parts covered up, it may be safely assumed that the head will be taken to be a woman's. The wavy locks on the forehead, and the others, which flow down the back approximately to the fourth or fifth dorsal vertebra, mark the head as more of a woman's than a man's.

'The woman's breast reveals two defects. The first indeed is an artistic one, for its outline gives it the appearance of a breast that is flabby and hangs down unpleasingly. The second defect is anatomical, for Leonardo the researcher had obviously been prevented by his fending off of sexuality from ever making a close examination of a nursing woman's nipples. Had he done so he would have been bound to notice that the milk flows out of a number of separate excretory ducts. Leonardo, however, drew only a single duct extending far down into the abdominal cavity and probably in his view drawing the milk from the *cisterna chyli* and perhaps also connected in some way with the sex organs. It must of course be taken into consideration that the study of the internal organs of the human body was at that time made extremely difficult, since the dissection of bodies was regarded as desecration of the dead and was most severely punished. Whether Leonardo, who had certainly only very little material for dissection at his disposal, knew anything at all of the existence of a lymph reservoir in the abdominal cavity is therefore in fact highly questionable, although in his drawing he included a cavity that is no doubt intended to be something of the sort. But from his making the lactiferous duct extend still further downwards till it reaches the internal sex organs we may suspect that he was trying to represent the synchronization of the beginning of the secretion of milk and the end of pregnancy by means of visible anatomical connections as well. However, even if we are ready to excuse the artist's defective knowledge of anatomy by referring it to the circumstances of his time, the striking fact still remains that it is precisely the female genital that Leonardo has treated so carelessly. The vagina and something that looks like the *portio uteri* can no doubt be made out, but the lines indicating the uterus itself are completely confused.

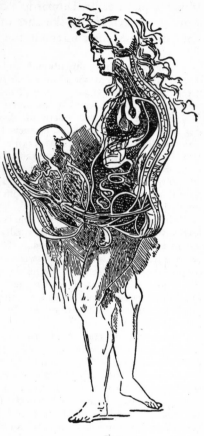

'The male genital on the other hand is depicted by Leonardo much more correctly. Thus, for instance, he was not satisfied with drawing the testis but also put in the epididymis, which he drew with perfect accuracy.

'What is especially remarkable is the posture in which Leonardo makes coitus take place. Pictures and drawings by famous artists exist which depict *coitus a tergo*, *a latere*, etc., but when it comes to a drawing of the sexual act being performed standing up, we must surely suppose that there was a sexual repression of quite special strength to have caused it to be represented in this isolated and almost grotesque way. If one wants to enjoy oneself it is usual to make oneself as comfortable as possible: this of course is true for both the primal instincts, hunger and love. Most of the peoples of antiquity took their meals in a lying position and it is normal in coitus to-day to lie down just as comfortably as

FIG. I

160

It is doubtful whether Leonardo ever embraced a woman
in passion; nor is it known that he had any intimate mental
relationship with a woman, such as Michelangelo's with
Vittoria Colonna. While he was still an apprentice, living in
the house of his master Verrocchio, a charge of forbidden
homosexual practices was brought against him, along with some
other young people, which ended in his acquittal. He seems
to have fallen under this suspicion because he had employed

---

did our ancestors. Lying down implies more or less a wish to stay in the desired
situation for some time.

'Moreover the features of the man with the feminine head are marked
by a resistance that is positively indignant. His brows are wrinkled and his
gaze is directed sideways with an expression of repugnance. The lips are
pressed together and their corners are then drawn down. In this face can
be seen neither the pleasure of love's blessings nor the happiness of indulgence:
it expresses only indignation and aversion.

'The clumsiest blunder, however, was made by Leonardo in drawing the
two lower extremities. The man's foot should in point of fact have been
his right one; for since Leonardo depicted the act of union in an anatomical
sagittal section it follows of course that the man's left foot would be above
the plane of the picture. Conversely, and for the same reason, the woman's
foot should have belonged to her left side. But in fact Leonardo has inter-
changed male and female. The male figure has a left foot and the female
one a right foot. This interchange is easiest to grasp if one recalls that
the big toes lie on the inner sides of the feet.

'This anatomical drawing alone would have made it possible to deduce
the repression of libido – a repression which threw the great artist and
investigator into something approaching confusion.'

[*Added* 1923:] These remarks of Reitler's have been criticized, it is true,
on the ground that such serious conclusions should not be drawn from a
hasty sketch, and that it is not even certain whether the different parts of
the drawing really belong together. [The anatomical drawing discussed here
by Reitler, and assumed by him (and consequently by Freud) to be Leonardo's
original, is in fact, as has since been pointed out by Brian Farrell, a
reproduction of a lithograph by Wehrt which was published in 1830 and
had been made by copying an engraving by Bartolozzi, itself published in
1812. Bartolozzi put in the feet, which Leonardo himself had not drawn,
and Wehrt added the sour expression on the man's face. Leonardo's original
drawing, which is at Windsor Castle (*Quaderni d'Anatomia*, III folio, 3 v.),
shows the man's head with a calm, neutral expression.]

a boy of bad reputation as a model.[1] When he had become a Master, he surrounded himself with handsome boys and youths whom he took as pupils. The last of these pupils, Francesco Melzi, accompanied him to France, remained with him up to his death and was named by him as his heir. Without sharing in the certainty of his modern biographers, who naturally reject the possibility that there was a sexual relationship between him and his pupils as a baseless insult to the great man, we may take it as much more probable that Leonardo's affectionate relations with the young men who – as was the custom with pupils at that time – shared his existence did not extend to sexual activity. Moreover a high degree of sexual activity is not to be attributed to him.

There is only one way in which the peculiarity of this emotional and sexual life can be understood in connection with Leonardo's double nature as an artist and as a scientific investigator. Among his biographers, to whom a psychological approach is often very alien, there is to my knowledge only one, Edmondo Solmi, who has approached the solution of the problem; but a writer who has chosen Leonardo as the hero of a great historical novel, Dmitry Sergeyevich Merezhkovsky, has made a similar reading of this unusual man the basis of his portrait and has given clear expression to his conception, not indeed in plain language, but (after the way of writers of imagination) in plastic terms.[2] Solmi's verdict on Leonardo is as follows (1908, 46): 'But his insatiable desire to understand everything around him, and to fathom in a spirit of cold superiority the deepest secret of all that is perfect, had

1. According to Scognamiglio (1900, 49) there is a reference to this episode in an obscure and even variously read passage in the *Codex Atlanticus*: 'Quando io feci Domeneddio putto voi mi metteste in prigione, ora s'io lo fo grande, voi mi farete peggio.' ['When I represented the Lord God as a baby, you put me in prison; now if I represent him as an adult you will do worse to me.']

2. Merezhkovsky: *Leonardo da Vinci* (German trans., 1903). This forms the second work of a great historical trilogy entitled *Christ and Antichrist*. The two other volumes are *Julian the Apostate* and *Peter and Alexis*.

condemned Leonardo's work to remain for ever unfinished.'

In an essay in the *Conferenze Fiorentine* the following pro-nouncement of Leonardo's is quoted, which represents his con-fession of faith and provides the key to his nature: 'Nessuna cosa si può amare nè odiare, se prima non si ha cognition di quella.'[1] That is to say: One has no right to love or hate anything if one has not acquired a thorough knowledge of its nature. And the same is repeated by Leonardo in a passage in the treatise on painting where he seems to be defending himself against the charge of irreligion: 'But such carping critics would do better to keep silent. For that (line of conduct) is the way to become acquainted with the Creator of so many wonderful things, and this is the way to love so great an Inventor. For in truth great love springs from great knowledge of the beloved object, and if you know it but little you will be able to love it only a little or not at all ...'[2]

The value of these remarks of Leonardo's is not to be looked for in their conveying an important psychological fact; for what they assert is obviously false, and Leonardo must have known this as well as we do. It is not true that human beings delay loving or hating until they have studied and become familiar with the nature of the object to which these affects apply. On the contrary they love impulsively, from emotional motives which have nothing to do with knowledge, and whose opera-tion is at most weakened by reflection and consideration. Leonardo, then, could only have meant that the love practised by human beings was not of the proper and unobjectionable kind: one *should* love in such a way as to hold back the affect, subject it to the process of reflection and only let it take its course when it has stood up to the test of thought. And at the same time we understand that he wishes to tell us that it happens so in his case and that it would be worth while for everyone else to treat love and hatred as he does.

And in his case it really seems to have been so. His affects were controlled and subjected to the instinct for research; he

1. Bottazzi (1910, 193) [J. P. Richter (1939, 2, 244)].
2. *Trattato della Pittura* [Ludwig (1909, 54)].

did not love and hate, but asked himself about the origin and significance of what he was to love or hate. Thus he was bound at first to appear indifferent to good and evil, beauty and ugliness. During this work of investigation love and hate threw off their positive or negative signs and were both alike transformed into intellectual interest. In reality Leonardo was not devoid of passion; he did not lack the divine spark which is directly or indirectly the driving force – *il primo motore* – behind all human activity. He had merely converted his passion into a thirst for knowledge; he then applied himself to investigation with the persistence, constancy and penetration which is derived from passion, and at the climax of intellectual labour, when knowledge had been won, he allowed the long restrained affect to break loose and to flow away freely, as a stream of water drawn from a river is allowed to flow away when its work is done. When, at the climax of a discovery, he could survey a large portion of the whole nexus, he was overcome by emotion, and in ecstatic language praised the splendour of the part of creation that he had studied, or – in religious phraseology – the greatness of his Creator. This process of transformation in Leonardo has been rightly understood by Solmi. After quoting a passage of this sort in which Leonardo celebrates the sublime law of nature ('O mirabile necessità ...'), he writes (1910, 11): 'Tale trasfigurazione della scienza della natura in emozione, quasi direi, religiosa, è uno dei tratti caratteristici de' manoscritti vinciani, e si trova cento e cento volte espressa ...'[1]

Because of his insatiable and indefatigable thirst for knowledge Leonardo has been called the Italian Faust. But quite apart from doubts about a possible transformation of the instinct to investigate back into an enjoyment of life – a transformation which we must take as fundamental in the tragedy of Faust – the view may be hazarded that Leonardo's development approaches Spinoza's mode of thinking.

1. ['Such a transfiguration of natural science into a sort of religious emotion is one of the characteristic features of Leonardo's manuscripts, and there are hundreds and hundreds of examples of it.']

A conversion of psychical instinctual force into various forms of activity can perhaps no more be achieved without loss than a conversion of physical forces. The example of Leonardo teaches us how many other things we have to take into account in connection with these processes. The postponement of loving until full knowledge is acquired ends in a substitution of the latter for the former. A man who has won his way to a state of knowledge cannot properly be said to love and hate; he remains beyond love and hatred. He has investigated instead of loving. And that is perhaps why Leonardo's life was so much poorer in love than that of other great men, and of other artists. The stormy passions of a nature that inspires and consumes, passions in which other men have enjoyed their richest experience, appear not to have touched him.

There are some further consequences. Investigating has taken the place of acting and creating as well. A man who has begun to have an inkling of the grandeur of the universe with all its complexities and its laws readily forgets his own insignificant self. Lost in admiration and filled with true humility, he all too easily forgets that he himself is a part of those active forces and that in accordance with the scale of his personal strength the way is open for him to try to alter a small portion of the destined course of the world – a world in which the small is still no less wonderful and significant than the great.

Leonardo's researches had perhaps first begun, as Solmi believes, in the service of his art;[1] he directed his efforts to the properties and laws of light, colours, shadows and perspective in order to ensure mastery in the imitation of nature and to point the same way to others. It is probable that at that time he already overrated the value to the artist of these

---

1. Solmi (1910, 8): 'Leonardo aveva posto, come regola al pittore, lo studio della natura ..., poi la passione dello studio era divenuta dominante, egli aveva voluto acquistare non più la scienza per l'arte, ma la scienza per la scienza.' ['Leonardo had prescribed the study of nature as a rule for the painter ..., then the passion for study had become dominant, he had no longer wished to acquire learning for the sake of art, but learning for the sake of learning.']

branches of knowledge. Still constantly following the lead given by the requirements of his painting he was then driven to investigate the painter's subjects, animals and plants, and the proportions of the human body, and, passing from their exterior, to proceed to gain a knowledge of their internal structure and their vital functions, which indeed also find expression in their appearance and have a claim to be depicted in art. And finally the instinct, which had become over-whelming, swept him away until the connection with the demands of his art was severed, so that he discovered the general laws of mechanics and divined the history of the stratification and fossilization in the Arno valley, and until he could enter in large letters in his book the discovery: *Il sole non si move*.[1] His investigations extended to practically every branch of natural science, and in every single one he was a discoverer or at least a prophet and pioneer.[2] Yet his urge for knowledge was always directed to the external world; something kept him far away from the investigation of the human mind. In the 'Academia Vinciana' [p. 222], for which he drew some cleverly intertwined emblems, there was little room for psychology.

Then, when he made the attempt to return from investigation to his starting point, the exercise of his art, he found himself disturbed by the new direction of his interests and the changed nature of his mental activity. What interested him in a picture was above all a problem; and behind the first one he saw countless other problems arising, just as he used to in his endless and inexhaustible investigation of nature. He was no longer able to limit his demands, to see the work of art in isolation and to tear it from the wide context to which he knew it belonged. After the most exhausting efforts to bring to expression in it everything which was connected with it in his

1. ['The sun does not move.' *Quaderni d'Anatomia*, 1–6, Royal Library, Windsor, V, 25.]

2. See the enumeration of his scientific achievements in the fine biographical introduction by Marie Herzfeld (1906), in the various essays of the *Conferenze Fiorentine* (1910), and elsewhere.

thoughts, he was forced to abandon it in an unfinished state or to declare that it was incomplete.

The artist had once taken the investigator into his service to assist him; now the servant had become the stronger and suppressed his master.

When we find that in the picture presented by a person's character a single instinct has developed an excessive strength, as did the craving for knowledge in Leonardo, we look for the explanation in a special disposition – though about its determinants (which are probably organic) scarcely anything is yet known. Our psychoanalytic studies of neurotic people have, however, led us to form two further expectations which it would be gratifying to find confirmed in each particular case. We consider it probable that an instinct like this of excessive strength was already active in the subject's earliest childhood, and that its supremacy was established by impressions in the child's life. We make the further assumption that it found reinforcement from what were originally sexual instinctual forces, so that later it could take the place of a part of the subject's sexual life. Thus a person of this sort would, for example, pursue research with the same passionate devotion that another would give to his love, and he would be able to investigate instead of loving. We would venture to infer that it is not only in the example of the instinct to investigate that there has been a sexual reinforcement, but also in most other cases where an instinct is of special intensity.

Observation of men's daily lives shows us that most people succeed in directing very considerable portions of their sexual instinctual forces to their professional activity. The sexual instinct is particularly well fitted to make contributions of this kind since it is endowed with a capacity for sublimation: that is, it has the power to replace its immediate aim by other aims which may be valued more highly and which are not sexual. We accept this process as proved whenever the history of a person's childhood – that is, the history of his mental development – shows that in childhood this over-powerful instinct was in the service of sexual interests. We find further confirmation if a striking atrophy occurs in the sexual life of maturity, as though a portion of sexual activity had now been replaced by the activity of the over-powerful instinct.

There seem to be special difficulties in applying these expectations to the case of an over-powerful instinct for investigation, since precisely in the case of children there is a reluctance to credit them with either this serious instinct or any noteworthy sexual interests. However, these difficulties are easily overcome. The curiosity of small children is manifested in their untiring love of asking questions; this is bewildering to the adult so long as he fails to understand that all these questions are merely circumlocutions and that they cannot come to an end because the child is only trying to make them take the place of a question which he does *not* ask. When he grows bigger and becomes better informed this expression of curiosity often comes to a sudden end. Psychoanalytic investigation provides us with a full explanation by teaching us that many, perhaps most children, or at least the most gifted ones, pass through a period, beginning when they are about three, which may be called the period of *infantile sexual researches*. So far as we know, the curiosity of children of this age does not awaken spontaneously, but is aroused by the impression made by some important event – by the actual birth of a little brother or sister, or by a fear of it based on external experiences – in which the child perceives a threat to his selfish interests. Researches are directed to the question of where babies come from, exactly as if the child were looking for ways and means to avert so undesired an event. In this way we have been astonished to learn that children refuse to believe the bits of information that are given them – for example, that they energetically reject the fable of the stork with its wealth of mythological meaning, that they date their intellectual independence from this act of disbelief, and that they often feel in serious opposition to adults and in fact never afterwards forgive them for having deceived them here about the true facts of the case. They investigate along their own lines, divine the baby's presence inside its mother's body, and following the lead of the impulses of their own sexuality form theories of babies originating from eating, of their being born through the bowels, and of the obscure part played by the father. By that time they already have a notion of the sexual act, which appears to them to be something hostile and violent. But since their own sexual constitution has not yet reached the point of being able to produce babies, their investigation of where babies come from must inevitably come to nothing too and be abandoned as insoluble. The impression caused by this failure in the first attempt at intellectual independence appears to be of a lasting and deeply depressing kind.[1]

When the period of infantile sexual researches has been terminated by a wave of energetic sexual repression, the instinct for research has three distinct possible vicissitudes open to it owing to its early connection with sexual interests. In the first of these, research shares the fate of sexuality; thenceforward curiosity remains inhibited and the free activity of intelligence may be limited for the whole of the subject's lifetime, especially as shortly after this the powerful religious inhibition of thought is brought into play by education. This is the type characterized by neurotic inhibition. We know very well that the intellectual weakness which has been acquired in this way gives an effective impetus to the outbreak of a neurotic illness. In a second type the intellectual development is sufficiently strong to resist the sexual repression which has hold of it. Some time after the infantile sexual researches have come to an end, the intelligence, having grown stronger, recalls the old association and offers its help in evading sexual repression, and the suppressed sexual activities of research return from the unconscious in the form

1. These improbable-sounding assertions can be confirmed from a study of my 'Analysis of a Phobia in a Five-Year-Old Boy' (1909b) [P.F.L., 8, 165 ff.] and of similar observations. [Before 1924 these last words ran: 'and of the similar observation in Volume II of the *Jahrbuch für psychoanalytische und psychopathologische Forschungen*' – a reference to Jung (1910).] In a paper on 'The Sexual Theories of Children' (1908c) I wrote: 'This brooding and doubting, however, becomes the prototype of all later intellectual work directed towards the solution of problems, and the first failure has a crippling effect on the child's whole future.' [P.F.L., 7, 196.]

of compulsive brooding, naturally in a distorted and unfree form, but sufficiently powerful to sexualize thinking itself and to colour intellectual operations with the pleasure and anxiety that belong to sexual processes proper. Here investigation becomes a sexual activity, often the exclusive one, and the feeling that comes from settling things in one's mind and explaining them replaces sexual satisfaction; but the interminable character of the child's researches is also repeated in the fact that this brooding never ends and that the intellectual feeling, so much desired, of having found a solution recedes more and more into the distance.

In virtue of a special disposition, the third type, which is the rarest and most perfect, escapes both inhibition of thought and neurotic compulsive thinking. It is true that here too sexual repression comes about, but it does not succeed in relegating a component instinct of sexual desire to the unconscious. Instead, the libido evades the fate of repression by being sublimated from the very beginning into curiosity and by becoming attached to the powerful instinct for research as a reinforcement. Here, too, the research becomes to some extent compulsive and a substitute for sexual activity; but owing to the complete difference in the underlying psychical processes (sublimation instead of an irruption from the unconscious) the quality of neurosis is absent; there is no attachment to the original complexes of infantile sexual research, and the instinct can operate freely in the service of intellectual interest. Sexual repression, which has made the instinct so strong through the addition to it of sublimated libido, is still taken into account by the instinct, in that it avoids any concern with sexual themes.

If we reflect on the concurrence in Leonardo of his over-powerful instinct for research and the atrophy of his sexual life (which was restricted to what is called ideal [sublimated] homosexuality) we shall be disposed to claim him as a model instance of our third type. The core of his nature, and the secret of it, would appear to be that after his curiosity had been activated in infancy in the service of sexual interests he succeeded in sublimating the greater part of his libido into an urge for research. But it is not easy, to be sure, to prove that this view is right. To do so we should need some picture of his mental development in the first years of his childhood, and it seems foolish to hope for material of that sort when the accounts of his life are so meagre and so unreliable, and when moreover it is a question of information about circumstances that escape the attention of observers even in relation to people of our own generation.

About Leonardo's youth we know very little. He was born in 1452 in the little town of Vinci between Florence and Empoli; he was an illegitimate child, which in those days was certainly not considered a grave social stigma; his father was Ser Piero da Vinci, a notary and descended from a family of notaries and farmers who took their name from the locality of Vinci; his mother was a certain Caterina, probably a peasant girl, who later married another native of Vinci. This mother does not occur again in the history of Leonardo's life, and it is only Merezhkovsky – the novelist – who believes that he has succeeded in finding some trace of her. The only definite piece of information about Leonardo's childhood comes in an official document of the year 1457; it is a Florentine land register for the purpose of taxation, which mentions Leonardo among the members of the household of the Vinci family as the five-year-old illegitimate child of Ser Piero.[1] The marriage of Ser Piero with a certain Donna Albiera remained childless, and it was therefore possible for the young Leonardo to be brought up in his father's house. He did not leave this house till – at what age is not known – he entered Andrea del Verrocchio's studio as an apprentice. In the year 1472 Leonardo's name was already to be found in the list of members of the 'Compagnia dei Pittori'. That is all.

1. Scognamiglio (1900, 15).

II

THERE is, so far as I know, only one place in his scientific notebooks where Leonardo inserts a piece of information about his childhood. In a passage about the flight of vultures he suddenly interrupts himself to pursue a memory from very early years which had sprung to his mind:

'It seems that I was always destined to be so deeply concerned with vultures; for I recall as one of my very earliest memories that while I was in my cradle a vulture came down to me, and opened my mouth with its tail, and struck me many times with its tail against my lips.'[1]

What we have here then is a childhood memory; and certainly one of the strangest sort. It is strange on account of its content and on account of the age to which it is assigned. That a person should be able to retain a memory of his suckling period is perhaps not impossible, but it cannot by any means be regarded as certain. What, however, this memory of Leonardo's asserts – namely that a vulture opened the child's mouth with its tail – sounds so improbable, so fabulous, that another view of it, which at a single stroke puts an end to both difficulties, has more to commend it to our judgement. On this view the scene with the vulture would not be a memory

1. 'Questo scriver si distintamente del nibio par che sia mio destino, perchè nella mia prima ricordatione della mia infantia e' mi parea che, essendo io in culla, che un nibio venissi a me e mi aprissi la bocca colla sua coda e molte volte mi percuotesse con tal coda dentro alle labbra.' (*Codex Atlanticus*, F. 65 v., as given by Scognamiglio [1900, 22].) [In the German text Freud quotes Herzfeld's translation of the Italian original, and our version above is a rendering of the German. There are in fact two inaccuracies in the German: '*nibio*' should be 'kite', not 'vulture' (see Editor's Note, p. 147), and '*dentro*', 'within', is omitted. This last omission is in fact rectified by Freud himself below (p. 177).]

of Leonardo's but a phantasy, which he formed at a later date and transposed to his childhood.[1]

This is often the way in which childhood memories originate. Quite unlike conscious memories from the time of maturity, they are not fixed at the moment of being experienced and afterwards repeated, but are only elicited at a later age when childhood is already past; in the process they are altered and falsified, and are put into the service of later trends, so that generally speaking they cannot be sharply distinguished from phantasies. Their nature is perhaps best illustrated by a comparison with the way in which the writing of history originated among the peoples of antiquity. As long as a nation was small and weak it gave no thought to the writing of its history. Men tilled the soil of their land, fought for their existence against their neighbours, and tried to gain territory from them and to acquire wealth. It was an age of heroes, not of historians. Then came another age, an age of reflection: men felt themselves to be rich and powerful, and now felt a need to learn where they had come from and how they had developed. Historical writing, which had begun to keep a continuous

1. [*Footnote added* 1919:] In a friendly notice of this book Havelock Ellis (1910) has challenged the view put forward above. He objects that this memory of Leonardo's may very well have had a basis of reality, since children's memories often reach very much further back than is commonly supposed; the large bird in question need not of course have been a vulture. This is a point that I will gladly concede, and as a step towards lessening the difficulty I in turn will offer a suggestion – namely that his mother observed the large bird's visit to her child – an event which may easily have had the significance of an omen in her eyes – and repeatedly told him about it afterwards. As a result, I suggest, he retained the memory of his mother's story, and later, as so often happens, it became possible for him to take it for a memory of an experience of his own. However, this alteration does no damage to the force of my general account. It happens, indeed, as a general rule that the phantasies about their childhood which people construct at a late date are attached to trivial but real events of this early, and normally forgotten, period. There must thus have been some secret reason for bringing into prominence a real event of no importance and for elaborating it in the sort of way Leonardo did in his story of the bird, which he dubbed a vulture, and of its remarkable behaviour.

record of the present, now also cast a glance back to the past, gathered traditions and legends, interpreted the traces of antiquity that survived in customs and usages, and in this way created a history of the past. It was inevitable that this early history should have been an expression of present beliefs and wishes rather than a true picture of the past; for many things had been dropped from the nation's memory, while others were distorted, and some remains of the past were given a wrong interpretation in order to fit in with contemporary ideas. Moreover, people's motive for writing history was not objective curiosity but a desire to influence their contemporaries, to encourage and inspire them, or to hold a mirror up before them. A man's conscious memory of the events of his maturity is in every way comparable to the first kind of historical writing [which was a chronicle of current events]; while the memories that he has of his childhood correspond, as far as their origins and reliability are concerned, to the history of a nation's earliest days, which was compiled later and for tendentious reasons.[1]

If, then, Leonardo's story about the vulture that visited him in his cradle is only a phantasy from a later period, one might suppose it could hardly be worth while spending much time on it. One might be satisfied with explaining it on the basis of his inclination, of which he makes no secret, to regard his preoccupation with the flight of birds as pre-ordained by destiny. Yet in underrating this story one would be committing just as great an injustice as if one were carelessly to reject the body of legends, traditions and interpretations found in a nation's early history. In spite of all the distortions and misunderstandings, they still represent the reality of the past: they are what a people forms out of the experience of its early days and under the dominance of motives that were once powerful and still operate to-day; and if it were only possible, by a knowledge of all the forces at work, to undo these distortions,

1. [Chapter IV of *The Psychopathology of Everyday Life* (1901*b*) deals with childhood memories and screen-memories, and, in an addition made to it in 1907, Freud makes the same comparison with historical writing. Cf. *P.F.L.*, **5**, 83 ff., 88.]

there would be no difficulty in disclosing the historical truth lying behind the legendary material. The same holds good for the childhood memories or phantasies of an individual. What someone thinks he remembers from his childhood is not a matter of indifference; as a rule the residual memories – which he himself does not understand – cloak priceless pieces of evidence about the most important features in his mental development.[1] As we now possess in the techniques of psychoanalysis excellent methods for helping us to bring this concealed

1. [*Footnote added* 1919:] Since I wrote the above words I have attempted to make similar use of an unintelligible memory dating from the childhood of another man of genius. In the account of his life that Goethe wrote when he was about sixty ('*Dichtung und Wahrheit*') there is a description in the first few pages of how, with the encouragement of his neighbours, he slung first some small and then some large pieces of crockery out of the window into the street, so that they were smashed to pieces. This is, indeed, the only scene that he reports from the earliest years of childhood. The sheer inconsequentiality of its content, the way in which it corresponded with the childhood memories of other human beings who did not become particularly great, and the absence in this passage of any mention of the young brother who was born when Goethe was three and three-quarters, and who died when he was nearly ten – all this induced me to undertake an analysis of this childhood memory. (This child is in fact mentioned at a later point in the book, where Goethe dwells on the many illnesses of childhood.) I hoped to be able as a result to replace it by something which would be more in keeping with the context of Goethe's account and whose content would make it worthy of preservation and of the place he has given it in the history of his life. The short analysis ['A Childhood Recollection from *Dichtung und Wahrheit*' (1917b), p. 323 ff. below] made it possible for the throwing-out of the crockery to be recognized as a magical act directed against a troublesome intruder; and at the place in the book where he describes the episode the intention is to triumph over the fact that a second son was not in the long run permitted to disturb Goethe's close relation with his mother. If the earliest memory of childhood, preserved in disguises such as these, should be concerned – in Goethe's case as well as in Leonardo's – with the mother, what would be so surprising in that? – [In the 1919 edition the phrase 'and the absence in this passage of any mention of the young brother ...' ran '... and the remarkable absence of any mention whatever of a young brother ...' It was given its present form, and the parenthesis that follows it was added, in 1923. The alteration is explained in a footnote added in 1924 to the Goethe paper (1917b), p. 328 *n.* 1 below.]

material to light, we may venture to fill in the gap in Leonardo's life story by analysing his childhood phantasy. And if in doing so we remain dissatisfied with the degree of certainty which we achieve, we shall have to console ourselves with the reflection that so many other studies of this great and enigmatic man have met with no better fate.

If we examine with the eyes of a psychoanalyst Leonardo's phantasy of the vulture, it does not appear strange for long. We seem to recall having come across the same sort of thing in many places, for example in dreams; so that we may venture to translate the phantasy from its own special language into words that are generally understood. The translation is then seen to point to an erotic content. A tail, 'coda', is one of the most familiar symbols and substitutive expressions for the male organ, in Italian no less than in other languages; the situation in the phantasy, of a vulture opening the child's mouth and beating about inside it vigorously with its tail, corresponds to the idea of an act of fellatio, a sexual act in which the penis is put into the mouth of the person involved. It is strange that this phantasy is so completely passive in character; moreover it resembles certain dreams and phantasies found in women or passive homosexuals (who play the part of the woman in sexual relations).

I hope the reader will restrain himself and not allow a surge of indignation to prevent his following psychoanalysis any further because it leads to an unpardonable aspersion on the memory of a great and pure man the very first time it is applied to his case. Such indignation, it is clear, will never be able to tell us the significance of Leonardo's childhood phantasy; at the same time Leonardo has acknowledged the phantasy in the most unambiguous fashion, and we cannot abandon our expectation – or, if it sounds better, our prejudice – that a phantasy of this kind must have *some* meaning, in the same way as any other psychical creation: a dream, a vision or a delirium. Let us rather therefore give a fair hearing for a while to the work of analysis, which indeed has not yet spoken its last word.

The inclination to take a man's sexual organ into the mouth and suck at it, which in respectable society is considered a loathsome sexual perversion, is nevertheless found with great frequency among women of to-day – and of earlier times as well, as ancient sculptures show – and in the state of being in love it appears completely to lose its repulsive character. Phantasies derived from this inclination are found by doctors even in women who have not become aware of the possibilities of obtaining sexual satisfaction in this way by reading Krafft-Ebing's *Psychopathia sexualis* [1893] or from other sources of information. Women, it seems, find no difficulty in producing this kind of wishful phantasy spontaneously.[1] Further investigation informs us that this situation, which morality condemns with such severity, may be traced to an origin of the most innocent kind. It only repeats in a different form a situation in which we all once felt comfortable – when we were still in our suckling days (*'essendo io in culla'*)[2] and took our mother's (or wet-nurse's) nipple into our mouth and sucked at it. The organic impression of this experience – the first source of pleasure in our life – doubtless remains indelibly printed on us; and when at a later date the child becomes familiar with the cow's udder whose function is that of a nipple, but whose shape and position under the belly make it resemble a penis, the preliminary stage has been reached which will later enable him to form the repellent sexual phantasy.[3]

Now we understand why Leonardo assigned the memory of his supposed experience with the vulture to his suckling period. What the phantasy conceals is merely a reminiscence of sucking – or being suckled – at his mother's breast, a scene of human beauty that he, like so many artists, undertook to depict with his brush, in the guise of the mother of God and her child. There is indeed another point which we do not yet understand and which we must not lose sight of: this

1. On this point compare my 'Fragment of an Analysis of a Case of Hysteria' (1905e) [*P.F.L.*, **8**, 85].
2. ['While I was in my cradle.' See footnote 1, p. 172 above.]
3. [Cf. the analysis of 'Little Hans' (1909b), *P.F.L.*, **8**, 171.]

reminiscence, which has the same importance for both sexes, has been transformed by the man Leonardo into a passive homosexual phantasy. For the time being we shall put aside the question of what there may be to connect homosexuality with sucking at the mother's breast, merely recalling that tradition does in fact represent Leonardo as a man with homosexual feelings. In this connection, it is irrelevant to our purpose whether the charge brought against the young Leonardo [p. 161] was justified or not. What decides whether we describe someone as an invert[1] is not his actual behaviour, but his emotional attitude.

Our interest is next claimed by another unintelligible feature of Leonardo's childhood phantasy. We interpret the phantasy as one of being suckled by his mother, and we find his mother replaced by – a vulture. Where does this vulture come from and how does it happen to be found in its present place?

At this point a thought comes to the mind from such a remote quarter that it would be tempting to set it aside. In the hieroglyphics of the ancient Egyptians the mother is represented by a picture of a vulture.[2] The Egyptians also worshipped a Mother Goddess, who was represented as having a vulture's head, or else several heads, of which at least one was a vulture's.[3] This goddess's name was pronounced *Mut*. Can the similarity to the sound of our word *Mutter* ['mother'] be merely a coincidence? There is, then, some real connection between vulture and mother – but what help is that to us? For have we any right to expect Leonardo to know of it, seeing that the first man who succeeded in reading hieroglyphics was François Champollion (1790–1832)?[4]

It would be interesting to inquire how it could be that the ancient Egyptians came to choose the vulture as a symbol of

1. [In 1910 only: 'a homosexual'.]
2. Horapollo (*Hieroglyphica* I, 11): 'Μητέρα δὲ γράφοντες ... γῦπα ζωγραφοῦσιν.' ['To denote a mother ... they delineate a vulture.']
3. Roscher (1884–97), Lanzone (1882).
4. Hartleben (1906).

motherhood. Now the religion and civilization of the Egyptians were objects of scientific curiosity even to the Greeks and the Romans: and long before we ourselves were able to read the monuments of Egypt we had at our disposal certain pieces of information about them derived from the extant writings of classical antiquity. Some of these writings were by well-known authors, such as Strabo, Plutarch and Ammianus Marcellinus; while others bear unfamiliar names and are uncertain in their source of origin and their date of composition, like the *Hieroglyphica* of Horapollo Nilus and the book of oriental priestly wisdom which has come down to us under the name of the god Hermes Trismegistos. We learn from these sources that the vulture was regarded as a symbol of motherhood because only female vultures were believed to exist; there were, it was thought, no males of this species.[1] A counterpart to this restriction to one sex was also known to the natural history of antiquity: in the case of the scarabaeus beetle, which the Egyptians worshipped as divine, it was thought that only males existed.[2]

How then were vultures supposed to be impregnated if all of them were female? This is a point fully explained in a passage in Horapollo.[3] At a certain time these birds pause in mid-flight, open their vagina and are impregnated by the wind.

1. 'γῦπα δὲ ἄρρενα οὔ φασι γινέσθαι ποτε, ἀλλὰ θηλείας ἁπάσας.' ['They say that no male vulture has ever existed but all are females.' Aelian, *De Natura Animalium*, II, 46.] Quoted by von Römer (1903, 732).

2. Plutarch: 'Veluti scarabaeos mares tantum esse putarunt Aegyptii sic inter vultures mares non inveniri statuerunt.' ['Just as they believed that only male scarabs existed, so the Egyptians concluded that no male vultures were to be found.' Freud has here inadvertently attributed to Plutarch a sentence which is in fact a gloss by Leemans (1835, 171) on Horapollo.]

3. *Horapollonis Niloi Hieroglyphica*, ed. Leemans (1835, 14). The words that refer to the vulture's sex run: 'μητέρα μέν, ἐπειδὴ ἄρρεν ἐν τούτῳ τῷ γένει τῶν ζώων οὐχ ὑπάρχει.' ['(They use the picture of a vulture to denote) a mother, because in this race of creatures there are no males.' – It seems as though the wrong passage from Horapollo is quoted here. The phrase in the text implies that what we should have here is the myth of the vulture's impregnation by the wind.]

We have now unexpectedly reached a position where we can take something as very probable which only a short time before we had to reject as absurd. It is quite possible that Leonardo was familiar with the scientific fable which was responsible for the vulture being used by the Egyptians as a pictorial representation of the idea of mother. He was a wide reader and his interest embraced all branches of literature and learning. In the *Codex Atlanticus* we find a catalogue of all the books he possessed at a particular date,[1] and in addition numerous jottings on other books that he had borrowed from friends; and if we may judge by the extracts from his notes by Richter [1883],[2] the extent of his reading can hardly be overestimated. Early works on natural history were well represented among them in addition to contemporary books; and all of them were already in print at the time. Milan was in fact the leading city in Italy for the new art of printing.

On proceeding further we come across a piece of information which can turn the probability that Leonardo knew the fable of the vulture into a certainty. The learned editor and commentator on Horapollo has the following note on the text already quoted above [Leemans, 1835, 172]: 'Caeterum hanc fabulam de vulturibus cupide amplexi sunt Patres Ecclesiastici, ut ita argumento ex rerum natura petito refutarent eos, qui Virginis partum negabant; itaque apud omnes fere hujus rei mentio occurrit.'[3]

So the fable of the single sex of vultures and their mode of conception remained something very far from an unimportant anecdote like the analogous tale of the scarabaeus beetle; it had been seized on by the Fathers of the Church so that they could have at their disposal a proof drawn from natural history to confront those who doubted sacred history.

1. Müntz (1899, 282).
2. Müntz (ibid.).
3. ['But this story about the vulture was eagerly taken up by the Fathers of the Church, in order to refute, by means of a proof drawn from the natural order, those who denied the Virgin Birth. The subject is therefore mentioned in almost all of them.']

If vultures were described in the best accounts of antiquity as depending on the wind for impregnation, why could not the same thing have also happened on one occasion with a human female? Since the fable of the vulture could be turned to this account 'almost all' the Fathers of the Church made a practice of telling it, and thus it can hardly be doubted that Leonardo too came to know of it through its being favoured by so wide a patronage.

We can now reconstruct the origin of Leonardo's vulture phantasy. He once happened to read in one of the Fathers or in a book on natural history the statement that all vultures were females and could reproduce their kind without any assistance from a male: and at that point a memory sprang to his mind, which was transformed into the phantasy we have been discussing, but which meant to signify that he also had been such a vulture child – he had had a mother, but no father. With this memory was associated, in the only way in which impressions of so great an age can find expression, an echo of the pleasure he had had at his mother's breast. The allusion made by the Fathers of the Church to the idea of the Blessed Virgin and her child – an idea cherished by every artist – must have played its part in helping the phantasy to appear valuable and important to him. Indeed in this way he was able to identify himself with the child Christ, the comforter and saviour not of this one woman alone.

Our aim in dissecting a childhood phantasy is to separate the real memory that it contains from the later motives that modify and distort it. In Leonardo's case we believe that we now know the real content of the phantasy: the replacement of his mother by the vulture indicates that the child was aware of his father's absence and found himself alone with his mother. The fact of Leonardo's illegitimate birth is in harmony with his vulture phantasy; it was only on this account that he could compare himself to a vulture child. But the next reliable fact that we possess about his youth is that by the time he was five he had been received into his father's household. We are completely ignorant when that happened – whether it was a few months after his birth or whether it was a few weeks before the drawing-up of the land register [p. 171]. It is here that the interpretation of the vulture phantasy comes in: Leonardo, it seems to tell us, spent the critical first years of his life not by the side of his father and stepmother, but with his poor, forsaken, real mother, so that he had time to feel the absence of his father. This seems a slender and yet a somewhat daring conclusion to have emerged from our psychoanalytic efforts, but its significance will increase as we continue our investigation. Its certainty is reinforced when we consider the circumstances that did in fact operate in Leonardo's childhood. In the same year that Leonardo was born, the sources tell us, his father, Ser Piero da Vinci, married Donna Albiera, a lady of good birth; it was to the childlessness of this marriage that the boy owed his reception into his father's (or rather his grandfather's) house – an event which had taken place by the time he was five years old, as the document attests. Now it is not usual at the start of a marriage to put an illegitimate offspring into the care of the young bride who still expects to be blessed with children of her own. Years of disappointment must surely first have elapsed before it was decided to adopt the illegitimate child – who had probably grown up an attractive young boy – as a compensation for the absence of the legitimate children that had been hoped for. It fits in best with the interpretation of the vulture phantasy if at least three years of Leonardo's life, and perhaps five, had elapsed before he could exchange the solitary person of his mother for a parental couple. And by then it was too late. In the first three or four years of life certain impressions become fixed and ways of reacting to the outside world are established which can never be deprived of their importance by later experiences.

If it is true that the unintelligible memories of a person's childhood and the phantasies that are built on them invariably emphasize the most important elements in his mental development, then it follows that the fact which the vulture phantasy confirms, namely that Leonardo spent the first years of his life alone with his mother, will have been of decisive influence in the formation of his inner life. An inevitable effect of this state of affairs was that the child – who was confronted in his early life with one problem more than other children – began to brood on this riddle with special intensity, and so at a tender age became a researcher, tormented as he was by the great question of where babies come from and what the father has to do with their origin.[1] It was a vague suspicion that his researches and the history of his childhood were connected in this way which later prompted him to exclaim that he had been destined from the first to investigate the problem of the flight of birds since he had been visited by a vulture as he lay in his cradle. Later on it will not be difficult to show how his curiosity about the flight of birds was derived from the sexual researches of his childhood.

1. [Cf. 'The Sexual Theories of Children' (1908c), *P.F.L.*, **7**, 183 ff.]

III

In Leonardo's childhood phantasy we have taken the element of the vulture to represent the real content of his memory, while the context in which Leonardo himself placed his phantasy has thrown a bright light on the importance which that content had for his later life. In proceeding with our work of interpretation we now come up against the strange problem of why this content has been recast into a homosexual situation. The mother who suckles her child – or to put it better, at whose breast the child sucks – has been turned into a vulture that puts its tail into the child's mouth. We have asserted that, according to the usual way in which language makes use of substitutes, the vulture's '*coda*' cannot possibly signify anything other than a male genital, a penis. But we do not understand how imaginative activity can have succeeded in endowing precisely this bird which is a mother with the distinguishing mark of masculinity; and in view of this absurdity we are at a loss how to reduce this creation of Leonardo's phantasy to any rational meaning.

However, we should not despair, as we reflect on the number of apparently absurd dreams that we have in the past compelled to give up their meaning. Is there any reason why a memory of childhood should offer us more difficulty than a dream?

Remembering that it is unsatisfactory when a peculiar feature is found singly, let us hasten to add another to it which is even more striking.[1]

The vulture-headed Egyptian goddess Mut, a figure without any personal character according to Drexler's article in Roscher's lexicon, was often merged with other mother-goddesses of a more strongly marked individuality, like Isis and Hathor, but at the same time she maintained her separate existence and cult. A special feature of the Egyptian pantheon

1. [Cf. some similar remarks by Freud in *The Interpretation of Dreams* (1900*a*), P.F.L., **4**, 216.]

was that the individual gods did not disappear in the process of syncretization. Alongside the fusion of gods the individual divinities continued to exist in independence. Now this vulture-headed mother-goddess was usually represented by the Egyptians with a phallus;[1] her body was female, as the breasts indicated, but it also had a male organ in a state of erection.

In the goddess Mut, then, we find the same combination of maternal and masculine characteristics as in Leonardo's phantasy of the vulture. Are we to explain this coincidence by assuming that from studying his books Leonardo had also learnt of the androgynous nature of the maternal vulture? Such a possibility is more than questionable; it appears that the sources to which he had access contained no information about this remarkable feature. It is more plausible to trace the correspondence back to a common factor operative in both cases but still unknown.

Mythology can teach us that an androgynous structure, a combination of male and female sex characters, was an attribute not only of Mut but also of other deities like Isis and Hathor – though perhaps of these only in so far as they too had a maternal nature and became amalgamated with Mut (Römer, 1903). It teaches us further that other Egyptian deities, like Neith of Sais – from whom the Greek Athene was later derived – were originally conceived of as androgynous, i.e. as hermaphrodite, and that the same was true of many of the *Greek* gods, especially of those associated with Dionysus, but also of Aphrodite, who was later restricted to the role of a female goddess of love. Mythology may then offer the explanation that the addition of a phallus to the female body is intended to denote the primal creative force of nature, and that all these hermaphrodite divinities are expressions of the idea that only a combination of male and female elements can give a worthy representation of divine perfection. But none of these considerations gives us an explanation of the puzzling psychological fact that the human imagination does not boggle at endowing a figure which is intended to embody the essence

1. See the illustrations in Lanzone (1882, Plates CXXXVI–VIII).

of the mother with the mark of male potency which is the opposite of everything maternal.

Infantile sexual theories provide the explanation. There was once a time when the male genital was found compatible with the picture of the mother.[1] When a male child first turns his curiosity to the riddles of sexual life, he is dominated by his interest in his own genital. He finds that part of his body too valuable and too important for him to be able to believe that it could be missing in other people whom he feels he resembles so much. As he cannot guess that there exists another type of genital structure of equal worth, he is forced to make the assumption that all human beings, women as well as men, possess a penis like his own. This preconception is so firmly planted in the youthful investigator that it is not destroyed even when he first observes the genitals of little girls. His perception tells him, it is true, that there is something different from what there is in him, but he is incapable of admitting to himself that the content of this perception is that he cannot find a penis in girls. That the penis could be missing strikes him as an uncanny and intolerable idea, and so in an attempt at a compromise he comes to the conclusion that little girls have a penis as well, only it is still very small; it will grow later.[2] If it seems from later observations that this expectation is not realized, he has another remedy at his disposal: little girls too had a penis, but it was cut off and in its place was left a wound. This theoretical advance already makes use of personal experiences of a distressing kind: the boy in the meantime has heard the threat that the organ which is so dear to him will be taken away from him if he shows his interest in it too plainly. Under the influence of this threat of castration he now sees the notion he has gained of the female genitals in a new light; henceforth he

1. [Cf. 'The Sexual Theories of Children' (1908c), *P.F.L.*, **7**, 193.]

2. Compare the observations in the *Jahrbuch für psychoanalytische und psychopathologische Forschungen* [i.e. Freud, 1909b ('Little Hans'), *P.F.L.*, **8**, 175, and Jung, 1910. – *Added* 1919:], in the *Internationale Zeitschrift für ärztliche Psychoanalyse* and in [the section dealing with children in] *Imago*.

will tremble for his masculinity, but at the same time he will despise the unhappy creatures on whom the cruel punishment has, as he supposes, already fallen.[1]

Before the child comes under the dominance of the castration complex – at a time when he still holds women at full value – he begins to display an intense desire to look, as an erotic instinctual activity. He wants to see other people's genitals, at first in all probability to compare them with his own. The erotic attraction that comes from his mother soon culminates in a longing for her genital organ, which he takes to be a penis. With the discovery, which is not made till later, that women do not have a penis, this longing often turns into its opposite and gives place to a feeling of disgust which in the years of puberty can become the cause of psychical impotence, misogyny and permanent homosexuality. But the fixation on the object that was once strongly desired, the woman's penis, leaves indelible traces on the mental life of the child, who has pursued that portion of his infantile sexual researches with particular thoroughness. Fetishistic reverence for a woman's foot and shoe appears to take the foot merely as a substitutive symbol for the woman's penis which was once revered and later missed; without knowing it, 'coupeurs de nattes'[2] play the part of people who carry out an act of castration on the female genital organ.

People will not reach a proper understanding of the activities of children's sexuality and will probably take refuge in declaring that what has been said here is incredible, so long as they cling to the attitude taken up by our civilization of depreciating the genitals and the sexual functions. To under-

1. [*Footnote added* 1919:] The conclusion strikes me as inescapable that here we may also trace one of the roots of the anti-semitism which appears with such elemental force and finds such irrational expression among the nations of the West. Circumcision is unconsciously equated with castration. If we venture to carry our conjectures back to the primaeval days of the human race we can surmise that originally circumcision must have been a milder substitute, designed to take the place of castration. [Further discussion on this will be found in a footnote to the analysis of 'Little Hans' (1909*b*), *P.F.L.*, 8, 198 *n.* 2, and in *Moses and Monotheism* (1939*a*), ibid., 13, 336 and *n.* 1.]

2. [Perverts who enjoy cutting off females' hair.]

stand the mental life of children we require analogies from primitive times. Through a long series of generations the genitals have been for us the '*pudenda*', objects of shame, and even (as a result of further successful sexual repression) of disgust. If one makes a broad survey of the sexual life of our time and in particular of the classes who sustain human civilization, one is tempted to declare that[1] it is only with reluctance that the majority of those alive to-day obey the command to propagate their kind; they feel that their dignity as human beings suffers and is degraded in the process. What is to be found among us in the way of another view of sexual life is confined to the uncultivated lower strata of society; among the higher and more refined classes it is concealed, since it is considered culturally inferior, and it ventures to put itself into practice only in the face of a bad conscience. In the primaeval days of the human race it was a different story. The laborious compilations of the student of civilization provide convincing evidence that originally the genitals were the pride and hope of living beings; they were worshipped as gods and transmitted the divine nature of their functions to all newly learned human activities. As a result of the sublimation of their basic nature there arose innumerable divinities; and at the time when the connection between official religions and sexual activity was already hidden from the general consciousness, secret cults devoted themselves to keeping it alive among a number of initiates. In the course of cultural development so much of the divine and sacred was ultimately extracted from sexuality that the exhausted remnant fell into contempt. But in view of the indelibility that is characteristic of all mental traces, it is surely not surprising that even the most primitive forms of genital worship can be shown to have existed in very recent times and that the language, customs and superstitions of mankind to-day contain survivals from every phase of this process of development.[2]

1. [The sentence up to this point was added in 1919.]
2. Cf. Knight [1883].

Impressive analogies from biology have prepared us to find that the individual's mental development repeats the course of human development in an abbreviated form; and the conclusions which psychoanalytic research into the child's mind has reached concerning the high value set on the genitals in infancy will not therefore strike us as improbable. The child's assumption that his mother has a penis is thus the common source from which are derived the androgynously-formed mother-goddesses such as the Egyptian Mut and the vulture's *'coda'* in Leonardo's childhood phantasy. It is in fact only due to a misunderstanding that we describe these representations of gods as hermaphrodite in the medical sense of the word. In none of them is there a combination of the true genitals of both sexes – a combination which, to the abhorrence of all beholders, is found in some cases of malformation; all that has happened is that the male organ has been added to the breasts which are the mark of a mother, just as it was present in the child's first idea of his mother's body. This form of the mother's body, the revered creation of primaeval phantasy, has been preserved for the faithful by mythology. We can now provide the following translation of the emphasis given to the vulture's tail in Leonardo's phantasy: 'That was a time when my fond curiosity was directed to my mother, and when I still believed she had a genital organ like my own.' Here is more evidence of Leonardo's early sexual researches, which in our opinion had a decisive effect on the whole of his later life.

At this point a little reflection will remind us that we ought not to feel satisfied yet with the way the vulture's tail in Leonardo's childhood phantasy has been explained. Something more seems to be contained in it which we do not yet understand. Its most striking feature, after all, was that it changed sucking at the mother's breast into being suckled, that is, into passivity, and thus into a situation whose nature is undoubtedly homosexual. When we remember the historical probability of Leonardo having behaved in his life as one who was emotionally homosexual, the question is forced upon us whether this phantasy does not indicate the existence of a causal connection between Leonardo's relation with his mother in childhood and his later manifest, if ideal [sublimated], homosexuality. We should not venture to infer a connection of this sort from Leonardo's distorted reminiscence if we did not know from the psychoanalytic study of homosexual patients that such a connection does exist and is in fact an intimate and necessary one.

Homosexual men, who have in our times taken vigorous action against the restrictions imposed by law on their sexual activity, are fond of representing themselves, through their theoretical spokesmen, as being from the outset a distinct sexual species, as an intermediate sexual stage, as a 'third sex'. They are, they claim, men who are innately compelled by organic determinants to find pleasure in men and have been debarred from obtaining it in women. Much as one would be glad on grounds of humanity to endorse their claims, one must treat their theories with some reserve, for they have been advanced without regard for the psychical genesis of homosexuality. Psychoanalysis offers the means of filling this gap and of putting the assertions of homosexuals to the test. It has succeeded in the task only in the case of a small number of persons, but all the investigations undertaken so far have yielded the same surprising result.[1] In all our male homosexual cases the subjects had had a very intense erotic attachment to a female person, as a rule their mother, during the first period of childhood, which is afterwards forgotten; this attachment was evoked or encouraged by too much tenderness on the part of the mother herself, and further reinforced by the small part played by the father during their childhood. Sadger emphasizes the fact that the mothers of his homosexual patients were frequently masculine women, women with energetic traits of character, who were able to push the father out of his proper place. I

1. I refer in particular to the investigations of I. Sadger, which I can in the main confirm from my own experience. I am also aware that Wilhelm Stekel of Vienna and Sándor Ferenczi of Budapest have arrived at the same results.

have occasionally seen the same thing, but I was more strongly impressed by cases in which the father was absent from the beginning or left the scene at an early date, so that the boy found himself left entirely under feminine influence. Indeed it almost seems as though the presence of a strong father would ensure that the son made the correct decision in his choice of object, namely someone of the opposite sex.[1]

After this preliminary stage a transformation sets in whose mechanism is known to us but whose motive forces we do not yet understand. The child's love for his mother cannot continue to develop consciously any further; it succumbs to repression. The boy represses his love for his mother: he puts himself in her place, identifies himself with her, and takes his own person as a model in whose likeness he chooses the new objects of his love. In this way he has become a homosexual. What he has in fact done is to slip back to auto-erotism: for the boys whom he now loves as he grows up are after all only substitutive figures and revivals of himself in childhood – boys whom he loves in the way in which his mother loved *him* when he was a child. He finds the objects of his love along the path of *narcissism*, as we say; for Narcissus, according to the Greek legend, was a youth who preferred his own reflection to every-

---

1. [*Footnote added* 1919:] Psychoanalytic research has contributed two facts that are beyond question to the understanding of homosexuality, without at the same time supposing that it has exhausted the causes of this sexual aberration. The first is the fixation of the erotic needs on the mother which has been mentioned above; the other is contained in the statement that everyone, even the most normal person, is capable of making a homosexual object-choice, and has done so at some time in his life, and either still adheres to it in his unconscious or else protects himself against it by vigorous counter-attitudes. These two discoveries put an end both to the claim of homosexuals to be regarded as a 'third sex' and to what has been believed to be the important distinction between innate and acquired homosexuality. The presence of somatic characters of the other sex (the quota provided by physical hermaphroditism) is highly conducive to the homosexual object-choice becoming manifest; but it is not decisive. It must be stated with regret that those who speak for the homosexuals in the field of science have been incapable of learning anything from the established findings of psychoanalysis.

thing else and who was changed into the lovely flower of that name.[1]

Psychological considerations of a deeper kind justify the assertion that a man who has become a homosexual in this way remains unconsciously fixated to the mnemic image of his mother. By repressing his love for his mother he preserves it in his unconscious and from now on remains faithful to her. While he seems to pursue boys and to be their lover, he is in reality running away from the other women, who might cause him to be unfaithful. In individual cases direct observation has also enabled us to show that the man who gives the appearance of being susceptible only to the charms of men is in fact attracted by women in the same way as a normal man; but on each occasion he hastens to transfer the excitation he has received from women on to a male object, and in this manner he repeats over and over again the mechanism by which he acquired his homosexuality.

We are far from wishing to exaggerate the importance of these explanations of the psychical genesis of homosexuality. It is quite obvious that they are in sharp contrast to the official theories of those who speak for homosexuals, but we know that they are not sufficiently comprehensive to make a conclusive explanation of the problem possible. What is for practical reasons called homosexuality may arise from a whole variety of psychosexual inhibitory processes; the particular process we have singled out is perhaps only one among many, and is perhaps related to only one type of 'homosexuality'. We must also admit that the number of cases of our homosexual type in which it is possible to point to the determinants which we require far exceeds the number of those where the deduced effect actually takes place; so that we too cannot reject the part played by unknown constitutional factors, to which the whole of homosexuality is usually traced. We should not have had

1. [Freud's first published reference to narcissism had appeared only a few months before, in a footnote added to the second (1910) edition of his *Three Essays* (1905*d*), *P.F.L.*, **7**, 56 *n*. 1. For a full discussion of the subject, see 'On Narcissism: an Introduction' (1914*c*), ibid., **11**, 59 ff.]

any cause at all for entering into the psychical genesis of the form of homosexuality we have studied if there were not a strong presumption that Leonardo, whose phantasy of the vulture was our starting point, was himself a homosexual of this very type.[1]

Few details are known about the sexual behaviour of the great artist and scientist, but we may place confidence in the probability that the assertions of his contemporaries were not grossly erroneous. In the light of these traditions, then, he appears as a man whose sexual need and activity were exceptionally reduced, as if a higher aspiration had raised him above the common animal need of mankind. It may remain open to doubt whether he ever sought direct sexual satisfaction – and if so, in what manner – or whether he was able to dispense with it altogether. We are, however, justified in looking in him too for the emotional currents which drive other men imperatively on to perform the sexual act; for we cannot imagine the mental life of any human being in the formation of which sexual desire in the broadest sense – libido – did not have its share, even if that desire has departed far from its original aim, or has refrained from putting itself into effect.

We cannot expect to find in Leonardo anything more than traces of untransformed sexual inclination. But these point in one direction and moreover allow him to be reckoned as a homosexual. It has always been emphasized that he took only strikingly handsome boys and youths as pupils. He treated them with kindness and consideration, looked after them, and when they were ill nursed them himself, just as a mother nurses her children and just as his own mother might have tended him. As he had chosen them for their beauty and not for their talent, none of them – Cesare da Sesto, Boltraffio, Andrea Salaino,

1. [A more general discussion of homosexuality and its genesis will be found in the first of Freud's *Three Essays* (1905*d*), particularly in a long footnote added between 1910 and 1920; *P.F.L.*, **7**, 56–9. Among later discussions of the subject may be mentioned his case history of a female homosexual (1920*a*), ibid., **9**, 367 ff., and 'Some Neurotic Mechanisms in Jealousy, Paranoia and Homosexuality' (1922*b*), ibid., **10**, 195 ff.]

Francesco Melzi and others – became a painter of importance. Generally they were unable to make themselves independent of their master, and after his death they disappeared without having left any definite mark on the history of art. The others, whose works entitled them to be called his pupils, like Luini and Bazzi, called Sodoma, he probably did not know personally.

We realize that we shall have to meet the objection that Leonardo's behaviour towards his pupils has nothing at all to do with sexual motives and that it allows no conclusions to be drawn about his particular sexual inclination. Against this we wish to submit with all caution that our view explains some peculiar features of the artist's behaviour which would otherwise have to remain a mystery. Leonardo kept a diary; he made entries in his small hand (written from right to left) which were meant only for himself. It is noteworthy that in this diary he addressed himself in the second person. 'Learn the multiplication of roots from Master Luca.' (Solmi, 1908, 152). 'Get Master d'Abacco to show you how to square the circle.' (Loc. cit.) Or on the occasion of a journey: 'I am going to Milan on business to do with my garden ... Have two baggage trunks made. Get Boltraffio to show you the turning-lathe and get him to polish a stone on it. Leave the book for Master Andrea il Todesco.' (Ibid., 203.)[1] Or a resolution of very different importance: 'You have to show in your treatise that the earth is a star, like the moon or something like it, and thus prove the nobility of our world.' (Herzfeld, 1906, 141.)

In this diary, which, by the way, like the diaries of other mortals, often dismisses the most important events of the day in a few words or else passes them over in complete silence, there are some entries which on account of their strangeness are quoted by all Leonardo's biographers. They are notes of small sums of money spent by the artist – notes recorded with

1. Leonardo is behaving here like someone whose habit it was to make his daily confession to another person and who uses his diary as a substitute for him. For a conjecture as to who this person may have been, see Merezhkovsky (1903, 367).

a minute exactness, as if they were made by a pedantically strict and parsimonious head of a household. There is on the other hand no record of the expenditure of larger sums or any other evidence that the artist was at home in keeping accounts. One of these notes has to do with a new cloak which he bought for his pupil Andrea Salaino:[1]

Silver brocade.	15 lire	4 soldi
Crimson velvet for trimming	9 ,,	— ,,
Braid	— ,,	9 ,,
Buttons.	— ,,	12 ,,

Another very detailed note brings together all the expenses he incurred through the bad character and thievish habits of another pupil:[2] 'On the twenty-first day of April 1490 I began this book and made a new start on the horse.[3] Jacomo came to me on St Mary Magdalen's day, 1490: he is ten years old.' (Marginal note: 'thievish, untruthful, selfish, greedy.') 'On the second day I had two shirts cut out for him, a pair of trousers and a jacket, and when I put the money aside to pay for these things, he stole the money from my purse, and it was never possible to make him own up, although I was absolutely sure of it.' (Marginal note: '4 lire ...') The report of the child's misdeeds runs on in this way and ends with the reckoning of expenses: 'In the first year, a cloak, 2 lire; 6 shirts, 4 lire; 3 jackets, 6 lire; 4 pairs of stockings, 7 lire; etc.'[4]

Nothing is further from the wishes of Leonardo's biographers than to try to solve the problems in their hero's mental life by starting from his small weaknesses and peculiarities; and the usual comment that they make on these singular accounts is one which lays stress on the artist's kindness and consideration for his pupils. They forget that what calls for explanation is not Leonardo's behaviour, but the fact that he left these pieces of evidence of it behind him. As it is impossible to believe

1. The text is that given by Merezhkovsky (1903, 282).
2. Or model.
3. For the equestrian statue of Francesco Sforza.
4. The full text is to be found in Herzfeld (1906, 45).

LEONARDO DA VINCI

that his motive was that of letting proofs of his good nature fall into our hands, we must assume that it was another motive, an affective one, which led him to write these notes down. What motive it was is not easy to guess, and we should be unable to suggest one if there were not another account found among Leonardo's papers which throws a vivid light on these strangely trifling notes about his pupils' clothing, etc.:

Expenses after Caterina's death for her funeral . . .	27	florins
2 pounds of wax	18	,,
For transporting and erecting the cross	12	,,
Catafalque	4	,,
Pall-bearers	8	,,
For 4 priests and 4 clerks	20	,,
Bell-ringing	2	,,
For the grave-diggers	16	,,
For the licence – to the officials	1	,,

Total   108 florins

Previous expenses

For the doctor . . . . 4 florins
For sugar and candles . . 12   ,,

16 florins

Grand total   124 florins.[1]

The novelist Merezhkovsky alone is able to tell us who this

1. Merezhkovsky (1903, 372). – As a melancholy example of the uncertainty that surrounds the information, which is in any case scanty enough, about Leonardo's private life, I may mention the fact that the same account is quoted by Solmi (1908, 104) with considerable variations. The most serious one is that soldi are given instead of florins. It may be assumed that florins in this account do not mean the old 'gold florins' but the monetary units which were used later and were worth $1\frac{2}{3}$ lire or $33\frac{1}{3}$ soldi. Solmi makes Caterina a servant who had looked after Leonardo's household for some time. The source from which the two versions of these accounts were taken was not accessible to me. [The figures given actually vary to some extent in the different editions of Freud's own book. The cost of the catafalque is given in 1910 as '12', in 1919 and 1923 as '19' and from 1925 as '4'. Before 1925 the cost of transporting and erecting the cross was given as '4'. For a recent version of the whole text, in Italian and English, see J. P. Richter (1939, 2, 379).]

Caterina was. From two other short notes[1] he concludes that Leonardo's mother, the poor peasant woman of Vinci, came to Milan in 1493 to visit her son, who was then forty-one; that she fell ill there, was taken to hospital by Leonardo, and when she died was honoured by him with this costly funeral.

This interpretation by the psychological novelist cannot be put to the proof, but it can claim so much inner probability, and is so much in harmony with all that we otherwise know of Leonardo's emotional activity, that I cannot refrain from accepting it as correct. He had succeeded in subjecting his feelings to the yoke of research and in inhibiting their free utterance; but even for him there were occasions when what had been suppressed obtained expression forcibly. The death of the mother he had once loved so dearly was one of these. What we have before us in the account of the costs of the funeral is the expression – distorted out of all recognition – of his mourning for his mother. We wonder how such distortion could come about, and indeed we cannot understand it if we treat it as a normal mental process. But similar processes are well known to us in the abnormal conditions of neurosis and especially of what is known as 'obsessional neurosis'. There we can see how the expression of intense feelings, which have however become unconscious through repression, is displaced on to trivial and even foolish actions. The expression of these repressed feelings has been lowered by the forces opposed to them to such a degree that one would have had to form a most insignificant estimate of their intensity; but the imperative compulsiveness with which this trivial expressive act is performed betrays the real force of the impulses – a force which is rooted in the unconscious and which consciousness would like to deny. Only a comparison such as this with what happens in obsessional neurosis can explain Leonardo's account of the expenses of his mother's funeral. In his unconscious he was still

1. 'Caterina arrived on 16 July 1493.' – 'Giovannina – a fabulous face – Call on Caterina in the hospital and make inquiries.' [The second note is actually mistranslated by Merezhkovsky. It should read: 'Giovannina – a fabulous face – is at the hospital of Santa Caterina.']

tied to her by erotically coloured feelings, as he had been in childhood. The opposition that came from the subsequent repression of this childhood love did not allow him to set up a different and worthier memorial to her in his diary. But what emerged as a compromise from this neurotic conflict had to be carried out; and thus it was that the account was entered in the diary, and has come to the knowledge of posterity as something unintelligible.

It does not seem a very extravagant step to apply what we have learnt from the funeral account to the reckonings of the pupils' expenses. They would then be another instance of the scanty remnants of Leonardo's libidinal impulses finding expression in a compulsive manner and in a distorted form. On that view, his mother and his pupils, the likenesses of his own boyish beauty, had been his sexual objects – so far as the sexual repression which dominated his nature allows us so to describe them – and the compulsion to note in laborious detail the sums he spent on them betrayed in this strange way his rudimentary conflicts. From this it would appear that Leonardo's erotic life did really belong to the type of homosexuality whose psychical development we have succeeded in disclosing, and the emergence of the homosexual situation in his phantasy of the vulture would become intelligible to us: for its meaning was exactly what we have already asserted of that type. We should have to translate it thus: 'It was through this erotic relation with my mother that I became a homosexual.'[1]

---

1. The forms of expression in which Leonardo's repressed libido was allowed to show itself – circumstantiality and concern over money – are among the traits of character which result from anal erotism. See my 'Character and Anal Erotism' (1908b). [P.F.L., 7, 205 ff.]

IV

WE have not yet done with Leonardo's vulture phantasy. In words which only too plainly recall a description of a sexual act ('and struck me many times with its tail against[1] my lips'), Leonardo stresses the intensity of the erotic relations between mother and child. From this linking of his mother's (the vulture's) activity with the prominence of the mouth zone it is not difficult to guess that a second memory is contained in the phantasy. This may be translated: 'My mother pressed innumerable passionate kisses on my mouth.' The phantasy is compounded from the memory of being suckled and being kissed by his mother.

Kindly nature has given the artist the ability to express his most secret mental impulses, which are hidden even from himself, by means of the works that he creates; and these works have a powerful effect on others who are strangers to the artist, and who are themselves unaware of the source of their emotion. Can it be that there is nothing in Leonardo's life work to bear witness to what his memory preserved as the strongest impression of his childhood? One would certainly expect there to be something. Yet if one considers the profound transformations through which an impression in an artist's life has to pass before it is allowed to make its contribution to a work of art, one will be bound to keep any claim to certainty in one's demonstration within very modest limits; and this is especially so in Leonardo's case.

Anyone who thinks of Leonardo's paintings will be reminded of a remarkable smile, at once fascinating and puzzling, which he conjured up on the lips of his female subjects. It is an unchanging smile, on long, curved lips; it has become a mark of his style and the name 'Leonardesque' has been chosen for

1. [See footnote 1, p. 172.]

199

it.[1] In the strangely beautiful face of the Florentine Mona Lisa del Giocondo it has produced the most powerful and confusing effect on whoever looks at it. [See Plate 2.] This smile has called for an interpretation, and it has met with many of the most varied kinds, none of which has been satisfactory. 'Voilà quatre siècles bientôt que Monna Lisa fait perdre la tête à tous ceux qui parlent d'elle, après l'avoir longtemps regardée.'[2]

Muther (1909, 1, 314) writes: 'What especially casts a spell on the spectator is the daemonic magic of this smile. Hundreds of poets and authors have written about this woman who now appears to smile on us so seductively, and now to stare coldly and without soul into space; and no one has solved the riddle of her smile, no one has read the meaning of her thoughts. Everything, even the landscape, is mysteriously dream-like, and seems to be trembling in a kind of sultry sensuality.'

The idea that two distinct elements are combined in Mona Lisa's smile is one that has struck several critics. They accordingly find in the beautiful Florentine's expression the most perfect representation of the contrasts which dominate the erotic life of women; the contrast between reserve and seduction, and between the most devoted tenderness and a sensuality that is ruthlessly demanding – consuming men as if they were alien beings. This is the view of Müntz (1899, 417): 'On sait quelle énigme indéchiffrable et passionnante Monna Lisa Gioconda ne cesse depuis bientôt quatre siècles de proposer aux admirateurs pressés devant elle. Jamais artiste (j'emprunte la plume du délicat écrivain qui se cache sous le pseudonyme de Pierre de Corlay) "a-t-il traduit ainsi l'essence même de la féminité: tendresse et coquetterie, pudeur et sourde volupté,

---

1. [*Footnote added* 1919:] The connoisseur of art will think here of the peculiar fixed smile found in archaic Greek sculptures – in those, for example, from Aegina; he will perhaps also discover something similar in the figures of Leonardo's teacher Verrocchio and therefore have some misgivings in accepting the arguments that follow.

2. ['For almost four centuries now Mona Lisa has caused all who talk of her, after having gazed on her for long, to lose their heads.'] The words are Gruyer's, quoted by von Seidlitz (1909, 2, 280).

tout le mystère d'un cœur qui se réserve, d'un cerveau qui réfléchit, d'une personnalité qui se garde et ne livre d'elle-même que son rayonnement ..." '[1] The Italian writer Angelo Conti (1910, 93) saw the picture in the Louvre brought to life by a ray of sunshine. 'La donna sorrideva in una calma regale: i suoi istinti di conquista, di ferocia, tutta l'eredità della specie, la volontà della seduzione e dell' agguato, la grazia del inganno, la bontà che cela un proposito crudele, tutto ciò appariva alternativamente e scompariva dietro il velo ridente e si fondeva nel poema del suo sorriso ... Buona e malvagia, crudele e compassionevole, graziosa e felina, ella rideva ...'[2]

Leonardo spent four years painting at this picture, perhaps from 1503 to 1507, during his second period of residence in Florence, when he was over fifty. According to Vasari he employed the most elaborate artifices to keep the lady amused during the sittings and to retain the famous smile on her features. In its present condition the picture has preserved but little of all the delicate details which his brush reproduced on the canvas at that time; while it was being painted it was considered to be the highest that art could achieve, but it is certain that Leonardo himself was not satisfied with it, declaring it to be incomplete, and did not deliver it to the person who had commissioned it, but took it to France with him, where his patron, Francis I, acquired it from him for the Louvre.

1. ['We know what an insoluble and enthralling enigma Mona Lisa Gioconda has never ceased through nearly four centuries to pose to the admirers that throng in front of her. No artist (I borrow the words from the sensitive writer who conceals himself behind the pseudonym of Pierre de Corlay) "has ever expressed so well the very essence of femininity: tenderness and coquetry, modesty and secret sensuous joy, all the mystery of a heart that holds aloof, a brain that meditates, a personality that holds back and yields nothing of itself save its radiance".']

2. ['The lady smiled in regal calm: her instincts of conquest, of ferocity, all the heredity of the species, the will to seduce and to ensnare, the charm of deceit, the kindness that conceals a cruel purpose, – all this appeared and disappeared by turns behind the laughing veil and buried itself in the poem of her smile ... Good and wicked, cruel and compassionate, graceful and feline, she laughed ...']

Let us leave unsolved the riddle of the expression on Mona Lisa's face, and note the indisputable fact that her smile exercised no less powerful a fascination on the artist than on all who have looked at it for the last four hundred years. From that date the captivating smile reappears in all his pictures and in those of his pupils. As Leonardo's Mona Lisa is a portrait, we cannot assume that he added on his own account such an expressive feature to her face – a feature that she did not herself possess. The conclusion seems hardly to be avoided that he found this smile in his model and fell so strongly under its spell that from then on he bestowed it on the free creations of his phantasy. This interpretation, which cannot be called far-fetched, is put forward, for example, by Konstantinowa (1907, 44):

'During the long period in which the artist was occupied with the portrait of Mona Lisa del Giocondo, he had entered into the subtle details of the features on this lady's face with such sympathetic feeling that he transferred its traits – in particular the mysterious smile and the strange gaze – to all the faces that he painted or drew afterwards. The Gioconda's peculiar facial expression can even be perceived in the picture of John the Baptist in the Louvre; but above all it may be clearly recognized in the expression on Mary's face in the "Madonna and Child with St Anne".'[1] [See Plate 3.]

Yet this situation may also have come about in another way. The need for a deeper reason behind the attraction of La Gioconda's smile, which so moved the artist that he was never again free from it, has been felt by more than one of his biographers. Walter Pater, who sees in the picture of Mona Lisa a 'presence ... expressive of what in the ways of a thousand years men had come to desire' [1873, 118], and who writes very sensitively of 'the unfathomable smile, always with a touch of something sinister in it, which plays over all Leonardo's

1. [The title of this subject in German is *'heilige Anna Selbdritt'*, literally 'St Anne with Two Others'.]

work' [ibid., 117], leads us to another clue when he declares (loc. cit.):

'Besides, the picture is a portrait. From childhood we see this image defining itself on the fabric of his dreams; and but for express historical testimony, we might fancy that this was but his ideal lady, embodied and beheld at last ...'

Marie Herzfeld (1906, 88) has no doubt something very similar in mind when she declares that in the Mona Lisa Leonardo encountered his own self and for this reason was able to put so much of his own nature into the picture 'whose features had lain all along in mysterious sympathy within Leonardo's mind'.

Let us attempt to clarify what is suggested here. It may very well have been that Leonardo was fascinated by Mona Lisa's smile for the reason that it awoke something in him which had for long lain dormant in his mind – probably an old memory. This memory was of sufficient importance for him never to get free of it when it had once been aroused; he was continually forced to give it new expression. Pater's confident assertion that we can see, from childhood, a face like Mona Lisa's defining itself on the fabric of his dreams seems convincing and deserves to be taken literally.

Vasari mentions that 'teste di femmine, che ridono'[1] formed the subject of Leonardo's first artistic endeavours. The passage – which, since it is not intended to prove anything, is quite beyond suspicion – runs more fully according to Schorn's translation (1843, 3, 6): 'In his youth he made some heads of laughing women out of clay, which were reproduced in plaster, and some children's heads which were as beautiful as if they had been modelled by the hand of a master ...'

Thus we learn that he began his artistic career by portraying two kinds of objects; and these cannot fail to remind us of the two kinds of sexual objects that we have inferred from the analysis of his vulture phantasy. If the beautiful children's heads were reproductions of his own person as it was in his childhood, then the smiling women are nothing other than

1. ['Heads of laughing women.'] Quoted by Scognamiglio (1900, 32).

repetitions of his mother Caterina, and we begin to suspect the possibility that it was his mother who possessed the mysterious smile – the smile that he had lost and that fascinated him so much when he found it again in the Florentine lady.[1]

The painting of Leonardo's which stands nearest to the Mona Lisa in point of time is the so-called 'St Anne with Two Others', St Anne with the Madonna and child. [See Plate 3.] In it the Leonardesque smile is most beautifully and markedly portrayed on both the women's faces. It is not possible to discover how long before or after the painting of the Mona Lisa Leonardo began to paint this picture. As both works extended over years, it may, I think, be assumed that the artist was engaged on them at the same time. It would best agree with our expectations if it was the intensity of Leonardo's preoccupation with the features of Mona Lisa which stimulated him to create the composition of St Anne out of his phantasy. For if the Gioconda's smile called up in his mind the memory of his mother, it is easy to understand how it drove him at once to create a glorification of motherhood, and to give back to his mother the smile he had found in the noble lady. We may therefore permit our interest to pass from Mona Lisa's portrait to this other picture – one which is hardly less beautiful, and which to-day also hangs in the Louvre.

St Anne with her daughter and her grandchild is a subject that is rarely handled in Italian painting. At all events Leonardo's treatment of it differs widely from all other known versions. Muther (1909, **I**, 309) writes:

'Some artists, like Hans Fries, the elder Holbein and Girolamo dai Libri, made Anne sit beside Mary and put the child between them. Others, like Jakob Cornelisz in his Berlin picture, painted what was truly a "St Anne with Two Others";[2]

1. The same assumption is made by Merezhkovsky. But the history of Leonardo's childhood as he imagines it departs at the essential points from the conclusions we have drawn from the phantasy of the vulture. Yet if the smile had been that of Leonardo himself [as Merezhkovsky also assumes] tradition would hardly have failed to inform us of the coincidence.

2. [I.e., St Anne was the most prominent figure in the picture.]

in other words, they represented her as holding in her arms the small figure of Mary upon which the still smaller figure of the child Christ is sitting.' In Leonardo's picture Mary is sitting on her mother's lap, leaning forward, and is stretching out both arms towards the boy, who is playing with a young lamb and perhaps treating it a little unkindly. The grandmother rests on her hip the arm that is not concealed and gazes down on the pair with a blissful smile. The grouping is certainly not entirely unconstrained. But although the smile that plays on the lips of the two women is unmistakably the same as that in the picture of Mona Lisa, it has lost its uncanny and mysterious character; what it expresses is inward feeling and quiet blissfulness.[1]

After we have studied this picture for some time, it suddenly dawns on us that only Leonardo could have painted it, just as only he could have created the phantasy of the vulture. The picture contains the synthesis of the history of his childhood: its details are to be explained by reference to the most personal impressions in Leonardo's life. In his father's house he found not only his kind stepmother, Donna Albiera, but also his grandmother, his father's mother, Monna Lucia, who – so we will assume – was no less tender to him than grandmothers usually are. These circumstances might well suggest to him a picture representing childhood watched over by mother and grandmother. Another striking feature of the picture assumes even greater significance. St Anne, Mary's mother and the boy's grandmother, who must have been a matron, is here portrayed as being perhaps a little more mature and serious than the Virgin Mary, but as still being a young woman of unfaded beauty. In point of fact Leonardo has given the boy two mothers, one who stretches her arms out to him, and another in the background; and both are endowed with the blissful smile of the joy of motherhood. This peculiarity of the picture has not failed

1. Konstantinowa (1907 [44]): 'Mary gazes down full of inward feeling on her darling, with a smile that recalls the mysterious expression of La Gioconda.' In another passage [ibid., 52] she says of Mary: 'The Gioconda's smile hovers on her features.'

to surprise those who have written about it: Muther, for example, is of the opinion that Leonardo could not bring himself to paint old age, lines and wrinkles, and for this reason made Anne too into a woman of radiant beauty. But can we be satisfied with this explanation? Others have had recourse to denying that there is any similarity in age between the mother and daughter.[1] But Muther's attempt at an explanation is surely enough to prove that the impression that St Anne has been made more youthful derives from the picture and is not an invention for an ulterior purpose.

Leonardo's childhood was remarkable in precisely the same way as this picture. He had had two mothers: first, his true mother Caterina, from whom he was torn away when he was between three and five, and then a young and tender step-mother, his father's wife, Donna Albiera. By his combining this fact about his childhood with the one mentioned above (the presence of his mother and grandmother)[2] and by his condensing them into a composite unity, the design of 'St Anne with Two Others' took shape for him. The maternal figure that is further away from the boy – the grandmother – corresponds to the earlier and true mother, Caterina, in its appearance and in its special relation to the boy. The artist seems to have used the blissful smile of St Anne to disavow and to cloak the envy which the unfortunate woman felt when she was forced to give up her son to her better-born rival, as she had once given up his father as well.[3]

1. Von Seidlitz (1909, **2**, 274, notes).

2. [The words in parentheses were added in 1923.]

3. [*Footnote added* 1919:] If an attempt is made to separate the figures of Anne and Mary in this picture and to trace the outline of each, it will not be found altogether easy. One is inclined to say that they are fused with each other like badly condensed dream-figures, so that in some places it is hard to say where Anne ends and where Mary begins. But what appears to a critic's eye [in 1919 only: 'to an artist's eye'] as a fault, as a defect in composition, is vindicated in the eyes of analysis by reference to its secret meaning. It seems that for the artist the two mothers of his childhood were melted into a single form.

[*Added* 1923:] It is especially tempting to compare the 'St Anne with Two Others' of the Louvre with the celebrated London cartoon, where the same material is used to form a different composition. [See Fig. 2.] Here the forms of the two mothers are fused even more closely and their separate outlines are even harder to make out, so that critics, far removed from any attempt to offer an interpretation, have been forced to say that it seems 'as if two heads were growing from a single body'.

FIG. 2

Most authorities are in agreement in pronouncing the London cartoon to be the earlier work and in assigning its origin to Leonardo's first period in Milan (before 1500). Adolf Rosenberg (1898), on the other hand, sees the composition of the cartoon as a later – and more successful – version of the same theme, and follows Anton Springer [1895] in dating it even after the Mona Lisa. It would fit in excellently with our arguments if the cartoon were to be much the earlier work. It is also not hard to imagine how the picture in the Louvre arose out of the cartoon, while the reverse course of events would make no sense. If we take the composition shown in the cartoon as our starting point, we can see how Leonardo may have felt the need to undo the dream-like fusion of the two women – a fusion corresponding to his childhood memory – and to separate the two heads in space. This came about as follows: From the group formed by the mothers he detached Mary's head and the upper part of her body and bent them downwards. To provide a reason for this displacement the child Christ had to come down from her lap on to the ground. There was then no room for the little St John, who was replaced by the lamb.

[*Added* 1919:] A remarkable discovery has been made in the Louvre picture by Oskar Pfister, which is of undeniable interest, even if one may not feel inclined to accept it without reserve. In Mary's curiously arranged and rather confusing drapery he has discovered the *outline of a vulture* and he interprets it as an *unconscious picture-puzzle*:

'In the picture that represents the artist's mother *the vulture, the symbol of motherhood*, is perfectly clearly visible.

'In the length of blue cloth, which is visible around the hip of the woman in front and which extends in the direction of her lap and her right knee, one can see the vulture's extremely characteristic head, its neck and the sharp curve where its body begins. Hardly any observer whom I have confronted with my little find has been able to resist the evidence of this picture-puzzle.' (Pfister, 1913, 147.)

At this point the reader will not, I feel sure, grudge the effort of looking at the accompanying illustration, to see if he can find in it the outlines of the vulture seen by Pfister. The piece of blue cloth, whose border marks the edges of the picture-puzzle, stands out in the reproduction as a light grey field against the darker ground of the rest of the drapery. [See Plate 3 and Fig. 3.]

FIG. 3

We thus find a confirmation in another of Leonardo's works of our suspicion that the smile of Mona Lisa del Giocondo had awakened in him as a grown man the memory of the mother of his earliest childhood. From that time onward, madonnas and aristocratic ladies were depicted in Italian painting humbly bowing their heads and smiling the strange, blissful smile of Caterina, the poor peasant girl who had brought into the world the splendid son who was destined to paint, to search and to suffer.

If Leonardo was successful in reproducing on Mona Lisa's face the double meaning which this smile contained, the promise of unbounded tenderness and at the same time sinister menace (to quote Pater's phrase), then here too he had remained true to the content of his earliest memory. For his mother's tenderness was fateful for him; it determined his destiny and the privations that were in store for him. The violence of the caresses, to which his phantasy of the vulture points, was only too natural. In her love for her child the poor forsaken mother had to give vent to all her memories of the caresses she had enjoyed as well as her longing for new ones; and she was forced to do so not only to compensate herself for having no husband, but also to compensate her child for having no father to fondle him. So, like all unsatisfied mothers, she took her little son in place of her husband, and by the too early maturing of his erotism robbed him of a part of his masculinity. A mother's

---

Pfister continues: 'The important question however is: How far does the picture-puzzle extend? If we follow the length of cloth, which stands out so sharply from its surroundings, starting at the middle of the wing and continuing from there, we notice that one part of it runs down to the woman's foot, while the other part extends in an upward direction and rests on her shoulder and on the child. The former of these parts might more or less represent the vulture's wing and tail, as it is in nature; the latter might be a pointed belly and – especially when we notice the radiating lines which resemble the outlines of feathers – a bird's outspread tail, whose right-hand end, *exactly as in Leonardo's fateful childhood dream* [sic], *leads to the mouth of the child, i.e. of Leonardo himself.*'

The author goes on to examine the interpretation in greater detail, and discusses the difficulties to which it gives rise.

love for the infant she suckles and cares for is something far more profound than her later affection for the growing child. It is in the nature of a completely satisfying love-relation, which not only fulfils every mental wish but also every physical need; and if it represents one of the forms of attainable human happiness, that is in no little measure due to the possibility it offers of satisfying, without reproach, wishful impulses which have long been repressed and which must be called perverse.[1] In the happiest young marriage the father is aware that the baby, especially if he is a baby son, has become his rival, and this is the starting-point of an antagonism towards the favourite which is deeply rooted in the unconscious.

When, in the prime of life, Leonardo once more encountered the smile of bliss and rapture which had once played on his mother's lips as she fondled him, he had for long been under the dominance of an inhibition which forbade him ever again to desire such caresses from the lips of women. But he had become a painter, and therefore he strove to reproduce the smile with his brush, giving it to all his pictures (whether he in fact executed them himself or had them done by his pupils under his direction) – to Leda, to John the Baptist and to Bacchus. The last two are variants of the same type. 'Leonardo has turned the locust-eater of the Bible', says Muther [1909, I, 314], 'into a Bacchus, a young Apollo, who, with a mysterious smile on his lips, and with his smooth legs crossed, gazes at us with eyes that intoxicate the senses.' These pictures breathe a mystical air into whose secret one dares not penetrate; at the very most one can attempt to establish their connection with Leonardo's earlier creations. The figures are still androgynous, but no longer in the sense of the vulture phantasy. They are beautiful youths of feminine delicacy and with effeminate forms; they do not cast their eyes down, but gaze in mysterious triumph, as if they knew of a great achievement of happiness, about which silence must be kept. The familiar smile of fascination leads one to guess that it is a secret of love. It is

1. See my *Three Essays on the Theory of Sexuality* (1905d) [*P.F.L.*, **7**, 145.]

possible that in these figures Leonardo has denied the unhappi-
ness of his erotic life and has triumphed over it in his art, by
representing the wishes of the boy, infatuated with his mother,
as fulfilled in this blissful union of the male and female natures.

AMONG the entries in Leonardo's notebooks there is one which catches the reader's attention owing to the importance of what it contains and to a minute formal error.

In July 1504 he writes:

'Adì 9 di Luglio 1504 mercoledi a ore 7 morì Ser Piero da Vinci, notalio al palazzo del Potestà, mio padre, a ore 7. Era d'età d'anni 80, lasciò 10 figlioli maschi e 2 femmine.'[1]

As we see, the note refers to the death of Leonardo's father. The small error in its form consists of the repetition of the time of day 'a ore 7' [at 7 o'clock], which is given twice, as if Leonardo had forgotten at the end of the sentence that he had already written it at the beginning. It is only a small detail, and anyone who was not a psychoanalyst would attach no importance to it. He might not even notice it, and if his attention was drawn to it he might say that a thing like that can happen to anyone in a moment of distraction or of strong feeling, and that it has no further significance.

The psychoanalyst thinks differently. To him nothing is too small to be a manifestation of hidden mental processes. He has learnt long ago that such cases of forgetting or repetition are significant, and that it is the 'distraction' which allows impulses that are otherwise hidden to be revealed.

We would say that this note, like the account for Caterina's funeral and the bills of the pupils' expenses, is a case in which Leonardo was unsuccessful in suppressing his affect and in which something that had long been concealed forcibly obtained a distorted expression. Even the form is similar: there is the same

1. ['On 9 July 1504, Wednesday at 7 o'clock died Ser Piero da Vinci, notary at the palace of the Podestà, my father, at 7 o'clock. He was 80 years old, and left 10 sons and 2 daughters.'] After Müntz (1899, 13 *n*.).

pedantic exactness, and the same prominence given to numbers.[1]

We call a repetition of this kind a perseveration. It is an excellent means of indicating affective colour. One recalls, for example, St Peter's tirade in Dante's *Paradiso* against his unworthy representative on earth:

> Quegli ch'usurpa in terra il luogo mio,
> Il luogo mio, il luogo mio, che vaca
> Nella presenza del Figliuol di Dio,
>
> Fatto ha del cimiterio mio cloaca.[2]

Without Leonardo's affective inhibition the entry in his diary might have run somewhat as follows: 'To-day at 7 o'clock my father died – Ser Piero da Vinci, my poor father!' But the displacement of the perseveration on to the most indifferent detail in the report of his death, the hour at which he died, robs the entry of all emotion, and further lets us see that here was something to be concealed and suppressed.

Ser Piero da Vinci, notary and descendant of notaries, was a man of great energy who reached a position of esteem and prosperity. He was married four times. His first two wives died childless, and it was only his third wife who presented him with his first legitimate son, in 1476, by which time Leonardo had reached the age of twenty-four and had long ago exchanged his father's home for the studio of his master Verrocchio. By his fourth and last wife, whom he married when he was already in his fifties, he had nine more sons and two daughters.[3]

It cannot be doubted that his father too came to play an

---

1. I am leaving on one side a greater error made by Leonardo in this note by giving his father's age as eighty instead of seventy-seven. [See also *n*. 3 below.]

2. ['He who usurps on earth my place, my place, my place, which in the presence of the Son of God is vacant, has made a sewer of the ground where I am buried.'] Canto XXVII, 22–5.

3. Leonardo has apparently made a further mistake in this passage in his diary over the number of his brothers and sisters – a remarkable contrast to the apparent exactness of the passage.

important part in Leonardo's psychosexual development, and not only negatively by his absence during the boy's first childhood years, but also directly by his presence in the later part of Leonardo's childhood. No one who as a child desires his mother can escape wanting to put himself in his father's place, can fail to identify himself with him in his imagination, and later to make it his task in life to gain ascendancy over him. When Leonardo was received into his grandfather's house before he had reached the age of five, his young stepmother Albiera must certainly have taken his mother's place where his feelings were concerned, and he must have found himself in what may be called the normal relationship of rivalry with his father. As we know, a decision in favour of homosexuality only takes place round the years of puberty. When this decision had been arrived at in Leonardo's case, his identification with his father lost all significance for his sexual life, but it nevertheless continued in other spheres of non-erotic activity. We hear that he was fond of magnificence and fine clothes, and kept servants and horses, although, in Vasari's words, 'he possessed almost nothing and did little work'. The responsibility for these tastes is not to be attributed solely to his feeling for beauty: we recognize in them at the same time a compulsion to copy and to outdo his father. His father had been a great gentleman to the poor peasant girl, and the son, therefore, never ceased to feel the spur to play the great gentleman as well, the urge 'to out-herod Herod',[1] to show his father what a great gentleman really looks like.

There is no doubt that the creative artist feels towards his work like a father. The effect which Leonardo's identification with his father had on his paintings was a fateful one. He created them and then cared no more about them, just as his father had not cared about him. His father's later concern could change nothing in this compulsion; for the compulsion derived from the impressions of the first years of childhood, and what has been repressed and has remained unconscious cannot be corrected by later experiences.

1. [The last three words are in English in the original.]

In the days of the Renaissance – and even much later – every artist stood in need of a gentleman of rank, a benefactor and patron, who gave him commissions and in whose hands his fortune rested. Leonardo found his patron in Lodovico Sforza, called Il Moro, a man of ambition and a lover of splendour, astute in diplomacy, but of erratic and unreliable character. At his court in Milan Leonardo passed the most brilliant period of his life, and in his service his creative power attained its most uninhibited expansion, to which the Last Supper and the equestrian statue of Francesco Sforza bore witness. He left Milan before catastrophe overtook Lodovico Sforza, who died a prisoner in a French dungeon. When the news of his patron's fate reached Leonardo, he wrote in his diary: 'The duke lost his dukedom and his property and his liberty, and none of the works that he undertook was completed.'[1] It is remarkable, and certainly not without significance, that he here cast the same reproach at his patron which posterity was to bring against himself. It is as if he wanted to make someone from the class of his fathers responsible for the fact that he himself left his works unfinished. In point of fact he was not wrong in what he said about the duke.

But if his imitation of his father did him damage as an artist, his rebellion against his father was the infantile determinant of what was perhaps an equally sublime achievement in the field of scientific research. In Merezhkovsky's admirable simile (1903, 348), he was like a man who had awoken too early in the darkness, while everyone else was still asleep. He dared to utter the bold assertion which contains within itself the justification for all independent research: *'He who appeals to authority when there is a difference of opinion works with his memory rather than with his reason.'*[2] Thus he became the first modern natural scientist, and an abundance of discoveries and suggestive ideas rewarded his courage for being the first man since the

1. 'Il duca perse lo stato e la roba e libertà e nessuna sua opera si finì per lui.' Quoted by von Seidlitz (1909, **2**, 270).

2. 'Chi disputa allegando l'autorità non adopra l'ingegno ma piuttosto la memoria.' Quoted by Solmi (1910, 13). [*Codex Atlanticus*, F. 76r.a.]

LEONARDO DA VINCI

time of the Greeks to probe the secrets of nature while relying
solely on observation and his own judgement. But in teaching
that authority should be looked down on and that imitation
of the 'ancients' should be repudiated, and in constantly urging
that the study of nature was the source of all truth, he was
merely repeating – in the highest sublimation attainable by
man – the one-sided point of view which had already forced
itself on the little boy as he gazed in wonder on the world.
If we translate scientific abstraction back again into concrete
individual experience, we see that the 'ancients' and authority
simply correspond to his father, and nature once more becomes
the tender and kindly mother who had nourished him. In most
other human beings – no less to-day than in primaeval times
– the need for support from an authority of some sort is so
compelling that their world begins to totter if that authority
is threatened. Only Leonardo could dispense with that support;
he would not have been able to do so had he not learnt in
the first years of his life to do without his father. His later
scientific research, with all its boldness and independence, pre-
supposed the existence of infantile sexual researches uninhibited
by his father, and was a prolongation of them with the sexual
element excluded.

When anyone has, like Leonardo, escaped being intimidated
by his father during his earliest childhood, and has in his
researches cast away the fetters of authority, it would be in
the sharpest contradiction to our expectation if we found that
he had remained a believer and had been unable to escape from
dogmatic religion. Psychoanalysis has made us familiar with
the intimate connection between the father-complex and belief
in God; it has shown us that a personal God is, psychologically,
nothing other than an exalted father, and it brings us evidence
every day of how young people lose their religious beliefs as
soon as their father's authority breaks down. Thus we recognize
that the roots of the need for religion are in the parental complex; the almighty and just God, and kindly Nature, appear
to us as grand sublimations of father and mother, or rather
as revivals and restorations of the young child's ideas of them.

Biologically speaking, religiousness is to be traced to the small human child's long-drawn-out helplessness and need of help; and when at a later date he perceives how truly forlorn and weak he is when confronted with the great forces of life, he feels his condition as he did in childhood, and attempts to deny his own despondency by a regressive revival of the forces which protected his infancy. The protection against neurotic illness, which religion vouchsafes to those who believe in it, is easily explained: it removes their parental complex, on which the sense of guilt in individuals as well as in the whole human race depends, and disposes of it, while the unbeliever has to grapple with the problem on his own.[1]

It does not seem as if the instance of Leonardo could show this view of religious belief to be mistaken. Accusations charging him with unbelief or (what at that time came to the same thing) with apostasy from Christianity were brought against him while he was still alive, and are clearly described in the first biography which Vasari [1550] wrote of him. (Müntz, 1899, 292 ff.) In the second (1568) edition of his *Vite* Vasari omitted these observations. In view of the extraordinary sensitiveness of his age where religious matters were in question, we can understand perfectly why even in his notebooks Leonardo should have refrained from directly stating his attitude to Christianity. In his researches he did not allow himself to be led astray in the slightest degree by the account of the Creation in Holy Writ; he challenged, for example, the possibility of a universal Deluge, and in geology he calculated in terms of hundreds of thousands of years with no more hesitation than men in modern times.

Among his 'prophecies' there are some things that would have been bound to offend the sensitive feelings of a Christian believer. Take for example, 'On the practice of praying to the images of saints':

'Men will speak to men that perceive nothing, that have

1. [This last sentence was added in 1919. – This point is mentioned again in *Group Psychology* (1921c), *P.F.L.*, **12**, 176, *The Future of an Illusion* (1927c), ibid., 227, and *Civilization and its Discontents* (1930a), ibid., 273.]

their eyes open and see nothing; they will talk to them and receive no answer; they will implore the grace of those that have ears and hear not; they will kindle lights for one that is blind.' (After Herzfeld, 1906, 292.)

Or 'On the mourning on Good Friday':

'In every part of Europe great peoples will weep for the death of a single man who died in the East.' (Ibid., 297.)

The view has been expressed about Leonardo's art that he took from the sacred figures the last remnant of their connection with the Church and made them human, so as to represent by their means great and beautiful human emotions. Muther praises him for overcoming the prevailing mood of decadence and for restoring to man his right to sensuality and the joy of living. In the notes that show Leonardo engrossed in fathoming the great riddles of nature there is no lack of passages where he expresses his admiration for the Creator, the ultimate cause of all these noble secrets; but there is nothing which indicates that he wished to maintain any personal relation with this divine power. The reflections in which he has recorded the deep wisdom of his last years of life breathe the resignation of the human being who subjects himself to Ἀνάγκη [Ananke: 'Necessity'], to the laws of nature, and who expects no alleviation from the goodness or grace of God. There is scarcely any doubt that Leonardo had prevailed over both dogmatic and personal religion, and had by his work of research removed himself far from the position from which the Christian believer surveys the world.

The findings, mentioned above [p. 186], which we have reached concerning the development of the mental life of children suggest the view that in Leonardo's case too the first researches of childhood were concerned with the problems of sexuality. Indeed he himself gives this away in a transparent disguise by connecting his urge for research with the vulture phantasy, and by singling out the problem of the flight of birds as one to which, as the result of a special chain of circumstances, he was destined to turn his attention. A highly obscure passage in his notes which is concerned with the flight of birds, and which sounds like a prophecy, gives a very good demonstration of the degree of affective interest with which he clung to his wish to succeed in imitating the art of flying himself: 'The great bird will take its first flight from the back of its Great Swan; it will fill the universe with stupefaction, and all writings with renown, and be the eternal glory of the nest where it was born.'[1] He probably hoped that he himself would be able to fly one day, and we know from wish-fulfilling dreams what bliss is expected from the fulfilment of that hope.

But why do so many people dream of being able to fly? The answer that psychoanalysis gives is that to fly or to be a bird is only a disguise for another wish, and that more than one bridge, involving words or things, leads us to recognize what it is. When we consider that inquisitive children are told that babies are brought by a large bird, such as the stork; when we find that the ancients represented the phallus as having wings; that the commonest expression in German for male sexual activity is *'vögeln'* ['to bird': *'Vogel'* is the German for 'bird']; that the male organ is actually called *'l'uccello'* ['the bird'] in Italian – all of these are only small fragments from a whole mass of connected ideas, from which we learn that in dreams the wish to be able to fly is to be understood as nothing else than a longing to be capable of sexual performance.[2] This is an early infantile wish. When an adult recalls his childhood it seems to him to have been a happy time, in which one enjoyed the moment and looked to the future without any wishes; it is for this reason that he envies children. But if children themselves were able to give us information earlier they would probably tell a different story. It seems that childhood is not the blissful idyll into which we distort it in retrospect, and that, on the contrary, children are goaded on through the years of

1. After Herzfeld (1906, 32). 'The Great Swan' seems to mean Monte Cecero, a hill near Florence [now Monte Ceceri: *'Cecero'* is Italian for 'swan'].

2. [*Footnote added* 1919:] This statement is based on the researches of Paul Federn [1914] and of Mourly Vold (1912), a Norwegian man of science who had no contact with psychoanalysis. [See also *The Interpretation of Dreams* (1900a), *P.F.L.*, 4, 518.]

childhood by the one wish to get big and do what grown-ups do. This wish is the motive of all their games. Whenever children feel in the course of their sexual researches that in the province which is so mysterious but nevertheless so important there is something wonderful of which adults are capable but which they are forbidden to know of and do, they are filled with a violent wish to be able to do it, and they dream of it in the form of flying, or they prepare this disguise of their wish to be used in their later flying dreams. Thus aviation, too, which in our day is at last achieving its aim, has its infantile erotic roots.

In admitting to us that ever since his childhood he felt bound up in a special and personal way with the problem of flight, Leonardo gives us confirmation that his childhood researches were directed to sexual matters; and this is what we were bound to expect as a result of our investigations on children in our own time. Here was one problem at least which had escaped the repression that later estranged him from sexuality. With slight changes in meaning, the same subject continued to interest him from his years of childhood until the time of his most complete intellectual maturity; and it may very well be that the skill that he desired was no more attainable by him in its primary sexual sense than in its mechanical one, and that he remained frustrated in both wishes.

Indeed, the great Leonardo remained like a child for the whole of his life in more than one way; it is said that all great men are bound to retain some infantile part. Even as an adult he continued to play, and this was another reason why he often appeared uncanny and incomprehensible to his contemporaries. It is only we who are unsatisfied that he should have constructed the most elaborate mechanical toys for court festivities and ceremonial receptions, for we are reluctant to see the artist turning his power to such trifles. He himself seems to have shown no unwillingness to spend his time thus, for Vasari tells us that he made similar things when he had not been commissioned to do so: 'There (in Rome) he got a soft lump of wax, and made very delicate animals out of it, filled with air; when he blew into them they flew around, and when the air ran out they fell to the ground. For a peculiar lizard which was found by the wine-grower of Belvedere he made wings from skin torn from other lizards, and filled them with quick-silver, so that they moved and quivered when it walked. Next he made eyes, a beard and horns for it, tamed it and put it in a box and terrified all his friends with it.'[1] Such ingenuities often served to express thoughts of a serious kind. 'He often had a sheep's intestines cleaned so carefully that they could have been held in the hollow of the hand. He carried them into a large room, took a pair of blacksmith's bellows into an adjoining room, fastened the intestines to them and blew them up, until they took up the whole room and forced people to take refuge in a corner. In this way he showed how they gradually became transparent and filled with air; and from the fact that at first they were limited to a small space and gradually spread through the whole breadth of the room, he compared them to genius.'[2] The same playful delight in harmlessly con-cealing things and giving them ingenious disguises is illustrated by his fables and riddles. The latter are cast into the form of 'prophecies': almost all are rich in ideas and to a striking degree devoid of any element of wit.

The games and pranks which Leonardo allowed his imagina-tion have in some cases led his biographers, who misunderstood this side of his character, grievously astray. In Leonardo's Milanese manuscripts there are, for example, some drafts of letters to the 'Diodario of Sorio (Syria), Viceroy of the Holy Sultan of Babylonia', in which Leonardo presents himself as an engineer sent to those regions of the East to construct certain works; defends himself against the charge of laziness; supplies geographical descriptions of towns and mountains, and con-cludes with an account of a great natural phenomenon that occurred while he was there.[3]

1. Vasari, from Schorn's translation (1843, 39) [ed. Poggi, 1919, 41].
2. Ibid., 39 [ed. Poggi, 41].
3. For these letters and the various questions connected with them see Müntz (1899, 82 ff.); the actual texts and other related notes will be found in Herzfeld (1906, 223 ff.).

In 1883 an attempt was made by J. P. Richter to prove from these documents that it was really a fact that Leonardo had made these observations while travelling in the service of the Sultan of Egypt, and had even adopted the Mohammedan religion when in the East. On this view his visit there took place in the period before 1483 – that is, before he took up residence at the court of the Duke of Milan. But the acumen of other authors has had no difficulty in recognizing the evidences of Leonardo's supposed Eastern journey for what they are – imaginary productions of the youthful artist, which he created for his own amusement and in which he may have found expression for a wish to see the world and meet with adventures.

Another probable example of a creation of his imagination is to be found in the 'Academia Vinciana' which has been postulated from the existence of five or six emblems, intertwined patterns of extreme intricacy, which contain the Academy's name. Vasari mentions these designs but not the Academy.[1] Müntz, who put one of these ornaments on the cover of his large work on Leonardo, is among the few who believe in the reality of an 'Academia Vinciana'.

It is probable that Leonardo's play instinct vanished in his maturer years, and that it too found its way into the activity of research which represented the latest and highest expansion of his personality. But its long duration can teach us how slowly anyone tears himself from his childhood if in his childhood days he has enjoyed the highest erotic bliss, which is never again attained.

---

1. 'Besides, he lost some time by even making a drawing of knots of cords, in which it was possible to trace the thread from one end to the other until it formed a completely circular figure. A very complex and beautiful design of this sort is engraved on copper; in the middle can be read the words "Leonardus Vinci Academia".' Schorn (1843, 8) [ed. Poggi, 5].

VI

IT would be futile to blind ourselves to the fact that readers to-day find all pathography unpalatable. They clothe their aversion in the complaint that a pathographical review of a great man never results in an understanding of his importance and his achievements, and that it is therefore a piece of useless impertinence to make a study of things in him that could just as easily be found in the first person one came across. But this criticism is so manifestly unjust that it is only understandable when taken as a pretext and a disguise. Pathography does not in the least aim at making the great man's achievements intelligible; and surely no one should be blamed for not carrying out something he has never promised to do. The real motives for the opposition are different. We can discover them if we bear in mind that biographers are fixated on their heroes in a quite special way. In many cases they have chosen their hero as the subject of their studies because — for reasons of their personal emotional life — they have felt a special affection for him from the very first. They then devote their energies to a task of idealization, aimed at enrolling the great man among the class of their infantile models – at reviving in him, perhaps, the child's idea of his father. To gratify this wish they obliterate the individual features of their subject's physiognomy; they smooth over the traces of his life's struggles with internal and external resistances, and they tolerate in him no vestige of human weakness or imperfection. They thus present us with what is in fact a cold, strange, ideal figure, instead of a human being to whom we might feel ourselves distantly related. That they should do this is regrettable, for they thereby sacrifice truth to an illusion, and for the sake of their infantile phantasies abandon the opportunity of penetrating the most fascinating secrets of human nature.[1]

1. This criticism applies quite generally and is not to be taken as being aimed at Leonardo's biographers in particular.

Leonardo himself, with his love of truth and his thirst for knowledge, would not have discouraged an attempt to take the trivial peculiarities and riddles in his nature as a starting-point, for discovering what determined his mental and intellectual development. We do homage to him by learning from him. It does not detract from his greatness if we make a study of the sacrifices which his development from childhood must have entailed, and if we bring together the factors which have stamped him with the tragic mark of failure.

We must expressly insist that we have never reckoned Leonardo as a neurotic or a 'nerve case', as the awkward phrase goes. Anyone who protests at our so much as daring to examine him in the light of discoveries gained in the field of pathology is still clinging to prejudices which we have to-day rightly abandoned. We no longer think that health and illness, normal and neurotic people, are to be sharply distinguished from each other, and that neurotic traits must necessarily be taken as proofs of a general inferiority. To-day we know that neurotic symptoms are structures which are substitutes for certain achievements of repression that we have to carry out in the course of our development from a child to a civilized human being. We know too that we all produce such substitutive structures, and that it is only their number, intensity and distribution which justify us in using the practical concept of illness and in inferring the presence of constitutional inferiority. From the slight indications we have about Leonardo's personality we should be inclined to place him close to the type of neurotic that we describe as 'obsessional'; and we may compare his researches to the 'obsessive brooding' of neurotics, and his inhibitions to what are known as their 'abulias'.

The aim of our work has been to explain the inhibitions in Leonardo's sexual life and in his artistic activity. With this in view we may be allowed to summarize what we have been able to discover about the course of his psychical development.

We have no information about the circumstances of his heredity; on the other hand we have seen that the accidental conditions of his childhood had a profound and disturbing effect on him. His illegitimate birth deprived him of his father's influence until perhaps his fifth year, and left him open to the tender seductions of a mother whose only solace he was. After being kissed by her into a precocious sexual maturity, he must no doubt have embarked on a phase of infantile sexual activity of which only one single manifestation is definitely attested – the intensity of his infantile sexual researches. The instinct to look and the instinct to know were those most strongly excited by the impressions of his early childhood; the erotogenic zone of the mouth was given an emphasis which it never afterwards surrendered. From his later behaviour in the contrary direction, such as his exaggerated sympathy for animals, we can conclude that there was no lack of strong sadistic traits in this period of his childhood.

A powerful wave of repression brought this childhood excess to an end, and established the dispositions which were to become manifest in the years of puberty. The most obvious result of the transformation was the avoidance of every crudely sensual activity; Leonardo was enabled to live in abstinence and to give the impression of being an asexual human being. When the excitations of puberty came in their flood upon the boy they did not, however, make him ill by forcing him to develop substitutive structures of a costly and harmful kind. Owing to his very early inclination towards sexual curiosity the greater portion of the needs of his sexual instinct could be sublimated into a general urge to know, and thus evaded repression. A much smaller portion of his libido continued to be devoted to sexual aims and represented a stunted adult sexual life. Because his love for his mother had been repressed, this portion was driven to take up a homosexual attitude and manifested itself in ideal love for boys. The fixation on his mother and on the blissful memories of his relations with her continued to be preserved in the unconscious, but for the time being it remained in an inactive state. In this way repression, fixation and sublimation all played their part in disposing of the contributions which the sexual instinct made to Leonardo's mental life.

Leonardo emerges from the obscurity of his boyhood as an artist, a painter and a sculptor, owing to a specific talent which may have been reinforced by the precocious awakening in the first years of childhood of his scopophilic instinct. We should be most glad to give an account of the way in which artistic activity derives from the primal instincts of the mind if it were not just here that our capacities fail us. We must be content to emphasize the fact – which it is hardly any longer possible to doubt – that what an artist creates provides at the same time an outlet for his sexual desire; and in Leonardo's case we can point to the information, which comes from Vasari [1550], that heads of laughing women and beautiful boys – in other words, representations of his sexual objects – were notable among his first artistic endeavours. In the bloom of his youth Leonardo appears at first to have worked without inhibition. Just as he modelled himself on his father in the outward conduct of his life, so too he passed through a period of masculine creative power and artistic productiveness in Milan, where a kindly fate enabled him to find a father-substitute in the duke Lodovico Moro. But soon we find confirmation of our experience that the almost total suppression of a real sexual life does not provide the most favourable conditions for the exercise of sublimated sexual trends. The pattern imposed by sexual life made itself felt. His activity and his ability to form quick decisions began to fail; his tendency towards deliberation and delay was already noticeable as a disturbing element in the 'Last Supper', and by influencing his technique it had a decisive effect on the fate of that great painting. Slowly there occurred in him a process which can only be compared to the regressions in neurotics. The development that turned him into an artist at puberty was overtaken by the process which led him to be an investigator, and which had its determinants in early infancy. The second sublimation of his erotic instinct gave place to the original sublimation for which the way had been prepared on the occasion of the first repression. He became an investigator, at first still in the service of his art, but later independently of it and away from it. With the loss of his patron, the substitute for his father, and with the increasingly sombre colours which his life took on, this regressive shift assumed larger and larger proportions. He became *'impacientissimo al pennello'*,[1] as we are told by a correspondent of the Countess Isabella d'Este, who was extremely eager to possess a painting from his hand. His infantile past had gained control over him. But the research which now took the place of artistic creation seems to have contained some of the features which distinguish the activity of unconscious instincts − insatiability, unyielding rigidity and the lack of an ability to adapt to real circumstances.

At the summit of his life, when he was in his early fifties − a time when in women the sexual characters have already undergone involution and when in men the libido not infrequently makes a further energetic advance − a new transformation came over him. Still deeper layers of the contents of his mind became active once more; but this further regression was to the benefit of his art, which was in the process of becoming stunted. He met the woman who awakened his memory of his mother's happy smile of sensual rapture; and, influenced by this revived memory, he recovered the stimulus that guided him at the beginning of his artistic endeavours, at the time when he modelled the smiling women. He painted the Mona Lisa, the 'St Anne with Two Others' and the series of mysterious pictures which are characterized by the enigmatic smile. With the help of the oldest of all his erotic impulses he enjoyed the triumph of once more conquering the inhibition in his art. This final development is obscured from our eyes in the shadows of approaching age. Before this his intellect had soared upwards to the highest realizations of a conception of the world that left his epoch far behind it.

In the preceding chapters I have shown what justification can be found for giving this picture of Leonardo's course of development − for proposing these subdivisions of his life and for explaining his vacillation between art and science in this way. If in making these statements I have provoked the criticism, even from friends of psychoanalysis and from those

1. ['Very impatient of painting.'] Von Seidlitz (1909, **2**, 271).

who are expert in it, that I have merely written a psychoanalytic novel, I shall reply that I am far from overestimating the certainty of these results. Like others I have succumbed to the attraction of this great and mysterious man, in whose nature one seems to detect powerful instinctual passions which can nevertheless only express themselves in so remarkably subdued a manner.

But whatever the truth about Leonardo's life may be, we cannot desist from our endeavour to find a psychoanalytic explanation for it until we have completed another task. We must stake out in a quite general way the limits which are set to what psychoanalysis can achieve in the field of biography: otherwise every explanation that is not forthcoming will be held up to us as a failure. The material at the disposal of a psychoanalytic inquiry consists of the data of a person's life history: on the one hand the chance circumstances of events and background influences, and, on the other hand, the subject's reported reactions. Supported by its knowledge of psychical mechanisms it then endeavours to establish a dynamic basis for his nature on the strength of his reactions, and to disclose the original motive forces of his mind, as well as their later transformations and developments. If this is successful the behaviour of a personality in the course of his life is explained in terms of the combined operation of constitution and fate, of internal forces and external powers. Where such an undertaking does not provide any certain results – and this is perhaps so in Leonardo's case – the blame rests not with the faulty or inadequate methods of psychoanalysis, but with the uncertainty and fragmentary nature of the material relating to him which tradition makes available. It is therefore only the author who is to be held responsible for the failure, by having forced psychoanalysis to pronounce an expert opinion on the basis of such insufficient material.

But even if the historical material at our disposal were very abundant, and if the psychical mechanisms could be dealt with with the greatest assurance, there are two important points at which a psychoanalytic inquiry would not be able to make us understand how inevitable it was that the person concerned should have turned out in the way he did and in no other way. In Leonardo's case we have had to maintain the view that the accident of his illegitimate birth and the excessive tenderness of his mother had the most decisive influence on the formation of his character and on his later fortune, since the sexual repression which set in after this phase of childhood caused him to sublimate his libido into the urge to know, and established his sexual inactivity for the whole of his later life. But this repression after the first erotic satisfactions of childhood need not necessarily have taken place or might have assumed much less extensive proportions. We must recognize here a degree of freedom which cannot be resolved any further by psycho-analytic means. Equally, one has no right to claim that the consequence of this wave of repression was the only possible one. It is probable that another person would not have succeeded in withdrawing the major portion of his libido from repression by sublimating it into a craving for knowledge; under the same influences he would have sustained a permanent injury to his intellectual activity or have acquired an in-surmountable disposition to obsessional neurosis. We are left, then, with these two characteristics of Leonardo which are inexplicable by the efforts of psychoanalysis: his quite special tendency towards instinctual repressions, and his extraordinary capacity for sublimating the primitive instincts.

Instincts and their transformations are at the limit of what is discernible by psychoanalysis. From that point it gives place to biological research. We are obliged to look for the source of the tendency to repression and the capacity for sublimation in the organic foundations of character on which the mental structure is only afterwards erected. Since artistic talent and capacity are intimately connected with sublimation we must admit that the nature of the artistic function is also inaccessible to us along psychoanalytic lines. The tendency of biological research to-day is to explain the chief features in a person's organic constitution as being the result of the blending of male and female dispositions, based on [chemical] substances. Leonardo's physical beauty and his left-handedness might be quoted in support of this view.[1] We will not, however, leave the ground of purely psychological research. Our aim remains that of demonstrating the connection along the path of instinctual activity between a person's external experiences and his reactions. Even if psychoanalysis does not throw light on the fact of Leonardo's artistic power, it at least renders its manifestations and its limitations intelligible to us. It seems at any rate as if only a man who had had Leonardo's childhood experiences could have painted the Mona Lisa and the St Anne, have secured so melancholy a fate for his works and have embarked on such an astonishing career as a natural scientist, as if the key to all his achievements and misfortunes lay hidden in the childhood phantasy of the vulture.

But may one not take objection to the findings of an inquiry which ascribes to accidental circumstances of his parental constellation so decisive an influence on a person's fate – which, for example, makes Leonardo's fate depend on his illegitimate birth and on the barrenness of his first stepmother Donna Albiera? I think one has no right to do so. If one considers chance to be unworthy of determining our fate, it is simply a relapse into the pious view of the universe which Leonardo himself was on the way to overcoming when he wrote that the sun does not move. We naturally feel hurt that a just God and a kindly Providence do not protect us better from such influences during the most defenceless period of our lives. At the same time we are all too ready to forget that in fact everything to do with our life is chance, from our origin out of the meeting of spermatozoon and ovum onwards – chance which nevertheless has a share in the law and necessity of nature, and which merely lacks any connection with our wishes and illusions. The apportioning of the determining factors of our life between the 'necessities' of our constitution and the

1. [This is no doubt an allusion to the views of Fliess by which Freud had been greatly influenced. Cf. his *Three Essays* (1905d), *P.F.L.*, **7**, 137 n. 1. On the particular question of bilaterality, however, they had not been in complete agreement. See above, p. 145 n. 1.]

'chances' of our childhood may still be uncertain in detail; but in general it is no longer possible to doubt the importance precisely of the first years of our childhood. We all still show too little respect for Nature which (in the obscure words of Leonardo which recall Hamlet's lines) 'is full of countless causes ['*ragioni*'] that never enter experience'.[1]

Every one of us human beings corresponds to one of the countless experiments in which these '*ragioni*' of nature force their way into experience.

1. '*La natura è piena d'infinite ragioni che non furono mai in isperienza*' (Herzfeld, 1906, 11). – [The allusion seems to be to Hamlet's familiar words:

There are more things in heaven and earth, Horatio,
Than are dreamt of in your philosophy.

(Act I, Scene 5)]

THE THEME OF THE
THREE CASKETS
(1913)

DAS MOTIV DER KÄSTCHENWAHL

(A) German Editions:

1913   *Imago*, **2** (3), 257–66.
1918   *S.K.S.N.*, **4**, 470–85. (1922, 2nd ed.)
1924   *Dichtung und Kunst*, 15–28.
1946   *Gesammelte Werke*, **10**, 24–37.

(B) English Translations:

'The Theme of the Three Caskets'

1925   *Collected Papers*, **4**, 244–56. (Tr. C. J. M. Hubback.)
1958   *Standard Edition*, **12**, 289–301. (Based on translation of 1925.)

The present edition is a reprint of the *Standard Edition* version.

Freud's correspondence (quoted in Jones, 1955, 405) shows that the underlying idea of this paper occurred to him in June 1912, though the work was only published a year later. In a letter to Ferenczi of 7 July 1913, he connected the 'subjective determinant' of the paper with his own three daughters (Freud, 1960*a*).

THE THEME OF THE
THREE CASKETS

I

Two scenes from Shakespeare, one from a comedy and the other from a tragedy, have lately given me occasion for posing and solving a small problem.

The first of these scenes is the suitors' choice between the three caskets in *The Merchant of Venice*. The fair and wise Portia is bound at her father's bidding to take as her husband only that one of her suitors who chooses the right casket from among the three before him. The three caskets are of gold, silver and lead: the right casket is the one that contains her portrait. Two suitors have already departed unsuccessful: they have chosen gold and silver. Bassanio, the third, decides in favour of lead; thereby he wins the bride, whose affection was already his before the trial of fortune. Each of the suitors gives reasons for his choice in a speech in which he praises the metal he prefers and depreciates the other two. The most difficult task thus falls to the share of the fortunate third suitor; what he finds to say in glorification of lead as against gold and silver is little and has a forced ring. If in psychoanalytic practice we were confronted with such a speech, we should suspect that there were concealed motives behind the unsatisfying reasons produced.

Shakespeare did not himself invent this oracle of the choice of a casket; he took it from a tale in the *Gesta Romanorum*,[1] in which a girl has to make the same choice to win the Emperor's son.[2] Here too the third metal, lead, is the bringer of fortune. It is not hard to guess that we have here an ancient theme, which requires to be interpreted, accounted for and traced back

1. [A medieval collection of stories of unknown authorship.]
2. Brandes (1896).

to its origin. A first conjecture as to the meaning of this choice between gold, silver and lead is quickly confirmed by a statement of Stucken's,[1] who has made a study of the same material over a wide field. He writes: 'The identity of Portia's three suitors is clear from their choice: the Prince of Morocco chooses the gold casket – he is the sun; the Prince of Arragon chooses the silver casket – he is the moon; Bassanio chooses the leaden casket – he is the star youth.' In support of this explanation he cites an episode from the Estonian folk epic 'Kalewipoeg', in which the three suitors appear undisguisedly as the sun, moon and star youths (the last being 'the Pole star's eldest boy') and once again the bride falls to the lot of the third.

Thus our little problem has led us to an astral myth! The only pity is that with this explanation we are not at the end of the matter. The question is not exhausted, for we do not share the belief of some investigators that myths were read in the heavens and brought down to earth; we are more inclined to judge with Otto Rank[2] that they were projected on to the heavens after having arisen elsewhere under purely human conditions. It is in this human content that our interest lies.

Let us look once more at our material. In the Estonian epic, just as in the tale from the *Gesta Romanorum*, the subject is a girl choosing between three suitors; in the scene from *The Merchant of Venice* the subject is apparently the same, but at the same time something appears in it that is in the nature of an inversion of the theme: a *man* chooses between three – caskets. If what we were concerned with were a dream, it would occur to us at once that caskets are also women, symbols of what is essential in woman, and therefore of a woman herself – like coffers, boxes, cases, baskets, and so on.[3] If we boldly assume that there are symbolic substitutions of the same kind in myths as well, then the casket scene in *The Merchant of Venice* really becomes the inversion we suspected. With a wave of the wand, as though we were in a fairy tale, we have stripped

1. Stucken (1907, 655).
2. Rank (1909, 8 ff.).
3. [See *The Interpretation of Dreams* (1900a), P.F.L., **4**, 471.]

the astral garment from our theme; and now we see that the theme is a human one, *a man's choice between three women.*

This same content, however, is to be found in another scene of Shakespeare's, in one of his most powerfully moving dramas; not the choice of a bride this time, yet linked by many hidden similarities to the choice of the casket in *The Merchant of Venice.* The old King Lear resolves to divide his kingdom while he is still alive among his three daughters, in proportion to the amount of love that each of them expresses for him. The two elder ones, Goneril and Regan, exhaust themselves in asseverations and laudations of their love for him; the third, Cordelia, refuses to do so. He should have recognized the unassuming, speechless love of his third daughter and rewarded it, but he does not recognize it. He disowns Cordelia, and divides the kingdom between the other two, to his own and the general ruin. Is not this once more the scene of a choice between three women, of whom the youngest is the best, the most excellent one?

There will at once occur to us other scenes from myths, fairy tales and literature, with the same situation as their content. The shepherd Paris has to choose between three goddesses, of whom he declares the third to be the most beautiful. Cinderella, again, is a youngest daughter, who is preferred by the prince to her two elder sisters. Psyche, in Apuleius's story, is the youngest and fairest of three sisters. Psyche is, on the one hand, revered as Aphrodite in human form; on the other, she is treated by that goddess as Cinderella was treated by her stepmother and is set the task of sorting a heap of mixed seeds, which she accomplishes with the help of small creatures (doves in the case of Cinderella, ants in the case of Psyche).[1] Anyone who cared to make a wider survey of the material would undoubtedly discover other versions of the same theme preserving the same essential features.

Let us be content with Cordelia, Aphrodite, Cinderella and

1. I have to thank Dr Otto Rank for calling my attention to these similarities. [Cf. a reference to this in *Group Psychology* (1921c), *P.F.L.*, **12**, 169–70.]

Psyche. In all the stories the three women, of whom the third is the most excellent one, must surely be regarded as in some way alike if they are represented as sisters. (We must not be led astray by the fact that Lear's choice is between three *daughters*; this may mean nothing more than that he has to be represented as an old man. An old man cannot very well choose between three women in any other way. Thus they become his daughters.)

But who are these three sisters and why must the choice fall on the third? If we could answer this question, we should be in possession of the interpretation we are seeking. We have once already made use of an application of psychoanalytic technique, when we explained the three caskets symbolically as three women. If we have the courage to proceed in the same way, we shall be setting foot on a path which will lead us first to something unexpected and incomprehensible, but which will perhaps, by a devious route, bring us to a goal.

It must strike us that this excellent third woman has in several instances certain peculiar qualities besides her beauty. They are qualities that seem to be tending towards some kind of unity; we must certainly not expect to find them equally well marked in every example. Cordelia makes herself unrecognizable, inconspicuous like lead, she remains dumb, she 'loves and is silent'.[1] Cinderella hides so that she cannot be found. We may perhaps be allowed to equate concealment and dumbness. These would of course be only two instances out of the five we have picked out. But there is an intimation of the same thing to be found, curiously enough, in two other cases. We have decided to compare Cordelia, with her obstinate refusal, to lead. In Bassanio's short speech while he is choosing the casket, he says of lead (without in any way leading up to the remark):

'Thy paleness[2] moves me more than eloquence.'

That is to say: 'Thy plainness moves me more than the blatant

1. [From an aside of Cordelia's, Act I, Scene 1.]
2. 'Plainness' according to another reading.

nature of the other two.' Gold and silver are 'loud'; lead is dumb – in fact like Cordelia, who 'loves and is silent'.[1]

In the ancient Greek accounts of the Judgement of Paris, nothing is said of any such reticence on the part of Aphrodite. Each of the three goddesses speaks to the youth and tries to win him by promises. But, oddly enough, in a quite modern handling of the same scene this characteristic of the third one which has struck us makes its appearance again. In the libretto of Offenbach's *La Belle Hélène*, Paris, after telling of the solicitations of the other two goddesses, describes Aphrodite's behaviour in this competition for the beauty-prize:

> La troisième, ah! la troisième . . .
> La troisième ne dit rien.
> Elle eut le prix tout de même . . .[2]

If we decide to regard the peculiarities of our 'third one' as concentrated in her 'dumbness', then psychoanalysis will tell us that in dreams dumbness is a common representation of death.[3]

More than ten years ago a highly intelligent man told me a dream which he wanted to use as evidence of the telepathic nature of dreams. In it he saw an absent friend from whom he had received no news for a very long time, and reproached him energetically for his silence. The friend made no reply. It afterwards turned out that he had met his death by suicide at about the time of the dream. Let us leave the problem of telepathy on one side:[4] there seems, however, not to be any

---

1. In Schlegel's translation this allusion is quite lost; indeed, it is given the opposite meaning: 'Dein schlichtes Wesen spricht beredt mich an.' ['Thy plainness speaks to me with eloquence.']

2. [Literally: 'The third one, ah! the third one . . . the third one said nothing. She won the prize all the same.' – The quotation is from Act I, Scene 7, of Meilhac and Halévy's libretto. In the German version used by Freud 'the third one' *'blieb stumm'* – 'remained dumb'.]

3. In Stekel's *Sprache des Traumes*, too, dumbness is mentioned among the 'death' symbols (1911, 351). [Cf. *The Interpretation of Dreams* (1900a), *P.F.L.*, **4**, 475.]

4. [Cf. Freud's later paper on 'Dreams and Telepathy' (1922a), *Standard Ed.*, **18**, 197.]

doubt that here the dumbness in the dream represented death. Hiding and being unfindable – a thing which confronts the prince in the fairy tale of Cinderella three times, is another unmistakable symbol of death in dreams; so, too, is a marked pallor, of which the 'paleness' of the lead in one reading of Shakespeare's text is a reminder.[1] It would be very much easier for us to transpose these interpretations from the language of dreams to the mode of expression used in the myth that is now under consideration if we could make it seem probable that dumbness must be interpreted as a sign of being dead in productions other than dreams.

At this point I will single out the ninth story in Grimms' *Fairy Tales*, which bears the title 'The Twelve Brothers'.[2] A king and a queen have twelve children, all boys. The king declares that if the thirteenth child is a girl, the boys will have to die. In expectation of her birth he has twelve coffins made. With their mother's help the twelve sons take refuge in a hidden wood, and swear death to any girl they may meet. A girl is born, grows up, and learns one day from her mother that she has had twelve brothers. She decides to seek them out, and in the wood she finds the youngest; he recognizes her, but is anxious to hide her on account of the brothers' oath. The sister says: 'I will gladly die, if by so doing I can save my twelve brothers.' The brothers welcome her affectionately, however, and she stays with them and looks after their house for them. In a little garden beside the house grow twelve lilies. The girl picks them and gives one to each brother. At that moment the brothers are changed into ravens, and disappear, together with the house and garden. (Ravens are spirit-birds; the killing of the twelve brothers by their sister is represented by the picking of the flowers, just as it is at the beginning of the story by the coffins and the disappearance of the brothers.) The girl, who is once more ready to save her brothers from death, is now told that as a condition she must be dumb for seven years, and not speak a single word. She submits to the test, which

1. Stekel (1911), loc. cit.
2. ['Die zwölf Brüder.' Grimm, 1918, I, 42.]

brings her herself into mortal danger. She herself, that is, dies for her brothers, as she promised to do before she met them. By remaining dumb she succeeds at last in setting the ravens free.

In the story of 'The Six Swans'[1] the brothers who are changed into birds are set free in exactly the same way – they are restored to life by their sister's dumbness. The girl has made a firm resolve to free her brothers, 'even if it should cost her her life'; and once again (being the wife of the king) she risks her own life because she refuses to give up her dumbness in order to defend herself against evil accusations.

It would certainly be possible to collect further evidence from fairy tales that dumbness is to be understood as representing death. These indications would lead us to conclude that the third one of the sisters between whom the choice is made is a dead woman. But she may be something else as well – namely, Death itself, the Goddess of Death. Thanks to a displacement that is far from infrequent, the qualities that a deity imparts to men are ascribed to the deity himself. Such a displacement will surprise us least of all in relation to the Goddess of Death, since in modern versions and representations, which these stories would thus anticipate, Death itself is nothing other than a dead man.

But if the third of the sisters is the Goddess of Death, the sisters are known to us. They are the Fates, the Moerae, the Parcae or the Norns, the third of whom is called Atropos, the inexorable.

II

We will for the time being put aside the task of inserting the interpretation that we have found into our myth, and listen to what the mythologists have to teach us about the role and origin of the Fates.[2]

1. ['Die sechs Schwäne.' Grimm, 1918, I, 217. (No. 49.)]
2. What follows is taken from Roscher's lexicon [1884–97], under the relevant headings.

The earliest Greek mythology (in Homer) only knew a single Μοῖρα, personifying inevitable fate. The further development of this one Moera into a company of three (or less often two) sister-goddesses probably came about on the basis of other divine figures to which the Moerae were closely related – the Graces and the Horae [the Seasons].

The Horae were originally goddesses of the waters of the sky, dispensing rain and dew, and of the clouds from which rain falls; and, since the clouds were conceived of as something that has been spun, it came about that these goddesses were looked upon as spinners, an attribute that then became attached to the Moerae. In the sun-favoured Mediterranean lands it is the rain on which the fertility of the soil depends, and thus the Horae became vegetation goddesses. The beauty of flowers and the abundance of fruit was their doing, and they were accredited with a wealth of agreeable and charming traits. They became the divine representatives of the Seasons, and it is possibly owing to this connection that there were three of them, if the sacred nature of the number three is not a sufficient explanation. For the peoples of antiquity at first distinguished only three seasons: winter, spring and summer. Autumn was only added in late Graeco-Roman times, after which the Horae were often represented in art as four in number.

The Horae retained their relation to time. Later they presided over the times of day, as they did at first over the times of the year; and at last their name came to be merely a designation of the hours (*heure, ora*). The Norns of German mythology are akin to the Horae and the Moerae and exhibit this time signification in their names.[1] It was inevitable, however, that a deeper view should come to be taken of the essential nature of these deities, and that their essence should be transposed on to the regularity with which the seasons change. The Horae thus became the guardians of natural law and of the divine Order which causes the same thing to recur in Nature in an unalterable sequence.

This discovery of Nature reacted on the conception of human

1. [Their names may be rendered: 'What was', 'What is', 'What shall be'.]

life. The nature myth changed into a human myth: the weather-goddesses became goddesses of Fate. But this aspect of the Horae found expression only in the Moerae, who watch over the necessary ordering of human life as inexorably as do the Horae over the regular order of nature. The ineluctable severity of Law and its relation to death and dissolution, which had been avoided in the charming figures of the Horae, were now stamped upon the Moerae, as though men had only perceived the full seriousness of natural law when they had to submit their own selves to it.

The names of the three spinners, too, have been significantly explained by mythologists. Lachesis, the name of the second, seems to denote 'the accidental that is included in the regularity of destiny'[1] – or, as we should say, 'experience'; just as Atropos stands for 'the ineluctable' – Death. Clotho would then be left to mean the innate disposition with its fateful implications.

But now it is time to return to the theme which we are trying to interpret – the theme of the choice between three sisters. We shall be deeply disappointed to discover how unintelligible the situations under review become and what contradictions of their apparent content result, if we apply to them the interpretation that we have found. On our supposition the third of the sisters is the Goddess of Death, Death itself. But in the Judgement of Paris she is the Goddess of Love, in the tale of Apuleius she is someone comparable to the goddess for her beauty, in *The Merchant of Venice* she is the fairest and wisest of women, in *King Lear* she is the one loyal daughter. We may ask whether there can be a more complete contradiction. Perhaps, improbable though it may seem, there is a still more complete one lying close at hand. Indeed, there certainly is; since, whenever our theme occurs, the choice between the women is free, and yet it falls on death. For, after all, no one chooses death, and it is only by a fatality that one falls a victim to it.

However, contradictions of a certain kind – replacements by the precise opposite – offer no serious difficulty to the work

1. Roscher [ibid.], quoting Preller, ed. Robert (1894).

of analytic interpretation. We shall not appeal here to the fact that contraries are so often represented by one and the same element in the modes of expression used by the unconscious, as for instance in dreams.[1] But we shall remember that there are motive forces in mental life which bring about replacement by the opposite in the form of what is known as reaction-formation; and it is precisely in the revelation of such hidden forces as these that we look for the reward of this inquiry. The Moerae were created as a result of a discovery that warned man that he too is a part of nature and therefore subject to the immutable law of death. Something in man was bound to struggle against this subjection, for it is only with extreme unwillingness that he gives up his claim to an exceptional position. Man, as we know, makes use of his imaginative activity in order to satisfy the wishes that reality does not satisfy. So his imagination rebelled against the recognition of the truth embodied in the myth of the Moerae, and constructed instead the myth derived from it, in which the Goddess of Death was replaced by the Goddess of Love and by what was equivalent to her in human shape. The third of the sisters was no longer Death; she was the fairest, best, most desirable and most lovable of women. Nor was this substitution in any way technically difficult: it was prepared for by an ancient ambivalence, it was carried out along a primaeval line of connection which could not long have been forgotten. The Goddess of Love herself, who now took the place of the Goddess of Death, had once been identical with her. Even the Greek Aphrodite had not wholly relinquished her connection with the underworld, although she had long surrendered her chthonic role to other divine figures, to Persephone, or to the tri-form Artemis-Hecate. The great mother-goddesses of the oriental peoples, however, all seem to have been both creators and destroyers – both goddesses of life and fertility and goddesses of death. Thus the replacement by a wishful opposite in our theme harks back to a primaeval identity.

The same consideration answers the question how the feature

1. [Cf. *The Interpretation of Dreams* (1900a), *P.F.L.*, **4**, 429–30.]

of a choice came into the myth of the three sisters. Here again there has been a wishful reversal. Choice stands in the place of necessity, of destiny. In this way man overcomes death, which he has recognized intellectually. No greater triumph of wish-fulfilment is conceivable. A choice is made where in reality there is obedience to a compulsion; and what is chosen is not a figure of terror, but the fairest and most desirable of women.

On closer inspection we observe, to be sure, that the original myth is not so thoroughly distorted that traces of it do not show through and betray its presence. The free choice between the three sisters is, properly speaking, no free choice, for it must necessarily fall on the third if every kind of evil is not to come about, as it does in *King Lear*. The fairest and best of women, who has taken the place of the Death-goddess, has kept certain characteristics that border on the uncanny, so that from them we have been able to guess at what lies beneath.[1]

So far we have been following out the myth and its trans-formation, and it is to be hoped that we have correctly indicated the hidden causes of the transformation. We may now turn our interest to the way in which the dramatist has made use of the theme. We get an impression that a reduction of the theme to the original myth is being carried out in his work, so that we once more have a sense of the moving significance which had been weakened by the distortion. It is by means of this reduction of the distortion, this partial return to the

1. The Psyche of Apuleius's story has kept many traits that remind us of her relation with death. Her wedding is celebrated like a funeral, she has to descend into the underworld, and afterwards she sinks into a death-like sleep (Otto Rank). – On the significance of Psyche as goddess of the spring and as 'Bride of Death', cf. Zinzow (1881). – In another of Grimms' Tales ('The Goose-girl at the Fountain' ['Die Gänsehirtin am Brunnen', 1918, 2, 300], No. 179) there is, as in 'Cinderella', an alternation between the beautiful and the ugly aspect of the third sister, in which one may no doubt see an indication of her double nature – before and after the substitution. This third daughter is repudiated by her father, after a test which is almost the same as the one in *King Lear*. Like her sisters, she has to declare how fond she is of their father, but can find no expression for her love but a comparison with salt. (Kindly communicated by Dr Hanns Sachs.)

original, that the dramatist achieves his more profound effect upon us.

To avoid misunderstandings, I should like to say that it is not my purpose to deny that King Lear's dramatic story is intended to inculcate two wise lessons: that one should not give up one's possessions and rights during one's lifetime, and that one must guard against accepting flattery at its face value. These and similar warnings are undoubtedly brought out by the play; but it seems to me quite impossible to explain the overpowering effect of *King Lear* from the impression that such a train of thought would produce, or to suppose that the dramatist's personal motives did not go beyond the intention of teaching these lessons. It is suggested, too, that his purpose was to present the tragedy of ingratitude, the sting of which he may well have felt in his own heart, and that the effect of the play rests on the purely formal element of its artistic presentation; but this cannot, so it seems to me, take the place of the understanding brought to us by the explanation we have reached of the theme of the choice between the three sisters.

Lear is an old man. It is for this reason, as we have already said, that the three sisters appear as his daughters. The relationship of a father to his children, which might be a fruitful source of many dramatic situations, is not turned to further account in the play. But Lear is not only an old man: he is a dying man. In this way the extraordinary premiss of the division of his inheritance loses all its strangeness. But the doomed man is not willing to renounce the love of women; he insists on hearing how much he is loved. Let us now recall the moving final scene, one of the culminating points of tragedy in modern drama. Lear carries Cordelia's dead body on to the stage. Cordelia is Death. If we reverse the situation it becomes intelligible and familiar to us. She is the Death-goddess who, like the Valkyrie in German mythology, carries away the dead hero from the battlefield. Eternal wisdom, clothed in the primaeval myth, bids the old man renounce love, choose death and make friends with the necessity of dying.

The dramatist brings us nearer to the ancient theme by representing the man who makes the choice between the three sisters as aged and dying. The regressive revision which he has thus applied to the myth, distorted as it was by wishful transformation, allows us enough glimpses of its original meaning to enable us perhaps to reach as well a superficial allegorical interpretation of the three female figures in the theme. We might argue that what is represented here are the three inevitable relations that a man has with a woman – the woman who bears him, the woman who is his mate and the woman who destroys him; or that they are the three forms taken by the figure of the mother in the course of a man's life – the mother herself, the beloved one who is chosen after her pattern, and lastly the Mother Earth who receives him once more. But it is in vain that an old man yearns for the love of woman as he had it first from his mother; the third of the Fates alone, the silent Goddess of Death, will take him into her arms.

THE MOSES OF MICHELANGELO
(1914)

DER MOSES DES MICHELANGELO

(A) German Editions:

1914   *Imago*, **3** (1), 15–36.
1924   *Dichtung und Kunst*, 29–58.
1946   *Gesammelte Werke*, **10**, 172–201.

'Nachtrag zur Arbeit über den Moses des
Michelangelo'

1927   *Imago*, **13** (4), 552–3.
1948   *Gesammelte Werke*, **14**, 321–2.

(B) English Translations:

'The Moses of Michelangelo'

1925   *Collected Papers*, **4**, 257–87. (Tr. Alix Strachey.)
1955   *Standard Edition*, **13**, 209–36. (Corrected version of
above.)

'Postscript to my Paper on the Moses of Michelangelo'

1951   *International Journal of Psycho-Analysis*, **32**, 94. (Tr. Alix
Strachey.)
1955   *Standard Edition*, **13**, 237–8. (Corrected version of
above.)

The present edition is a reprint of the *Standard Edition* version,
with a few editorial changes.

Freud's interest in Michelangelo's statue was of old standing.
He went to see it on the fourth day of his very first visit to
Rome in September 1901, as well as on many later occasions.

He was already planning the present paper in 1912, and on 25 September he wrote from Rome to his wife: 'I ... pay a visit every day to the Moses in S. Pietro in Vincoli, about which I may perhaps write a few words' (Freud, 1960a). But it was not written until the autumn of 1913. Many years later, referring to the paper in a letter of 12 April 1933 to Edoardo Weiss, Freud wrote: 'Every day for three lonely weeks of September 1913 [a slip for 1912], I stood in the church in front of the statue, studying it, measuring it and drawing it until there dawned on me that understanding which I expressed in my essay, though I only dared to do so anonymously. It was only much later that I legitimized this non-analytical child' (Freud, 1970a). An account of his long hesitation over publishing the essay, and of his final decision to do so anonymously, is given in Jones's biography (Jones, 1955, 410).

Freud's preoccupation with the historical Moses is, of course, well known from the last work that he published in his lifetime: *Moses and Monotheism* (1939a), *P.F.L.*, **13**, 237 ff.

THE MOSES OF MICHELANGELO[1]

I MAY say at once that I am no connoisseur in art, but simply a layman. I have often observed that the subject-matter of works of art has a stronger attraction for me than their formal and technical qualities, though to the artist their value lies first and foremost in these latter. I am unable rightly to appreciate many of the methods used and the effect obtained in art. I state this so as to secure the reader's indulgence for the attempt I propose to make here.

Nevertheless, works of art do exercise a powerful effect on me, especially those of literature and sculpture, less often of painting. This has occasioned me, when I have been contemplating such things, to spend a long time before them trying to apprehend them in my own way, i.e. to explain to myself what their effect is due to. Wherever I cannot do this, as for instance with music, I am almost incapable of obtaining any pleasure. Some rationalistic, or perhaps analytic, turn of mind in me rebels against being moved by a thing without knowing why I am thus affected and what it is that affects me.

This has brought me to recognize the apparently paradoxical fact that precisely some of the grandest and most overwhelming creations of art are still unsolved riddles to our understanding. We admire them, we feel overawed by them, but we are unable

1. [The following footnote, obviously drafted by Freud himself, was attached to the title when the paper made its first, anonymous, appearance in *Imago*:

'Although this paper does not, strictly speaking, conform to the conditions under which contributions are accepted for publication in this Journal, the editors have decided to print it, since the author, who is personally known to them, moves in psychoanalytic circles, and since his mode of thought has in point of fact a certain resemblance to the methodology of psychoanalysis.']

to say what they represent to us. I am not sufficiently well-read to know whether this fact has already been remarked upon; possibly, indeed, some writer on aesthetics has discovered that this state of intellectual bewilderment is a necessary condition when a work of art is to achieve its greatest effects. It would be only with the greatest reluctance that I could bring myself to believe in any such necessity.

I do not mean that connoisseurs and lovers of art find no words with which to praise such objects to us. They are eloquent enough, it seems to me. But usually in the presence of a great work of art each says something different from the other; and none of them says anything that solves the problem for the unpretending admirer. In my opinion, what grips us so powerfully can only be the artist's intention, in so far as he has succeeded in expressing it in his work and in getting us to understand it. I realize that this cannot be merely a matter of intellectual comprehension; what he aims at is to awaken in us the same emotional attitude, the same mental constellation as that which in him produced the impetus to create. But why should the artist's intention not be capable of being communicated and comprehended in words, like any other fact of mental life? Perhaps where great works of art are concerned this would never be possible without the application of psychoanalysis. The product itself after all must admit of such an analysis, if it really is an effective expression of the intentions and emotional activities of the artist. To discover his intention, though, I must first find out the meaning and content of what is represented in his work; I must, in other words, be able to *interpret* it. It is possible, therefore, that a work of art of this kind needs interpretation, and that until I have accomplished that interpretation I cannot come to know why I have been so powerfully affected. I even venture to hope that the effect of the work will undergo no diminution after we have succeeded in thus analysing it.

Let us consider Shakespeare's masterpiece, *Hamlet*, a play now over three centuries old.[1] I have followed the literature of

1. Perhaps first performed in 1602.

psychoanalysis closely, and I accept its claim that it was not until the material of the tragedy had been traced back by psychoanalysis to the Oedipus theme that the mystery of its effect was at last explained. [Cf. *The Interpretation of Dreams*, *P.F.L.*, **4**, 366–8.] But before this was done, what a mass of differing and contradictory interpretative attempts, what a variety of opinions about the hero's character and the dramatist's intentions! Does Shakespeare claim our sympathies on behalf of a sick man, or of an ineffectual weakling, or of an idealist who is merely too good for the real world? And how many of these interpretations leave us cold! – so cold that they do nothing to explain the effect of the play and rather incline us to the view that its magical appeal rests solely upon the impressive thoughts in it and the splendour of its language. And yet, do not those very endeavours speak for the fact that we feel the need of discovering in it some source of power beyond them alone?

Another of these inscrutable and wonderful works of art is the marble statue of Moses, by Michelangelo, in the Church of San Pietro in Vincoli in Rome. As we know, it was only a fragment of the gigantic tomb which the artist was to have erected for the powerful Pope Julius II.[1] It always delights me to read an appreciative sentence about this statue, such as that it is 'the crown of modern sculpture' (Grimm [1900, 189]). For no piece of statuary has ever made a stronger impression on me than this. How often have I mounted the steep steps from the unlovely Corso Cavour to the lonely piazza where the deserted church stands, and have essayed to support the angry scorn of the hero's glance! Sometimes I have crept cautiously out of the half-gloom of the interior as though I myself belonged to the mob upon whom his eye is turned – the mob which can hold fast no conviction, which has neither faith nor patience, and which rejoices when it has regained its illusory idols.

But why do I call this statue inscrutable? There is not the

1. According to Henry Thode [1908, 194], the statue was made between the years 1512 and 1516.

slightest doubt that it represents Moses, the Law-giver of the Jews, holding the Tables of the Ten Commandments. That much is certain, but that is all. As recently as 1912 an art critic, Max Sauerlandt, has said, 'No other work of art in the world has been judged so diversely as the Moses with the head of Pan. The mere interpretation of the figure has given rise to completely opposed views. . . .' Basing myself on an essay published only five years ago,[1] I will first set out the doubts which are associated with this figure of Moses; and it will not be difficult to show that behind them lies concealed all that is most essential and valuable for the comprehension of this work of art.

I

The Moses of Michelangelo is represented as seated; his body faces forward, his head with its mighty beard looks to the left, his right foot rests on the ground and his left leg is raised so that only the toes touch the ground. His right arm links the Tables of the Law with a portion of his beard; his left arm lies in his lap. [See Plate 4.] Were I to give a more detailed description of his attitude, I should have to anticipate what I want to say later on. The descriptions of the figure given by various writers are, by the way, curiously inapt. What has not been understood has been inaccurately perceived or reproduced. Grimm [1900, 189] says that the right hand, 'under whose arm the Tables rest, grasps his beard'. So also Lübke [1863, 666]: 'Profoundly shaken, he grasps with his right hand his magnificent, flowing beard . . .'; and Springer [1895, 33]: 'Moses presses one (the left) hand against his body, and thrusts the other, as though unconsciously, into the mighty locks of his beard.' Justi [1900, 326] thinks that the fingers of his (right) hand are playing with his beard, 'as an agitated man nowadays might play with his watch-chain.' Müntz [1895, 391 *n*.], too, lays stress on this playing with the beard. Thode [1908, 205] speaks of the 'calm, firm posture of the right hand upon the

1. Thode (1908).

Plate 1.   Bas–relief of 'Gradiva'.
(*Vatican Museum, Rome*)

Plate 2.   Leonardo's 'Mona Lisa'.
(*Louvre, Paris*)

Plate 3.   Leonardo's 'Madonna and Child with St Anne'.
(*Louvre, Paris*)

Plate 4.   The 'Moses' of Michelangelo.
(*San Pietro in Vincoli, Rome*)

Plate 5. Detail from the 'Moses' of Michelangelo

Plate 6. Statuette of Moses, attributed to Nicholas of Verdun, twelfth century.
(*Ashmolean Museum, Oxford*)

Plate 7.   The first appearance of the Devil to Christoph Haizmann.
(*Österreichische Nationalbibliothek, Vienna*)

Plate 8.   The second appearance of the Devil to Christoph Haizmann.
(*Österreichische Nationalbibliothek, Vienna*)

Tables resting against his side'. He does not recognize any sign of excitement even in the right hand, as Justi and also Boito [1883] do. 'The hand remains grasping his beard, in the position it was in before the Titan turned his head to one side.' Jakob Burckhardt [1927, 634] complains that 'the celebrated left arm has no other function in reality than to press his beard to his body'.

If mere descriptions do not agree we shall not be surprised to find a divergence of view as to the meaning of various features of the statue. In my opinion we cannot better characterize the facial expression of Moses than in the words of Thode [1908, 205], who reads in it 'a mixture of wrath, pain and contempt', – 'wrath in his threatening contracted brows, pain in his glance, and contempt in his protruded under-lip and in the down-drawn corners of his mouth'. But other admirers must have seen with other eyes. Thus Dupaty says, 'His august brow seems to be but a transparent veil only half concealing his great mind'.[1] Lübke [1863, 666–7], on the other hand, declares that 'one would look in vain in that head for an expression of higher intelligence; his down-drawn brow speaks of nothing but a capacity for infinite wrath and an all-compelling energy'. Guillaume (1876 [96]) differs still more widely in his interpretation of the expression of the face. He finds no emotion in it 'only a proud simplicity, an inspired dignity, a living faith. The eye of Moses looks into the future, he foresees the lasting survival of his people, the immutability of his law.' Similarly, to Müntz [1895, 391], 'the eyes of Moses rove far beyond the race of men. They are turned towards those mysteries which he alone has descried.' To Steinmann [1899, 169], indeed, this Moses is 'no longer the stern Law-giver, no longer the terrible enemy of sin, armed with the wrath of Jehovah, but the royal priest, whom age may not approach, beneficent and prophetic, with the reflection of eternity upon his brow, taking his last farewell of his people'.

There have even been some for whom the Moses of Michel-angelo had nothing at all to say, and who are honest enough

1. Quoted by Thode, ibid., 197.

to admit it. Thus a critic in the *Quarterly Review* of 1858 [103, 469]: 'There is an absence of meaning in the general conception, which precludes the idea of a self-sufficing whole ...' And we are astonished to learn that there are yet others who find nothing to admire in the Moses, but who revolt against it and complain of the brutality of the figure and the animal cast of the head.

Has then the master-hand indeed traced such a vague or ambiguous script in the stone that so many different readings of it are possible?

Another question, however, arises, which covers the first one. Did Michelangelo intend to create a 'timeless study of character and mood' in this Moses, or did he portray him at a particular moment of his life and, if so, at a highly significant one? The majority of judges have decided in the latter sense and are able to tell us what episode in his life it is which the artist has immortalized in stone. It is the descent from Mount Sinai, where Moses has received the Tables from God, and it is the moment when he perceives that the people have meanwhile made themselves a Golden Calf and are dancing around it and are rejoicing. This is the scene upon which his eyes are turned, this is the spectacle which calls out the feelings depicted in his countenance – feelings which in the next instant will launch his great frame into violent action. Michelangelo has chosen this last moment of hesitation, of calm before the storm, for his representation. In the next instant Moses will spring to his feet – his left foot is already raised from the ground – dash the Tables to the earth, and let loose his rage upon his faithless people.

Once more many individual differences of opinion exist among those who support this interpretation.

Burckhardt [1927, 634] writes: 'Moses seems to be shown at that moment at which he catches sight of the worship of the Golden Calf, and is springing to his feet. His form is animated by the inception of a mighty movement and the physical strength with which he is endowed causes us to await it with fear and trembling.'

Lübke [1863, 666] says: 'It is as if at this moment his flashing eye were perceiving the sin of the worship of the Golden Calf and a mighty inward movement were running through his whole frame. Profoundly shaken, he grasps with his right hand his magnificent, flowing beard, as though to master his actions for one instant longer, only for the explosion of his wrath to burst out with more shattering force the next.'

Springer [1895, 33] agrees with this view, but not without mentioning one misgiving, which will engage our attention later in this paper. He says, 'Burning with energy and zeal, it is with difficulty that the hero subdues his inward emotion … We are thus involuntarily reminded of a dramatic situation and are brought to believe that Moses is represented at the moment at which he sees the people of Israel worshipping the Golden Calf and is about to start up in wrath. Such an impression, it is true, is not easy to reconcile with the artist's real intention, since the figure of Moses, like the other five seated figures on the upper part of the Papal tomb, is meant primarily to have a decorative effect. But it testifies very convincingly to the vitality and individuality portrayed in the figure of Moses.'

One or two writers, without actually accepting the Golden Calf theory, do nevertheless agree on its main point, namely, that Moses is just about to spring to his feet and take action.

According to Grimm [1900, 189], 'The form' (of Moses) 'is filled with a majesty, a self-assurance, a feeling that all the thunders of heaven are at his command, and that yet he is holding himself in check before loosing them, waiting to see whether the foes whom he means to annihilate will dare to attack him. He sits there as if on the point of starting to his feet, his proud head carried high on his shoulders; the hand under whose arm the Tables rest grasps his beard, which falls in heavy waves over his breast, his nostrils distended and his lips shaped as though words were trembling upon them.'

Heath Wilson [1876, 450] declares that Moses' attention has been excited, and he is about to leap to his feet, but is still hesitating; and that his glance of mingled scorn and indignation is still capable of changing into one of compassion.

Wölfflin [1899, 72] speaks of 'inhibited movement'. The cause of this inhibition, he says, lies in the will of the man himself; it is the last moment of self-control before he lets himself go and leaps to his feet.

Justi [1900, 326–7] has gone the furthest of all in his interpretation of the statue as Moses in the act of perceiving the Golden Calf, and he has pointed out details hitherto unobserved in it and worked them into his hypothesis. He directs our attention to the position of the two Tables – an unusual one, for they are about to slip down on to the stone seat. 'He' (Moses) 'might therefore be looking in the direction from which the clamour was coming with an expression of evil foreboding, or it might be the actual sight of the abomination which has dealt him a stunning blow. Quivering with horror and pain he has sunk down.[1] He has sojourned on the mountain forty days and nights and he is weary. A horror, a great turn of fortune, a crime, even happiness itself, can be perceived in a single moment, but not grasped in its essence, its depths or its consequences. For an instant it seems to Moses that his work is destroyed and he despairs utterly of his people. In such moments the inner emotions betray themselves involuntarily in small movements. He lets the Tables slip from his right hand on to the stone seat; they have come to rest on their corner there and are pressed by his forearm against the side of his body. His hand, however, comes in contact with his breast and beard and thus, by the turning of the head to the spectator's right, it draws the beard to the left and breaks the symmetry of that masculine adornment. It looks as though his fingers were playing with his beard as an agitated man nowadays might play with his watch-chain. His left hand is buried in his garment over the lower part of his body – in the Old Testament the viscera are the seat of the emotions – but the left leg is already drawn back and the right put forward; in the next instant he

1. It should be remarked that the careful arrangement of the mantle over the knees of the sitting figure invalidates this first part of Justi's view. On the contrary, this would lead us to suppose that Moses is represented as sitting there in calm repose until he is startled by some sudden perception.

will leap up, his mental energy will be transposed from feeling into action, his right arm will move, the Tables will fall to the ground, and the shameful trespass will be expiated in torrents of blood ...' 'This is not yet the moment of tension of an act. Pain of mind still dominates him and almost paralyses him.'

Knapp [1906, xxxii] takes the same view, except that he does not introduce the doubtful point at the beginning of the description,[1] and carries the idea of the slipping Tables further. 'He who just now was alone with his God is distracted by earthly sounds. He hears a noise; the noise of singing and dancing wakes him from his dream; he turns his eyes and his head in the direction of the clamour. In one instant fear, rage and unbridled passion traverse his huge frame. The Tables begin to slip down, and will fall to the ground and break when he leaps to his feet and hurls the angry thunder of his words into the midst of his backsliding people ... This is the moment of highest tension which is chosen ...' Knapp, therefore, emphasizes the element of preparation for action, and disagrees with the view that what is being represented is an initial inhibition due to an overmastering agitation.

It cannot be denied that there is something extraordinarily attractive about attempts at an interpretation of the kind made by Justi and Knapp. This is because they do not stop short at the general effect of the figure, but are based on separate features in it; these we usually fail to notice, being overcome by the total impression of the statue and as it were paralysed by it. The marked turn of the head and eyes to the left, whereas the body faces forwards, supports the view that the resting Moses has suddenly seen something on that side to rivet his attention. His lifted foot can hardly mean anything else but that he is preparing to spring up;[2] and the very unusual way in which the Tables are held (for they are most sacred objects and are not to be brought into the composition like any

1. [Cf. previous note.]

2. Although the left foot of the reposeful seated figure of Giuliano in the Medici Chapel is similarly raised from the ground.

ordinary accessory) is fully accounted for if we suppose they have slipped down as a result of the agitation of their bearer and will fall to the ground. According to this view we should believe that the statue represents a special and important moment in the life of Moses, and we should be left in no doubt of what that moment is.

But two remarks of Thode's deprive us of the knowledge we thought to have gained. This critic says that to his eye the Tables are not slipping down but are 'firmly lodged'. He notes the 'calm, firm pose of the right hand upon the resting Tables'. If we look for ourselves we cannot but admit unreservedly that Thode is right. The Tables are firmly placed and in no danger of slipping. Moses' right hand supports them or is supported by them. This does not explain the position in which they are held, it is true, but that position cannot be used in favour of the interpretation of Justi and others. [Thode (1908), 205.]

The second observation is still more final. Thode reminds us that 'this statue was planned as one of six, and is intended to be seated. Both facts contradict the view that Michelangelo meant to record a particular historical moment. For, as regards the first consideration, the plan of representing a row of seated figures as types of human beings – as the *vita activa* and the *vita contemplativa* – excluded a representation of a particular historic episode. And, as regards the second, the representation of a seated posture – a posture necessitated by the artistic conception of the whole monument – contradicts the nature of that episode, namely, the descent of Moses from Mount Sinai into the camp.'

If we accept Thode's objection we shall find that we can add to its weight. The figure of Moses was to have decorated the base of the tomb together with five other statues (or according to a later sketch, with three). Its immediate counterpart was to have been a figure of Paul. One other pair, representing the *vita activa* and the *vita contemplativa* in the shape of Leah and Rachel – standing, it is true – has been executed on the tomb as it still exists in its sadly aborted form. The

Moses thus forms part of a whole and we cannot imagine that the figure was meant to arouse an expectation in the spectator that it was on the point of leaping up from its seat and rushing away to create a disturbance on its own account. If the other figures were not also represented as about to take violent action – and it seems very improbable that they were – then it would create a very bad impression for one of them to give us the illusion that it was going to leave its place and its companions, in fact to abandon its role in the general scheme. Such an intention would have a chaotic effect and we could not charge a great artist with it unless the facts drove us to it. A figure in the act of instant departure would be utterly at variance with the state of mind which the tomb is meant to induce in us.

The figure of Moses, therefore, cannot be supposed to be springing to his feet; he must be allowed to remain as he is in sublime repose like the other figures and like the proposed statue of the Pope (which was not, however, executed by Michelangelo himself). But then the statue we see before us cannot be that of a man filled with wrath, of Moses when he came down from Mount Sinai and found his people faithless and threw down the Holy Tables so that they were broken. And, indeed, I can recollect my own disillusionment when, during my first visits to San Pietro in Vincoli, I used to sit down in front of the statue in the expectation that I should now see how it would start up on its raised foot, dash the Tables of the Law to the ground and let fly its wrath. Nothing of the kind happened. Instead, the stone image became more and more transfixed, an almost oppressively solemn calm emanated from it, and I was obliged to realize that something was represented here that could stay without change; that this Moses would remain sitting like this in his wrath for ever.

But if we have to abandon our interpretation of the statue as showing Moses just before his outburst of wrath at the sight of the Golden Calf, we have no alternative but to accept one of the hypotheses which regard it as a study of character. Thode's view seems to be the least arbitrary and to have the closest reference to the meaning of its movements. He says, 'Here, as always, he [Michelangelo] is concerned with representing a certain type of character. He creates the image of a passionate leader of mankind who, conscious of his divine mission as Law-giver, meets the uncomprehending opposition of men. The only means of representing a man of action of this kind was to accentuate the power of his will, and this was done by a rendering of movement pervading the whole of his apparent quiet, as we see in the turn of his head, the tension of his muscles and the position of his left foot. These are the same distinguishing marks that we find again in the *vir activus* of the Medici Chapel in Florence. This general character of the figure is further heightened by laying stress on the conflict which is bound to arise between such a reforming genius and the rest of mankind. Emotions of anger, contempt and pain are typified in him. Without them it would not have been possible to portray the nature of a superman of this kind. Michelangelo has created, not a historical figure, but a character-type, embodying an inexhaustible inner force which tames the recalcitrant world; and he has given a form not only to the Biblical narrative of Moses, but to his own inner experiences, and to his impressions both of the individuality of Julius himself, and also, I believe, of the underlying springs of Savonarola's perpetual conflicts.' [1908, 206.]

This view may be brought into connection with Knackfuss's remark [1900, 69] that the great secret of the effect produced by the Moses lies in the artistic contrast between the inward fire and the outward calm of his bearing.

For myself, I see nothing to object to in Thode's explanation; but I feel the lack of something in it. Perhaps it is the need to discover a closer parallel between the state of mind of the hero as expressed in his attitude, and the contrast above-mentioned between his 'outward' calm and 'inward' emotion.

II

Long before I had any opportunity of hearing about psycho-analysis, I learnt that a Russian art connoisseur, Ivan Lermo-lieff,[1] had caused a revolution in the art galleries of Europe by questioning the authorship of many pictures, showing how to distinguish copies from originals with certainty, and con-structing hypothetical artists for those works whose former supposed authorship had been discredited. He achieved this by insisting that attention should be diverted from the general impression and main features of a picture, and by laying stress on the significance of minor details, of things like the drawing of the fingernails, of the lobe of an ear, of halos and such un-considered trifles which the copyist neglects to imitate and yet which every artist executes in his own characteristic way. I was then greatly interested to learn that the Russian pseudonym concealed the identity of an Italian physician called Morelli, who died in 1891 with the rank of Senator of the Kingdom of Italy. It seems to me that his method of inquiry is closely related to the technique of psychoanalysis. It, too, is accustomed to divine secret and concealed things from despised or un-noticed features, from the rubbish-heap, as it were, of our observations.

Now in two places in the figure of Moses there are certain details which have hitherto not only escaped notice but, in fact, have not even been properly described. These are the attitude of his right hand and the position of the two Tables of the Law. We may say that this hand forms a very singular, un-natural link, and one which calls for explanation, between the Tables and the wrathful hero's beard. He has been described as running his fingers through his beard and playing with its locks, while the outer edge of his hand rests on the Tables. But this is plainly not so. It is worth while examining more closely what those fingers of the right hand are doing, and describing more minutely the mighty beard with which they are in contact. [Cf. Plate 5.]

1. His first essays were published in German between 1874 and 1876.

We now quite clearly perceive the following things: the thumb of the hand is concealed and the index finger alone is in effective contact with the beard. It is pressed so deeply against the soft masses of hair that they bulge out beyond it both above and below, that is, both towards the head and towards the abdomen. The other three fingers are propped upon the wall of his chest and are bent at the upper joints; they are barely touched by the extreme right-hand lock of the beard which falls past them. They have, as it were, withdrawn from the beard. It is therefore not correct to say that the right hand is playing with the beard or plunged in it; the simple truth is that the index finger is laid over part of the beard and makes a deep trough in it. It cannot be denied that to press one's beard with one finger is an extraordinary gesture and one not easy to understand.

The much-admired beard of Moses flows from his cheeks, chin and upper lip in a number of waving strands which are kept distinct from one another all the way down. One of the strands on his extreme right, growing from the cheek, falls down to the inward-pressing index finger, by which it is retained. We may assume that it resumes its course between that finger and the concealed thumb. The corresponding strand on his left side falls practically unimpeded far down over his breast. What has received the most unusual treatment is the thick mass of hair on the inside of this latter strand, the part between it and the middle line. It is not suffered to follow the turn of the head to the left; it is forced to roll over loosely and form part of a kind of scroll which lies across and over the strands on the inner right side of the beard. This is because it is held fast by the pressure of the right index finger, although it grows from the left side of the face and is, in fact, the main portion of the whole left side of the beard. Thus, the main mass of the beard is thrown to the right of the figure, whereas the head is sharply turned to the left. At the place where the right index finger is pressed in, a kind of whorl of hairs is formed; strands of hair coming from the left lie over strands coming from the right, both caught in by that despotic finger.

It is only beyond this place that the masses of hair, deflected from their course, flow freely once more, and now they fall vertically until their ends are gathered up in Moses' left hand as it lies open on his lap.

I have no illusions as to the clarity of my description, and venture no opinion whether the sculptor really does invite us to solve the riddle of that knot in the beard of his statue. But apart from this, the fact remains that the pressure of the *right* index finger affects mainly the strands of hair from the *left* side; and that this oblique hold prevents the beard from accompanying the turn of the head and eyes to the left. Now we may be allowed to ask what this arrangement means and to what motives it owes its existence. If it was indeed considerations of linear and spatial design which caused the sculptor to draw the downward-streaming wealth of hair across to the right of the figure which is looking to its left, how strangely unsuitable as a means does the pressure of a single finger appear to be! And what man who, for some reason or other, has drawn his beard over to the other side, would take it into his head to hold down the one half across the other by the pressure of one finger? Yet may not these minute particulars mean nothing in reality, and may we not be racking our brains about things which were of no moment to their creator?

But let us proceed on the assumption that even these details have significance. There is a solution which will remove our difficulties and afford a glimpse of a new meaning. If the *left* side of Moses' beard lies under the pressure of his *right* finger, we may perhaps take this pose as the last stage of some connection between his right hand and the left half of his beard, a connection which was a much more intimate one at some moment before that chosen for representation. Perhaps his hand had seized his beard with far more energy, had reached across to its left edge, and, in returning to that position in which the statue shows it, had been followed by a part of his beard which now testifies to the movement which has just taken place. The loop of the beard would thus be an indication of the path taken by this hand.

Thus we shall have inferred that there had been a retreating motion of the right hand. This one assumption necessarily brings others with it. In imagination we complete the scene of which this movement, established by the evidence of the beard, is a part; and we are brought back quite naturally to the hypothesis according to which the resting Moses is startled by the clamour of the people and the spectacle of the Golden Calf. He was sitting there calmly, we will suppose, his head with its flowing beard facing forward, and his hand in all probability not near it at all. Suddenly the clamour strikes his ear; he turns his head and eyes in the direction from which the disturbance comes, sees the scene and takes it in. Now wrath and indignation lay hold of him; and he would fain leap up and punish the wrongdoers, annihilate them. His rage, distant as yet from its object, is meanwhile directed in a gesture against his own body. His impatient hand, ready to act, clutches at his beard which has moved with the turn of his head, and presses it between his thumb and palm in the iron grasp of his closing fingers. It is a gesture whose power and vehemence remind us of other creations of Michelangelo's. But now an alteration takes place, as yet we do not know how or why. The hand that had been put forward and had sunk into his beard is hastily withdrawn and unclasped, and the fingers let go their hold; but so deeply have they been plunged in that in their withdrawal they drag a great piece of the left side of the beard across to the right, and this piece remains lodged over the hair of the right under the weight of one finger, the longest and uppermost one of the hand. And this new position, which can only be understood with reference to the former one, is now retained.

It is time now to pause and reflect. We have assumed that the right hand was, to begin with, away from the beard; that then it reached across to the left of the figure in a moment of great emotional tension and seized the beard; and that it was finally drawn back again, taking a part of the beard with it. We have disposed of this right hand as though we had the free use of it. But may we do this? Is the hand indeed so free?

Must it not hold or support the Tables? Are not such mimetic evolutions as these prohibited by its important function? And furthermore, what could have occasioned its withdrawal if the motive which made it leave its original position was such a strong one?

Here are indeed fresh difficulties. It is undeniable that the right hand is responsible for the Tables; and also that we have no motive to account for the withdrawal we have ascribed to it. But what if both difficulties could be solved together, and if then and then only they presented a clear and connected sequence of events? What if it is precisely something which is happening to the Tables that explains the movements of the hand?

If we look at the drawing in Fig. 7 we shall see that the Tables present one or two notable features hitherto not deemed worthy of remark. It has been said that the right hand rests upon the Tables; or again that it supports them. And we can

FIG. 4   FIG. 5

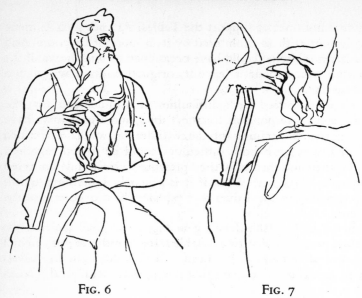

FIG. 6   FIG. 7

see at once that the two apposed, rectangular tablets stand on one corner. If we look closer we shall notice that the lower edge is a different shape from the upper one, which is obliquely inclined forward. The upper edge is straight, whereas the lower one has a protuberance like a horn on the part nearest to us, and the Tables touch the stone seat precisely with this protuberance. What can be the meaning of this detail?[1] It can hardly be doubted that this projection is meant to mark the actual top side of the Tables, as regards the writing. It is only the top edge of rectangular tablets of this kind that is curved or notched. Thus we see that the Tables are upside-down. This is a singular way to treat such sacred objects. They are stood on their heads and practically balanced on one corner. What consideration of form could have led Michelangelo to put them in such a position? Or was this detail as well of no importance to the artist?

1. Which, by the way, is quite incorrectly reproduced in a larger plaster cast in the collection of the Vienna Academy of Fine Arts.

We begin to suspect that the Tables too have arrived at their present position.as the result of a previous movement; that this movement was a consequence of the change of place of the right hand that we have postulated, and in its turn compelled that hand to make its subsequent retreat. The movements of the hand and of the Tables can be co-ordinated in this way: at first the figure of Moses, while it was still sitting quietly, carried the Tables perpendicularly under its right arm. Its right hand grasped their lower edge and found a hold in the projection on their front part. (The fact that this made them easier to carry sufficiently accounts for the upside-down position in which the Tables were held.) Then came the moment when Moses' calm was broken by the disturbance. He turned his head in its direction, and when he saw the spectacle he lifted his foot preparatory to starting up, let go the Tables with his hand and plunged it to the left and upwards into his beard, as though to turn his violence against his own body. The Tables were now consigned to the pressure of his arm, which had to squeeze them against his side. But this support was not sufficient and the Tables began to slip in a forward and downward direction. The upper edge, which had been held horizontally, now began to face forwards and downwards; and the lower edge, deprived of its stay, was nearing the stone seat with its front corner. Another instant and the Tables would have pivoted upon this new point of support, have hit the ground with the upper edge foremost, and been shattered to pieces. It is *to prevent this* that the right hand retreated, let go the beard, a part of which was drawn back with it unintentionally, came against the upper edge of the Tables in time and held them near the hind corner, which had now come uppermost. Thus the singularly constrained air of the whole – beard, hand and tilted Tables – can be traced to that one passionate movement of the hand and its natural consequences. If we wish to reverse the effects of those stormy movements, we must raise the upper front corner of the Tables and push it back, thus lifting their lower front corner (the one with the protuberance) from the stone seat; and then lower the right hand and bring it under the now horizontal lower edge of the Tables.

I have procured from the hand of an artist three drawings to illustrate my meaning. Fig. 6 reproduces the statue as it actually is; Figs. 4 and 5 represent the preceding stages according to my hypothesis – the first that of calm, the second that of highest tension, in which the figure is preparing to spring up and has abandoned its hold of the Tables, so that these are beginning to slip down. Now it is remarkable how the two postures in the imaginary drawings vindicate the incorrect descriptions of earlier writers. Condivi, a contemporary of Michelangelo's, says: 'Moses, the captain and leader of the Hebrews, is seated in the attitude of a contemplative sage, holding the Tables of the Law under his right arm, and leaning his chin on his left hand(!), as one who is weary and full of care.' No such attitude is to be seen in Michelangelo's statue, but it describes almost exactly the view on which the first drawing is based. Lübke writes, together with other critics: 'Profoundly shaken, he grasps with his right hand his magnificent, flowing beard.' This is incorrect if we look at the reproduction of the actual statue, but it is true of the second sketch (Fig. 5). Justi and Knapp have observed, as we have seen, that the Tables are about to slip down and are in danger of being broken. Thode set them right and showed that the Tables were securely held by the right hand; yet they would have been correct if they had been describing not the statue itself but the middle stage of our reconstructed action. It almost seems as if they had emancipated themselves from the visual image of the statue and had unconsciously begun an analysis of the motive forces behind it, and that that analysis had led them to make the same claim as we have done more consciously and more explicitly.

III

We may now, I believe, permit ourselves to reap the fruits of our endeavours. We have seen how many of those who

have felt the influence of this statue have been impelled to
interpret it as representing Moses agitated by the spectacle of
his people fallen from grace and dancing around an idol. But
this interpretation had to be given up, for it made us expect
to see him spring up in the next moment, break the Tables
and accomplish the work of vengeance. Such a conception,
however, would fail to harmonize with the design of making
this figure, together with three (or five) more seated figures,
a part of the tomb of Julius II. We may now take up again
the abandoned interpretation, for the Moses we have reconstructed will neither leap up nor cast the Tables from him.
What we see before us is not the inception of a violent action
but the remains of a movement that has already taken place.
In his first transport of fury, Moses desired to act, to spring
up and take vengeance and forget the Tables; but he has overcome the temptation, and he will now remain seated and still,
in his frozen wrath and in his pain mingled with contempt.
Nor will he throw away the Tables so that they will break
on the stones, for it is on their especial account that he has
controlled his anger; it was to preserve them that he kept his
passion in check. In giving way to his rage and indignation,
he had to neglect the Tables, and the hand which upheld them
was withdrawn. They began to slide down and were in danger
of being broken. This brought him to himself. He remembered
his mission and for its sake renounced an indulgence of his
feelings. His hand returned and saved the unsupported Tables
before they had actually fallen to the ground. In this attitude
he remained immobilized, and in this attitude Michelangelo
has portrayed him as the guardian of the tomb.

As our eyes travel down it the figure exhibits three distinct
emotional strata. The lines of the face reflect the feelings which
have won the ascendancy; the middle of the figure shows the
traces of suppressed movement; and the foot still retains the
attitude of the projected action. It is as though the controlling
influence had proceeded downwards from above. No mention
has been made so far of the left arm, and it seems to claim
a share in our interpretation. The hand is laid in the lap in

a mild gesture and holds as though in a caress the end of the flowing beard. It seems as if it is meant to counteract the violence with which the other hand had misused the beard a few moments ago.

But here it will be objected that after all this is not the Moses of the Bible. For that Moses did actually fall into a fit of rage and did throw away the Tables and break them. This Moses must be a quite different man, a new Moses of the artist's conception; so that Michelangelo must have had the presumption to emend the sacred text and to falsify the character of that holy man. Can we think him capable of a boldness which might almost be said to approach the act of blasphemy?

The passage in the Holy Scriptures which describes Moses' action at the scene of the Golden Calf is as follows:[1] (*Exodus*, xxxii, 7) 'And the Lord said unto Moses, Go, get thee down; for thy people, which thou broughtest out of the land of Egypt, have corrupted themselves: (8) They have turned aside quickly out of the way which I commanded them: they have made them a molten calf, and have worshipped it, and have sacrificed thereunto, and said, These be thy gods, O Israel, which brought thee up out of the land of Egypt. (9) And the Lord said unto Moses, I have seen this people, and, behold, it is a stiff-necked people: (10) Now therefore let me alone, that my wrath may wax hot against them, and that I may consume them; and I will make of thee a great nation. (11) And Moses besought the Lord his God, and said, Lord, why doth thy wrath wax hot against thy people, which thou hast brought forth out of the land of Egypt with great power, and with a mighty hand? ...

'(14) And the Lord repented of the evil which he thought to do unto his people. (15) And Moses turned, and went down from the mount, and the two tables of the testimony were in his hand: the tables were written on both their sides; on the one side and on the other were they written. (16) And the tables were the work of God, and the writing was the

---

1. [In the original, Freud apologizes for his 'anachronistic use of Luther's translation'. What follows is from the Authorized Version.]

writing of God, graven upon the tables. (17) And when Joshua heard the noise of the people as they shouted, he said unto Moses, There is a noise of war in the camp. (18) And he said, It is not the voice of them that shout for mastery, neither is it the voice of them that cry for being overcome; but the noise of them that sing do I hear. (19) And it came to pass, as soon as he came nigh unto the camp, that he saw the calf, and the dancing: and Moses' anger waxed hot, and he cast the tables out of his hands, and brake them beneath the mount. (20) And he took the calf which they had made, and burnt it in the fire, and ground it to powder, and strawed it upon the water, and made the children of Israel drink of it. . . .

'(30) And it came to pass on the morrow, that Moses said unto the people, Ye have sinned a great sin: and now I will go up unto the Lord; peradventure I shall make an atonement for your sin. (31) And Moses returned unto the Lord, and said, Oh! this people have sinned a great sin, and have made them gods of gold! (32) Yet now, if thou wilt forgive their sin —; and if not, blot me, I pray thee, out of thy book which thou hast written. (33) And the Lord said unto Moses, Whosoever hath sinned against me, him will I blot out of my book. (34) Therefore now go, lead the people unto the place of which I have spoken unto thee. Behold, mine Angel shall go before thee: nevertheless, in the day when I visit, I will visit their sin upon them. (35) And the Lord plagued the people, because they made the calf which Aaron made.'

It is impossible to read the above passage in the light of modern criticism of the Bible without finding evidence that it has been clumsily put together from various sources. In verse 8 the Lord Himself tells Moses that his people have fallen away and made themselves an idol; and Moses intercedes for the wrongdoers. And yet he speaks to Joshua as though he knew nothing of this (18), and is suddenly aroused to wrath as he sees the scene of the worshipping of the Golden Calf (19). In verse 14 he has already gained a pardon from God for his erring people, yet in verse 31 he returns into the mountain to implore this forgiveness, tells God about his people's sin and is assured of the postponement of the punishment. Verse 35 speaks of a visitation of his people by the Lord about which nothing more is told us; whereas the verses 20–30 describe the punishment which Moses himself dealt out. It is well known that the historical parts of the Bible, dealing with the Exodus, are crowded with still more glaring incongruities and contradictions.

The age of the Renaissance had naturally no such critical attitude towards the text of the Bible, but had to accept it as a consistent whole, with the result that the passage in question was not a very good subject for representation. According to the Scriptures Moses was already instructed about the idolatry of his people and had ranged himself on the side of mildness and forgiveness; nevertheless, when he saw the Golden Calf and the dancing crowd, he was overcome by a sudden frenzy of rage. It would therefore not surprise us to find that the artist, in depicting the reaction of his hero to that painful surprise, had deviated from the text from inner motives. Moreover, such deviations from the scriptural text on a much slighter pretext were by no means unusual or disallowed to artists. A celebrated picture by Parmigiano possessed by his native town depicts Moses sitting on the top of a mountain and dashing the Tables to the ground, although the Bible expressly says that he broke them 'beneath the mount'.[1] Even the representation of a seated Moses finds no support in the text and seems rather to bear out those critics who maintain that Michelangelo's statue is not meant to record any particular moment in the prophet's life.

More important than his infidelity to the text of the Scriptures is the alteration which Michelangelo has, in our supposition, made in the character of Moses. The Moses of legend

1. [The picture referred to here is without doubt Parmigianino's monochrome panel on the vaulting of the Chiesa della Steccata in Parma. As Professor Quentin Bell has pointed out, however, close inspection of the picture does not bear out the assumption that Moses is depicted on the top of a mountain. The nine studies for the Moses (cf. Popham, 1953) suggest even more clearly that a generalized architectural setting for the figure was intended.]

and tradition had a hasty temper and was subject to fits of passion. It was in a transport of divine wrath of this kind that he slew an Egyptian who was maltreating an Israelite, and had to flee out of the land into the wilderness; and it was in a similar passion that he broke the Tables of the Law, inscribed by God Himself. Tradition, in recording such a characteristic, is unbiased, and preserves the impression of a great personality who once lived. But Michelangelo has placed a different Moses on the tomb of the Pope, one superior to the historical or traditional Moses. He has modified the theme of the broken Tables; he does not let Moses break them in his wrath, but makes him be influenced by the danger that they will be broken and makes him calm that wrath, or at any rate prevent it from becoming an act. In this way he has added something new and more than human to the figure of Moses; so that the giant frame with its tremendous physical power becomes only a concrete expression of the highest mental achievement that is possible in a man, that of struggling successfully against an inward passion for the sake of a cause to which he has devoted himself.

We have now completed our interpretation of Michelangelo's statue, though it can still be asked what motives prompted the sculptor to select the figure of Moses, and a so greatly altered Moses, as an adornment for the tomb of Julius II. In the opinion of many these motives are to be found in the character of the Pope and in Michelangelo's relations with him. Julius II was akin to Michelangelo in this, that he attempted to realize great and mighty ends, and especially designs on a grand scale. He was a man of action and he had a definite purpose, which was to unite Italy under the Papal supremacy. He desired to bring about single-handed what was not to happen for several centuries, and then only through the conjunction of many alien forces; and he worked alone, with impatience, in the short span of sovereignty allowed him, and used violent means. He could appreciate Michelangelo as a man of his own kind, but he often made him smart under his sudden anger and his utter lack of consideration for others. The artist felt

the same violent force of will in himself, and, as the more intro-
spective thinker, may have had a premonition of the failure
to which they were both doomed. And so he carved his Moses
on the Pope's tomb, not without a reproach against the dead
pontiff, as a warning to himself, thus, in self-criticism, rising
superior to his own nature.

IV

In 1863 an Englishman, Watkiss Lloyd, devoted a little book
to the Moses of Michelangelo. I succeeded in getting hold of
this short essay of forty-six pages, and read it with mixed
feelings. I once more had an opportunity of experiencing in
myself what unworthy and puerile motives enter into our
thoughts and acts even in a serious cause. My first feeling was
one of regret that the author should have anticipated so much
of my thought, which seemed precious to me because it was
the result of my own efforts; and it was only in the second
instance that I was able to get pleasure from its unexpected
confirmation of my opinion. Our views, however, diverge on
one very important point.

Lloyd remarks in the first place that the usual descriptions
of the figure are incorrect, and that Moses is not in the act
of rising[1] – that the right hand is not grasping the beard, but
that the index finger alone is resting upon it.[2] Lloyd also
recognizes, and this is much more important, that the attitude
portrayed can only be explained by postulating a foregoing
one, which is not represented, and that the drawing of the left
lock of the beard across to the right signifies that the right
hand and the left side of the beard have at a previous stage

1. 'But he is not rising or preparing to rise; the bust is fully upright, not
thrown forward for the alteration of balance preparatory for such a movement....' (Lloyd, 1863, 10).

2. 'Such a description is altogether erroneous; the fillets of the beard are
detained by the right hand but they are not held, nor grasped, enclosed or
taken hold of. They are even detained but momentarily – momentarily
engaged, they are on the point of being free for disengagement' (ibid., 11).

been in closer and more natural contact. But he suggests another way of reconstructing the earlier contact which must necessarily be assumed. According to him, it was not the hand which had been plunged into the beard, but the beard which had been where the hand now is. We must, he says, imagine that just before the sudden interruption the head of the statue was turned far round to its right over the hand which, then as now, was holding the Tables of the Law. The pressure (of the Tables) against the palm of the hand caused the fingers to open naturally beneath the flowing locks of the beard, and the sudden turn of the head to the other side resulted in a part of the beard being detained for an instant by the motionless hand and forming the loop of hair which is to be looked on as a mark of the course it has taken – its 'wake', to use Lloyd's own word.

In rejecting the other possibility, that of the right hand having previously been in contact with the left side of the beard, Lloyd has allowed himself to be influenced by a consideration which shows how near he came to our interpretation. He says that it was not possible for the prophet, even in very great agitation, to have put out his hand to draw his beard across to the right. For in that case his fingers would have been in an entirely different position; and, moreover, such a movement would have allowed the Tables to slip down, since they are only supported by the pressure of the right arm – unless, in Moses' endeavour to save them at the last moment, we think of them as being 'clutched by a gesture so awkward that to imagine it is profanation'.

It is easy to see what the writer has overlooked. He has correctly interpreted the anomalies of the beard as indicating a preceding movement, but he has omitted to apply the same explanation to the no less unnatural details in the position of the Tables. He examines only the data connected with the beard and not those connected with the Tables, whose position he assumes to be the original one. In this way he closes the door to a conception like ours which, by examining certain insignificant details, has arrived at an unexpected interpretation of the meaning and aim of the figure as a whole.

But what if both of us have strayed on to a wrong path? What if we have taken too serious and profound a view of details which were nothing to the artist, details which he had introduced quite arbitrarily or for some purely formal reasons with no hidden intention behind? What if we have shared the fate of so many interpreters who have thought they saw quite clearly things which the artist did not intend either consciously or unconsciously? I cannot tell. I cannot say whether it is reasonable to credit Michelangelo – an artist in whose works there is so much thought striving for expression – with such an elementary want of precision, and especially whether this can be assumed in regard to the striking and singular features of the statue under discussion. And finally we may be allowed to point out, in all modesty, that the artist is no less responsible than his interpreters for the obscurity which surrounds his work. In his creations Michelangelo has often enough gone to the utmost limit of what is expressible in art; and perhaps in his statue of Moses he has not completely succeeded, if his purpose was to make the passage of a violent gush of passion visible in the signs left behind it in the ensuing calm.

POSTSCRIPT
(1927)

Several years after the publication of my paper on the Moses of Michelangelo, which appeared anonymously in *Imago* in 1914, Dr Ernest Jones very kindly sent me a copy of the April number of the *Burlington Magazine* of 1921 (Vol. 38), which could not fail to turn my interest once more to the interpretation of the statue which I had originally suggested. This number contains (pp. 157–66) a short article by H. P. Mitchell on two bronzes of the twelfth century, now in the Ashmolean Museum at Oxford, which are attributed to an outstanding artist of that day, Nicholas of Verdun. We possess other works by the same hand in Tournay, Arras and Klosterneuburg, near Vienna; his masterpiece is considered to be the Shrine of the Three Kings in Cologne.

One of the two statuettes described by Mitchell, which is just over 9 inches high, is identifiable beyond all doubt as a Moses, because of the two Tables of the Law which he holds in his hand. This Moses, too, is represented as seated, enveloped in a flowing robe. His face is expressive of strong passion, mixed, perhaps, with grief; and his hand grasps his long beard and presses its strands between palm and thumb as in a vice. He is, that is to say, making the very gesture which I postulated in Fig. 5 of my former paper as a preliminary stage of the attitude into which Michelangelo has cast him.

A glance at the accompanying illustration [Plate 6] will show the main difference between the two compositions, which are separated from each other by an interval of more than three centuries. The Moses of the Lorraine artist is holding the Tables by their top edge with his left hand, resting them on his knee. If we were to transfer them to the other side of his body and put them under his right arm we should have established the preliminary posture of Michelangelo's Moses. If my view of the thrusting of the hand into the beard is right, then the Moses of the year 1180 shows us an instant during his storm of feeling, whilst the statue in San Pietro in Vincoli depicts the calm when the storm is over.

In my opinion this new piece of evidence increases the probability that the interpretation which I attempted in 1914 was a correct one. Perhaps some connoisseur of art will be able to bridge the gulf in time between the Moses of Nicholas of Verdun and the Moses of the Master of the Italian Renaissance by telling us where examples of representations of Moses belonging to the intervening period are to be found.

ON TRANSIENCE
(1916 [1915])

VERGÄNGLICHKEIT

(A) German Editions:

1916   In *Das Land Goethes 1914–1916*. Stuttgart: Deutsche
         Verlagsanstalt.
1926   *Almanach 1927*, 39–42.
1946   *Gesammelte Werke*, **10**, 358–61.

(B) English Translations:

'On Transience'

1942   *International Journal of Psycho-Analysis*, **23** (2), 84–5.
         (Tr. James Strachey.)
1950   *Collected Papers*, **5**, 79–82. (Same translator.)
1957   *Standard Edition*, **14**, 303–7. (Slightly altered reprint of
         above.)

The present edition is a reprint of the *Standard Edition* version.

This essay was written in November 1915 at the invitation of
the Berliner Goethebund (the Berlin Goethe Society) for a
commemorative volume they issued in the following year
under the title of *Das Land Goethes* (Goethe's Country). This
elaborately produced volume included a large number of contributions from well-known writers and artists past and present,
such as von Bülow, von Brentano, Ricarda Huch, Hauptmann
and Liebermann. The German original (apart from the picture
it gives of Freud's feelings about the war, which was then in
its second year) is excellent evidence of his literary powers.
It is of interest to note that the essay includes a statement of

the theory of mourning contained in 'Mourning and Melancholia' (1917*e*; *P.F.L.*, **11**, 251 ff.), which Freud had written some months before, but which was not published until two years later.

ON TRANSIENCE

NOT long ago I went on a summer walk through a smiling countryside in the company of a taciturn friend and of a young but already famous poet.[1] The poet admired the beauty of the scene around us but felt no joy in it. He was disturbed by the thought that all this beauty was fated to extinction, that it would vanish when winter came, like all human beauty and all the beauty and splendour that men have created or may create. All that he would otherwise have loved and admired seemed to him to be shorn of its worth by the transience which was its doom.

The proneness to decay of all that is beautiful and perfect can, as we know, give rise to two different impulses in the mind. The one leads to the aching despondency felt by the young poet, while the other leads to rebellion against the fact asserted. No! it is impossible that all this loveliness of Nature and Art, of the world of our sensations and of the world outside, will really fade away into nothing. It would be too senseless and too presumptuous to believe it. Somehow or other this loveliness must be able to persist and to escape all the powers of destruction.

But this demand for immortality is a product of our wishes too unmistakable to lay claim to reality: what is painful may none the less be true. I could not see my way to dispute the transience of all things, nor could I insist upon an exception in favour of what is beautiful and perfect. But I did dispute the pessimistic poet's view that the transience of what is beautiful involves any loss in its worth.

1. [Freud spent part of August 1913 in the Dolomites, but the identity of his companions cannot be established.]

On the contrary, an increase! Transience value is scarcity value in time. Limitation in the possibility of an enjoyment raises the value of the enjoyment. It was incomprehensible, I declared, that the thought of the transience of beauty should interfere with our joy in it. As regards the beauty of Nature, each time it is destroyed by winter it comes again next year, so that in relation to the length of our lives it can in fact be regarded as eternal. The beauty of the human form and face vanish for ever in the course of our own lives, but their evanescence only lends them a fresh charm. A flower that blossoms only for a single night does not seem to us on that account less lovely. Nor can I understand any better why the beauty and perfection of a work of art or of an intellectual achievement should lose its worth because of its temporal limitation. A time may indeed come when the pictures and statues which we admire to-day will crumble to dust, or a race of men may follow us who no longer understand the works of our poets and thinkers, or a geological epoch may even arrive when all animate life upon the earth ceases; but since the value of all this beauty and perfection is determined only by its significance for our own emotional lives, it has no need to survive us and is therefore independent of absolute duration.

These considerations appeared to me incontestable; but I noticed that I had made no impression either upon the poet or upon my friend. My failure led me to infer that some power-ful emotional factor was at work which was disturbing their judgement, and I believed later that I had discovered what it was. What spoilt their enjoyment of beauty must have been a revolt in their minds against mourning. The idea that all this beauty was transient was giving these two sensitive minds a foretaste of mourning over its decease; and, since the mind instinctively recoils from anything that is painful, they felt their enjoyment of beauty interfered with by thoughts of its transience.

Mourning over the loss of something that we have loved or admired seems so natural to the layman that he regards it as self-evident. But to psychologists mourning is a great riddle, one of those phenomena which cannot themselves be explained but to which other obscurities can be traced back. We possess, as it seems, a certain amount of capacity for love – what we call libido – which in the earliest stages of development is directed towards our own ego. Later, though still at a very early time, this libido is diverted from the ego on to objects, which are thus in a sense taken into our ego. If the objects are destroyed or if they are lost to us, our capacity for love (our libido) is once more liberated; and it can then either take other objects instead or can temporarily return to the ego. But why it is that this detachment of libido from its objects should be such a painful process is a mystery to us and we have not hitherto been able to frame any hypothesis to account for it. We only see that libido clings to its objects and will not renounce those that are lost even when a substitute lies ready to hand. Such then is mourning.

My conversation with the poet took place in the summer before the war. A year later the war broke out and robbed the world of its beauties. It destroyed not only the beauty of the countrysides through which it passed and the works of art which it met with on its path but it also shattered our pride in the achievements of our civilization, our admiration for many philosophers and artists and our hopes of a final triumph over the differences between nations and races. It tarnished the lofty impartiality of our science, it revealed our instincts in all their nakedness and let loose the evil spirits within us which we thought had been tamed for ever by centuries of continuous education by the noblest minds. It made our country small again and made the rest of the world far remote. It robbed us of very much that we had loved, and showed us how ephemeral were many things that we had regarded as change-less.

We cannot be surprised that our libido, thus bereft of so many of its objects, has clung with all the greater intensity to what is left to us, that our love of our country, our affection for those nearest us and our pride in what is common to us have suddenly grown stronger. But have those other possessions, which we have now lost, really ceased to have any worth for us because they have proved so perishable and so unresistant? To many of us this seems to be so, but once more wrongly, in my view. I believe that those who think thus, and seem ready to make a permanent renunciation because what was precious has proved not to be lasting, are simply in a state of mourning for what is lost. Mourning, as we know, however painful it may be, comes to a spontaneous end. When it has renounced everything that has been lost, then it has consumed itself, and our libido is once more free (in so far as we are still young and active) to replace the lost objects by fresh ones equally or still more precious. It is to be hoped that the same will be true of the losses caused by this war. When once the mourning is over, it will be found that our high opinion of the riches of civilization has lost nothing from our discovery of their fragility. We shall build up again all that war has destroyed, and perhaps on firmer ground and more lastingly than before.

SOME CHARACTER-TYPES MET WITH IN PSYCHOANALYTIC WORK
(1916)

EINIGE CHARAKTERTYPEN AUS DER
PSYCHOANALYTISCHEN ARBEIT

(A) German Editions:

1916   *Imago*, **4** (6), 317–36.
1918   *S.K.S.N.*, **4**, 521–52. (1922, 2nd ed.)
1924   *Dichtung und Kunst*, 59–86.
1946   *Gesammelte Werke*, **10**, 364–91.

(B) English Translations:

'Some Character-Types Met with in Psycho-Analytic Work'

1925   *Collected Papers*, **4**, 318–44. (Tr. E. C. Mayne.)
1957   *Standard Edition*, **14**, 309–33. (Based on above.)

The present edition is a reprint of the *Standard Edition* version, with some editorial changes.

These three essays were published in the last issue of *Imago* for the year 1916. The third of them, although the shortest, has produced as many repercussions as any of Freud's non-medical writings, for it has thrown an entirely fresh light on the problems of the psychology of crime.

SOME CHARACTER-TYPES MET
WITH IN PSYCHOANALYTIC
WORK

WHEN a doctor carries out the psychoanalytic treatment of a neurotic, his interest is by no means directed in the first instance to the patient's character. He would much rather know what the symptoms mean, what instinctual impulses are concealed behind them and are satisfied by them, and what course was followed by the mysterious path that has led from the instinctual wishes to the symptoms. But the technique which he is obliged to follow soon compels him to direct his immediate curiosity towards other objectives. He observes that his investigation is threatened by resistances set up against him by the patient, and these resistances he may justly count as part of the latter's character. This now acquires the first claim on his interest.

What opposes the doctor's efforts is not always those traits of character which the patient recognizes in himself and which are attributed to him by people round him. Peculiarities in him which he had seemed to possess only to a modest degree are often brought to light in surprisingly increased intensity, or attitudes reveal themselves in him which had not been betrayed in other relations of life. The pages which follow will be devoted to describing and tracing back a few of these surprising traits of character.

I

THE 'EXCEPTIONS'

PSYCHOANALYTIC work is continually confronted with the task of inducing the patient to renounce an immediate and directly attainable yield of pleasure. He is not asked to renounce all pleasure; that could not, perhaps, be expected of any human being, and even religion is obliged to support its demand that earthly pleasure shall be set aside by promising that it will provide instead an incomparably greater amount of superior pleasure in another world. No, the patient is only asked to renounce such satisfactions as will inevitably have detrimental consequences. His privation is only to be temporary; he has only to learn to exchange an immediate yield of pleasure for a better assured, even though a postponed one. Or, in other words, under the doctor's guidance he is asked to make the advance from the pleasure principle to the reality principle by which the mature human being is distinguished from the child. In this educative process, the doctor's clearer insight can hardly be said to play a decisive part; as a rule, he can only tell his patient what the latter's own reason can tell him. But it is not the same to know a thing in one's mind and to hear it from someone outside. The doctor plays the part of this effective outsider; he makes use of the influence which one human being exercises over another. Or – recalling that it is the habit of psychoanalysis to replace what is derivative and etiolated by what is original and basic – let us say that the doctor, in his educative work, makes use of one of the components of love. In this work of after-education, he is probably doing no more than repeat the process which made education of any kind possible in the first instance. Side by side with the exigencies of life, love is the great educator; and it is by the love of those nearest him that the incomplete human being is induced to respect the decrees of necessity and to spare himself the punishment that follows any infringement of them.

When in this way one asks the patient to make a provisional renunciation of some pleasurable satisfaction, to make a sacrifice, to show his readiness to accept some temporary suffering for the sake of a better end, or even merely to make up his mind to submit to a necessity which applies to everyone, one comes upon individuals who resist such an appeal on a special ground. They say that they have renounced enough and suffered enough, and have a claim to be spared any further demands; they will submit no longer to any disagreeable necessity, for they are *exceptions* and, moreover, intend to remain so. In one such patient this claim was magnified into a conviction that a special providence watched over him, which would protect him from any painful sacrifices of the sort. The doctor's arguments will achieve nothing against an inner confidence which expresses itself as strongly as this; even *his* influence, indeed, is powerless at first, and it becomes clear to him that he must discover the sources from which this damaging prepossession is being fed.

Now it is no doubt true that everyone would like to consider himself an 'exception' and claim privileges over others. But precisely because of this there must be a particular reason, and one not universally present, if someone actually proclaims himself an exception and behaves as such. This reason may be of more than one kind; in the cases I investigated I succeeded in discovering a common peculiarity in the earlier experiences of these patients' lives. Their neuroses were connected with some experience or suffering to which they had been subjected in their earliest childhood, one in respect of which they knew themselves to be guiltless, and which they could look upon as an unjust disadvantage imposed upon them. The privileges that they claimed as a result of this injustice, and the rebelliousness it engendered, had contributed not a little to intensifying the conflicts leading to the outbreak of their neurosis. In one of these patients, a woman, the attitude towards life which I am discussing came to a head when she learnt that a painful organic trouble, which had hindered her from attaining her aims in life, was of congenital origin. So long as she looked upon this trouble as an accidental and late acquisition, she bore it patiently; as soon as she found that it was part of an innate inheritance, she became rebellious. The young man who believed that he was watched over by a special providence had in his infancy been the victim of an accidental infection from his wet-nurse, and had spent his whole later life making claims for compensation, an accident pension, as it were, without having any idea on what he based those claims. In his case the analysis, which constructed this event out of obscure mnemic residues and interpretations of the symptoms, was confirmed objectively by information from his family.

For reasons which will be easily understood I cannot communicate very much about these or other case histories. Nor do I propose to go into the obvious analogy between deformities of character resulting from protracted sickliness in childhood and the behaviour of whole nations whose past history has been full of suffering. Instead, however, I will take the opportunity of pointing to a figure created by the greatest of poets – a figure in whose character the claim to be an exception is closely bound up with and is motivated by the circumstance of congenital disadvantage.

In the opening soliloquy to Shakespeare's *Richard III*, Gloucester, who subsequently becomes King, says:

> But I, that am not shaped for sportive tricks,
> Nor made to court an amorous looking-glass;
> I that am rudely stamp'd, and want love's majesty
> To strut before a wanton ambling nymph;
> I, that am curtail'd of this fair proportion,
> Cheated of feature by dissembling Nature,
> Deform'd, unfinish'd, sent before my time
> Into this breathing world, scarce half made up,
> And that so lamely and unfashionable,
> That dogs bark at me as I halt by them;

> * * * * * * *

> And therefore, since I cannot prove a lover,
> To entertain these fair well-spoken days,
> I am determined to prove a villain,
> And hate the idle pleasures of these days.

296

At a first glance this tirade may perhaps seem unrelated to our present theme. Richard seems to say nothing more than: 'I find these idle times tedious, and I want to enjoy myself. As I cannot play the lover on account of my deformity, I will play the villain; I will intrigue, murder and do anything else I please.' Such a frivolous motivation could not but stifle any stirring of sympathy in the audience if it were not a screen for something much more serious. Otherwise the play would be psychologically impossible, for the writer must know how to furnish us with a secret background of sympathy for his hero, if we are to admire his boldness and adroitness without inward protest; and such sympathy can only be based on understanding or on a sense of a possible inner fellow-feeling for him.

I think, therefore, that Richard's soliloquy does not say everything; it merely gives a hint, and leaves us to fill in what it hints at. When we do so, however, the appearance of frivolity vanishes, the bitterness and minuteness with which Richard has depicted his deformity make their full effect, and we clearly perceive the fellow-feeling which compels our sympathy even with a villain like him. What the soliloquy thus means is: 'Nature has done me a grievous wrong in denying me the beauty of form which wins human love. Life owes me reparation for this, and I will see that I get it. I have a right to be an exception, to disregard the scruples by which others let themselves be held back. I may do wrong myself, since wrong has been done to me.' And now we feel that we ourselves might become like Richard; that on a small scale, indeed, we are already like him. Richard is an enormous magnification of something we find in ourselves as well. We all think we have reason to reproach Nature and our destiny for congenital and infantile disadvantages; we all demand reparation for early wounds to our narcissism, our self-love. Why did not Nature give us the golden curls of Balder or the strength of Siegfried or the lofty brow of genius or the noble profile of aristocracy? Why were we born in a middle-class home instead of in a royal palace? We could carry off beauty and distinction quite as well as any of those whom we are now obliged to envy for these qualities.

It is, however, a subtle economy of art in the poet that he does not permit his hero to give open and complete expression to all his secret motives. By this means he obliges us to supplement them; he engages our intellectual activity, diverts it from critical reflection and keeps us firmly identified with his hero. A bungler in his place would give conscious expression to all that he wishes to reveal to us, and would then find himself confronted by our cool, untrammelled intelligence, which would preclude any deepening of the illusion.

Before leaving the 'exceptions', however, we may point out that the claim of women to privileges and to exemption from so many of the importunities of life rests upon the same foundation. As we learn from psychoanalytic work, women regard themselves as having been damaged in infancy, as having been undeservedly cut short of something and unfairly treated; and the embitterment of so many daughters against their mother derives, ultimately, from the reproach against her of having brought them into the world as women instead of as men.

THOSE WRECKED BY SUCCESS

PSYCHOANALYTIC work has furnished us with the thesis that people fall ill of a neurosis as a result of *frustration*.[1] What is meant is the frustration of the satisfaction of their libidinal wishes, and some digression is necessary in order to make the thesis intelligible. For a neurosis to be generated there must be a conflict between a person's libidinal wishes and the part of his personality we call his ego, which is the expression of his instinct of self-preservation and which also includes his *ideals* of his personality. A pathogenic conflict of this kind takes place only when the libido tries to follow paths and aims which the ego has long since overcome and condemned and has therefore prohibited for ever; and this the libido only does if it is deprived of the possibility of an ideal ego-syntonic satisfaction. Hence privation, frustration of a real satisfaction, is the first condition for the generation of a neurosis, although, indeed, it is far from being the only one.

So much the more surprising, and indeed bewildering, must it appear when as a doctor one makes the discovery that people occasionally fall ill precisely when a deeply-rooted and long-cherished wish has come to fulfilment. It seems then as though they were not able to tolerate their happiness; for there can be no question that there is a causal connection between their success and their falling ill.

I had an opportunity of obtaining an insight into a woman's history, which I propose to describe as typical of these tragic occurrences. She was of good birth and well brought-up, but as quite a young girl she could not restrain her zest for life; she ran away from home and roved about the world in search of adventures, till she made the acquaintance of an artist who could appreciate her feminine charms but could also divine,

1. [See 'Types of Onset of Neurosis' (1912c), *P.F.L.*, **10**, 115 ff.]

in spite of what she had fallen to, the finer qualities she possessed. He took her to live with him, and she proved a faithful companion to him, and seemed only to need social rehabilitation to achieve complete happiness. After many years of life together, he succeeded in getting his family reconciled to her, and was then prepared to make her his legal wife. At that moment she began to go to pieces. She neglected the house of which she was now about to become the rightful mistress, imagined herself persecuted by his relatives, who wanted to take her into the family, debarred her lover, through her senseless jealousy, from all social intercourse, hindered him in his artistic work, and soon succumbed to an incurable mental illness.

On another occasion I came across the case of a most respectable man who, himself an academic teacher, had for many years cherished the natural wish to succeed the master who had initiated him into his own studies. When this older man retired, and his colleagues informed him that it was he who was chosen as successor, he began to hesitate, depreciated his merits, declared himself unworthy to fill the position designed for him, and fell into a melancholia which unfitted him for all activity for some years.

Different as these two cases are in other respects, they yet agree in this one point: the illness followed close upon the fulfilment of a wish and put an end to all enjoyment of it.

The contradiction between such experiences and the rule that what induces illness is frustration is not insoluble. It disappears if we make a distinction between an *external* and an *internal* frustration. If the object in which the libido can find its satisfaction is withheld *in reality*, this is an external frustration. In itself it is inoperative, not pathogenic, until an internal frustration is joined to it. This latter must proceed from the ego, and must dispute the access by the libido to other objects, which it now seeks to get hold of. Only then does a conflict arise, and the possibility of a neurotic illness, i.e. of a substitutive satisfaction reached circuitously by way of the repressed unconscious. Internal frustration is potentially present, therefore, in every case, only it does not come into operation until external, real frustration has prepared the ground for it. In those exceptional cases in which people are made ill by success, the internal frustration has operated by itself; indeed it has only made its appearance after an external frustration has been replaced by fulfilment of a wish. At first sight there is something strange about this; but on closer consideration we shall reflect that it is not at all unusual for the ego to tolerate a wish as harmless so long as it exists in phantasy alone and seems remote from fulfilment, whereas the ego will defend itself hotly against such a wish as soon as it approaches fulfilment and threatens to become a reality. The distinction between this and familiar situations in neurosis formation is merely that ordinarily it is internal intensifications of the libidinal cathexis that turn the phantasy, which has hitherto been thought little of and tolerated, into a dreaded opponent; while in these cases of ours the signal for the outbreak of conflict is given by a real external change.

Analytic work has no difficulty in showing us that it is forces of conscience which forbid the subject to gain the long hoped-for advantage from the fortunate change in reality. It is a difficult task, however, to discover the essence and origin of these judging and punishing trends, which so often surprise us by their existence where we do not expect to find them. For the usual reasons I shall not discuss what we know or conjecture on the point in relation to cases of clinical observation, but in relation to figures which great writers have created from the wealth of their knowledge of the mind.

We may take as an example of a person who collapses on reaching success, after striving for it with single-minded energy, the figure of Shakespeare's Lady Macbeth. Beforehand there is no hesitation, no sign of any internal conflict in her, no endeavour but that of overcoming the scruples of her ambitious and yet tender-minded husband. She is ready to sacrifice even her womanliness to her murderous intention, without reflecting on the decisive part which this womanliness must play when the question afterwards arises of preserving the aim of her ambition, which has been attained through a crime.

> Come, you spirits
> That tend on mortal thoughts, unsex me here
> ... Come to my woman's breasts,
> And take my milk for gall, you murdering ministers!
>
> (Act I, Scene 5)

> ... I have given suck, and know
> How tender 'tis to love the babe that milks me:
> I would, while it was smiling in my face,
> Have pluck'd my nipple from his boneless gums,
> And dashed the brains out, had I so sworn as you
> Have done to this.
>
> (Act I, Scene 7)

One solitary faint stirring of reluctance comes over her before the deed:

> ... Had he not resembled
> My father as he slept, I had done it ...
>
> (Act II, Scene 2)

Then, when she has become queen through the murder of Duncan, she betrays for a moment something like disappointment, something like disillusionment. We cannot tell why.

> ... Nought's had, all's spent,
> Where our desire is got without content:
> 'Tis safer to be that which we destroy,
> Than by destruction dwell in doubtful joy.
>
> (Act III, Scene 2)

Nevertheless, she holds out. In the banqueting scene which follows on these words, she alone keeps her head, cloaks her husband's state of confusion and finds a pretext for dismissing the guests. And then she disappears from view. We next see her in the sleep-walking scene in the last Act, fixated to the impressions of the night of the murder. Once again, as then, she seeks to put heart into her husband:

> 'Fie, my lord, fie! a soldier, and afeard? What need we fear who knows it, when none can call our power to account?'
>
> (Act V, Scene 1)

· She hears the knocking at the door, which terrified her husband after the deed. But at the same time she strives to 'undo the deed which cannot be undone'. She washes her hands, which are blood-stained and smell of blood, and is conscious of the futility of the attempt. She who had seemed so remorseless seems to have been borne down by remorse. When she dies, Macbeth, who meanwhile has become as inexorable as she had been in the beginning, can only find a brief epitaph for her:

> She should have died hereafter;
> There would have been a time for such a word.
>
> (Act V, Scene 5)

And now we ask ourselves what it was that broke this character which had seemed forged from the toughest metal? Is it only disillusionment – the different aspect shown by the accomplished deed[1] – and are we to infer that even in Lady Macbeth an originally gentle and womanly nature had been worked up to a concentration and high tension which could not endure for long, or ought we to seek for signs of a deeper motivation which will make this collapse more humanly intelligible to us?

It seems to me impossible to come to any decision. Shakespeare's *Macbeth* is a *pièce d'occasion*, written for the accession of James, who had hitherto been King of Scotland. The plot was ready-made, and had been handled by other contemporary writers, whose work Shakespeare probably made use of in his customary manner. It offered remarkable analogies to the actual situation. The 'virginal' Elizabeth, of whom it was rumoured that she had never been capable of child-bearing and who had once described herself as 'a barren stock',[2] in an anguished outcry at the news of James's birth, was obliged by this very child-

1. [An allusion to two lines in Schiller's *Die Braut von Messina*, Act IV, Scene 5.]

2. Cf. *Macbeth*, Act III, Scene 1:

> Upon my head they placed a fruitless crown,
> And put a barren sceptre in my gripe,
> Thence to be wrenched with an unlineal hand,
> No son of mine succeeding ...

lessness of hers to make the Scottish king her successor. And he was the son of Mary Stuart whose execution she, even though reluctantly, had ordered, and who, in spite of the clouding of their relations by political concerns, was never-theless of her blood and might be called her guest.

The accession of James I was like a demonstration of the curse of unfruitfulness and the blessings of continuous genera-tion. And the action of Shakespeare's *Macbeth* is based on this same contrast.[1]

The Weird Sisters assured Macbeth that he himself should be king, but to Banquo they promised that his children should succeed to the crown. Macbeth is incensed by this decree of destiny. He is not content with the satisfaction of his own ambition. He wants to found a dynasty – not to have murdered for the benefit of strangers. This point is overlooked if Shake-speare's play is regarded only as a tragedy of ambition. It is clear that Macbeth cannot live for ever, and thus there is but one way for him to invalidate the part of the prophecy which opposes him – namely, to have children himself who can succeed him. And he seems to expect them from his indomitable wife:

> Bring forth men–children only!
> For thy undaunted mettle should compose
> Nothing but males . . .
>
> (Act I, Scene 7)

And equally it is clear that if he is deceived in this expectation he must submit to destiny; otherwise his actions lose all purpose and are transformed into the blind fury of one doomed to destruction, who is resolved to destroy beforehand all that he can reach. We watch Macbeth pass through this development, and at the height of the tragedy we hear Macduff's shattering cry, which has so often been recognized to be ambiguous and which may perhaps contain the key to the change in Macbeth:

1. [Freud had already suggested this in the first edition of *The Interpretation of Dreams* (1900a), *P.F.L.*, **4**, 368.]

He has no children!

(Act IV, Scene 3)

There is no doubt that this means: 'Only because he is himself childless could he murder my children.' But more may be implied in it, and above all it might lay bare the deepest motive which not only forces Macbeth to go far beyond his own nature, but also touches the hard character of his wife at its only weak point. If one surveys the whole play from the summit marked by these words of Macduff's, one sees that it is sown with references to the father–children relation. The murder of the kindly Duncan is little else than parricide; in Banquo's case, Macbeth kills the father while the son escapes him; and in Macduff's, he kills the children because the father has fled from him. A bloody child, and then a crowned one, are shown him by the witches in the apparition scene; the armed head which is seen earlier is no doubt Macbeth himself. But in the background rises the sinister form of the avenger, Macduff, who is himself an exception to the laws of generation, since he was not born of his mother but ripp'd from her womb.

It would be a perfect example of poetic justice in the manner of the talion if the childlessness of Macbeth and the barrenness of his Lady were the punishment for their crimes against the sanctity of generation – if Macbeth could not become a father because he had robbed children of their father and a father of his children, and if Lady Macbeth suffered the unsexing she had demanded of the spirits of murder. I believe Lady Macbeth's illness, the transformation of her callousness into penitence, could be explained directly as a reaction to her childlessness, by which she is convinced of her impotence against the decrees of nature, and at the same time reminded that it is through her own fault if her crime has been robbed of the better part of its fruits.

In Holinshed's *Chronicle* (1577), from which Shakespeare took the plot of *Macbeth*, Lady Macbeth is only once mentioned as the ambitious wife who instigates her husband to murder in order that she may herself become queen. There is no mention of her subsequent fate and of the development of her character. On the other hand, it would seem that the change of Macbeth's character into a bloodthirsty tyrant is ascribed to the same motives as we have suggested here. For in Holinshed *ten years* pass between the murder of Duncan, through which Macbeth becomes king, and his further misdeeds; and in these ten years he is shown as a stern but just ruler. It is not until after this lapse of time that the change begins in him, under the influence of the tormenting fear that the prophecy to Banquo may be fulfilled just as the prophecy of his own destiny has been. Only then does he contrive the murder of Banquo, and, as in Shakespeare, is driven from one crime to another. It is not expressly stated in Holinshed that it was his childlessness which urged him to these courses, but enough time and room is given for that plausible motive. Not so in Shakespeare. Events crowd upon us in the tragedy with breathless haste so that, to judge by the statements made by the characters in it, the course of its action covers about *one week*.[1] This acceleration takes the ground from under all our constructions of the motives for the change in the characters of Macbeth and his wife. There is no time for a long-drawn-out disappointment of their hopes of offspring to break the woman down and drive the man to defiant rage; and the contradiction remains that though so many subtle interrelations in the plot, and between it and its occasion, point to a common origin of them in the theme of childlessness, nevertheless the economy of time in the tragedy expressly precludes a development of character from any motives but those inherent in the action itself.

What, however, these motives can have been which in so short a space of time could turn the hesitating, ambitious man into an unbridled tyrant, and his steely-hearted instigator into a sick woman gnawed by remorse, it is, in my view, impossible to guess. We must, I think, give up any hope of penetrating the triple layer of obscurity into which the bad preservation of the text, the unknown intention of the dramatist, and the hidden purport of the legend have become condensed. But I should not subscribe to the objection that investigations like

1. Darmesteter (1881, lxxv).

these are idle in the face of the powerful effect which the tragedy has upon the spectator. The dramatist can indeed, during the representation, overwhelm us by his art and paralyse our powers of reflection; but he cannot prevent us from attempting subsequently to grasp its effect by studying its psychological mechanism. Nor does the contention that a dramatist is at liberty to shorten at will the natural chronology of the events he brings before us, if by the sacrifice of common probability he can enhance the dramatic effect, seem to me relevant in this instance. For such a sacrifice is justified only when it merely interferes with probability,[1] and not when it breaks the causal connection; moreover, the dramatic effect would hardly have suffered if the passage of time had been left indeterminate, instead of being expressly limited to a few days.

One is so unwilling to dismiss a problem like that of *Macbeth* as insoluble that I will venture to bring up a fresh point, which may offer another way out of the difficulty. Ludwig Jekels, in a recent Shakespearean study,[2] thinks he has discovered a particular technique of the poet's, and this might apply to *Macbeth*. He believes that Shakespeare often splits a character up into two personages, which, taken separately, are not completely understandable and do not become so until they are brought together once more into a unity. This might be so with Macbeth and Lady Macbeth. In that case it would of course be pointless to regard her as an independent character and seek to discover the motives for her change, without considering the Macbeth who completes her. I shall not follow this clue any further, but I should, nevertheless, like to point out something which strikingly confirms this view: the germs of fear which break out in Macbeth on the night of the murder do not develop further in *him* but in *her*.[3] It is he who has the

1. As in Richard III's wooing of Anne beside the bier of the King whom he has murdered.

2. [This does not appear to have been published. In a later paper on *Macbeth* Jekels (1917) barely refers to this theory, apart from quoting the present paragraph. In a still later paper, on 'The Psychology of Comedy', Jekels (1926) returns to the subject, but again very briefly.]

3. Cf. Darmesteter (1881, lxxv).

hallucination of the dagger before the crime; but it is she who afterwards falls ill of a mental disorder. It is he who after the murder hears the cry in the house: 'Sleep no more! Macbeth does murder sleep ...' and so 'Macbeth shall sleep no more'; but we never hear that *he* slept no more, while the Queen, as we see, rises from her bed and, talking in her sleep, betrays her guilt. It is he who stands helpless with bloody hands, lamenting that 'all great Neptune's ocean' will not wash them clean, while she comforts him: 'A little water clears us of this deed'; but later it is she who washes her hands for a quarter of an hour and cannot get rid of the bloodstains: 'All the perfumes in Arabia will not sweeten this little hand.' Thus what he feared in his pangs of conscience is fulfilled in her; she becomes all remorse and he all defiance. Together they exhaust the possibilities of reaction to the crime, like two disunited parts of a single psychical individuality, and it may be that they are both copied from a single prototype.

If we have been unable to give any answer to the question why Lady Macbeth should collapse after her success, we may perhaps have a better chance when we turn to the creation of another great dramatist, who loves to pursue problems of psychological responsibility with unrelenting rigour.

Rebecca Gamvik, the daughter of a midwife, has been brought up by her adopted father, Dr West, to be a freethinker and to despise the restrictions which a morality founded on religious belief seeks to impose on the desires of life. After the doctor's death she finds a position at Rosmersholm, the home for many generations of an ancient family whose members know nothing of laughter and have sacrificed joy to a rigid fulfilment of duty. Its occupants are Johannes Rosmer, a former pastor, and his invalid wife, the childless Beata. Overcome by 'a wild, uncontrollable passion'[1] for the love of the high-born Rosmer, Rebecca resolves to remove the wife who stands in her way, and to this end makes use of her 'fearless, free' will,

1. [The quotations are based on William Archer's English translation.]

which is restrained by no scruples. She contrives that Beata shall read a medical book in which the aim of marriage is represented to be the begetting of offspring, so that the poor woman begins to doubt whether her own marriage is justifiable. Rebecca then hints that Rosmer, whose studies and ideas she shares, is about to abandon the old faith and join the 'party of enlightenment'; and, after she has thus shaken the wife's confidence in her husband's moral integrity, gives her finally to understand that she, Rebecca, will soon leave the house in order to conceal the consequences of her illicit intercourse with Rosmer. The criminal scheme succeeds. The poor wife, who has passed for depressed and irresponsible, throws herself from the path beside the mill into the mill-race, possessed by the sense of her own worthlessness and wishing no longer to stand between her beloved husband and his happiness.

For more than a year Rebecca and Rosmer have been living alone at Rosmersholm in a relationship which he wishes to regard as a purely intellectual and ideal friendship. But when this relationship begins to be darkened from outside by the first shadow of gossip, and at the same time tormenting doubts arise in Rosmer about the motives for which his wife put an end to herself, he begs Rebecca to become his second wife, so that they may counter the unhappy past with a new living reality (Act II). For an instant she exclaims with joy at his proposal, but immediately afterwards declares that it can never be, and that if he urges her further she will 'go the way Beata went'. Rosmer cannot understand this rejection; and still less can we, who know more of Rebecca's actions and designs. All we can be certain of is that her 'no' is meant in earnest.

How could it come about that the adventuress with the 'fearless, free will', who forged her way ruthlessly to her desired goal, should now refuse to pluck the fruit of success when it is offered to her? She herself gives us the explanation in the fourth Act: '*This* is the terrible part of it: that now, when all life's happiness is within my grasp – my heart is changed and my own past cuts me off from it.' That is to say, she has in the meantime become a different being; her conscience has awakened, she has acquired a sense of guilt which debars her from enjoyment.

And what has awakened her conscience? Let us listen to her herself, and then consider whether we can believe her entirely. 'It is the Rosmer view of life – or your view of life at any rate – that has infected my will ... And made it sick. Enslaved it to laws that had no power over me before. You – life with you – has ennobled my mind.'

This influence, we are further to understand, has only become effective since she has been able to live alone with Rosmer: 'In quiet – in solitude – when you showed me all your thoughts without reserve – every tender and delicate feeling, just as it came to you – *then* the great change came over me.'

Shortly before this she has lamented the other aspect of the change: 'Because Rosmersholm has sapped my strength. My old fearless will has had its wings clipped here. It is crippled! The time is past when I had courage for anything in the world. I have lost the power of action, Rosmer.'

Rebecca makes this declaration after she had revealed herself as a criminal in a voluntary confession to Rosmer and Rector Kroll, the brother of the woman she has got rid of. Ibsen has made it clear by small touches of masterly subtlety that Rebecca does not actually tell lies, but is never entirely straightforward. Just as, in spite of all her freedom from prejudices, she has understated her age by a year, so her confession to the two men is incomplete, and as a result of Kroll's insistence it is supplemented on some important points. Hence it is open to us to suppose that her explanation of her renunciation exposes one motive only to conceal another.

Certainly, we have no reason to disbelieve her when she declares that the atmosphere of Rosmersholm and her association with the high-minded Rosmer have ennobled – and crippled – her. She is here expressing what she knows and has felt. But this is not necessarily all that has happened in her, nor need she have understood all that has happened. Rosmer's influence may only have been a cloak, which concealed another influence that was operative, and a remarkable indication points in this other direction.

Even after her confession, Rosmer, in their last conversation which brings the play to an end, again beseeches her to be his wife. He forgives her the crime she has committed for love of him. And now she does not answer, as she should, that no forgiveness can rid her of the feeling of guilt she has incurred from her malignant deception of poor Beata; but she charges herself with another reproach which affects us as coming strangely from this freethinking woman, and is far from deserving the importance which Rebecca attaches to it: 'Dear – never speak of this again! It is impossible! For you must know, Rosmer, I have a – a past behind me.' She means, of course, that she has had sexual relations with another man; and we do not fail to observe that these relations, which occurred at a time when she was free and accountable to nobody, seem to her a greater hindrance to the union with Rosmer than her truly criminal behaviour to his wife.

Rosmer refuses to hear anything about this past. We can guess what it was, though everything that refers to it in the play is, so to speak, subterranean and has to be pieced together from hints. But nevertheless they are hints inserted with such art that it is impossible to misunderstand them.

Between Rebecca's first refusal and her confession something occurs which has a decisive influence on her future destiny. Rector Kroll arrives one day at the house on purpose to humiliate Rebecca by telling her that he knows she is an illegitimate child, the daughter of the very Dr West who adopted her after her mother's death. Hate has sharpened his perceptions, yet he does not suppose that this is any news to her. 'I really did not suppose you were ignorant of this, otherwise it would have been very odd that you should have let Dr West adopt you ...' 'And then he takes you into his house – as soon as your mother dies. He treats you harshly. And yet you stay with him. You know that he won't leave you a halfpenny – as a matter of fact you got only a case of books – and yet you stay on; you bear with him; you nurse him to the last' . . . 'I attribute your care for him to the natural filial instinct of a daughter. Indeed, I believe your whole conduct is a natural result of your origin.'

But Kroll is mistaken. Rebecca had no idea at all that she could be Dr West's daughter. When Kroll began with dark hints at her past, she must have thought he was referring to something else. After she has gathered what he means, she can still retain her composure for a while, for she is able to suppose that her enemy is basing his calculations on her age, which she had given falsely on an earlier visit of his. But Kroll demolishes this objection by saying: 'Well, so be it, but my calculation may be right, none the less; for Dr West was up there on a short visit the year before he got the appointment.' After this new information, she loses her self-possession. 'It is not true!' She walks about wringing her hands. 'It is impossible. You want to cheat me into believing it. This can never, never be true. It cannot be true. Never in this world! –' Her agitation is so extreme that Kroll cannot attribute it to his information alone.

'KROLL: But, my dear Miss West – why in Heaven's name are you so terribly excited? You quite frighten me. What am I to think – to believe – ?

'REBECCA: Nothing. You are to think and believe nothing.

'KROLL: Then you must really tell me how you can take this affair – this possibility – so terribly to heart.

'REBECCA (controlling herself): It is perfectly simple, Rector Kroll. I have no wish to be taken for an illegitimate child.'

The enigma of Rebecca's behaviour is susceptible of only one solution. The news that Dr West was her father is the heaviest blow that can befall her, for she was not only his adopted daughter, but had been his mistress. When Kroll began to speak, she thought that he was hinting at these relations, the truth of which she would probably have admitted and justified by her emancipated ideas. But this was far from the Rector's intention; he knew nothing of the love-affair with Dr West, just as she knew nothing of Dr West's being her father. She *cannot* have had anything else in her mind but this love-affair when she accounted for her final rejection of Rosmer on the ground that she had a past which made her unworthy to be his wife. And probably, if Rosmer had consented to hear of that past, she would have confessed half her secret only and have kept silence on the more serious part of it.

But now we understand, of course, that this past must seem to her the more serious obstacle to their union – the more serious crime.

After she has learnt that she has been the mistress of her own father, she surrenders herself wholly to her now overmastering sense of guilt. She makes the confession to Rosmer and Kroll which stamps her as a murderess; she rejects for ever the happiness to which she has paved the way by crime, and prepares for departure. But the true motive of her sense of guilt, which results in her being wrecked by success, remains a secret. As we have seen, it is something quite other than the atmosphere of Rosmersholm and the refining influence of Rosmer.

At this point no one who has followed us will fail to bring forward an objection which may justify some doubts. Rebecca's first refusal of Rosmer occurs before Kroll's second visit, and therefore before his exposure of her illegitimate origin and at a time when she as yet knows nothing of her incest – if we have rightly understood the dramatist. Yet this first refusal is energetic and seriously meant. The sense of guilt which bids her renounce the fruit of her actions is thus effective before she knows anything of her cardinal crime; and if we grant so much, we ought perhaps entirely to set aside her incest as a source of that sense of guilt.

So far we have treated Rebecca West as if she were a living person and not a creation of Ibsen's imagination, which is always directed by the most critical intelligence. We may therefore attempt to maintain the same position in dealing with the objection that has been raised. The objection is valid: before the knowledge of her incest, conscience was already in part awakened in Rebecca; and there is nothing to prevent our making the influence which is acknowledged and blamed by Rebecca herself responsible for this change. But this does not exempt us from recognizing the second motive. Rebecca's behaviour when she hears what Kroll has to tell her, the confession which is her immediate reaction, leave no doubt that then only does the stronger and decisive motive for renunciation begin to take effect. It is in fact a case of multiple motivation, in which a deeper motive comes into view behind the more superficial one. Laws of poetic economy necessitate this way of presenting the situation, for this deeper motive could not be explicitly enunciated. It had to remain concealed, kept from the easy perception of the spectator or the reader; otherwise serious resistances, based on the most distressing emotions, would have arisen, which might have imperilled the effect of the drama.

We have, however, a right to demand that the explicit motive shall not be without an internal connection with the concealed one, but shall appear as a mitigation of, and a derivation from, the latter. And if we may rely on the fact that the dramatist's conscious creative combination arose logically from unconscious premisses, we may now make an attempt to show that he has fulfilled this demand. Rebecca's feeling of guilt has its source in the reproach of incest, even before Kroll, with analytical perspicacity, has made her conscious of it. If we reconstruct her past, expanding and filling in the author's hints, we may feel sure that she cannot have been without some inkling of the intimate relation between her mother and Dr West. It must have made a great impression on her when she became her mother's successor with this man. She stood under the domination of the Oedipus complex, even though she did not know that this universal phantasy had in her case become a reality. When she came to Rosmersholm, the inner force of this first experience drove her into bringing about, by vigorous action, the same situation which had been realized in the original instance through no doing of hers – into getting rid of the wife and mother, so that she might take her place with the husband and father. She describes with a convincing insistence how, against her will, she was obliged to proceed, step by step, to the removal of Beata.

'You think then that I was cool and calculating and self-possessed all the time! I was not the same woman then that I am now, as I stand here telling it all. Besides, there are two sorts of will in us, I believe! I wanted Beata away, by one means or another; but I never really believed that it would come to pass. As I felt my way forward, at each step I ventured, I seemed to hear something within me cry out: No farther! Not a step farther! And yet I *could* not stop. I *had* to venture the least little bit farther. And only one hair's-breadth more. And then one more – and always one more. And then it happened. – That is the way such things come about.'

That is not an embellishment, but an authentic description. Everything that happened to her at Rosmersholm, her falling in love with Rosmer and her hostility to his wife, was from the first a consequence of the Oedipus complex – an inevitable replica of her relations with her mother and Dr West.

And so the sense of guilt which first causes her to reject Rosmer's proposal is at bottom no different from the greater one which drives her to her confession after Kroll has opened her eyes. But just as under the influence of Dr West she had become a freethinker and despiser of religious morality, so she is transformed by her love for Rosmer into a being of conscience and nobility. This much of the mental processes within her she herself understands, and so she is justified in describing Rosmer's influence as the motive for her change – the motive that had become accessible to her.

The practising psychoanalytic physician knows how frequently, or how invariably, a girl who enters a household as servant, companion or governess will consciously or unconsciously weave a day-dream, which derives from the Oedipus complex, of the mistress of the house disappearing and the master taking the newcomer as his wife in her place.[1] *Rosmersholm* is the greatest work of art of the class that treats of this common phantasy in girls. What makes it into a tragic drama is the extra circumstance that the heroine's day-dream

1. [Cf. the case of Miss Lucy R. in the *Studies on Hysteria* (1895*d*), P.F.L., 3, 180 ff.]

had been preceded in her childhood by a precisely corresponding reality.[1]

After this long digression into literature, let us return to clinical experience – but only to establish in a few words the complete agreement between them. Psychoanalytic work teaches that the forces of conscience which induce illness in consequence of success, instead of, as normally, in consequence of frustration, are closely connected with the Oedipus complex, the relation to father and mother – as perhaps, indeed, is our sense of guilt in general.[2]

1. The presence of the theme of incest in *Rosmersholm* has already been demonstrated by the same arguments as mine in Otto Rank's extremely comprehensive *Das Inzest-Motiv in Dichtung und Sage* (1912 [404–5]).

2. [Some twenty years later, in his Open Letter to Romain Rolland describing his first visit to the Acropolis at Athens (1936a), *P.F.L.*, **11**, 443 ff., Freud compared the feeling of something being 'too good to be true' with the situation analysed in the present paper.]

CRIMINALS FROM A SENSE OF GUILT

IN telling me about their early youth, particularly before puberty, people who have afterwards often become very respectable have informed me of forbidden actions which they committed at that time – such as thefts, frauds and even arson. I was in the habit of dismissing these statements with the comment that we are familiar with the weakness of moral inhibitions at that period of life, and I made no attempt to find a place for them in any more significant context. But eventually I was led to make a more thorough study of such incidents by some glaring and more accessible cases in which the misdeeds were committed while the patients were actually under my treatment, and were no longer so youthful. Analytic work then brought the surprising discovery that such deeds were done principally because they were forbidden, and because their execution was accompanied by mental relief for their doer. He was suffering from an oppressive feeling of guilt, of which he did not know the origin, and after he had committed a misdeed this oppression was mitigated. His sense of guilt was at least attached to something.

Paradoxical as it may sound, I must maintain that the sense of guilt was present before the misdeed, that it did not arise from it, but conversely – the misdeed arose from the sense of guilt. These people might justly be described as criminals from a sense of guilt. The pre-existence of the guilty feeling had of course been demonstrated by a whole set of other manifestations and effects.

But scientific work is not satisfied with the establishment of a curious fact. There are two further questions to answer: what is the origin of this obscure sense of guilt before the deed, and is it probable that this kind of causation plays any considerable part in human crime?

An examination of the first question held out the promise of bringing us information about the source of mankind's sense of guilt in general. The invariable outcome of analytic work was to show that this obscure sense of guilt derived from the Oedipus complex and was a reaction to the two great criminal intentions of killing the father and having sexual relations with the mother. In comparison with these two, the crimes committed in order to fix the sense of guilt to something came as a relief to the sufferers. We must remember in this connection that parricide and incest with the mother are the two great human crimes, the only ones which, as such, are pursued and abhorred in primitive communities. And we must remember, too, how close other investigations have brought us to the hypothesis that the conscience of mankind, which now appears as an inherited mental force, was acquired in connection with the Oedipus complex.

In order to answer the second question we must go beyond the scope of psychoanalytic work. With children it is easy to observe that they are often 'naughty' on purpose to provoke punishment, and are quiet and contented after they have been punished. Later analytic investigation can often put us on the track of the guilty feeling which induced them to seek punishment. Among adult criminals we must no doubt except those who commit crimes without any sense of guilt, who have either developed no moral inhibitions or who, in their conflict with society, consider themselves justified in their action. But as regards the majority of other criminals, those for whom punitive measures are really designed, such a motivation for crime might very well be taken into consideration; it might throw light on some obscure points in the psychology of the criminal, and furnish punishment with a new psychological basis.

A friend has since called my attention to the fact that the 'criminal from a sense of guilt' was known to Nietzsche too. The pre-existence of the feeling of guilt, and the utilization of a deed in order to rationalize this feeling, glimmer before us in Zarathustra's sayings[1] 'On the Pale Criminal'. Let us leave it to future research to decide how many criminals are to be reckoned among these 'pale' ones.

1. [In the editions before 1924, 'obscure sayings'. − A hint at the idea of the sense of guilt being a motive for misdeeds is already to be found in the case history of 'Little Hans' (1909b), P.F.L., 8, 204, as well as in that of the 'Wolf Man' (1918b), ibid., 9, 257−8, which, though published later than the present paper, was in fact mostly written in the year before it. In this latter passage the complicating factor of masochism is introduced.]

A CHILDHOOD RECOLLECTION FROM *DICHTUNG UND WAHRHEIT*
(1917)

EINE KINDHEITSERINNERUNG AUS
DICHTUNG UND WAHREIT

(A) German Editions:

1917   *Imago*, **5** (2), 49–57.
1918   *S.K.S.N.*, **4**, 564–77 (1922, 2nd ed.).
1924   *Dichtung und Kunst*, 87–98.
1947   *Gesammelte Werke*, **12**, 15–26.

(B) English Translations:

'A Childhood Recollection from *Dichtung und Wahrheit*'

1925   *Collected Papers*, **4**, 357–67. (Tr. C. J. M. Hubback.)
1955   *Standard Edition*, **17**, 145–56. (Considerably modified
        version of above.)

The present edition is a corrected reprint of the *Standard Edition* version.

Freud gave the first part of this paper before the Vienna Psycho-Analytical Society on 13 December 1916 and the second part before the same society on 18 April 1917. The paper was not actually written by him until September 1917, in the train on his way back from a summer holiday in the Tatra Mountains in Hungary. The date of publication is uncertain, since *Imago* appeared very irregularly at that time, owing to war conditions. A summary of his conclusions will be found in a long footnote which he added in 1919 to Chapter II of his study of a childhood memory of Leonardo da Vinci's (1910*c*), p. 175 *n*. 1 above.

A CHILDHOOD RECOLLECTION
FROM
DICHTUNG UND WAHRHEIT

'IF we try to recollect what happened to us in the earliest years of childhood, we often find that we confuse what we have heard from others with what is really a possession of our own derived from what we ourselves witnessed.' This remark is found on one of the first pages of Goethe's account of his life [*Dichtung und Wahrheit*], which he began to write at the age of sixty. It is preceded only by some information about his birth, which 'took place on 28 August 1749, at mid-day on the stroke of twelve'. The stars were in a favourable conjunction and may well have been the cause of his survival, for at his entry into the world he was 'as though dead', and it was only after great efforts that he was brought to life. There follows on this a short description of the house and of the place in it where the children – he and his younger sister – best liked to play. After this, however, Goethe relates in fact only one single event which can be assigned to the 'earliest years of child-hood' (the years up to four?) and of which he seems to have preserved a recollection of his own.

The account of it runs as follows: 'And three brothers (von Ochsenstein by name) who lived over the way became very fond of me; they were orphan sons of the late magistrate, and they took an interest in me and used to tease me in all sorts of ways.

'My people used to like to tell of all kinds of pranks in which these men, otherwise of a serious and retiring disposition, used to encourage me. I will quote only one of these exploits. The crockery-fair was just over, and not only had the kitchen been fitted up from it with what would be needed for some time to come, but miniature utensils of the same sort had been bought for us children to play with. One fine afternoon, when all was quiet in the house, I was playing with my dishes and pots in the hall' (a place which had already been described, opening on to the street) 'and, since this seemed to lead to nothing, I threw a plate into the street, and was overjoyed to see it go to bits so merrily. The von Ochsensteins, who saw how delighted I was and how joyfully I clapped my little hands, called out "Do it again!" I did not hesitate to sling out a pot on to the paving-stones, and then, as they kept crying "Another!", one after another all my little dishes, cooking-pots and pans. My neighbours continued to show their approval and I was highly delighted to be amusing them. But my stock was all used up, and still they cried "Another!" So I ran off straight into the kitchen and fetched the earthenware plates, which made an even finer show as they smashed to bits. And thus I ran backwards and forwards, bringing one plate after another, as I could reach them in turn from the dresser; and, as they were not content with that, I hurled every piece of crockery I could get hold of to the same destruction. Only later did someone come and interfere and put a stop to it all. The damage was done, and to make up for so much broken earthenware there was at least an amusing story, which the rascals who had been its instigators enjoyed to the end of their lives.'

In pre-analytic days it was possible to read this without finding occasion to pause and without feeling surprised, but later on the analytic conscience became active. We had formed definite opinions and expectations about the memories of earliest childhood, and would have liked to claim universal validity for them. It should not be a matter of indifference or entirely without meaning which detail of a child's life had escaped the general oblivion. It might on the contrary be conjectured that what had remained in memory was the most significant element in that whole period of life, whether it had possessed such an importance at the time, or whether it had gained subsequent importance from the influence of later events.

The high value of such childish recollections was, it is true, obvious only in a few cases. Generally they seemed indifferent, worthless even, and it remained at first incomprehensible why just these memories should have resisted amnesia; nor could the person who had preserved them for long years as part of his own store of memories see more in them than any stranger to whom he might relate them. Before their significance could be appreciated, a certain work of interpretation was necessary. This interpretation either showed that their content required to be replaced by some other content, or revealed that they were related to some other unmistakably important experiences and had appeared in their place as what are known as 'screen memories'.[1]

In every psychoanalytic investigation of a life-history it is always possible to explain the meaning of the earliest childhood memories along these lines. Indeed, it usually happens that the very recollection to which the patient gives precedence, which he relates first, with which he introduces the story of his life, proves to be the most important, the very one that holds the key to the secret pages of his mind.[2] But the little childish episode related in *Dichtung und Wahrheit* does not rise to our expectations. The ways and means that with our patients lead to interpretation are of course not available to us here; the episode does not seem in itself to admit of any traceable connection with important impressions at a later date. A mischievous trick with damaging effects on the household economy, carried out under the spur of outside encouragement, is certainly no fitting headpiece for all that Goethe has to tell us of his richly filled life. An impression of utter innocence and irrelevance clings to this childhood memory, and it might be taken as a warning not to stretch the claims of psychoanalysis too far nor to apply it in unsuitable places.

The little problem, therefore, had long since slipped out of my mind, when one day chance brought me a patient in whom

1. [See Chapter IV of *The Psychopathology of Everyday Life* (1901*b*), P.F.L., **5**, 83 ff.]
2. [Cf. the 'Rat Man' case (1909*d*), P.F.L., **9**, 41 *n*. 2.]

a similar childhood memory appeared in a clearer connection. He was a man of twenty-seven, highly educated and gifted, whose life at that time was entirely filled with a conflict with his mother that affected all his interests, and from the effects of which his capacity for love and his ability to lead an independent existence had suffered greatly. This conflict went far back into his childhood; certainly to his fourth year. Before that he had been a very weakly child, always ailing, and yet that sickly period was glorified into a paradise in his memory; for then he had had exclusive, uninterrupted possession of his mother's affection. When he was not yet four, a brother, who is still living, was born, and in his reaction to that disturbing event he became transformed into an obstinate, unmanageable boy, who perpetually provoked his mother's severity. Moreover, he never regained the right path.

When he came to me for treatment – by no means the least reason for his coming was that his mother, a religious bigot, had a horror of psychoanalysis – his jealousy of the younger brother (which had once actually been manifested as a murderous attack on the infant in its cradle) had long been forgotten. He now treated his brother with great consideration; but certain curious fortuitous actions of his (which involved sudden and severe injuries to favourite animals, like his sporting dog or birds which he had carefully reared) were probably to be understood as echoes of these hostile impulses against the little brother.

Now this patient related that, at about the time of the attack on the baby he so much hated, he had thrown all the crockery he could lay hands on out of the window of their country house into the road – the very same thing that Goethe relates of his childhood in *Dichtung und Wahrheit*! I may remark that my patient was of foreign nationality and was not acquainted with German literature; he had never read Goethe's autobiography.

This communication naturally suggested to me that an attempt might be made to explain Goethe's childhood memory on the lines forced upon us by my patient's story. But could the necessary conditions for this explanation be shown to exist in the poet's childhood? Goethe himself, it is true, makes the instigation of the von Ochsenstein brothers responsible for his childish prank. But from his own narrative it can be seen that these grown-up neighbours merely encouraged him to go on with what he was doing. The beginning was on his own initiative, and the reason he gives for this beginning – 'since this (the game) seemed to lead to nothing' – is surely, without any forcing of its meaning, a confession that at the time of writing it down and probably for many years previously he was not aware of any adequate motive for his behaviour.

It is well known that Johann Wolfgang and his sister Cornelia were the eldest survivors of a considerable family of very weakly children. Dr Hanns Sachs has been so kind as to supply me with the following details concerning these brothers and sisters of Goethe's, who died in childhood:

(a) Hermann Jakob, baptized Monday, 27 November 1752; reached the age of six years and six weeks; buried 13 January 1759.

(b) Katharina Elisabetha, baptized Monday, 9 September 1754; buried Thursday, 22 December 1755. (One year and four months old.)

(c) Johanna Maria, baptized Tuesday, 29 March 1757, and buried Saturday, 11 August 1759. (Two years and four months old.) (This was doubtless the very pretty and attractive little girl celebrated by her brother.)

(d) Georg Adolph, baptized Sunday, 15 June 1760; buried, eight months old, Wednesday, 18 February 1761.

Goethe's next-youngest sister, Cornelia Friederica Christiana, was born on 7 December 1750, when he was fifteen months old. This slight difference in age almost excludes the possibility of her having been an object of jealousy. It is known that, when their passions awake, children never develop such violent reactions against the brothers and sisters they find already in existence, but direct their hostility against the new-comers. Nor is the scene we are endeavouring to interpret reconcilable with Goethe's tender age at the time of, or shortly after, Cornelia's birth.

At the time of the birth of the first little brother, Hermann Jakob, Johann Wolfgang was three and a quarter years old. Nearly two years later, when he was about five years old, the second sister was born. Both ages come under consideration in dating the episode of the throwing out of the crockery. The earlier is perhaps to be preferred; and it would best agree with the case of my patient, who was about three and a quarter years old at the birth of his brother.

Moreover, Goethe's brother Hermann Jakob, to whom we are thus led in our attempt at interpretation, did not make so brief a stay in the family nursery as the children born afterwards. One might feel some surprise that the autobiography does not contain a word of remembrance of him.[1] He was over six, and Johann Wolfgang was nearly ten, when he died. Dr Hitschmann, who was kind enough to place his notes on this subject at my disposal, says:

'*Goethe, too, as a little boy saw a younger brother die without regret*. At least, according to Bettina Brentano his mother gave the following account: "It struck her as very extraordinary that he shed no tears at the death of his younger brother Jakob who was his playfellow; he seemed on the contrary to feel annoyance at the grief of his parents and sisters. When, later on, his mother asked the young rebel if he had not been fond of his brother, he ran into his room and brought out from under the bed a heap of papers on which lessons and little stories were written, saying that he had done all this to teach his brother." So it seems all the same that the elder brother enjoyed playing father to the younger and showing him his superiority.'

The opinion might thus be formed that the throwing of crockery out of the window was a symbolic action, or, to put

1. [*Footnote added* 1924:] I take this opportunity of withdrawing an incorrect statement which should not have been made. In a later passage in this first volume the younger brother *is* mentioned and described. It occurs in connection with memories of the serious illnesses of childhood, from which this brother also suffered 'not a little'. 'He was a delicate child, quiet and self-willed, and we never had much to do with each other. Besides, he hardly survived the years of infancy.'

it more correctly, a *magic* action, by which the child (Goethe as well as my patient) gave violent expression to his wish to get rid of a disturbing intruder. There is no need to dispute a child's enjoyment of smashing things; if an action is pleasurable in itself, that is not a hindrance but rather an inducement to repeat it in obedience to other purposes as well. It is unlikely, however, that it could have been the pleasure in the crash and the breaking which ensured the childish prank a lasting place in adult memory. Nor is there any objection to complicating the motivation of the action by adding a further factor. A child who breaks crockery knows quite well that he is doing something naughty for which grown-ups will scold him, and if he is not restrained by that knowledge, he probably has a grudge against his parents that he wants to satisfy; he wants to show naughtiness.

The pleasure in breaking and in broken things would be satisfied, too, if the child simply threw the breakable object on the ground. The hurling them out of the window into the street would still remain unexplained. This 'out!' seems to be an essential part of the magic action and to arise directly from its hidden meaning. The new baby must be *got rid of* – through the window, perhaps because he came in through the window. The whole action would thus be equivalent to the verbal response, already familiar to us, of a child who was told that the stork had brought a little brother. 'The stork can take him away again!' was his verdict.[1]

All the same, we are not blind to the objections – apart from any internal uncertainties – against basing the interpretation of a childhood act on a single parallel. For this reason I had for years kept back my theory about the little scene in *Dichtung und Wahrheit*. Then one day I had a patient who began his analysis with the following remarks, which I set down word for word: 'I am the eldest of a family of eight or nine children.[2]

---

1. [See *The Interpretation of Dreams* (1900*a*), *P.F.L.*, **4**, 351.]

2. A momentary error of a striking character. It was probably induced by the influence of the intention, which was already showing itself, to get rid of a brother. (Cf. Ferenczi, 1912, 'Transitory Symptom-Constructions during the Analysis'.)

One of my earliest recollections is of my father sitting on the bed in his night-shirt and telling me laughingly that I had a new brother. I was then three and three-quarter years old; that is the difference in age between me and my next younger brother. I know, too, that a short time after (or was it a year before?)[1] I threw a lot of things, brushes – or was it only one brush? – shoes and other things, out of the window into the street. I have a still earlier recollection. When I was two years old, I spent a night with my parents in a hotel bedroom at Linz on the way to the Salzkammergut. I was so restless in the night and made such a noise that my father had to beat me.'

After hearing this statement I threw all doubts to the winds. When in analysis two things are brought out one immediately after the other, as though in one breath, we have to interpret this proximity as a connection of thought. It was, therefore, as if the patient had said, '*Because* I found that I had got a new brother, I shortly afterwards threw these things into the street.' The act of flinging the brushes, shoes and so on, out of the window must be recognized as a reaction to the birth of the brother. Nor is it a matter for regret that in this instance the objects thrown out were not crockery but other things, probably anything the child could reach at the moment. – The hurling out (through the window into the street) thus proves to be the essential thing in the act, while the pleasure in the smashing and the noise, and the class of object on which 'execution is done', are variable and unessential points.

Naturally, the principle of there being a connection of thought must be applied as well to the patient's third childhood recollection, which is the earliest, though it was put at the end of the short series. This can easily be done. Evidently the two-year-old child was so restless because he could not bear his parents being in bed together. On the journey it was no doubt impossible to avoid the child being a witness of this. The feelings

1. This doubt, attaching to the essential point of the communication for purposes of resistance, was shortly afterwards withdrawn by the patient of his own accord.

which were aroused at that time in the jealous little boy left him with an embitterment against women which persisted and permanently interfered with the development of his capacity for love.

After making these two observations I expressed the opinion at a meeting of the Vienna Psycho-Analytical Society that occurrences of the same kind might be not infrequent among young children; in response, Frau Dr von Hug-Hellmuth placed two further observations at my disposal, which I append here.

I

'At the age of about three and a half, little Erich quite suddenly acquired the habit of throwing everything he did not like out of the window. He also did it, however, with things that were not in his way and did not concern him. On his father's birthday – he was three years and four and a half months old – he snatched a heavy rolling-pin from the kitchen, dragged it into the living-room and threw it out of the window of the third-floor flat into the street. Some days later he sent after it the kitchen-pestle, and then a pair of heavy mountaineering boots of his father's, which he had first to take out of the cupboard.[1]

'At that time his mother had a miscarriage, in the seventh or eighth month of pregnancy, and after that the child was "sweet and quiet and so good that he seemed quite changed". In the fifth or sixth month he repeatedly said to his mother, "Mummy, I'll jump on your tummy" – or, "I'll push your tummy in." And shortly before the miscarriage, in October, he said, "If I must have a brother, at least I don't want him till after Christmas."'

1. 'He always chose heavy objects.'

II

'A young lady of nineteen told me spontaneously that her earliest recollection was as follows: "I see myself, frightfully naughty, sitting under the table in the dining-room, ready to creep out. My cup of coffee is standing on the table – I can still see the pattern on the china quite plainly – and Granny comes into the room just as I am going to throw it out of the window.

' "For the fact was that no one had been bothering about me, and in the meantime a skin had formed on the coffee, which was always perfectly dreadful to me and still is.

' "On that day my brother, who is two and a half years younger than I am, was born, and so no one had had any time to spare for me.

' "They always tell me that I was insupportable on that day: at dinner I threw my father's favourite glass on the floor, I dirtied my frock several times, and was in the worst temper from morning to night. In my rage I tore a bath-doll to pieces." '

These two cases scarcely call for a commentary. They establish without further analytic effort that the bitterness children feel about the expected or actual appearance of a rival finds expression in throwing objects out of the window and in other acts of naughtiness and destructiveness. In the first case the 'heavy objects' probably symbolized the mother herself, against whom the child's anger was directed so long as the new baby had not yet appeared. The three-and-a-half-year-old boy knew about his mother's pregnancy and had no doubt that she had got the baby in her body. 'Little Hans'[1] and his special dread of heavily loaded carts may be recalled here.[2] In the second

1. Cf. 'Analysis of a Phobia in a Five-Year-Old Boy' (1909b) [P.F.L., 8, 250–51, 285–6].

2. Further confirmation of this pregnancy symbolism was given me some time ago by a lady of over fifty. She had often been told that as a little child, when she could hardly talk, she used to drag her father to the window

case the very young age of the child, two and a half years, is noteworthy.

If we now return to Goethe's childhood memory and put in the place it occupies in *Dichtung und Wahrheit* what we believe we have obtained through observations of other children, a perfectly valid train of thought emerges which we should not otherwise have discovered. It would run thus: 'I was a child of fortune: destiny preserved my life, although I came into the world as though dead. Even more, destiny removed my brother, so that I did not have to share my mother's love with him.' The train of thought [in *Dichtung und Wahrheit*] then goes on to someone else who died in those early days – the grandmother who lived like a quiet friendly spirit in another part of the house.

I have, however, already remarked elsewhere[1] that if a man has been his mother's undisputed darling he retains throughout life the triumphant feeling, the confidence in success, which not seldom brings actual success along with it. And Goethe might well have given some such heading to his autobiography as: 'My strength has its roots in my relation to my mother.'

---

in great agitation whenever a heavy furniture-van was passing along the street. In view of other recollections of the houses they had lived in, it became possible to establish that she was then younger than two and three-quarter years. At about that time the brother next to her was born, and in consequence of this addition to the family a move was made. At about the same time, she often had an alarming feeling before going to sleep of something uncannily large, that came up to her, and 'her hands got so thick'.

1. [In a footnote added in 1911 to Chapter VI (E) of *The Interpretation of Dreams* (1900a), P.F.L., 4, 523 n.]

THE 'UNCANNY'
(1919)

DAS UNHEIMLICHE

(A) GERMAN EDITIONS:

1919   *Imago*, **5** (5–6), 297–324.
1922   *S.K.S.N.*, **5**, 229–73.
1924   *Dichtung und Kunst*, 99–138.
1947   *Gesammelte Werke*, **12**, 229–68.

(B) ENGLISH TRANSLATIONS:

'The "Uncanny"'

1925   *Collected Papers*, **4**, 368–407. (Tr. Alix Strachey.)
1955   *Standard Edition*, **17**, 217–52. (Considerably modified version of above.)

The present edition is a corrected reprint of the *Standard Edition* version.

This paper, published in the autumn of 1919, is mentioned by Freud in a letter to Ferenczi of 12 May of the same year, in which he says he has dug an old paper out of a drawer and is rewriting it. Nothing is known as to when it was originally written or how much it was changed, though the footnote quoted from *Totem and Taboo* (1912–13) shows that the subject was present in his mind as early as 1913. The passages dealing with the 'compulsions to repeat' must in any case have formed part of the revision. They include a summary of much of the contents of *Beyond the Pleasure Principle* (1920*g*) and speak of it as 'already completed', though it was not in fact published for another year. (See *P.F.L.*, **11**, 269 ff.)

The first section of the present paper, with its lengthy quotation from a German dictionary, raises special difficulties for the translator. It is to be hoped that readers will not allow themselves to be discouraged by this preliminary obstacle, for the paper is full of interesting and important material, and travels far beyond merely linguistic topics.

THE 'UNCANNY'

I

IT is only rarely that a psychoanalyst feels impelled to investigate the subject of aesthetics, even when aesthetics is understood to mean not merely the theory of beauty but the theory of the qualities of feeling. He works in other strata of mental life and has little to do with the subdued emotional impulses which, inhibited in their aims and dependent on a host of concurrent factors, usually furnish the material for the study of aesthetics. But it does occasionally happen that he has to interest himself in some particular province of that subject; and this province usually proves to be a rather remote one, and one which has been neglected in the specialist literature of aesthetics.

The subject of the 'uncanny'[1] is a province of this kind. It is undoubtedly related to what is frightening – to what arouses dread and horror; equally certainly, too, the word is not always used in a clearly definable sense, so that it tends to coincide with what excites fear in general. Yet we may expect that a special core of feeling is present which justifies the use of a special conceptual term. One is curious to know what this common core is which allows us to distinguish as 'uncanny' certain things which lie within the field of what is frightening.

As good as nothing is to be found upon this subject in comprehensive treatises on aesthetics, which in general prefer to concern themselves with what is beautiful, attractive and sublime – that is, with feelings of a positive nature – and with the circumstances and the objects that call them forth, rather

1. [The German word, translated throughout this paper by the English 'uncanny', is *unheimlich*, literally 'unhomely'. The English term is not, of course, an exact equivalent of the German one.]

than with the opposite feelings of repulsion and distress. I know of only one attempt in medico-psychological literature, a fertile but not exhaustive paper by Jentsch (1906). But I must confess that I have not made a very thorough examination of the literature, especially the foreign literature, relating to this present modest contribution of mine, for reasons which, as may easily be guessed, lie in the times in which we live; so that my paper is presented to the reader without any claim to priority.

In his study of the 'uncanny' Jentsch quite rightly lays stress on the obstacle presented by the fact that people vary so very greatly in their sensitivity to this quality of feeling. The writer of the present contribution, indeed, must himself plead guilty to a special obtuseness in the matter, where extreme delicacy of perception would be more in place. It is long since he has experienced or heard of anything which has given him an uncanny impression, and he must start by translating himself into that state of feeling, by awakening in himself the possibility of experiencing it. Still, such difficulties make themselves powerfully felt in many other branches of aesthetics; we need not on that account despair of finding instances in which the quality in question will be unhesitatingly recognized by most people.

Two courses are open to us at the outset. Either we can find out what meaning has come to be attached to the word 'uncanny' in the course of its history; or we can collect all those properties of persons, things, sense-impressions, experiences and situations which arouse in us the feeling of uncanniness, and then infer the unknown nature of the uncanny from what all these examples have in common. I will say at once that both courses lead to the same result: the uncanny is that class of the frightening which leads back to what is known of old and long familiar. How this is possible, in what circumstances the familiar can become uncanny and frightening, I shall show in what follows. Let me also add that my investigation was actually begun by collecting a number of individual cases, and was only later confirmed by an examination of linguistic usage. In this discussion, however, I shall follow the reverse course.

*

I. THE 'UNCANNY'

The German word *'unheimlich'* is obviously the opposite of *'heimlich'* ['homely'], *'heimisch'* ['native'] – the opposite of what is familiar; and we are tempted to conclude that what is 'uncanny' is frightening precisely because it is *not* known and familiar. Naturally not everything that is new and unfamiliar is frightening, however; the relation is not capable of inversion. We can only say that what is novel can easily become frightening and uncanny; some new things are frightening but not by any means all. Something has to be added to what is novel and unfamiliar in order to make it uncanny.

On the whole, Jentsch did not get beyond this relation of the uncanny to the novel and unfamiliar. He ascribes the essential factor in the production of the feeling of uncanniness to intellectual uncertainty; so that the uncanny would always, as it were, be something one does not know one's way about in. The better orientated in his environment a person is, the less readily will he get the impression of something uncanny in regard to the objects and events in it.

It is not difficult to see that this definition is incomplete, and we will therefore try to proceed beyond the equation 'uncanny' = 'unfamiliar'. We will first turn to other languages. But the dictionaries that we consult tell us nothing new, perhaps only because we ourselves speak a language that is foreign. Indeed, we get an impression that many languages are without a word for this particular shade of what is frightening.

I should like to express my indebtedness to Dr Theodor Reik for the following excerpts:

LATIN: (K. E. Georges, *Deutschlateinisches Wörterbuch*, 1898). An uncanny place: *locus suspectus*; at an uncanny time of night: *intempesta nocte* .

GREEK: (Rost's and Schenkl's Lexikons). ξένος (i.e. strange, foreign).

ENGLISH: (from the dictionaries of Lucas, Bellows, Flügel and Muret-Sanders). Uncomfortable, uneasy, gloomy, dismal, uncanny, ghastly; (of a house) haunted; (of a man) a repulsive fellow.

FRENCH: (Sachs–Villatte). *Inquiétant, sinistre, lugubre, mal à son aise.*

SPANISH: (Tollhausen, 1889). *Sospechoso, de mal agüero, lúgubre, siniestro.*

The Italian and Portuguese languages seem to content themselves with words which we should describe as circumlocutions. In Arabic and Hebrew 'uncanny' means the same as 'daemonic', 'gruesome'.

Let us therefore return to the German language. In Daniel Sanders's *Wörterbuch der Deutschen Sprache* (1860, 1, 729), the following entry, which I here reproduce in full, is to be found under the word *'heimlich'*. I have laid stress on one or two passages by italicizing them.[1]

Heimlich, adj., subst. *Heimlichkeit* (pl. *Heimlichkeiten*): I. Also *heimelich, heimelig*, belonging to the house, not strange, familiar, tame, intimate, friendly, etc.

(*a*) (Obsolete) belonging to the house or the family, or regarded as so belonging (cf. Latin *familiaris*, familiar): *Die Heimlichen*, the members of the household; *Der heimliche Rat* (*Genesis*, xli, 45; 2 *Samuel*, xxiii, 23; 1 *Chronicles*, xii, 25; *Wisdom*, viii, 4), now more usually *Geheimer Rat* [Privy Councillor].

(*b*) Of animals: tame, companionable to man. As opposed to wild, e.g. 'Animals which are neither wild nor *heimlich*', etc. 'Wild animals . . . that are trained to be *heimlich* and accustomed to men.' 'If these young creatures are brought up from early days among men they become quite *heimlich*, friendly' etc. So also: 'It (the lamb) is so *heimlich* and eats out of my hand.' 'Nevertheless, the stork is a beautiful, *heimelich* bird.'

(*c*) Intimate, friendlily comfortable; the enjoyment of quiet content, etc., arousing a sense of agreeable restfulness and security as in one within the four walls of his house.[2] 'Is it still *heimlich* to you in your country where strangers are felling

---

1. [In the translation which follows, a few details, mainly giving the sources of the quotations, have been omitted.]

2. [It may be remarked that the English 'canny', in addition to its more usual meaning of 'shrewd', can mean 'pleasant', 'cosy'.]

your woods?' 'She did not feel too *heimlich* with him.' 'Along a high, *heimlich*, shady path . . . , beside a purling, gushing and babbling woodland brook.' 'To destroy the *Heimlichkeit* of the home.' 'I could not readily find another spot so intimate and *heimlich* as this.' 'We pictured it so comfortable, so nice, so cosy and *heimlich*.' 'In quiet *Heimlichkeit*, surrounded by close walls.' 'A careful housewife, who knows how to make a pleasing *Heimlichkeit* (*Häuslichkeit* [domesticity]) out of the smallest means.' 'The man who till recently had been so strange to him now seemed to him all the more *heimlich*.' 'The protestant land-owners do not feel . . . *heimlich* among their catholic inferiors.' 'When it grows *heimlich* and still, and the evening quiet alone watches over your cell.' 'Quiet, lovely and *heimlich*, no place more fitted for their rest.' 'He did not feel at all *heimlich* about it.' – Also, [in compounds] 'The place was so peaceful, so lonely, so shadily-*heimlich*.' 'The in- and out-flowing waves of the current, dreamy and lullaby-*heimlich*.' Cf. in especial *Unheimlich* [see below]. Among Swabian Swiss authors in especial, often as a trisyllable: 'How *heimelich* it seemed to Ivo again of an evening, when he was at home.' 'It was so *heimelig* in the house.' 'The warm room and the *heimelig* afternoon.' 'When a man feels in his heart that he is so small and the Lord so great – that is what is truly *heimelig*.' 'Little by little they grew at ease and *heimelig* among themselves.' 'Friendly *Heimeligkeit*.' 'I shall be nowhere more *heimelich* than I am here.' 'That which comes from afar . . . assuredly does not live quite *heimelig* (*heimatlich* [at home], *freundnachbarlich* [in a neighbourly way]) among the people.' 'The cottage where he had once sat so often among his own people, so *heimelig*, so happy.' 'The sentinel's horn sounds so *heimelig* from the tower, and his voice invites so hospitably.' 'You go to sleep there so soft and warm, so wonderfully *heim'lig*.' – *This form of the word deserves to become general in order to protect this perfectly good sense of the word from becoming obsolete through an easy confusion with* II [see below]. Cf: '"The Zecks [a family name] are all 'heimlich'."* (in sense II) *"'Heimlich'? . . . What do you understand by 'heimlich'?" "Well, . . . they are like a buried spring or a dried-up pond. One cannot walk* *over it without always having the feeling that water might come up there again." "Oh, we call it 'unheimlich'; you call it 'heimlich'. Well, what makes you think that there is something secret and untrustworthy about this family?"'* (Gutzkow).

(*d*) Especially in Silesia: gay, cheerful; also of the weather.

II. Concealed, kept from sight, so that others do not get to know of or about it, withheld from others. To do something *heimlich*, i.e. behind someone's back; to steal away *heimlich*; *heimlich* meetings and appointments; to look on with *heimlich* pleasure at someone's discomfiture; to sigh or weep *heimlich*; to behave *heimlich*, as though there was something to conceal; *heimlich* love-affair, love, sin; *heimlich* places (which good manners oblige us to conceal) (1 *Samuel*, v, 6). 'The *heimlich* chamber' (privy) (2 *Kings*, x, 27). Also, 'the *heimlich* chair'. 'To throw into pits or *Heimlichkeiten*'. – 'Led the steeds *heimlich* before Laomedon.' – 'As secretive, *heimlich*, deceitful and malicious towards cruel masters ... as frank, open, sympathetic and helpful towards a friend in misfortune.' 'You have still to learn what is *heimlich* holiest to me.' 'The *heimlich* art' (magic). 'Where public ventilation has to stop, there *heimlich* machinations begin.' 'Freedom is the whispered watchword of *heimlich* conspirators and the loud battle-cry of professed revolutionaries.' 'A holy, *heimlich* effect.' 'I have roots that are most *heimlich*, I am grown in the deep earth.' 'My *heimlich* pranks.' 'If he is not given it openly and scrupulously he may seize it *heimlich* and unscrupulously.' 'He had achromatic telescopes constructed *heimlich* and secretly.' 'Henceforth I desire that there should be nothing *heimlich* any longer between us.' – To discover, disclose, betray someone's *Heimlichkeiten*; 'to concoct *Heimlichkeiten* behind my back'. 'In my time we studied *Heimlichkeit*.' 'The hand of understanding can alone undo the powerless spell of the *Heimlichkeit* (of hidden gold).' 'Say, where is the place of concealment ... in what place of hidden *Heimlichkeit*?' 'Bees, who make the lock of *Heimlichkeiten*' (i.e. sealing-wax). 'Learned in strange *Heimlichkeiten*' (magic arts).

For compounds see above, I*c*. Note especially the negative

'*un-*': eerie, weird, arousing gruesome fear: 'Seeming quite *un-heimlich* and ghostly to him.' 'The *unheimlich*, fearful hours of night.' 'I had already long since felt an *unheimlich*, even gruesome feeling.' 'Now I am beginning to have an *unheimlich* feeling' ... 'Feels an *unheimlich* horror.' '*Unheimlich* and motionless like a stone image.' 'The *unheimlich* mist called hill-fog.' 'These pale youths are *unheimlich* and are brewing heaven knows what mischief.' ' "*Unheimlich*" *is the name for everything that ought to have remained* ... *secret and hidden but has come to light*' (Schelling). — 'To veil the divine, to surround it with a certain *Unheimlichkeit*.' — *Unheimlich* is not often used as opposite to meaning II (above).

What interests us most in this long extract is to find that among its different shades of meaning the word '*heimlich*' exhibits one which is identical with its opposite, '*unheimlich*'. What is *heimlich* thus comes to be *unheimlich*. (Cf. the quotation from Gutzkow: 'We call it "*unheimlich*"; you call it "*heimlich*".') In general we are reminded that the word '*heimlich*' is not unambiguous, but belongs to two sets of ideas, which, without being contradictory, are yet very different: on the one hand it means what is familiar and agreeable, and on the other, what is concealed and kept out of sight.[1] '*Unheimlich*' is customarily used, we are told, as the contrary only of the first signification of '*heimlich*', and not of the second. Sanders tells us nothing concerning a possible genetic connection between these two meanings of *heimlich*. On the other hand, we notice that Schelling says something which throws quite a new light on the concept of the *Unheimlich*, for which we were certainly not prepared. According to him, everything is *unheimlich* that ought to have remained secret and hidden but has come to light.

Some of the doubts that have thus arisen are removed if

---

1. [According to the *Oxford English Dictionary*, a similar ambiguity attaches to the English 'canny', which may mean not only 'cosy' but also 'endowed with occult or magical powers'.]

we consult Grimms' dictionary (1877, **4**, Part 2, 873 ff.).

We read:

Heimlich; adj. and adv. *vernaculus, occultus*; MHG. heimelich, heimlich.

(P. 874.) In a slightly different sense: 'I feel *heimlich*, well, free from fear' ...

[3] (*b*) *Heimlich* is also used of a place free from ghostly influences ... familiar, friendly, intimate.

(P. 875: *β*) Familiar, amicable, unreserved.

4. *From the idea of 'homelike', 'belonging to the house', the further idea is developed of something withdrawn from the eyes of strangers, something concealed, secret; and this idea is expanded in many ways ...*

(P. 876.) 'On the left bank of the lake there lies a meadow *heimlich* in the wood.' (Schiller, *Wilhelm Tell*, I.4.) ... Poetic licence, rarely so used in modern speech ... *Heimlich* is used in conjunction with a verb expressing the act of concealing: 'In the secret of his tabernacle he shall hide me *heimlich*.' (*Psalms*, xxvii, 5.) ... *Heimlich* parts of the human body, *pudenda* ... 'the men that died not were smitten on their *heimlich* parts.' (*1 Samuel*, v, 12.) ...

(*c*) Officials who give important advice which has to be kept secret in matters of state are called *heimlich* councillors; the adjective, according to modern usage, has been replaced by *geheim* [secret] ... 'Pharaoh called Joseph's name "him to whom secrets are revealed"' (*heimlich* councillor). (*Genesis* xli, 45.)

(P. 878.) 6. *Heimlich*, as used of knowledge – mystic, allegorical: a *heimlich* meaning, *mysticus, divinus, occultus, figuratus*.

(P. 878.) *Heimlich* in a different sense, as withdrawn from knowledge, unconscious ... *Heimlich* also has the meaning of that which is obscure, inaccessible to knowledge ... 'Do you not see? They do not trust us; they fear the *heimlich* face of the Duke of Friedland.' (Schiller, *Wallensteins Lager*, Scene 2.)

9. *The notion of something hidden and dangerous, which is expressed in the last paragraph, is still further developed, so that 'heimlich' comes to have the meaning usually ascribed to 'unheimlich'.* Thus: 'At times I feel like a man who walks in the night and

believes in ghosts; every corner is *heimlich* and full of terrors for him'. (Klinger, *Theater*, **3**, 298.)

Thus *heimlich* is a word the meaning of which develops in the direction of ambivalence, until it finally coincides with its opposite, *unheimlich*. *Unheimlich* is in some way or other a sub-species of *heimlich*. Let us bear this discovery in mind, though we cannot yet rightly understand it, alongside of Schelling's definition of the *Unheimlich*. If we go on to examine individual instances of uncanniness, these hints will become intelligible to us.

II

When we proceed to review the things, persons, impressions, events and situations which are able to arouse in us a feeling of the uncanny in a particularly forcible and definite form, the first requirement is obviously to select a suitable example to start on. Jentsch has taken as a very good instance 'doubts whether an apparently animate being is really alive; or conversely, whether a lifeless object might not be in fact animate'; and he refers in this connection to the impression made by waxwork figures, ingeniously constructed dolls and automata. To these he adds the uncanny effect of epileptic fits, and of manifestations of insanity, because these excite in the spectator the impression of automatic, mechanical processes at work behind the ordinary appearance of mental activity. Without entirely accepting this author's view, we will take it as a starting-point for our own investigation because in what follows he reminds us of a writer who has succeeded in producing uncanny effects better than anyone else.

Jentsch writes: 'In telling a story, one of the most successful devices for easily creating uncanny effects is to leave the reader in uncertainty whether a particular figure in the story is a human being or an automaton, and to do it in such a way that his attention is not focused directly upon his uncertainty, so that he may not be led to go into the matter and clear it up immediately. That, as we have said, would quickly dissipate the peculiar emotional effect of the thing. E. T. A. Hoffmann has repeatedly employed this psychological artifice with success in his fantastic narratives.'

This observation, undoubtedly a correct one, refers primarily to the story of 'The Sand-Man' in Hoffmann's *Nachtstücken*,[1] which contains the original of Olympia, the doll that appears in the first act of Offenbach's opera, *Tales of Hoffmann*. But I cannot think – and I hope most readers of the story will agree with me – that the theme of the doll Olympia, who is to all appearances a living being, is by any means the only, or indeed the most important, element that must be held responsible for the quite unparalleled atmosphere of uncanniness evoked by the story. Nor is this atmosphere heightened by the fact that the author himself treats the episode of Olympia with a faint touch of satire and uses it to poke fun at the young man's idealization of his mistress. The main theme of the story is, on the contrary, something different, something which gives it its name, and which is always re-introduced at critical moments: it is the theme of the 'Sand-Man' who tears out children's eyes.

This fantastic tale opens with the childhood recollections of the student Nathaniel. In spite of his present happiness, he cannot banish the memories associated with the mysterious and terrifying death of his beloved father. On certain evenings his mother used to send the children to bed early, warning them that 'the Sand-Man was coming'; and, sure enough, Nathaniel would not fail to hear the heavy tread of a visitor, with whom his father would then be occupied for the evening. When questioned about the Sand-Man, his mother, it is true, denied that such a person existed except as a figure of speech; but his nurse could give him more definite information: 'He's a wicked

---

1. Hoffmann's *Sämtliche Werke*, Grisebach edition, 3. [A translation of 'The Sand-Man' is included in *Eight Tales of Hoffmann*, translated by J. M. Cohen, London, Pan Books, 1952.]

man who comes when children won't go to bed, and throws handfuls of sand in their eyes so that they jump out of their heads all bleeding. Then he puts the eyes in a sack and carries them off to the half-moon to feed his children. They sit up there in their nest, and their beaks are hooked like owls' beaks, and they use them to peck up naughty boys' and girls' eyes with.'

Although little Nathaniel was sensible and old enough not to credit the figure of the Sand-Man with such gruesome attributes, yet the dread of him became fixed in his heart. He determined to find out what the Sand-Man looked like; and one evening, when the Sand-Man was expected again, he hid in his father's study. He recognized the visitor as lawyer Coppelius, a repulsive person whom the children were frightened of when he occasionally came to a meal; and he now identified this Coppelius with the dreaded Sand-Man. As regards the rest of the scene, Hoffmann already leaves us in doubt whether what we are witnessing is the first delirium of the panic-stricken boy, or a succession of events which are to be regarded in the story as being real. His father and the guest are at work at a brazier with glowing flames. The little eavesdropper hears Coppelius call out: 'Eyes here! Eyes here!' and betrays himself by screaming aloud. Coppelius seizes him and is on the point of dropping bits of red-hot coal from the fire into his eyes, and then of throwing them into the brazier, but his father begs him off and saves his eyes. After this the boy falls into a deep swoon; and a long illness brings his experience to an end. Those who decide in favour of the rationalistic interpretation of the Sand-Man will not fail to recognize in the child's phantasy the persisting influence of his nurse's story. The bits of sand that are to be thrown into the child's eyes turn into bits of red-hot coal from the flames; and in both cases they are intended to make his eyes jump out. In the course of another visit of the Sand-Man's, a year later, his father is killed in his study by an explosion. The lawyer Coppelius disappears from the place without leaving a trace behind.

THE 'UNCANNY'

Nathaniel, now a student, believes that he has recognized this phantom of horror from his childhood in an itinerant optician, an Italian called Giuseppe Coppola, who at his university town, offers him weather-glasses for sale. When Nathaniel refuses, the man goes on: 'Not weather-glasses? not weather-glasses? also got fine eyes, fine eyes!' The student's terror is allayed when he finds that the proffered eyes are only harmless spectacles, and he buys a pocket spy-glass from Coppola. With its aid he looks across into Professor Spalanzani's house opposite and there spies Spalanzani's beautiful, but strangely silent and motionless daughter, Olympia. He soon falls in love with her so violently that, because of her, he quite forgets the clever and sensible girl to whom he is betrothed. But Olympia is an automaton whose clock-work has been made by Spalanzani, and whose eyes have been put in by Coppola, the Sand-Man. The student surprises the two masters quarrelling over their handiwork. The optician carries off the wooden eyeless doll; and the mechanician, Spalanzani, picks up Olympia's bleeding eyes from the ground and throws them at Nathaniel's breast, saying that Coppola had stolen them from the student. Nathaniel succumbs to a fresh attack of madness, and in his delirium his recollection of his father's death is mingled with this new experience. 'Hurry up! hurry up! ring of fire!' he cries. 'Spin about, ring of fire – Hurrah! Hurry up, wooden doll! lovely wooden doll, spin about –.' He then falls upon the professor, Olympia's 'father', and tries to strangle him.

Rallying from a long and serious illness, Nathaniel seems at last to have recovered. He intends to marry his betrothed, with whom he has become reconciled. One day he and she are walking through the city market-place, over which the high tower of the town hall throws its huge shadow. On the girl's suggestion, they climb the tower, leaving her brother, who is walking with them, down below. From the top, Clara's attention is drawn to a curious object moving along the street. Nathaniel looks at this thing through Coppola's spy-glass, which he finds in his pocket, and falls into a new attack of madness. Shouting 'Spin about, wooden doll!' he tries to throw the girl into the gulf below. Her brother, brought to her side by her cries, rescues her and hastens down with her to safety. On the tower above, the madman rushes round, shrieking 'Ring of fire, spin about!' – and we know the origin of the words. Among the people who begin to gather below there comes forward the figure of the lawyer Coppelius, who has suddenly returned. We may suppose that it was his approach, seen through the spy-glass, which threw Nathaniel into his fit of madness. As the onlookers prepare to go up and overpower the madman, Coppelius laughs and says: 'Wait a bit; he'll come down of himself.' Nathaniel suddenly stands still, catches sight of Coppelius, and with a wild shriek 'Yes! "Fine eyes – fine eyes"!' flings himself over the parapet. While he lies on the paving-stones with a shattered skull the Sand-Man vanishes in the throng.

This short summary leaves no doubt, I think, that the feeling of something uncanny is directly attached to the figure of the Sand-Man, that is, to the idea of being robbed of one's eyes, and that Jentsch's point of an intellectual uncertainty has nothing to do with the effect. Uncertainty whether an object is living or inanimate, which admittedly applied to the doll Olympia, is quite irrelevant in connection with this other, more striking instance of uncanniness. It is true that the writer creates a kind of uncertainty in us in the beginning by not letting us know, no doubt purposely, whether he is taking us into the real world or into a purely fantastic one of his own creation. He has, of course, a right to do either; and if he chooses to stage his action in a world peopled with spirits, demons and ghosts, as Shakespeare does in *Hamlet*, in *Macbeth* and, in a different sense, in *The Tempest* and *A Midsummer Night's Dream*, we must bow to his decision and treat his setting as though it were real for as long as we put ourselves into his hands. But this uncertainty disappears in the course of Hoffmann's story, and we perceive that he intends to make us, too, look through the demon optician's spectacles or spy-glass – perhaps, indeed, that the author in his very own person once peered through such an instrument. For the conclusion of the story makes it quite clear that Coppola the optician really *is* the lawyer Coppelius[1] and also, therefore, the Sand-Man.

There is no question, therefore, of any intellectual uncertainty here: we know now that we are not supposed to be looking on at the products of a madman's imagination, behind which we, with the superiority of rational minds, are able to detect the sober truth; and yet this knowledge does not lessen the impression of uncanniness in the least degree. The theory of intellectual uncertainty is thus incapable of explaining that impression.

We know from psychoanalytic experience, however, that the fear of damaging or losing one's eyes is a terrible one in children. Many adults retain their apprehensiveness in this respect, and no physical injury is so much dreaded by them as an injury to the eye. We are accustomed to say, too, that we will treasure a thing as the apple of our eye. A study of dreams, phantasies and myths has taught us that anxiety about one's eyes, the fear of going blind, is often enough a substitute for the dread of being castrated. The self-blinding of the mythical criminal, Oedipus, was simply a mitigated form of the punishment of castration – the only punishment that was adequate for him by the *lex talionis*. We may try on rationalistic grounds to deny that fears about the eye are derived from the fear of castration, and may argue that it is very natural that so precious an organ as the eye should be guarded by a proportionate dread. Indeed, we might go further and say that the fear of castration itself contains no other significance and no deeper secret than a justifiable dread of this rational kind. But this view does not account adequately for the substitutive relation between the eye and the male organ which is seen to exist in dreams and myths and phantasies; nor can it dispel the impression that the threat of being castrated in especial excites a peculiarly violent and obscure emotion, and that this emotion

---

1. Frau Dr Rank has pointed out the association of the name with '*coppella*' = crucible, connecting it with the chemical operations that caused the father's death; and also with '*coppo*' = eye-socket.

is what first gives the idea of losing other organs its intense colouring. All further doubts are removed when we learn the details of their 'castration complex' from the analysis of neurotic patients, and realize its immense importance in their mental life.

Moreover, I would not recommend any opponent of the psychoanalytic view to select this particular story of the Sand-Man with which to support his argument that anxiety about the eyes has nothing to do with the castration complex. For why does Hoffmann bring the anxiety about eyes into such intimate connection with the father's death? And why does the Sand-Man always appear as a disturber of love? He separates the unfortunate Nathaniel from his betrothed and from her brother, his best friend; he destroys the second object of his love, Olympia, the lovely doll; and he drives him into suicide at the moment when he has won back his Clara and is about to be happily united to her. Elements in the story like these, and many others, seem arbitrary and meaningless so long as we deny all connection between fears about the eye and castration; but they become intelligible as soon as we replace the Sand-Man by the dreaded father at whose hands castration is expected.[1]

---

1. In fact, Hoffmann's imaginative treatment of his material has not made such wild confusion of its elements that we cannot reconstruct their original arrangement. In the story of Nathaniel's childhood, the figures of his father and Coppelius represent the two opposites into which the father-imago is split by his ambivalence; whereas the one threatens to blind him – that is, to castrate him – the other, the 'good' father, intercedes for his sight. The part of the complex which is most strongly repressed, the death-wish against the 'bad' father, finds expression in the death of the 'good' father, and Coppelius is made answerable for it. This pair of fathers is represented later, in his student days, by Professor Spalanzani and Coppola the optician. The Professor is in himself a member of the father-series, and Coppola is recognized as identical with Coppelius the lawyer. Just as they used before to work together over the secret brazier, so now they have jointly created the doll Olympia; the Professor is even called the father of Olympia. This double occurrence of activity in common betrays them as divisions of the father-imago: both the mechanician and the optician were the father of Nathaniel (and of Olympia as well). In the frightening scene in childhood,

We shall venture, therefore, to refer the uncanny effect of
the Sand-Man to the anxiety belonging to the castration
complex of childhood. But having reached the idea that we
can make an infantile factor such as this responsible for feelings
of uncanniness, we are encouraged to see whether we can apply
it to other instances of the uncanny. We find in the story of
the Sand-Man the other theme on which Jentsch lays stress,
of a doll which appears to be alive. Jentsch believes that a
particularly favourable condition for awakening uncanny
feelings is created when there is intellectual uncertainty whether
an object is alive or not, and when an inanimate object becomes
too much like an animate one. Now, dolls are of course rather
closely connected with childhood life. We remember that in

Coppelius, after sparing Nathaniel's eyes, had screwed off his arms and legs
as an experiment; that is, he had worked on him as a mechanician would
on a doll. This singular feature, which seems quite outside the picture of
the Sand-Man, introduces a new castration equivalent; but it also points to
the inner identity of Coppelius with his later counterpart, Spalanzani the
mechanician, and prepares us for the interpretation of Olympia. This
automatic doll can be nothing else than a materialization of Nathaniel's
feminine attitude towards his father in his infancy. Her fathers, Spalanzani
and Coppola, are, after all, nothing but new editions, reincarnations of
Nathaniel's pair of fathers. Spalanzani's otherwise incomprehensible statement
that the optician has stolen Nathaniel's eyes (see above [p. 350]), so as to
set them in the doll, now becomes significant as supplying evidence of the
identity of Olympia and Nathaniel. Olympia is, as it were, a dissociated
complex of Nathaniel's which confronts him as a person, and Nathaniel's
enslavement to this complex is expressed in his senseless obsessive love for
Olympia. We may with justice call love of this kind narcissistic, and we
can understand why someone who has fallen victim to it should relinquish
the real, external object of his love. The psychological truth of the situation
in which the young man, fixated upon his father by his castration complex,
becomes incapable of loving a woman, is amply proved by numerous analyses
of patients whose story, though less fantastic, is hardly less tragic than that
of the student Nathaniel.

Hoffmann was the child of an unhappy marriage. When he was three
years old, his father left his small family, and was never united to them again.
According to Grisebach, in his biographical introduction to Hoffmann's
works, the writer's relation to his father was always a most sensitive subject
with him.

their early games children do not distinguish at all sharply
between living and inanimate objects, and that they are
especially fond of treating their dolls like live people. In fact,
I have occasionally heard a woman patient declare that even
at the age of eight she had still been convinced that her dolls
would be certain to come to life if she were to look at them
in a particular, extremely concentrated, way. So that here, too,
it is not difficult to discover a factor from childhood. But,
curiously enough, while the Sand-Man story deals with the
arousing of an early childhood fear, the idea of a 'living doll'
excites no fear at all; children have no fear of their dolls coming
to life, they may even desire it. The source of uncanny feelings
would not, therefore, be an infantile fear in this case, but rather
an infantile wish or even merely an infantile belief. There seems
to be a contradiction here; but perhaps it is only a complication,
which may be helpful to us later on.

Hoffmann is the unrivalled master of the uncanny in literature. His novel, *Die Elixiere des Teufels* [*The Devil's Elixir*],
contains a whole mass of themes to which one is tempted to
ascribe the uncanny effect of the narrative;[1] but it is too obscure
and intricate a story for us to venture upon a summary of it.
Towards the end of the book the reader is told the facts, hitherto
concealed from him, from which the action springs; with the

1. [Under the rubric 'Varia' in one of the issues of the *Internationale
Zeitschrift für Psychoanalyse* for 1919 (5, 308), the year in which the present
paper was first published, there appears over the initials 'S.F.' a short note
which it is not unreasonable to attribute to Freud. Its insertion here, though
strictly speaking irrelevant, may perhaps be excused. The note is headed:
'E. T. A. Hoffmann on the Function of Consciousness' and it proceeds: 'In
Die Elixiere des Teufels (Part II, p. 210, in Hesse's edition) – a novel rich
in masterly descriptions of pathological mental states – Schönfeld comforts
the hero, whose consciousness is temporarily disturbed, with the following
words: "And what do you get out of it? I mean out of the particular mental
function which we call consciousness, and which is nothing but the con-
founded activity of a damned toll-collector – excise-man – deputy-chief
customs officer, who has set up his infamous bureau in our top storey and
who exclaims, whenever any goods try to get out: 'Hi! hi! exports are
prohibited . . . they must stay here . . . here, in this country. . . .'" ']

result, not that he is at last enlightened, but that he falls into a state of complete bewilderment. The author has piled up too much material of the same kind. In consequence one's grasp of the story as a whole suffers, though not the impression it makes. We must content ourselves with selecting those themes of uncanniness which are most prominent, and with seeing whether they too can fairly be traced back to infantile sources. These themes are all concerned with the phenomenon of the 'double', which appears in every shape and in every degree of development. Thus we have characters who are to be considered identical because they look alike. This relation is accentuated by mental processes leaping from one of these characters to another — by what we should call telepathy — so that the one possesses knowledge, feelings and experience in common with the other. Or it is marked by the fact that the subject identifies himself with someone else, so that he is in doubt as to which his self is, or substitutes the extraneous self for his own. In other words, there is a doubling, dividing and interchanging of the self. And finally there is the constant recurrence of the same thing[1] — the repetition of the same features or character-traits or vicissitudes, of the same crimes, or even the same names through several consecutive generations.

The theme of the 'double' has been very thoroughly treated by Otto Rank (1914). He has gone into the connections which the 'double' has with reflections in mirrors, with shadows, with guardian spirits, with the belief in the soul and with the fear of death; but he also lets in a flood of light on the surprising evolution of the idea. For the 'double' was originally an insurance against the destruction of the ego, an 'energetic denial of the power of death', as Rank says; and probably the 'immortal' soul was the first 'double' of the body. This invention of doubling as a preservation against extinction has its counter-

---

1. [This phrase seems to be an echo from Nietzsche (e.g. from the last part of *Also Sprach Zarathustra*). In *Beyond the Pleasure Principle* (1920g), *P.F.L.*, **11**, 292, Freud puts a similar phrase, 'this perpetual recurrence of the same thing', into inverted commas.]

part in the language of dreams, which is fond of representing castration by a doubling or a multiplication of a genital symbol.[1] The same desire led the Ancient Egyptians to develop the art of making images of the dead in lasting materials. Such ideas, however, have sprung from the soil of unbounded self-love, from the primary narcissism which dominates the mind of the child and of primitive man. But when this stage has been surmounted, the 'double' reverses its aspect. From having been an assurance of immortality, it becomes the uncanny harbinger of death.

The idea of the 'double' does not necessarily disappear with the passing of primary narcissism, for it can receive fresh meaning from the later stages of the ego's development. A special agency is slowly formed there, which is able to stand over against the rest of the ego, which has the function of observing and criticizing the self and of exercising a censorship within the mind, and which we become aware of as our 'conscience'. In the pathological case of delusions of observation, this mental agency becomes isolated, dissociated from the ego, and discernible to the physician's eye. The fact that an agency of this kind exists, which is able to treat the rest of the ego like an object — the fact, that is, that man is capable of self-observation — renders it possible to invest the old idea of a 'double' with a new meaning and to ascribe a number of things to it — above all, those things which seem to self-criticism to belong to the old surmounted narcissism of earliest times.[2]

1. [Cf. *The Interpretation of Dreams* (1900a), P.F.L., **4**, 474.]

2. I believe that when poets complain that two souls dwell in the human breast, and when popular psychologists talk of the splitting of people's egos, what they are thinking of is this division (in the sphere of ego psychology) between the critical agency and the rest of the ego, and not the antithesis discovered by psychoanalysis between the ego and what is unconscious and repressed. It is true that the distinction between these two antitheses is to some extent effaced by the circumstance that foremost among the things that are rejected by the criticism of the ego are derivatives of the repressed. – [Freud had already discussed this critical agency at length in his paper on narcissism (1914c), P.F.L., **11**, 89–92, and it was soon to be further expanded into the 'ego ideal' and 'super-ego' in, respectively, *Group Psychology* (1921c), ibid., **12**, 161–6, and *The Ego and the Id* (1923b), ibid., **11**, 367–79.]

But it is not only this latter material, offensive as it is to the criticism of the ego, which may be incorporated in the idea of a double. There are also all the unfulfilled but possible futures to which we still like to cling in phantasy, all the strivings of the ego which adverse external circumstances have crushed, and all our suppressed acts of volition which nourish in us the illusion of free will.[1] [Cf. Freud, 1901*b*, *P.F.L.*, **5**, 316.]

But after having thus considered the *manifest* motivation of the figure of a 'double', we have to admit that none of this helps us to understand the extraordinarily strong feeling of something uncanny that pervades the conception; and our knowledge of pathological mental processes enables us to add that nothing in this more superficial material could account for the urge towards defence which has caused the ego to project that material outward as something foreign to itself. When all is said and done, the quality of uncanniness can only come from the fact of the 'double' being a creation dating back to a very early mental stage, long since surmounted – a stage, incidentally, at which it wore a more friendly aspect. The 'double' has become a thing of terror, just as, after the collapse of their religion, the gods turned into demons. (Heine, 'Die Götter im Exil'.)

The other forms of ego disturbance exploited by Hoffmann can easily be estimated along the same lines as the theme of the 'double'. They are a harking-back to particular phases in the evolution of the self-regarding feeling, a regression to a time when the ego had not yet marked itself off sharply from the external world and from other people. I believe that these factors are partly responsible for the impression of uncanniness, although it is not easy to isolate and determine exactly their share of it.

The factor of the repetition of the same thing will perhaps

1. In Ewers's *Der Student von Prag*, which serves as the starting-point of Rank's study on the 'double', the hero has promised his beloved not to kill his antagonist in a duel. But on his way to the duelling-ground he meets his 'double', who has already killed his rival. [Cf. Rank, 1914.]

not appeal to everyone as a source of uncanny feeling. From what I have observed, this phenomenon does undoubtedly, subject to certain conditions and combined with certain circumstances, arouse an uncanny feeling, which, furthermore, recalls the sense of helplessness experienced in some dream-states. As I was walking, one hot summer afternoon, through the deserted streets of a provincial town in Italy which was unknown to me, I found myself in a quarter of whose character I could not long remain in doubt. Nothing but painted women were to be seen at the windows of the small houses, and I hastened to leave the narrow street at the next turning. But after having wandered about for a time without inquiring my way, I suddenly found myself back in the same street, where my presence was now beginning to excite attention. I hurried away once more, only to arrive by another *détour* at the same place yet a third time. Now, however, a feeling overcame me which I can only describe as uncanny, and I was glad enough to find myself back at the piazza I had left a short while before, without any further voyages of discovery. Other situations which have in common with my adventure an unintended recurrence of the same situation, but which differ radically from it in other respects, also result in the same feeling of helplessness and of uncanniness. So, for instance, when, caught in a mist perhaps, one has lost one's way in a mountain forest, every attempt to find the marked or familiar path may bring one back again and again to one and the same spot, which one can identify by some particular landmark. Or one may wander about in a dark, strange room, looking for the door or the electric switch, and collide time after time with the same piece of furniture – though it is true that Mark Twain succeeded by wild exaggeration in turning this latter situation into something irresistibly comic.[1]

If we take another class of things, it is easy to see that there, too, it is only this factor of involuntary repetition which surrounds what would otherwise be innocent enough with an uncanny atmosphere, and forces upon us the idea of something

1. [Mark Twain, *A Tramp Abroad*, London, 1880, **1**, 107.]

fateful and inescapable when otherwise we should have spoken only of 'chance'. For instance, we naturally attach no importance to the event when we hand in an overcoat and get a cloakroom ticket with the number, let us say, 62; or when we find that our cabin on a ship bears that number. But the impression is altered if two such events, each in itself indifferent, happen close together – if we come across the number 62 several times in a single day, or if we begin to notice that everything which has a number – addresses, hotel rooms, compartments in railway trains – invariably has the same one, or at all events one which contains the same figures. We do feel this to be uncanny. And unless a man is utterly hardened and proof against the lure of superstition, he will be tempted to ascribe a secret meaning to this obstinate recurrence of a number; he will take it, perhaps, as an indication of the span of life allotted to him.[1] Or suppose one is engaged in reading the works of the famous physiologist, Hering,[2] and within the space of a few days receives two letters from two different countries, each from a person called Hering, though one has never before had any dealings with anyone of that name. Not long ago an ingenious scientist (Kammerer, 1919) attempted to reduce coincidences of this kind to certain laws, and so deprive them of their uncanny effect. I will not venture to decide whether he has succeeded or not.

How exactly we can trace back to infantile psychology the uncanny effect of such similar recurrences is a question I can only lightly touch on in these pages; and I must refer the reader instead to another work,[3] already completed, in which this has been gone into in detail, but in a different connection. For it is possible to recognize the dominance in the unconscious mind of a 'compulsion to repeat' proceeding from the instinctual impulses and probably inherent in the very nature of the instincts – a compulsion powerful enough to overrule the pleasure

1. [Freud had himself reached the age of sixty-two a year earlier, in 1918.]
2. [Ewald Hering (1834–1918); cf. *P.F.L.*, **11**, 211–12, 322.]
3. [This was *Beyond the Pleasure Principle* (1920*g*), ibid., **11**, 283–6, 288–94, where the 'compulsion to repeat' is enlarged upon.]

principle, lending to certain aspects of the mind their daemonic character, and still very clearly expressed in the impulses of small children; a compulsion, too, which is responsible for a part of the course taken by the analyses of neurotic patients. All these considerations prepare us for the discovery that whatever reminds us of this inner 'compulsion to repeat' is perceived as uncanny.

Now, however, it is time to turn from these aspects of the matter, which are in any case difficult to judge, and look for some undeniable instances of the uncanny, in the hope that an analysis of them will decide whether our hypothesis is a valid one.

In the story of 'The Ring of Polycrates',[1] the King of Egypt turns away in horror from his host, Polycrates, because he sees that his friend's every wish is at once fulfilled, his every care promptly removed by kindly fate. His host has become 'uncanny' to him. His own explanation, that the too fortunate man has to fear the envy of the gods, seems obscure to us; its meaning is veiled in mythological language. We will therefore turn to another example in a less grandiose setting. In the case history of an obsessional neurotic,[2] I have described how the patient once stayed in a hydropathic establishment and benefited greatly by it. He had the good sense, however, to attribute his improvement not to the therapeutic properties of the water, but to the situation of his room, which immediately adjoined that of a very accommodating nurse. So on his second visit to the establishment he asked for the same room, but was told that it was already occupied by an old gentleman, whereupon he gave vent to his annoyance in the words: 'I wish he may be struck dead for it.' A fortnight later the old gentleman really did have a stroke. My patient thought this an 'uncanny' experience. The impression of uncanniness would have been stronger still if less time had elapsed between his words and the untoward event, or if he had been able to report innumerable similar coincidences. As a matter of fact, he had

1. [Schiller's poem based on Herodotus.]
2. 'Notes upon a Case of Obsessional Neurosis' (1909*d*) [*P.F.L.*, **9**, 113–14].

no difficulty in producing coincidences of this sort; but then not only he but every obsessional neurotic I have observed has been able to relate analogous experiences. They are never surprised at their invariably running up against someone they have just been thinking of, perhaps for the first time for a long while. If they say one day 'I haven't had any news of so-and-so for a long time', they will be sure to get a letter from him the next morning, and an accident or a death will rarely take place without having passed through their mind a little while before. They are in the habit of referring to this state of affairs in the most modest manner, saying that they have 'presentiments' which 'usually' come true.

One of the most uncanny and widespread forms of superstition is the dread of the evil eye, which has been exhaustively studied by the Hamburg oculist Seligmann (1910–11). There never seems to have been any doubt about the source of this dread. Whoever possesses something that is at once valuable and fragile is afraid of other people's envy, in so far as he projects on to them the envy he would have felt in their place. A feeling like this betrays itself by a look[1] even though it is not put into words; and when a man is prominent owing to noticeable, and particularly owing to unattractive, attributes, other people are ready to believe that his envy is rising to a more than usual degree of intensity and that this intensity will convert it into effective action. What is feared is thus a secret intention of doing harm, and certain signs are taken to mean that that intention has the necessary power at its command.

These last examples of the uncanny are to be referred to the principle which I have called 'omnipotence of thoughts', taking the name from an expression used by one of my patients.[2] And now we find ourselves on familiar ground. Our analysis of instances of the uncanny has led us back to the old, animistic conception of the universe. This was characterized by the idea that the world was peopled with the spirits of human

1. ['The evil eye' in German is *der böse Blick*, literally 'the evil look'.]
2. [The obsessional patient referred to just above – the 'Rat Man' (1909*d*), P.F.L., **9**, 113–14 and *n*. 2.]

beings; by the subject's narcissistic overvaluation of his own mental processes; by the belief in the omnipotence of thoughts and the technique of magic based on that belief; by the attribution to various outside persons and things of carefully graded magical powers, or '*mana*'; as well as by all the other creations with the help of which man, in the unrestricted narcissism of that stage of development, strove to fend off the manifest prohibitions of reality. It seems as if each one of us has been through a phase of individual development corresponding to this animistic stage in primitive men, that none of us has passed through it without preserving certain residues and traces of it which are still capable of manifesting themselves, and that everything which now strikes us as 'uncanny' fulfils the condition of touching those residues of animistic mental activity within us and bringing them to expression.[1]

At this point I will put forward two considerations which, I think, contain the gist of this short study. In the first place, if psychoanalytic theory is correct in maintaining that every affect belonging to an emotional impulse, whatever its kind, is transformed, if it is repressed, into anxiety, then among instances of frightening things there must be one class in which the frightening element can be shown to be something repressed which *recurs*. This class of frightening things would then constitute the uncanny; and it must be a matter of indifference whether what is uncanny was itself originally frightening or whether it carried some *other* affect. In the second place, if this is indeed the secret nature of the uncanny, we can understand why linguistic usage has extended *das Heimliche* ['homely'] into its opposite, *das Unheimliche*; for this uncanny is in reality nothing new or alien, but something which is familiar and old-established in the mind and which has become alienated from

1. Cf. my book *Totem and Taboo* (1912–13), Essay III, 'Animism, Magic and the Omnipotence of Thoughts', where the following footnote will be found: 'We appear to attribute an "uncanny" quality to impressions that seek to confirm the omnipotence of thoughts and the animistic mode of thinking in general, after we have reached a stage at which, in our *judgement*, we have abandoned such beliefs.' [*P.F.L.*, **13**, 144 *n.* 1.]

it only through the process of repression. This reference to the factor of repression enables us, furthermore, to understand Schelling's definition [p. 345] of the uncanny as something which ought to have remained hidden but has come to light.

It only remains for us to test our new hypothesis on one or two more examples of the uncanny.

Many people experience the feeling in the highest degree in relation to death and dead bodies, to the return of the dead, and to spirits and ghosts. As we have seen, some languages in use to-day can only render the German expression 'an *unheimlich* house' by 'a *haunted* house'. We might indeed have begun our investigation with this example, perhaps the most striking of all, of something uncanny, but we refrained from doing so because the uncanny in it is too much intermixed with what is purely gruesome and is in part overlaid by it. There is scarcely any other matter, however, upon which our thoughts and feelings have changed so little since the very earliest times, and in which discarded forms have been so completely preserved under a thin disguise, as our relation to death. Two things account for our conservatism: the strength of our original emotional reaction to death and the insufficiency of our scientific knowledge about it. Biology has not yet been able to decide whether death is the inevitable fate of every living being or whether it is only a regular but yet perhaps avoidable event in life.[1] It is true that the statement 'All men are mortal' is paraded in text-books of logic as an example of a general proposition; but no human being really grasps it, and our unconscious has as little use now as it ever had for the idea of its own mortality.[2] Religions continue to dispute the importance of the undeniable fact of individual death and to postulate a life after death; civil governments still believe that they cannot maintain moral order among the living if they

1. [This problem figures prominently in *Beyond the Pleasure Principle* (1920*g*), on which Freud was engaged while writing the present paper. (Cf. *P.F.L.*, **11**, 316 ff.)]

2. [Freud had discussed the individual's attitude to death at greater length in 'Thoughts for the Times on War and Death' (1915*b*), ibid., **12**, 62, 79–89.]

do not uphold the prospect of a better life hereafter as a recompense for mundane existence. In our great cities, placards announce lectures that undertake to tell us how to get into touch with the souls of the departed; and it cannot be denied that not a few of the most able and penetrating minds among our men of science have come to the conclusion, especially towards the close of their own lives, that a contact of this kind is not impossible. Since almost all of us still think as savages do on this topic, it is no matter for surprise that the primitive fear of the dead is still so strong within us and always ready to come to the surface on any provocation. Most likely our fear still implies the old belief that the dead man becomes the enemy of his survivor and seeks to carry him off to share his new life with him. Considering our unchanged attitude towards death, we might rather inquire what has become of the repression, which is the necessary condition of a primitive feeling recurring in the shape of something uncanny. But repression is there, too. All supposedly educated people have ceased to believe officially that the dead can become visible as spirits, and have made any such appearances dependent on improbable and remote conditions; their emotional attitude towards their dead, moreover, once a highly ambiguous and ambivalent one, has been toned down in the higher strata of the mind into an unambiguous feeling of piety.[1]

We have now only a few remarks to add – for animism, magic and sorcery, the omnipotence of thoughts, man's attitude to death, involuntary repetition and the castration complex comprise practically all the factors which turn something frightening into something uncanny.

We can also speak of a living person as uncanny, and we do so when we ascribe evil intentions to him. But that is not all; in addition to this we must feel that his intentions to harm us are going to be carried out with the help of special powers. A good instance of this is the 'Gettatore',[2] that uncanny figure

1. Cf. *Totem and Taboo* [(1912–13), *P.F.L.*, **13**, 122.]
2. [Literally 'thrower' (of bad luck), or 'one who casts' (the evil eye). – Schaeffer's novel was published in 1918.]

of Romantic superstition which Schaeffer, with intuitive poetic feeling and profound psychoanalytic understanding, has transformed into a sympathetic character in his *Josef Montfort*. But the question of these secret powers brings us back again to the realm of animism. It was the pious Gretchen's intuition that Mephistopheles possessed secret powers of this kind that made him so uncanny to her.

> Sie fühlt, dass ich ganz sicher ein Genie,
> Vielleicht wohl gar der Teufel bin.[1]

The uncanny effect of epilepsy and of madness has the same origin. The layman sees in them the working of forces hitherto unsuspected in his fellow-men, but at the same time he is dimly aware of them in remote corners of his own being. The Middle Ages quite consistently ascribed all such maladies to the influence of demons, and in this their psychology was almost correct. Indeed, I should not be surprised to hear that psychoanalysis, which is concerned with laying bare these hidden forces, has itself become uncanny to many people for that very reason. In one case, after I had succeeded – though none too rapidly – in effecting a cure in a girl who had been an invalid for many years, I myself heard this view expressed by the patient's mother long after her recovery.

Dismembered limbs, a severed head, a hand cut off at the wrist, as in a fairy tale of Hauff's,[2] feet which dance by themselves, as in the book by Schaeffer which I mentioned above – all these have something peculiarly uncanny about them, especially when, as in the last instance, they prove capable of independent activity in addition. As we already know, this kind of uncanniness springs from its proximity to the castration complex. To some people the idea of being buried alive by mistake is the most uncanny thing of all. And yet psychoanalysis has

---

1.   [She feels that surely I'm a genius now, –
      Perhaps the very Devil indeed!
            Goethe, *Faust*, Part I, Scene 18 (Bayard Taylor's translation)]
   2. [*Die Geschichte von der abgehauenen Hand* ('The Story of the Severed Hand').]

taught us that this terrifying phantasy is only a transformation of another phantasy which had originally nothing terrifying about it at all, but was qualified by a certain lasciviousness – the phantasy, I mean, of intra-uterine existence.[1]

There is one more point of general application which I should like to add, though, strictly speaking, it has been included in what has already been said about animism and modes of working of the mental apparatus that have been surmounted; for I think it deserves special emphasis. This is that an uncanny effect is often and easily produced when the distinction between imagination and reality is effaced, as when something that we have hitherto regarded as imaginary appears before us in reality, or when a symbol takes over the full functions of the thing it symbolizes, and so on. It is this factor which contributes not a little to the uncanny effect attaching to magical practices. The infantile element in this, which also dominates the minds of neurotics, is the over-accentuation of psychical reality in comparison with material reality – a feature closely allied to the belief in the omnipotence of thoughts. In the middle of the isolation of war-time a number of the English *Strand Magazine* fell into my hands; and, among other somewhat redundant matter, I read a story about a young married couple who move into a furnished house in which there is a curiously shaped table with carvings of crocodiles on it. Towards evening an intolerable and very specific smell begins to pervade the house; they stumble over something in the dark; they seem to see a vague form gliding over the stairs – in short, we are given to understand that the presence of the table causes ghostly crocodiles to haunt the place, or that the wooden monsters come to life in the dark, or something of the sort. It was a naïve enough story, but the uncanny feeling it produced was quite remarkable.

To conclude this collection of examples, which is certainly not complete, I will relate an instance taken from psycho-analytic experience; if it does not rest upon mere coincidence,

1. [See Freud's analysis of the 'Wolf Man' (1918*b*), *P.F.L.*, **9**, 342 f.]

it furnishes a beautiful confirmation of our theory of the uncanny. It often happens that neurotic men declare that they
feel there is something uncanny about the female genital organs.
This *unheimlich* place, however, is the entrance to the former
Heim [home] of all human beings, to the place where each one
of us lived once upon a time and in the beginning. There is
a joking saying that 'Love is home-sickness'; and whenever a
man dreams of a place or a country and says to himself, while
he is still dreaming: 'this place is familiar to me, I've been here
before', we may interpret the place as being his mother's
genitals or her body.[1] In this case too, then, the *unheimlich* is
what was once *heimisch*, familiar; the prefix *'un'* ['un-'] is the
token of repression.[2]

III

In the course of this discussion the reader will have felt certain
doubts arising in his mind; and he must now have an opportunity of collecting them and bringing them forward.

It may be true that the uncanny [*unheimlich*] is something
which is secretly familiar [*heimlich–heimisch*], which has undergone repression and then returned from it, and that everything
that is uncanny fulfils this condition. But the selection of
material on this basis does not enable us to solve the problem
of the uncanny. For our proposition is clearly not convertible.
Not everything that fulfils this condition – not everything that
recalls repressed desires and surmounted modes of thinking
belonging to the prehistory of the individual and of the race
– is on that account uncanny.

Nor shall we conceal the fact that for almost every example
adduced in support of our hypothesis one may be found which
rebuts it. The story of the severed hand in Hauff's fairy tale
certainly has an uncanny effect, and we have traced that effect
back to the castration complex; but most readers will probably
agree with me in judging that no trace of uncanniness is

1. [Cf. *The Interpretation of Dreams* (1900a), P.F.L., **4**, 524.]
2. [See Freud's paper on 'Negation' (1925h), ibid., **11**, 437–8.]

provoked by Herodotus's story of the treasure of Rhampsinitus, in which the master-thief, whom the princess tries to hold fast by the hand, leaves his brother's severed hand behind with her instead. Again, the prompt fulfilment of the wishes of Polycrates undoubtedly affects us in the same uncanny way as it did the King of Egypt; yet our own fairy stories are crammed with instantaneous wish-fulfilments which produce no uncanny effect whatever. In the story of 'The Three Wishes', the woman is tempted by the savoury smell of a sausage to wish that she might have one too, and in an instant it lies on a plate before her. In his annoyance at her hastiness her husband wishes it may hang on her nose. And there it is, dangling from her nose. All this is very striking but not in the least uncanny. Fairy tales quite frankly adopt the animistic standpoint of the omnipotence of thoughts and wishes, and yet I cannot think of any genuine fairy story which has anything uncanny about it. We have heard that it is in the highest degree uncanny when an inanimate object – a picture or a doll – comes to life; nevertheless in Hans Andersen's stories the household utensils, furniture and tin soldiers are alive, yet nothing could well be more remote from the uncanny. And we should hardly call it uncanny when Pygmalion's beautiful statue comes to life.

Apparent death and the re-animation of the dead have been represented as most uncanny themes. But things of this sort too are very common in fairy stories. Who would be so bold as to call it uncanny, for instance, when Snow-White opens her eyes once more? And the resuscitation of the dead in accounts of miracles, as in the New Testament, elicits feelings quite unrelated to the uncanny. Then, too, the theme that achieves such an indubitably uncanny effect, the unintended recurrence of the same thing, serves other and quite different purposes in another class of cases. We have already come across one example [p. 359] in which it is employed to call up a feeling of the comic; and we could multiply instances of this kind. Or again, it works as a means of emphasis, and so on. And once more: what is the origin of the uncanny effect of silence, darkness and solitude? Do not these factors point to the part played by danger in the genesis of what is uncanny, notwithstanding that in children these same factors are the most frequent determinants of the expression of fear [rather than of the uncanny]? And are we after all justified in entirely ignoring intellectual uncertainty as a factor, seeing that we have admitted its importance in relation to death [p. 364]?

It is evident, therefore, that we must be prepared to admit that there are other elements besides those which we have so far laid down as determining the production of uncanny feelings. We might say that these preliminary results have satisfied *psychoanalytic* interest in the problem of the uncanny, and that what remains probably calls for an *aesthetic* inquiry. But that would be to open the door to doubts about what exactly is the value of our general contention that the uncanny proceeds from something familiar which has been repressed.

We have noticed one point which may help us to resolve these uncertainties: nearly all the instances that contradict our hypothesis are taken from the realm of fiction, of imaginative writing. This suggests that we should differentiate between the uncanny that we actually experience and the uncanny that we merely picture or read about.

What is *experienced* as uncanny is much more simply conditioned but comprises far fewer instances. We shall find, I think, that it fits in perfectly with our attempt at a solution, and can be traced back without exception to something familiar that has been repressed. But here, too, we must make a certain important and psychologically significant differentiation in our material, which is best illustrated by turning to suitable examples.

Let us take the uncanny associated with the omnipotence of thoughts, with the prompt fulfilment of wishes, with secret injurious powers and with the return of the dead. The condition under which the feeling of uncanniness arises here is unmistakable. We – or our primitive forefathers – once believed that these possibilities were realities, and were convinced that they actually happened. Nowadays we no longer believe in them, we have *surmounted* these modes of thought; but we do not feel quite sure of our new beliefs, and the old ones still exist within us ready to seize upon any confirmation. As soon as something *actually happens* in our lives which seems to confirm the old, discarded beliefs we get a feeling of the uncanny; it is as though we were making a judgement something like this: 'So, after all, it is *true* that one can kill a person by the mere wish!' or, 'So the dead *do* live on and appear on the scene of their former activities!' and so on. Conversely, anyone who has completely and finally rid himself of animistic beliefs will be insensible to this type of the uncanny. The most remarkable coincidences of wish and fulfilment, the most mysterious repetition of similar experiences in a particular place or on a particular date, the most deceptive sights and suspicious noises – none of these things will disconcert him or raise the kind of fear which can be described as 'a fear of something uncanny'. The whole thing is purely an affair of 'reality-testing', a question of the material reality of the phenomena.[1]

The state of affairs is different when the uncanny proceeds from repressed infantile complexes, from the castration complex, womb phantasies, etc.; but experiences which arouse this

---

1. Since the uncanny effect of a 'double' also belongs to this same group it is interesting to observe what the effect is of meeting one's own image unbidden and unexpected. Ernst Mach has related two such observations in his *Analyse der Empfindungen* (1900, 3). On the first occasion he was not a little startled when he realized that the face before him was his own. The second time he formed a very unfavourable opinion about the supposed stranger who entered the omnibus, and thought 'What a shabby-looking school-master that man is who is getting in!' – I can report a similar adventure. I was sitting alone in my *wagon-lit* compartment when a more than usually violent jolt of the train swung back the door of the adjoining washing-cabinet, and an elderly gentleman in a dressing-gown and a travelling cap came in. I assumed that in leaving the washing-cabinet, which lay between the two compartments, he had taken the wrong direction and come into my compartment by mistake. Jumping up with the intention of putting him right, I at once realized to my dismay that the intruder was nothing but my own reflection in the looking-glass on the open door. I can still recollect that I thoroughly disliked his appearance. Instead, therefore, of being *frightened* by our 'doubles', both Mach and I simply failed to recognize them as such. It is not possible, though, that our dislike of them was a vestigial trace of the archaic reaction which feels the 'double' to be something uncanny?

kind of uncanny feeling are not of very frequent occurrence in real life. The uncanny which proceeds from actual experience belongs for the most part to the first group [the group dealt with in the previous paragraph]. Nevertheless the distinction between the two is theoretically very important. Where the uncanny comes from infantile complexes the question of material reality does not arise; its place is taken by psychical reality. What is involved is an actual repression of some content of thought and a return of this repressed content, not a cessation of *belief in the reality* of such a content. We might say that in the one case what had been repressed is a particular ideational content, and in the other the belief in its (material) reality. But this last phrase no doubt extends the term 'repression' beyond its legitimate meaning. It would be more correct to take into account a psychological distinction which can be detected here, and to say that the animistic beliefs of civilized people are in a state of having been (to a greater or lesser extent) *surmounted* [rather than repressed]. Our conclusion could then be stated thus: an uncanny experience occurs either when infantile complexes which have been repressed are once more revived by some impression, or when primitive beliefs which have been surmounted seem once more to be confirmed. Finally, we must not let our predilection for smooth solutions and lucid exposition blind us to the fact that these two classes of uncanny experience are not always sharply distinguishable. When we consider that primitive beliefs are most intimately connected with infantile complexes, and are, in fact, based on them, we shall not be greatly astonished to find that the distinction is often a hazy one.

The uncanny as it is depicted in *literature*, in stories and imaginative productions, merits in truth a separate discussion. Above all, it is a much more fertile province than the uncanny in real life, for it contains the whole of the latter and something more besides, something that cannot be found in real life. The contrast between what has been repressed and what has been surmounted cannot be transposed on to the uncanny in fiction without profound modification; for the realm of phantasy depends for its effect on the fact that its content is not submitted to reality-testing. The somewhat paradoxical result is that *in the first place a great deal that is not uncanny in fiction would be so if it happened in real life; and in the second place that there are many more means of creating uncanny effects in fiction than there are in real life.*

The imaginative writer has this licence among many others, that he can select his world of representation so that it either coincides with the realities we are familiar with or departs from them in what particulars he pleases. We accept his ruling in every case. In fairy tales, for instance, the world of reality is left behind from the very start, and the animistic system of beliefs is frankly adopted. Wish-fulfilments, secret powers, omnipotence of thoughts, animation of inanimate objects, all the elements so common in fairy stories, can exert no uncanny influence here; for, as we have learnt, that feeling cannot arise unless there is a conflict of judgement as to whether things which have been 'surmounted' and are regarded as incredible may not, after all, be possible; and this problem is eliminated from the outset by the postulates of the world of fairy tales. Thus we see that fairy stories, which have furnished us with most of the contradictions to our hypothesis of the uncanny, confirm the first part of our proposition – that in the realm of fiction many things are not uncanny which would be so if they happened in real life. In the case of these stories there are other contributory factors, which we shall briefly touch upon later.

The creative writer can also choose a setting which though less imaginary than the world of fairy tales, does yet differ from the real world by admitting superior spiritual beings such as daemonic spirits or ghosts of the dead. So long as they remain within their setting of poetic reality, such figures lose any uncanniness which they might possess. The souls in Dante's *Inferno*, or the supernatural apparitions in Shakespeare's *Hamlet*, *Macbeth* or *Julius Caesar*, may be gloomy and terrible enough, but they are no more really uncanny than Homer's jovial world of gods. We adapt our judgement to the imaginary reality imposed on us by the writer, and regard souls, spirits and ghosts as though their existence had the same validity as our own has in material reality. In this case too we avoid all trace of the uncanny.

The situation is altered as soon as the writer pretends to move in the world of common reality. In this case he accepts as well all the conditions operating to produce uncanny feelings in real life; and everything that would have an uncanny effect in reality has it in his story. But in this case he can even increase his effect and multiply it far beyond what could happen in reality, by bringing about events which never or very rarely happen in fact. In doing this he is in a sense betraying us to the superstitiousness which we have ostensibly surmounted; he deceives us by promising to give us the sober truth, and then after all overstepping it. We react to his inventions as we would have reacted to real experiences; by the time we have seen through his trick it is already too late and the author has achieved his object. But it must be added that his success is not unalloyed. We retain a feeling of dissatisfaction, a kind of grudge against the attempted deceit. I have noticed this particularly after reading Schnitzler's *Die Weissagung* [*The Prophecy*] and similar stories which flirt with the supernatural. However, the writer has one more means which he can use in order to avoid our recalcitrance and at the same time to improve his chances of success. He can keep us in the dark for a long time about the precise nature of the presuppositions on which the world he writes about is based, or he can cunningly and ingeniously avoid any definite information on the point to the last. Speaking generally, however, we find a confirmation of the second part of our proposition – that fiction presents more opportunities for creating uncanny feelings than are possible in real life.

Strictly speaking, all these complications relate only to that class of the uncanny which proceeds from forms of thought that have been surmounted. The class which proceeds from repressed complexes is more resistant and remains as powerful in fiction as in real experience, subject to one exception [see below]. The uncanny belonging to the first class — that proceeding from forms of thought that have been surmounted — retains its character not only in experience but in fiction as well, so long as the setting is one of material reality; but where it is given an arbitrary and artificial setting in fiction, it is apt to lose that character.

We have clearly not exhausted the possibilities of poetic licence and the privileges enjoyed by story-writers in evoking or in excluding an uncanny feeling. In the main we adopt an unvarying passive attitude towards real experience and are subject to the influence of our physical environment. But the storyteller has a *peculiarly* directive power over us; by means of the moods he can put us into, he is able to guide the current of our emotions, to dam it up in one direction and make it flow in another, and he often obtains a great variety of effects from the same material. All this is nothing new, and has doubtless long since been fully taken into account by students of aesthetics. We have drifted into this field of research half involuntarily, through the temptation to explain certain instances which contradicted our theory of the causes of the uncanny. Accordingly we will now return to the examination of a few of those instances.

We have already asked why it is that the severed hand in the story of the treasure of Rhampsinitus has no uncanny effect in the way that the severed hand has in Hauff's story. The question seems to have gained in importance now that we have recognized that the class of the uncanny which proceeds from repressed complexes is the more resistant of the two. The answer is easy. In the Herodotus story our thoughts are concentrated much more on the superior cunning of the master-thief than on the feelings of the princess. The princess may very well have had an uncanny feeling, indeed she very probably fell into a swoon; but we have no such sensations, for we put ourselves in the thief's place, not in hers. In Nestroy's farce, *Der Zerrissene* [*The Torn Man*], another means is used to avoid any impression of the uncanny in the scene in which the fleeing man, convinced that he is a murderer, lifts up one trap-door after another and each time sees what he takes to be the ghost of his victim rising up out of it. He calls out in despair, 'But I've only killed *one* man. Why this ghastly multiplication?' We know what went before this scene and do not share his error, so what must be uncanny to him has an irresistibly comic effect on us. Even a 'real' ghost, as in Oscar Wilde's *Canterville Ghost*, loses all power of at least arousing *gruesome* feelings in us as soon as the author begins to amuse himself by being ironical about it and allows liberties to be taken with it. Thus we see how independent emotional effects can be of the actual subject-matter in the world of fiction. In fairy stories feelings of fear – including therefore uncanny feelings – are ruled out altogether. We understand this, and that is why we ignore any opportunities we find in them for developing such feelings.

Concerning the factors of silence, solitude and darkness, we can only say that they are actually elements in the production of the infantile anxiety from which the majority of human beings have never become quite free. This problem has been discussed from a psychoanalytic point of view elsewhere.[1]

1. [See the discussion of children's fear of the dark in Freud's *Three Essays* (1905*d*), *P.F.L.*, **7**, 147 *n*. 1.]

A SEVENTEENTH-CENTURY
DEMONOLOGICAL NEUROSIS
(1923 [1922])

EDITOR'S NOTE

EINE TEUFELSNEUROSE IM SIEBZEHNTEN JAHRHUNDERT

(A) GERMAN EDITIONS:

1923   *Imago*, **9** (1), 1–34.

1924   Leipzig, Vienna and Zürich: Internationaler Psychoanalytischer Verlag.

1928   'Bibliophiles' limited edition, with 7 plates. Same publishers.

1940   *Gesammelte Werke*, **13**, 317–53.

(B) ENGLISH TRANSLATIONS:

'A Neurosis of Demoniacal Possession in the Seventeenth Century'

1925   *Collected Papers*, **4**, 436–72. (Tr. E. Glover.)

1961   *Standard Edition*, **19**, 67–105. (Considerably modified version of above, with a new title.)

The present edition is a reprint of the *Standard Edition* version, with a few editorial changes.

The 'Bibliophiles' edition was produced for the 1928 Congress of German Bibliophiles in Vienna. It contained black-and-white reproductions of three of the paintings (representing the first, second and fifth appearances of the Devil) and of four folios of the manuscript.

This was written in the last months of 1922 (Jones, 1957, 105). The origin of the paper is sufficiently explained by Freud himself at the beginning of Section I. Freud's interest in witchcraft, possession and allied phenomena was of long standing. It seems possible that it was stimulated by his studies at the Salpêtrière in 1885–6. Charcot himself had paid much attention to the historical aspects of neurosis, a fact referred to at more than one point in Freud's 'Report' on his visit to Paris (1956a [1886]). There is an account of a sixteenth-century case of possession at the beginning of Lecture 16 in the first set of Charcot's lectures translated by Freud (1886f) and a discussion of the hysterical nature of medieval 'demonio-manias' in the seventh of the *Leçons du mardi* in the second set of Freud's translations (1892–4). Moreover, in his obituary of Charcot (1893f), he laid especial emphasis on this side of his teacher's work.

Two letters to Fliess, of 17 and 24 January 1897 (Freud, 1950a, Letters 56 and 57), which discuss witches and their relation to the Devil, show that this interest had not diminished; in the first of them, indeed, he speaks as though the topic was one which had often been discussed between him and Fliess. There is already a suggestion that the Devil may be a father-figure, and the part played by anal material in medieval beliefs about witches is particularly insisted upon. Both of these points recur in a short allusion to the subject in the paper on 'Character and Anal Erotism' (1908b), *P.F.L.*, **7**, 214. We learn from Jones (1957, 378) that on 27 January 1909 Hugo Heller, the Vienna bookseller and publisher, read a paper to the Vienna Psycho-Analytical Society on 'The History of the Devil' and that Freud spoke at length on the psychological composition of the belief in the Devil, evidently on much the same lines as in Section III of the present paper. In this section of the paper, too, Freud passes beyond the discussion of an individual case and of the limited demonological problem to a consideration of some of the wider questions involved in the adoption by males of a feminine attitude towards the father. And here he brings up the history of Dr Schreber (1911c; *P.F.L.*, **9**, 129 ff.) as a parallel, though he nowhere classifies the present case as one of paranoia.

The sumptuous volume brought out under the title *Schizophrenia 1677* (Macalpine and Hunter, 1956) includes a facsimile of the manuscript of the 'Trophy of Mariazell' and coloured reproductions of the nine paintings attached to it. An examination of these has made it possible to make one or two additions and corrections to Freud's account of the manuscript, which was no doubt based entirely on the transcription and report of Dr Payer-Thurn (1924). It must be added that the lengthy commentaries of Dr Macalpine and Dr Hunter are largely directed to criticism of Freud's views on the case; and it has unfortunately been impossible to adopt their translation of the many passages from the manuscript quoted by Freud, since at two or three important points their rendering of the original is inconsistent with Freud's.[1]

No attempt has been made in the present translation to imitate the style of the seventeenth-century German of the manuscript.

---

[1]. More recently, Dr G. Vandendriessche has discovered a quantity of historical material – unknown to Freud – relating to Christoph Haizmann, including further transcripts of sections of the *Trophaeum*, which has enabled him to make corrections to the text of the Vienna manuscript and reconstruct its damaged portions. His findings are incorporated in a critical examination of Freud's paper. (Cf. Vandendriessche, 1965.)

A SEVENTEENTH-CENTURY
DEMONOLOGICAL NEUROSIS[1]

[INTRODUCTION]

THE neuroses of childhood have taught us that a number of things can easily be seen in them with the naked eye which at a later age are only to be discovered after a thorough investigation. We may expect that the same will turn out to be true of neurotic illnesses in earlier centuries, provided that we are prepared to recognize them under names other than those of our present-day neuroses. We need not be surprised to find that, whereas the neuroses of our unpsychological modern days take on a hypochondriacal aspect and appear disguised as organic illnesses, the neuroses of those early times emerge in demonological trappings. Several authors, foremost among them Charcot, have, as we know, identified the manifestations of hysteria in the portrayals of possession and ecstasy that have been preserved for us in the productions of art. If more attention had been paid to the histories of such cases at the time, it would not have been difficult to retrace in them the subject-matter of a neurosis.

The demonological theory of those dark times has won in the end against all the somatic views of the period of 'exact' science. The states of possession correspond to our neuroses, for the explanation of which we once more have recourse to psychical powers. In our eyes, the demons are bad and

1. [In the English translation of 1925 the following footnote appeared at this point: 'The author wishes to add to the English translation two footnotes (which appear within square brackets), and to express his regret that they were omitted from the German version.' Actually what was in question were *additions* to two existing footnotes, on pp. 400 and 402. They were not included in later German editions.]

reprehensible wishes, derivatives of instinctual impulses that have been repudiated and repressed. We merely eliminate the projection of these mental entities into the external world which the Middle Ages carried out; instead, we regard them as having arisen in the patient's internal life, where they have their abode.

I

THE STORY OF CHRISTOPH HAIZMANN
THE PAINTER

I AM indebted to the friendly interest of Hofrat Dr Payer-Thurn, director of the former Imperial Fideikommissbibliothek[1] of Vienna, for the opportunity of studying a seventeenth-century demonological neurosis of this kind. Payer-Thurn had discovered a manuscript in this library which originated from the shrine of Mariazell[2] and in which there was a detailed account of a miraculous redemption from a pact with the Devil through the grace of the Blessed Virgin Mary. His interest was aroused by the resemblance of this story to the legend of Faust, and has led him to undertake the exhaustive publication and editing of the material. Finding, however, that the person whose redemption was described had been subject to convulsive seizures and visions he approached me for a medical opinion on the case. We came to an agreement to publish our investigations independently and separately.[3] I should like to take this opportunity of thanking him for his original suggestion and for the many ways in which he has assisted me in the study of the manuscript.

This demonological case history leads to really valuable findings which can be brought to light without much interpretation – much as a vein of pure metal may sometimes be struck which must elsewhere be laboriously smelted from the ore.

★

1. [A law library for the registration of entails (somewhat akin to the library of the Record Office in London), now included in the National Library of Austria.]

2. [A well-known place of pilgrimage, some eighty miles south-west of Vienna.]

3. [Cf. Payer-Thurn (1924).]

The manuscript, an exact copy of which lies before me, falls into two quite distinct sections. One is a report, written in Latin, by a monastic scribe or compiler; the other is a fragment from the patient's diary, written in German. The first section contains a preface and a description of the actual miraculous cure. The second can scarcely have been of any significance for the reverend Fathers but so much the more is it of value for us. It serves in large part to confirm our judgement of the case, which might otherwise have been hesitant, and we have good cause to be grateful to the clergy for having preserved the document although it added nothing to support the tenor of their views and, indeed, may rather have weakened it.

But before going further into the composition of this little manuscript brochure, which bears the title *Trophaeum Mariano-Cellense*, I must relate a part of its contents, which I take from the preface.

On 5 September 1677, the painter Christoph Haizmann, a Bavarian, was brought to Mariazell, with a letter of introduction from the village priest of Pottenbrunn (in lower Austria) not far away.[1] The letter states that the man had been staying in Pottenbrunn for some months, pursuing his occupation of painting. On 29 August, while in the church there, he had been seized with frightful convulsions. As these convulsions recurred during the following days, he had been examined by the *Praefectus Dominii Pottenbrunnensis*[2] with a view to discovering what it was that was oppressing him and whether perhaps he had entered into illicit traffic with the Evil Spirit.[3] Upon this, the man had admitted that nine years before, when he was in a state of despondency about his art and doubtful whether

---

1. No mention is anywhere made of the painter's age. The context suggests that he was a man of between thirty and forty, probably nearer the lower figure. He died, as we shall see, in 1700.

2. [Prefect of the Domain of Pottenbrunn.]

3. We will merely note in passing the possibility that this interrogation inspired in the sufferer — 'suggested' to him — the phantasy of his pact with the Devil.

he could support himself, he had yielded to the Devil, who had tempted him nine times, and that he had given him his bond in writing to belong to him in body and soul after a period of nine years. This period would expire on the twenty-fourth day of the current month.[1] The letter went on to say that the unfortunate man had repented and was convinced that only the grace of the Mother of God at Mariazell could save him, by compelling the Evil One to deliver up the bond, which had been written in blood. For this reason the village priest ventured to recommend *miserum hunc hominem omni auxilio destitutum*[2] to the benevolence of the Fathers of Mariazell.

So far the narrative of Leopoldus Braun, the village priest of Pottenbrunn, dated 1 September 1677.

We can now proceed with the analysis of the manuscript. It consists of three parts:

(1) A coloured title-page representing the scene of the signing of the pact and the scene of the redemption in the chapel of Mariazell. On the next sheet[3] are eight pictures, also coloured, representing the subsequent appearances of the Devil, with a short legend in German attached to each. These pictures are not the originals; they are copies – faithful copies, we are solemnly assured – of the original paintings by Christoph Haizmann.

(2) The actual *Trophaeum Mariano-Cellense* (in Latin), the work of a clerical compiler who signs himself at the foot 'P.A.E.' and appends to these intials four lines of verse containing his biography. The *Trophaeum* ends with a deposition by the Abbot Kilian of St Lambert,[4] dated 9[5] September 1729,

---

1. *Quorum et finis 24 mensis hujus futurus appropinquat.* [This refers to September, at the beginning of which the letter of introduction was written.]

2. ['This wretched man, who was bereft of all help.']

3. [In fact, the eight pictures and a triptych (Freud's 'title-page') occupy five folios of the manuscript (Macalpine and Hunter, 1956).]

4. [The monks of the Convent of St Lambert were in charge of the shrine.]

5. [So in the manuscript; wrongly given as '12 September' by Freud, as Vandendriessche (1965) points out.]

which is in a different handwriting from that of the compiler. It testifies to the exact correspondence of the manuscript and the pictures with the originals preserved in the archives. There is no mention of the year in which the *Trophaeum* was compiled. We are free to assume that it was done in the same year in which the Abbot Kilian made his deposition – that is, in 1729; or, since the last date mentioned in the text is 1714, we may put the compiler's work somewhere between the years 1714 and 1729. The miracle which was to be preserved from oblivion by this manuscript occurred in 1677 – that is to say, between thirty-seven and fifty-two years earlier.

(3) The painter's diary, written in German and covering the period from his redemption in the chapel till 13 January of the following year, 1678. It is inserted in the text of the *Trophaeum* near the end.

The core of the actual *Trophaeum* consists of two pieces of writing: the letter of introduction from the village priest, Leopold Braun of Pottenbrunn, dated 1 September 1677, and the report by the Abbot Franciscus of Mariazell and St Lambert, describing the miraculous cure. This is dated 12 September 1677, that is to say, only a few days later. The activity of the editor or compiler, P.A.E., has provided a preface which as it were fuses the contents of these two documents; he has also added some connecting passages of little importance, and, at the end, an account of the subsequent vicissitudes of the painter, based on inquiries made in the year 1714.[1]

The painter's previous history is thus told three times over in the *Trophaeum*: (1) in the village priest of Pottenbrunn's letter of introduction, (2) in the formal report by the Abbot Franciscus and (3) in the editor's preface. A comparison of these three sources discloses certain discrepancies which it will be not unimportant for us to follow up.

I can now continue with the painter's story. After he had undergone a prolonged period of penance and prayer at Mariazell, the Devil appeared to him in the sacred Chapel at

1. This would seem to suggest that the *Trophaeum*, too, dates from 1714.

midnight on 8 September, the Nativity of the Virgin, in the form of a winged dragon, and gave him back the pact, which was written in blood. We shall learn later, to our surprise, that *two* bonds with the Devil appear in Christoph Haizmann's story – an earlier one, written in black ink, and a later one, written in blood. The one referred to in the description of the scene of exorcism, as can also be seen from the picture on the title-page, is the one written in blood – that is, the later one.

At this point a doubt as to the credibility of the clerical reporters may well arise in our minds and warn us not to waste our labours on a product of monastic superstition. We are told that several clerics, mentioned by name, assisted at the exorcism and were present in the Chapel when the Devil appeared. If it had been asserted that they, too, saw the Devil appear in the form of a dragon and offer the painter the paper written in red (*Schedam sibi porrigentem conspexisset*),[1] we should be faced by several unpleasant possibilities, among which that of a collective hallucination would be the mildest. But the Abbot Franciscus's testimony dispels this doubt. Far from asserting that the assisting clerics saw the Devil too, he only states in straightforward and sober words that the painter suddenly tore himself away from the Fathers who were holding him, rushed into the corner of the Chapel where he saw the apparition, and then returned with the paper in his hand.[2]

The miracle was great, and the victory of the Holy Mother over Satan without question; but unfortunately the cure was not a lasting one. It is once more to the credit of the clergy that they have not concealed this. After a short time the painter left Mariazell in the best of health and went to Vienna, where he lived with a married sister. On 11 October fresh attacks

1. [See next footnote.]
2. '... [*poenitens*] *ipsumque Daemonem ad Aram Sac. Cellae per fenestrellam in cornu Epistolae, Schedam sibi porrigentem conspexisset, eo advolans e Religiosorum manibus, qui eum tenebant, ipsam Schedam ad manum obtinuit....*'
['... (the penitent) saw the Demon himself by the sacred altar of Zell through the little window on the Epistle side, offering him the paper; he rushed to the place from the hands of the Fathers who were holding him, and seized the same paper ...']

began, some of them very severe, and these are reported in the diary until 13 January [1678]. They consisted in visions and 'absences', in which he saw and experienced every kind of thing, in convulsive seizures accompanied by the most painful sensations, on one occasion in paralysis of the legs, and so on. This time, however, it was not the Devil who tormented him; it was by sacred figures that he was vexed – by Christ and by the Blessed Virgin herself. It is remarkable that he suffered no less through these heavenly manifestations and the punishments they inflicted on him than he had formerly through his traffic with the Devil. In his diary, indeed, he included these fresh experiences too as manifestations of the Devil; and when, in May 1678, he returned to Mariazell, he complained of *maligni Spiritûs manifestationes* ['manifestations of the Evil Spirit'].[1]

He told the reverend Fathers that his reason for returning was that he had to require the Devil to give him back another, earlier bond, which had been written in ink.[2] This time once more the Blessed Virgin and the pious Fathers helped him to obtain the fulfilment of his request. As to how this came about, however, the report is silent. It merely states shortly: *quâ iuxta votum redditâ* ['when this had been returned in accordance with his prayer'] – he prayed once again and received the pact back. After this he felt quite free and entered the Order of the Brothers Hospitallers.

We have occasion yet again to acknowledge that in spite of the obvious purpose of his efforts, the compiler has not been tempted into departing from the veracity required of a case history. For he does not conceal the outcome of the inquiry that was made in 1714 from the Superior of the Monastery of the Brothers Hospitallers [in Vienna] concerning the painter's later history. The Reverend Pater Provincialis reported that Brother Chrysostomus had again been repeatedly tempted by the Evil Spirit, who tried to seduce him into making a fresh

1. [The manuscript reads: *'de ... maligni Spiritûs infestatione* (of ... molestation by the Evil Spirit)'.]

2. This bond had been signed in September 1668, and by May 1678, nine and a half years later, it would long since have fallen due.

pact (though this only happened 'when he had drunk somewhat too much wine').[1] But by the grace of God, it had always been possible to repel these attempts. Brother Chrysostomus had died of a hectic fever 'peacefully and of good comfort'[2] in the year 1700 in the Monastery of the Order, at Neustatt on the Moldau.

1. ['Wenn er etwas mehrers von Wein getrunken.']
2. ['Sanft und trostreich.']

II

THE MOTIVE FOR THE PACT WITH
THE DEVIL

IF we look at this bond with the Devil as if it were the case history of a neurotic, our interest will turn in the first instance to the question of its motivation, which is, of course, intimately connected with its exciting cause. Why does anyone sign a bond with the Devil? Faust, it is true, asked contemptuously: 'Was willst du, armer Teufel, geben?' ['What hast thou to give, poor Devil?']¹ But he was wrong. In return for an immortal soul, the Devil has many things to offer which are highly prized by men: wealth, security from danger, power over mankind and the forces of nature, even magical arts, and, above all else, enjoyment – the enjoyment of beautiful women. These services performed or undertakings made by the Devil are usually mentioned specifically in the agreement made with him.² What, then, was the motive which induced Christoph Haizmann to make his pact?

Curiously enough, it was none of these very natural wishes. To put the matter beyond doubt, one has only to read the short

---

1. [*Faust*, Part I, Scene 4.]
2. Cf. *Faust*, Part I, Scene 4:
> Ich will mich *hier* zu deinem Dienst verbinden,
> Auf deinem Wink nicht rasten und nicht ruhn;
> Wenn wir uns *drüben* wiederfinden,
> So sollst du mir das Gleiche thun.

> [*Here*, an unwearied slave, I'll wear thy tether,
> And to thine every nod obedient be:
> When *There* again we come together,
> Then thou shalt do the same for me.

> (Bayard Taylor's translation)]

remarks attached by the painter to his illustrations of the apparitions of the Devil. For example, the caption to the third vision runs: 'On the third occasion within a year and a half, he appeared to me in this loathsome shape, with a book in his hand which was full of magic and black arts ...'[1] But from the legend attached to a later apparition we learn that the Devil reproached him violently for having 'burnt his before-mentioned book',[2] and threatened to tear him to pieces if he did not give it back.

At his fourth appearance the Devil showed him a large yellow money-bag and a great ducat and promised him to give him as many of these as he wanted at any time. But the painter is able to boast that he 'had taken nothing whatever of the kind'.[3]

Another time the Devil asked him to turn to enjoyment and entertainment,[4] and the painter remarks that 'this indeed came to pass at his desire; but I did not continue for more than three days and I was thereupon set free again'.[5]

Since he rejected magical arts, money and pleasures when they were offered him by the Devil, and still less made them conditions of the pact, it becomes really imperative to know what the painter in fact wanted from the Devil when he signed a bond with him. *Some* motive he must have had for his dealings with the Devil.

On this point, too, the *Trophaeum* provides us with reliable information. He had become low-spirited, was unable or un-willing to work properly and was worried about making a livelihood; that is to say, he was suffering from melancholic

---

1. ['Zum driten ist er mir in anderthalb Jahren in diser abscheühlichen Gestalt erschinen, mit einen Buuch in der Handt, darin lauter Zauberey und schwarze Kunst war begrüffen ...']

2. ['... sein vorgemeldtes Buuch verbrennt.']

3. ['... aber ich solliches gar nit angenomben.']

4. [There is some indication in the illustration to the original manuscript that this has a sexual meaning.]

5. ['... welliches zwar auch auf sein begehren geschehen aber ich yber drey Tag nit continuirt, vnd gleich widerumb aussgelöst worden.']

depression, with an inhibition in his work and (justified) fears about his future. We can see that what we are dealing with really is a case history. We learn, too, the exciting cause of the illness, which the painter himself, in the caption to one of his pictures of the Devil, actually calls a melancholia ('that I should seek diversion and banish melancholy'[1]). The first of our three sources of information, the village priest's letter of introduction, speaks, it is true, only of the state of depression ('*dum artis suae progressum emolumentumque secuturum* pusillanimis *perpenderet*'[2]), but the second source, the Abbot Franciscus's report, tells us the cause of this despondency or depression as well. He says: '*acceptâ aliquâ pusillanimitate* ex morte parentis';[3] and in the compiler's preface the same words are used, though in a reversed order: ('*ex morte parentis acceptâ aliquâ pusillanimitate*'). His father, then, had died and he had in consequence fallen into a state of melancholia; whereupon the Devil had approached him and asked him why he was so downcast and sad, and had promised 'to help him in every way and to give him support'.[4]

Here was a person, therefore, who signed a bond with the Devil in order to be freed from a state of depression. Undoubtedly an excellent motive, as anyone will agree who can have an understanding sense of the torments of such a state and who knows as well how little medicine can do to alleviate this ailment. Yet no one who has followed the story so far as this would be able to guess what the wording of this bond (or rather, of these two bonds)[5] with the Devil actually was.

1. ['... solte mich darmit belustigen und meläncoley vertreiben.']
2. ['... when he was feeling despondent about the progress of his art and his future earnings ...']
3. ['... having become somewhat despondent owing to the death of his parent ...']
4. ['... auf alle Weiss zu helfen und an die Handt zu gehen.'] – The first picture on the title-page and its caption represent the Devil in the form of an 'honest citizen' ['ersamer Bürger'. He is also so represented in the first of the eight separate pictures (cf. p. 399 and Plate 7).]
5. Since there were two of them – the first written in ink, and the second written about a year later in blood – both said still to be in the treasury of Mariazell and to be transcribed in the *Trophaeum*.

These bonds bring us two great surprises. In the first place, they mention no *undertaking* given by the Devil in return for whose fulfilment the painter pledges his eternal bliss, but only a *demand* made by the Devil which the painter must satisfy. It strikes us as quite illogical and absurd that this man should give up his soul, not for something he is to *get* from the Devil but for something he is to *do* for him. But the undertaking given by the *painter* seems even stranger.

The first 'syngrapha' [bond], written in ink, runs as follows: 'Ich Christoph Haizmann vndterschreibe mich disen Herrn sein leibeigener Sohn auff 9. Jahr. 1669 Jahr.'[1] The second, written in blood, runs:

'Anno 1669.

'Christoph Haizmann. Ich verschreibe mich disen Satan, ich sein leibeigner Sohn zu sein, und in 9. Jahr ihm mein Leib und Seel zuzugeheren.'[2]

All our astonishment vanishes, however, if we read the text of the bonds in the sense that what is represented in them as a demand made by the Devil is, on the contrary, a service performed by him – that is to say, it is a demand made by the *painter*. The incomprehensible pact would in that case have a straightforward meaning and could be paraphrased thus. The Devil undertakes to replace the painter's lost father for nine years. At the end of that time the painter becomes the property, body and soul, of the Devil, as was the usual custom in such bargains. The train of thought which motivated the painter in making the pact seems to have been this: his father's death had made him lose his spirits and his capacity to work; if he could only obtain a father-substitute he might hope to regain what he had lost.

A man who has fallen into a melancholia on account of his

1. ['I, Christoph Haizmann, subscribe myself to this Lord as his bounden son till the ninth year. Year 1669.']
2. ['Christoph Haizmann. I sign a bond with this Satan, to be his bounden son, and in the ninth year to belong to him body and soul.']

father's death must really have been fond of him. But, if so, it is very strange that such a man should have hit upon the idea of taking the Devil as a substitute for the father whom he loved.

III

THE DEVIL AS A FATHER-SUBSTITUTE

I FEAR that sober critics will not be prepared to admit that this fresh interpretation has made the meaning of this pact with the Devil clear. They will have two objections to make to it.

In the first place they will say that it is not necessary to regard the bond as a contract in which the undertakings of both parties have been set out. On the contrary, they will argue, it contains only the painter's undertaking; the Devil's is omitted from the text, and is, as it were, *sousentendu*: the painter gives *two* undertakings – firstly to be the Devil's son for nine years, and secondly to belong to him entirely after death. In this way one of the premisses on which our conclusion is built would be disposed of.

The second objection will be that we are not justified in attaching any special importance to the expression 'the Devil's bounden son'; that this is no more than a common figure of speech, which anyone could interpret in the same way as the reverend Fathers may have done. For in their Latin translation they did not mention the relationship of son promised in the bonds, but merely say that the painter *'mancipavit'* himself – made himself a bondslave – to the Evil One and had undertaken to lead a sinful life and to deny God and the Holy Trinity. Why depart from this obvious and natural view of the matter?[1] The position would simply be that a man, in the torment and perplexity of a melancholic depression, signs a bond with the Devil, to whom he ascribes the greatest therapeutic power. That

1. In point of fact, when we come to consider later [p. 412 ff.] at what time and for whom these bonds were drawn up, we shall realize that their text had to be expressed in unobtrusive and generally comprehensible terms. It is enough for us, however, that it contains an ambiguity which we can take as the starting-point of our discussion.

the depression was occasioned by his father's death would then be irrelevant; the occasion might quite as well have been something else.

All this sounds convincing and reasonable. Psychoanalysis has once more to meet the reproach that it makes hair-splitting complications in the simplest things and sees mysteries and problems where none exist, and that it does this by laying undue stress on insignificant and irrelevant details, such as occur everywhere, and making them the basis of the most far-reaching and strangest conclusions. It would be useless for us to point out that this rejection of our interpretation would do away with many striking analogies and break a number of subtle connections which we are able to demonstrate in this case. Our opponents will say that those analogies and connections do not in fact exist, but have been imported into the case by us with quite uncalled-for ingenuity.

I will not preface my reply with words, 'to be honest' or 'to be candid', for one must always be able to be these things without any special preliminaries. I will instead say quite simply that I know very well that no reader who does not already believe in the justifiability of the psychoanalytic mode of thought will acquire that belief from the case of the seventeenth-century painter, Christoph Haizmann. Nor is it my intention to make use of this case as evidence of the validity of psychoanalysis. On the contrary, I presuppose its validity and am employing it to throw light on the painter's demonological illness. My justification for doing so lies in the success of our investigations into the nature of the neuroses in general. We may say in all modesty that to-day even the more obtuse among our colleagues and contemporaries are beginning to realize that no understanding of neurotic states can be reached without the help of psychoanalysis.

> 'These shafts can conquer Troy, these shafts alone'

as Odysseus confesses in the *Philoctetes* of Sophocles.

If we are right in regarding our painter's bond with the Devil as a neurotic phantasy, there is no need for any further apology for considering it psychoanalytically. Even small indications have a meaning and importance, and quite specially when they are related to the conditions under which a neurosis originates. To be sure, it is as possible to overvalue as to undervalue them, and it is a matter of judgement how far one should go in exploiting them. But anyone who does not believe in psychoanalysis – or, for the matter of that, even in the Devil – must be left to make what he can of the painter's case, whether he is able to furnish an explanation of his own or whether he sees nothing in it that needs explaining.

We therefore come back to our hypothesis that the Devil with whom the painter signed the bond was a direct substitute for his father. And this is borne out by the shape in which the Devil first appeared to him – as an honest elderly citizen with a brown beard, dressed in a red cloak and leaning with his right hand on a stick, with a black dog beside him[1] (cf. the first picture). Later on his appearance grows more and more terrifying – more mythological, one might say. He is equipped with horns, eagle's claws and bat's wings. Finally he appears in the chapel as a flying dragon. We shall have to come back later to a particular detail of his bodily shape.

It does indeed sound strange that the Devil should be chosen as a substitute for a loved father. But this is only so at first sight, for we know a good many things which lessen our surprise. To begin with, we know that God is a father-substitute; or, more correctly, that he is an exalted father; or, yet again, that he is a copy of a father as he is seen and experienced in childhood – by individuals in their own childhood and by mankind in its prehistory as the father of the primitive and primal horde. Later on in life the individual sees his father as something different and lesser. But the ideational image belonging to his childhood is preserved and becomes

---

1. [Cf. Plate 7.] In Goethe [*Faust*, Part I, Scenes 2 and 3], a black dog like this turns into the Devil himself.

merged with the inherited memory-traces of the primal father
to form the individual's idea of God. We also know, from
the secret life of the individual which analysis uncovers, that
his relation to his father was perhaps ambivalent from the
outset, or, at any rate, soon became so. That is to say, it contained two sets of emotional impulses that were opposed to
each other: it contained not only impulses of an affectionate
and submissive nature, but also hostile and defiant ones. It is
our view that the same ambivalence governs the relations of
mankind to its Deity. The unresolved conflict between, on the
one hand, a longing for the father and, on the other, a fear
of him and a son's defiance of him, has furnished us with an
explanation of important characteristics of religion and decisive
vicissitudes in it.[1]

Concerning the Evil Demon, we know that he is regarded
as the antithesis of God and yet is very close to him in his
nature. His history has not been so well studied as that of God;
not all religions have adopted the Evil Spirit, the opponent
of God, and his prototype in the life of the individual has so
far remained obscure. One thing, however, is certain: gods can
turn into evil demons when new gods oust them. When one
people has been conquered by another, their fallen gods not
seldom turn into demons in the eyes of the conquerors. The
evil demon of the Christian faith – the Devil of the Middle
Ages – was, according to Christian mythology, himself a fallen
angel and of a godlike nature. It does not need much analytic
perspicacity to guess that God and the Devil were originally
identical – were a single figure which was later split into two
figures with opposite attributes.[2] In the earliest ages of religion
God himself still possessed all the terrifying features which were
afterwards combined to form a counterpart of him.

We have here an example of the process, with which we
are familiar, by which an idea that has a contradictory – an

1. Cf. *Totem and Taboo* (1912–13) [*P.F.L.*, **13**, 206–7] and Reik (1919).
2. Cf. Reik, 1923, Chapter VII [quoting Jones, 1912].

ambivalent – content becomes divided into two sharply contrasted opposites. The contradictions in the original nature of
God are, however, a reflection of the ambivalence which
governs the relation of the individual to his personal father.
If the benevolent and righteous God is a substitute for his father,
it is not to be wondered at that his hostile attitude to his father,
too, which is one of hating and fearing him and of making
complaints against him, should have come to expression in the
creation of Satan. Thus the father, it seems, is the individual
prototype of both God and the Devil. But we should expect
religions to bear ineffaceable marks of the fact that the primitive
primal father was a being of unlimited evil – a being less like
God than the Devil.

It is true that it is by no means easy to demonstrate the traces
of this satanic view of the father in the mental life of the individual. When a boy draws grotesque faces and caricatures,
we may no doubt be able to show that he is jeering at his
father in them; and when a person of either sex is afraid of
robbers and burglars at night, it is not hard to recognize these
as split-off portions of the father.[1] The animals, too, which
appear in children's animal phobias are most often father-
substitutes, as were the totem animals of primaeval times. But
that the Devil is a duplicate of the father and can act as a substitute for him has not been shown so clearly elsewhere as in
the demonological neurosis of this seventeenth-century painter.
That is why, at the beginning of this paper, I foretold that
a demonological case history of this kind would yield in the
form of pure metal material which, in the neuroses of a later
epoch (no longer superstitious but hypochondriacal instead),
has to be laboriously extracted by analytic work from the ore

---

1. In the familiar fairy tale of 'The Seven Little Goats', the Father Wolf
appears as a burglar. [This fairy tale figures prominently in the 'Wolf Man'
case history (1918*b*), *P.F.L.*, **9**, 254, 259 ff., 271 ff.]

of free associations and symptoms.[1] A deeper penetration into the analysis of our painter's illness will probably bring stronger conviction. It is no unusual thing for a man to acquire a melancholic depression and an inhibition in his work as a result of his father's death. When this happens, we conclude that the man had been attached to his father with an especially strong love, and we remember how often a severe melancholia appears as a neurotic form of mourning.[2]

In this we are undoubtedly right. But we are not right if we conclude further that this relation has been merely one of love. On the contrary, his mourning over the loss of his father is the more likely to turn into melancholia, the more his attitude to him bore the stamp of ambivalence. This emphasis on ambivalence, however, prepares us for the possibility of the father being subjected to a debasement, as we see happening in the painter's demonological neurosis. If we were able to learn as much about Christoph Haizmann as about a patient undergoing an analysis with us, it would be an easy matter to elicit this ambivalence, to get him to remember when and under what provocations he was given cause to fear and hate his father; and, above all, to discover what were the accidental factors that were added to the typical motives for a hatred of the father which are necessarily inherent in the natural relationship of son to father. Perhaps we might then find a special explanation

---

1. The fact that in our analyses we so seldom succeed in finding the Devil as a father-substitute may be an indication that for those who come to us for analysis this figure from medieval mythology has long since played out its part. For the pious Christian of earlier centuries belief in the Devil was no less a duty than belief in God. In point of fact, he needed the Devil in order to be able to keep hold of God. The later decrease in faith has, for various reasons, first and foremost affected the figure of the Devil.

If we are bold enough to apply this idea of the Devil as a father-substitute to cultural history, we may also be able to see the witch trials of the Middle Ages in a new light [as has already been shown by Ernest Jones in his chapter on witches in his book on the nightmare (1912). – Cf. the Editor's Note on pp. 379–81 above.]

2. [For this and the following paragraph, see 'Mourning and Melancholia' (1917e), P.F.L., 11, 251 ff.]

for the painter's inhibition to work. It is possible that his father had opposed his wish to become a painter. If that was so, his inability to practise his art after his father's death would on the one hand be an expression of the familiar phenomenon of 'deferred obedience';[1] and, on the other hand, by making him incapable of earning a livelihood, it would be bound to increase his longing for his father as a protector from the cares of life. In its aspect as deferred obedience it would also be an expression of remorse and a successful self-punishment.

Since, however, we cannot carry out an analysis of this sort with Christoph Haizmann, who died in the year 1700, we must content ourselves with bringing out those features of his case history which may point to the typical exciting causes of a negative attitude to the father. There are only a few such features, nor are they very striking, but they are of great interest.

Let us first consider the part played by the number nine. The pact with the Evil One was for nine years. On this point the unquestionably trustworthy report by the village priest of Pottenbrunn is quite clear: *pro novem annis Syngraphen scriptam tradidit.*[2] This letter of introduction, dated 1 September 1677, is also able to inform us that the appointed time was about to expire in a few days: *quorum et finis 24 mensis hujus futurus appropinquat.*[3] The pact would therefore have been signed on 24 September 1668.[4] In the same report, indeed, yet another use is made of the number nine. The painter claims to have withstood the temptations of the Evil One nine times – *'nonies'* – before he yielded to him. This detail is no longer mentioned in the later reports. In the Abbot's deposition the phrase '*post annos novem* [after nine years]' is used, and the compiler repeats

1. ['Deferred obedience' is also mentioned in the case histories of 'Little Hans' (1909*b*), *P.F.L.*, **8**, 198, and Schreber (1911*c*), ibid., **9**, 191. A sociological application of the concept appears in *Totem and Taboo* (1912–13), ibid., **13**, 205, 206.]

2. ['He handed over a pact signed for nine years.']

3. ['. . . the end of which is about to approach on the twenty-fourth of this month.']

4. The contradictory fact that both the pacts as transcribed bear the date 1669 will be considered later [p. 409 ff.].

'*ad novem annos* [for nine years]' in his summary – a proof that this number was not regarded as indifferent.

The number nine is well known to us from neurotic phantasies. It is the number of the months of pregnancy, and wherever it appears it directs our attention to a phantasy of pregnancy. In our painter's case, to be sure, the number refers to years, not months; and it will be objected that nine is a significant number in other ways as well. But who knows whether it may not in general owe a good deal of its sanctity to the part it plays in pregnancy? Nor need we be disconcerted by the change from nine months to nine years. We know from dreams[1] what liberties 'unconscious mental activity' takes with numbers. If, for instance, the number five occurs in a dream, this can invariably be traced back to a five that is important in waking life; but whereas in waking life the five was a five years' difference in age or a company of five people, it appeared in the dream as five bank-notes or five fruits. That is to say, the number is kept, but its denominator is changed according to the requirements of condensation and displacement. Nine years in a dream could thus easily correspond to nine months in real life. The dream-work plays about with the numbers of waking life in another way, too, for it shows a sovereign disregard for noughts and does not treat them as numbers at all. Five dollars in a dream can stand for fifty or five hundred or five thousand dollars in reality.[2]

Another detail in the painter's relations to the Devil has once more a sexual reference. On the first occasion, as I have mentioned, he saw the Evil One in the shape of an honest citizen. But already on the second occasion the Devil was naked and misshapen, and had two pairs of female breasts. [See Plate 8.] In none of his subsequent apparitions are the breasts absent, either as a single or a double pair. Only in one of them does the Devil exhibit, in addition to the breasts, a large penis ending

---

1. [Cf. *The Interpretation of Dreams* (1900a), *P.F.L.*, **4**, 540–44.]
2. [Noughts appended to numbers in dreams are therefore ignored in interpretation. Cf. 'Dreams in Folklore' (1957a), *Standard Ed.*, **12**, 177.]

in a snake. This stressing of the female sexual character by introducing large pendulous breasts (there is never any indication of the female genitals) is bound to appear to us as a striking contradiction of our hypothesis that the Devil had the meaning of a father-substitute for the painter. And, indeed, such a way of representing the Devil is in itself unusual. Where 'devil' is thought of in a generic sense, and devils appear in numbers, there is nothing strange about depicting female devils; but that *the* Devil, who is a great individuality, the Lord of Hell and the Adversary of God, should be represented otherwise than as a male, and, indeed, as a super-male, with horns, tail and a big penis-snake – this, I believe, is never found.

These two slight indications give us an idea of what the typical factor is which determines the negative side of the painter's relation to his father. What he is rebelling against is his feminine attitude to him which culminates in a phantasy of bearing him a child (the nine years). We have an accurate knowledge of this resistance from our analyses, where it takes on very strange forms in the transference and gives us a great deal of trouble. With the painter's mourning for his lost father, and the heightening of his longing for him, there also comes about in him a reactivation of his long-since repressed phantasy of pregnancy, and he is obliged to defend himself against it by a neurosis and by debasing his father.

But why should his father, after being reduced to the status of a Devil, bear this physical mark of a woman? The feature seems at first hard to interpret; but soon we find two explanations which compete with each other without being mutually exclusive. A boy's feminine attitude to his father undergoes repression as soon as he understands that his rivalry with a woman for his father's love has as a precondition the loss of his own male genitals – in other words, castration. Repudiation of the feminine attitude is thus the result of a revolt against castration. It regularly finds its strongest expression in the converse phantasy of castrating the father, of turning *him* into a woman. Thus the Devil's breasts would correspond to a projection of the subject's own femininity on to the father-substitute. The second explanation of these female additions to the Devil's body no longer has a hostile meaning but an affectionate one. It sees in the adoption of this shape an indication that the child's tender feelings towards his mother have been displaced on to his father; and this suggests that there has previously been a strong fixation on the mother, which, in its turn, is responsible for part of the child's hostility towards his father. Large breasts are the positive sexual characteristics of the mother even at a time when the negative characteristic of the female – her lack of a penis – is as yet unknown to the child.[1]

If our painter's repugnance to accepting castration made it impossible for him to appease his longing for his father, it is perfectly understandable that he should have turned for help and salvation to the image of his mother. This is why he declared that only the Holy Mother of God of Mariazell could release him from his pact with the Devil and why he obtained his freedom once more on the day of the Mother's Nativity (8 September). Whether the day on which the pact was made – 24 September – was not also determined in some similar way, we shall of course never know.

Among the observations made by psychoanalysis of the mental life of children there is scarcely one which sounds so repugnant and unbelievable to a normal adult as that of a boy's feminine attitude to his father and the phantasy of pregnancy that arises from it. It is only since Senatspräsident Daniel Paul Schreber, a judge presiding over a division of the Appeal Court of Saxony, published the history of his psychotic illness and his extensive recovery from it[2] that we can discuss the subject without trepidation or apology. We learn from this invaluable book that, somewhere about the age of fifty, the Senats-präsident became firmly convinced that God – who, inciden-tally, exhibited distinct traits of his father, the worthy physician,

1. Cf. *Leonardo da Vinci and a Memory of his Childhood* (1910c) [p. 189 above].
2. *Denkwürdigkeiten eines Nervenkranken*, 1903. See my analysis of his case (1911c) [*P.F.L.*, **9**, 129 ff.].

Dr Schreber – had decided to emasculate him, to use him as a woman, and to beget from him 'a new race of men born from the spirit of Schreber'.[1] (His own marriage was childless.) In his revolt against this intention of God's, which seemed to him highly unjust and 'contrary to the Order of Things', he fell ill with symptoms of paranoia, which, however, underwent a process of involution in the course of years, leaving only a small residue behind. The gifted author of his own case history could not have guessed that in it he had uncovered a typical pathogenic factor.

This revolt against castration or a feminine attitude has been torn out of its organic context by Alfred Adler. He has linked it superficially or falsely with the longing for power, and has postulated it as an independent 'masculine protest' [Adler, 1910]. Since a neurosis can only arise from a conflict between two trends, it is as justifiable to see the cause of 'every' neurosis in the masculine protest as it is to see it in the feminine attitude against which the protest is being made. It is quite true that this masculine protest plays a regular part in the formation of character – in some types of people a very large part – and that we meet it in the analysis of neurotic men as a vigorous resistance. Psychoanalysis has attached due importance to the masculine protest in connection with the castration complex, without being able to accept its omnipotence or its omni-presence in neuroses. The most marked case of a masculine protest with all its manifest reactions and character-traits that I have met with in analysis was that of a patient who came to me for treatment on account of an obsessional neurosis in whose symptoms the unresolved conflict between a masculine and a feminine attitude (fear of castration and desire for castra-tion) found clear expression. In addition, the patient had developed masochistic phantasies which were wholly derived from a wish to accept castration; and he had even gone beyond these phantasies to real satisfaction in perverse situations. The whole of his state rested – like Adler's theory itself – on the

1. [Ibid., **9**, 183, 195.]

repression and denial of early infantile fixations of love.[1]

Senatspräsident Schreber found the way to recovery when he decided to give up his resistance to castration and to accommodate himself to the feminine role cast for him by God. After this, he became lucid and calm, was able to put through his own discharge from the asylum and led a normal life – with the one exception that he devoted some hours every day to the cultivation of his femaleness, of whose gradual advance towards the goal determined by God he remained convinced.

1. [Freud discusses Adler's 'masculine protest' at greater length in 'A Child is Being Beaten' (1919e), *P.F.L.*, **10**, 189–92.]

IV

THE TWO BONDS

A REMARKABLE detail in our painter's story is the statement that he signed two different bonds with the Devil.

The first, written in black ink, ran as follows:[1]

'I, Chr. H., subscribe myself to this Lord as his bounden son till the ninth year.'

The second, written in blood, ran:

'Chr. H. I sign a bond with this Satan, to be his bounden son, and in the ninth year to belong to him body and soul.'

The originals of both are said to have been in the archives at Mariazell when the *Trophaeum* was compiled, and both bear the same date – 1669.

I have already made a number of references to the two bonds; and I now propose to deal with them in greater detail, although it is precisely here that the danger of overvaluing trifles seems especially great.

It is unusual for anyone to sign a bond with the Devil twice, in such a way that the first document is replaced by the second, but without losing its own validity. Perhaps this occurrence is less surprising to other people, who are more at home with demonological material. For my part, I could only look on it as a special peculiarity of our case, and my suspicions were aroused when I found that the reports were at variance precisely on this point. Examination of these discrepancies will afford us, unexpectedly, a deeper understanding of the case history.

The village priest of Pottenbrunn's letter of introduction describes a very simple and clear situation. In it mention is only made of one bond, which was written in blood by the painter nine years before and which was due to expire in a few days'

1. [The German versions will be found above on p. 395.]

time – on 24 September [1677]. It must therefore have been drawn up on 24 September 1668; unfortunately this date, although it can be inferred with certainty, is not explicitly stated.

The Abbot Franciscus's deposition, which was dated, as we know, a few days later (12 September 1677), already describes a more complicated state of affairs. It is plausible to assume that the painter had given more precise information in the interval. The deposition relates that the painter had signed two bonds: one in the year 1668 (a date which should also be the correct one according to the letter of introduction), written in black ink, and the other 'sequenti anno [in the following year] 1669', written in blood. The bond that he received back on the day of the Nativity of the Virgin [8 September] was the one written in blood – viz. the later bond, which had been signed in 1669. This does not emerge from the Abbot's deposition, for there it merely says later 'schedam redderet [should give back the paper]' and 'schedam sibi porrigentem conspexisset [saw him offering him the paper]' as if there could only be a single document in question. But it does follow from the subsequent course of the story, and also from the coloured title-page of the Trophaeum, where what is clearly a red script can be seen on the paper which the demon dragon is holding. The further course of the story is, as I have already related, that the painter returned to Mariazell in May 1678, after he had experienced further temptations from the Evil One in Vienna; and that he begged that, through a further act of grace on the part of the Holy Mother, the first document, written in ink, might also be given back to him. In what way this came about is not so fully described as on the first occasion. We are merely told: 'quâ iuxta votum redditâ [when this had been returned in accordance with his prayer]'; and in another passage the compiler says that this particular bond was thrown to the painter by the Devil 'crumpled up and torn into four pieces'[1] on 9 May 1678, at about nine o'clock in the evening.

Both bonds, however, bear the date of the same year – 1669.

---

1. [... 'in globum convolutam et in quatuor partes dilaceratam ...']

This incompatibility is either of no significance or may put us on the following track.

If we take as a starting-point the Abbot's account, as being the more detailed one, we are confronted with a number of difficulties. When Christoph Haizmann confessed to the village priest of Pottenbrunn that he was hard pressed by the Devil and that the time-limit would soon run out, he could only (in 1677) have been thinking of the bond which he had signed in 1668 – namely, the first one, written in black (which is referred to in the letter of introduction as the only one, but is described there as being written in blood). But a few days later, at Mariazell, he was only concerned to get back the later bond, in blood, which was not nearly due to expire then (1669–1677), and allowed the first one to become overdue. This latter was not reclaimed till 1678 – that is, when it had run into its tenth year. Furthermore, why are both the bonds dated in the same year (1669), when one of them is explicitly attributed to the following year ('*anno subsequenti*'[1])?

The compiler must have noticed these difficulties, for he made an attempt to remove them. In his preface he adopted the Abbot's version, but he modified it in one particular. The painter, he says, signed a bond with the Devil in 1669 in ink, but afterwards ('*deinde vero*') in blood. He thus overrode the express statement of both reports that one bond was signed in 1668, and he ignored the Abbot's remark in his deposition to the effect that there was a difference in the year-number between the two bonds. This he did in order to keep in harmony with the dating of the two documents that were given back by the Devil.

In the Abbot's deposition a passage appears in brackets after the words '*sequenti vero anno* [but in the following year] *1669*'. It runs: '*sumitur hic alter annus pro nondum completo, uti saepe in loquendo fieri solet, nam eundem annum indicant syngraphae, quarum atramento scripta ante praesentem attestationem nondum*

---

1. [This is derived from the compiler's preface. The 'sequenti anno' quoted above (p. 410) and again below is from the Abbot's deposition.]

habita fuit.'[1] This passage is clearly an interpolation by the compiler; for the Abbot, who had only seen one bond, could not have stated that both bore the same date. The placing of the passage in brackets, moreover, must have been intended to show that it was an addition to the text of the deposition.[2] It represents another attempt on the compiler's part to reconcile the incompatible evidence. He agrees that the first bond was signed in 1668; but he thinks that, since the year was already far advanced (it was September), the painter had post-dated it by a year so that both bonds were able to show the same year. His invoking the fact that people often do the same sort of thing in conversation seems to me to stamp his whole attempt at an explanation as no more than a feeble evasion.

I cannot tell whether my presentation of the case has made any impression on the reader and whether it has put him in a position to take an interest in these minute details. I myself have found it impossible to arrive with any certainty at the true state of affairs; but, in studying this confused business, I hit upon a notion which has the advantage of giving the most natural picture of the course of events, even though once more the written evidence does not entirely fit in with it.

My view is that when the painter first came to Mariazell he spoke only of *one* bond, written in the regular way in blood, which was about to fall due and which had therefore been signed in September 1668 – all exactly as described in the village priest's letter of introduction. In Mariazell, too, he presented this bond in blood as the one which the Demon had given back to him under compulsion from the Holy Mother. We know what happened subsequently. The painter left the shrine soon afterwards and went to Vienna, where he felt free till the middle of October. Then, however, he began once more

---

1. ['Here the second (later) year is taken instead of the one that was not yet completed, as is often done in conversation; for the same year is indicated by (both) syngraphae (bonds), of which the one written in ink had not yet been received back before the present deposition.']

2. [It is also written in very much smaller script than the rest of the Abbot's deposition.]

to be subjected to sufferings and apparitions, in which he saw the work of the Evil Spirit. He again felt in need of redemption, but was faced with the difficulty of explaining why the exorcism in the holy Chapel had not brought him a lasting deliverance. He would certainly not have been welcome at Mariazell if he had returned there uncured and relapsed. In this quandary, he invented an earlier, first bond, which, however, was to be written in ink, so that its supersession in favour of a later bond, written in blood, should seem more plausible. Having returned to Mariazell, he had this alleged first bond given back to him too. After this he was left in peace by the Evil One; but at the same time he did something else, which will show us what lay in the background of his neurosis.

The drawings he made were undoubtedly executed during his second stay at Mariazell: the title-page, which is a single composition, contains a representation of both the bond scenes. The attempt to make his new story tally with his earlier one may well have caused him embarrassment. It was unfortunate for him that his additional invention could only be of an earlier bond and not of a later one. Thus he could not avoid the awkward result that he had redeemed one – the blood bond – too soon (in the eighth year), and the other – the black bond – too late (in the tenth year). And he betrayed the double editing of the story by making a mistake in the dating of the bonds and attributing the earlier one as well as the later to the year 1669. This mistake has the significance of a piece of unintentional honesty: it enables us to guess that the supposedly earlier bond was fabricated at the later date. The compiler, who certainly did not begin revising the material before 1714, and perhaps not till 1729, had to do his best to resolve its not inconsiderable contradictions. Finding that both the bonds before him were dated 1669, he had recourse to the evasion which he interpolated in the Abbot's deposition.

It is easy to see where the weak spot lies in this otherwise attractive reconstruction. Reference is already made to the existence of two bonds, one in black and one in blood, in the Abbot's deposition. I therefore have the choice between accusing the compiler of having also made an alteration in the deposition, an alteration closely related to his interpolation, or confessing that I am unable to unravel the tangle.[1]

The reader will long ago have judged this whole discussion superfluous and the details concerned in it too unimportant. But the matter gains a new interest if it is pursued in a certain direction.

I have just expressed the view that, when the painter was disagreeably surprised by the course taken by his illness, he invented an earlier bond (the one in ink) in order to be able to maintain his position with the reverend Fathers at Mariazell.

1. The compiler, it seems to me, was between two fires. On the one hand, he found, in the village priest's letter of introduction as well as in the Abbot's deposition, the statement that the bond (or at any rate the first bond) had been signed in 1668; on the other hand, both bonds, which had been preserved in the archives, bore the date 1669. As he had two bonds before him, it seemed certain to him that two bonds had been signed. If, as I believe, the Abbot's deposition mentioned only one bond, he was obliged to insert in the deposition a reference to the other and then remove the contradiction by the hypothesis of the post-dating. The textual alteration which he made occurs immediately before the interpolation, which can only have been written by him. He was obliged to link the interpolation to the alteration with the words *'sequenti vero anno* [but in the following year] *1669'*, since the painter had expressly written in his (very much damaged) caption to the title-page:

'A year after He
... terrible threatenings in
... shape No. 2, was forced
... to sign a bond in blood.'
[*'Nach einem Jahr würdt Er*
... *schrökhliche betrohungen in ab-*
... *gestalt Nr. 2 bezwungen sich,*
... *n Bluot zu verschreiben.'*]

The painter's blunder [*Verschreiben*] in writing his *Syngraphae* – a blunder which I have been obliged to assume in my attempted explanation – appears to me to be no less interesting than are the actual bonds. [There is a pun here on the word *'Verschreiben'*, which means 'making a mistake in writing' as well as 'signing a bond'. – In *The Psychopathology of Everyday Life* (1901*b*), *P.F.L.*, **5**, 279, Freud points out that an accidental slip often reveals a deliberate falsification.]

Now I am writing for readers who, although they believe in psychoanalysis, do not believe in the Devil; and they might object that it was absurd for me to bring such an accusation against the poor wretch – *hunc miserum*, as he is called in the letter of introduction. For, they will say, the bond in blood was just as much a product of his phantasy as the allegedly earlier one in ink. In reality, no Devil appeared to him at all, and the whole business of pacts with the Devil only existed in his imagination. I quite realize this: the poor man cannot be denied the right to supplement his original phantasy with a new one, if altered circumstances seem to require it.

But here, too, the matter goes further. After all, the two bonds were not phantasies like the visions of the Devil. They were documents, preserved, according to the assurances of the copyist and the deposition of the later Abbot Kilian, in the archives of Mariazell, for all to see and touch. We are therefore in a dilemma. Either we must assume that both the papers which were supposed to have been given back to the painter through divine grace were written by him at the time when he needed them; or else, despite all the solemn assurances, the confirmatory evidence of witnesses, signed and sealed, and so on, we shall be obliged to deny the credibility of the reverend Fathers of Mariazell and St Lambert. I must admit that I am unwilling to cast doubts on the Fathers. I am inclined to think, it is true, that the compiler, in the interests of consistency, has falsified some things in the deposition made by the first Abbot; but a 'secondary revision' such as this does not go much beyond what is carried out even by modern lay historians, and at all events it was done in good faith. In another respect, the reverend Fathers have established a good claim to our confidence. As I have said already, there was nothing to prevent them from suppressing the accounts of the incompleteness of the cure and the continuance of the temptations. And even the description of the scene of exorcism in the Chapel, which one might have viewed with some apprehension, is soberly written and inspires belief. So there is nothing for it but to lay the blame on the painter. No doubt he had the red bond with him when he went to penitential prayer in the Chapel, and he produced it afterwards as he came back to his spiritual assistants from his meeting with the Demon. Nor need it have been the same paper which was later preserved in the archives, and, according to our construction, it may have borne the date 1668 (nine years before the exorcism).

V

THE FURTHER COURSE OF
THE NEUROSIS

BUT if this is so, we should be dealing not with a neurosis
but with a deception, and the painter would be a malingerer
and forger instead of a sick man suffering from possession. But
the transitional stages between neurosis and malingering are,
as we know, very fluid. Nor do I see any difficulty in supposing
that the painter wrote this paper and the later one, and took
them with him, in a peculiar state, similar to the one in which
he had his visions. Indeed there was no other course open to him
if he wished to carry into effect his phantasy of his pact with
the Devil and of his redemption.

On the other hand, the diary written in Vienna, which he
gave to the clerics on his second visit to Mariazell, bears the
stamp of veracity. It undoubtedly affords us a deep insight into
the motivation – or let us rather say, the exploitation – of the
neurosis.

The entries extend from the time of the successful exorcism
till 13[1] January of the following year, 1678.

Until 11 October he felt very well in Vienna, where he lived
with a married sister; but after that he had fresh attacks, with
visions, convulsions, loss of consciousness and painful sensations, and these finally led to his return to Mariazell in May
1678.

The story of his fresh illness falls into three phases. First,
temptation appeared in the form of a finely dressed cavalier,
who tried to persuade him to throw away the document attest-
ing his admission to the Brotherhood of the Holy Rosary.[2]

1. [In all the German editions except the first this is misprinted '15'.]
2. [A religious order to which he had been admitted on his arrival in Vienna.]

417

He resisted this temptation, whereupon the same thing happened next day; only this time the scene was laid in a magnificently decorated hall in which grand gentlemen were dancing with beautiful ladies. The same cavalier who had tempted him before made a proposal to him connected with painting[1] and promised to give him a handsome sum of money in return. After he had made this vision disappear by prayer, it was repeated once more a few days later, in a still more pressing form. This time the cavalier sent one of the most beautiful of the ladies who sat at the banqueting table to him to persuade him to join their company, and he had difficulty in defending himself from the temptress. Most terrifying of all, moreover, was the vision which occurred soon after this. He saw a still more magnificent hall, in which there was a 'throne built up of gold pieces'. Cavaliers were standing about awaiting the arrival of their king. The same person who had so often made proposals to him now approached him and summoned him to ascend the throne, for they 'wanted to have him for their King and to honour him for ever'. This extravagant phantasy concluded the first, perfectly transparent, phase of the story of his temptation.

There was bound to be a revulsion against this. An ascetic reaction reared its head. On 20 October a great light appeared, and a voice came from it, making itself known as Christ, and commanded him to forswear this wicked world and serve God in the wilderness for six years. The painter clearly suffered more from these holy apparitions than from the earlier demoniacal ones; it was only after two and a half hours that he awoke from this attack. In the next attack the holy figure surrounded by light was much more unfriendly. He issued threats against him for not having obeyed the divine behest and led him down into Hell so that he might be terrified by the fate of the damned. Evidently, however, this failed in its effect, for the apparitions of the figure surrounded by light, which purported to be Christ, were repeated several more times. Each time the painter underwent an *absence* and an ecstasy lasting for hours. In the grandest of these ecstasies the figure surrounded by light took him first

1. This passage is unintelligible to me.

into a town in whose streets people were perpetrating all the acts of darkness; and then, in contrast, took him to a lovely meadow in which anchorites were leading a godly life and were receiving tangible evidence of God's grace and care. There then appeared, instead of Christ, the Holy Mother herself, who, reminding him of what she had already done on his behalf, called on him to obey the command of her dear Son. 'Since he could not truly resolve so to do', Christ appeared to him again the next day and upbraided him soundly with threats and promises. At last he gave way and made up his mind to leave the world and to do what was required of him. With this decision, the second phase ended. The painter states that from this time onwards he had no more visions and no more temptations.

Nevertheless, his resolution cannot have been firm enough or he must have delayed its execution too long; for while he was in the midst of his devotions, on 26 December, in St Stephen's [Cathedral], catching sight of a strapping young woman accompanied by a smartly dressed gentleman, he could not fend off the thought that he might himself be in this gentleman's place. This called for punishment, and that very evening it overtook him like a thunderbolt. He saw himself in bright flames and sank down in a swoon. Attempts were made to rouse him but he rolled about in the room till blood flowed from his mouth and nose. He felt that he was surrounded by heat and noisome smells, and he heard a voice say that he had been condemned to this state as a punishment for his vain and idle thoughts. Later he was scourged with ropes by Evil Spirits, and was told that he would be tormented like this every day until he had decided to enter the Order of Anchorites. These experiences continued up to the last entry in his diary (13 January).

We see how our unfortunate painter's phantasies of temptation were succeeded by ascetic ones and finally by phantasies of punishment. The end of his tale of suffering we know already. In May he went to Mariazell, told his story of an earlier bond written in black ink, to which he explicitly attributed his continued torment by the Devil, received this bond back, too, and was cured.

During his second stay there he painted the pictures which are copied in the *Trophaeum*. Then he took a step which was in keeping with the demands of the ascetic phase of his diary. He did not, it is true, go into the wilderness to become an anchorite, but he joined the Order of the Brothers Hospitallers: *religiosus factus est*.

Reading the diary, we gain insight into another part of the story. It will be remembered that the painter signed a bond with the Devil because after his father's death, feeling depressed and unable to work, he was worried about making a livelihood. These factors of depression, inhibition in his work and mourning for his father are somehow connected with one another, whether in a simple or a complicated way. Perhaps the reason why the apparitions of the Devil were so over-generously furnished with breasts was that the Evil One was meant to become his foster-father. This hope was not fulfilled, and the painter continued to be in a bad state. He could not work properly, or he was out of luck and could not find enough employment. The village priest's letter of introduction speaks of him as *'hunc miserum omni auxilio destitutum'*. He was thus not only in moral straits but was suffering material want. In the account [in his diary] of his later visions, we find remarks here and there indicating – as do the contents of the scenes described – that even after the successful first exorcism, nothing had been changed in his situation. We come to know him as a man who fails in everything and who is therefore trusted by no one. In his first vision the cavalier asked him 'what he is going to do, since he has no one to stand by him'. The first series of visions in Vienna tallied completely with the wishful phantasies of a poor man, who had come down in the world and who hungered for enjoyment: magnificent halls, high living, a silver dinner-service and beautiful women. Here we find what was missing in his relations with the Devil made good. At that time he had been in a melancholia which made him unable to enjoy anything and obliged him to reject the most attractive offers. After the exorcism the melancholia seems to have been overcome and all his worldly-minded desires had once more become active.

In one of the ascetic visions he complained to his guide (Christ) that nobody had any faith in him, so that he was unable to carry out the commands laid upon him. The reply he was given is, unfortunately, obscure to us: 'Although they will not believe me, yet I know well what has happened, but I am not able to declare it.' Especially illuminating, however, are the experiences which his heavenly Guide made him have among the anchorites. He came to a cave in which an old man had been sitting for the last sixty years, and in answer to a question he learnt that this old man had been fed every day by God's angels. And then he saw for himself how an angel brought the old man food: 'Three dishes with food, a loaf, a dumpling and some drink.' After the anchorite had eaten, the angel collected everything and carried it away. We can see what the temptation was which the pious visions offered the painter: they were meant to induce him to adopt a mode of existence in which he need no longer worry about sustenance. The utterances of Christ in the last vision are also worthy of note. After threatening that, if he did not prove amenable, something would happen which would oblige him and the people to believe [in it[1]], Christ gave him a direct warning that 'I should not heed the people; even if they were to persecute me or give me no help, God would not abandon me'.

Christoph Haizmann was enough of an artist and a child of the world to find it difficult to renounce this sinful world. Nevertheless, in view of his helpless position, he did so in the end. He entered a holy order. With this, both his internal struggle and his material need came to an end. In his neurosis, this outcome was reflected in the fact of his seizures and visions being brought to an end by the return of an alleged first bond. Actually, both portions of his demonological illness had the

---

1. ['*Daran*', in square brackets in the German.]

same meaning. He wanted all along simply to make his life secure. He tried first to achieve this with the help of the Devil at the cost of his salvation; and when this failed and had to be given up, he tried to achieve it with the help of the clergy at the cost of his freedom and most of the possibilities of enjoyment in life. Perhaps he himself was only a poor devil who simply had no luck; perhaps he was too ineffective or too untalented to make a living, and was one of those types of people who are known as 'eternal sucklings' – who cannot tear themselves away from the blissful situation at the mother's breast, and who, all through their lives, persist in a demand to be nourished by someone else. – And so it was that, in this history of his illness, he followed the path which led from his father, by way of the Devil as a father-substitute, to the pious Fathers of the Church.

To superficial observation Haizmann's neurosis appears to be a masquerade which overlays a part of the serious, if commonplace, struggle for existence. This is not always the case, but it is not infrequently so. Analysts often discover how unprofitable it is to treat a business man who 'though otherwise in good health, has for some time shown signs of a neurosis'. The business catastrophe with which he feels himself threatened throws up the neurosis as a by-product; and this gives him the advantage of being able to conceal his worries about his real life behind his symptoms. But apart from this the neurosis serves no useful purpose whatever, since it uses up forces which would have been more profitably employed in dealing rationally with the dangerous situation.

In a far greater number of cases the neurosis is more autonomous and more independent of the interest of self-preservation and self-maintenance. In the conflict which creates the neurosis, what are at stake are either solely libidinal interests or libidinal interests in intimate connections with self-preservative ones. In all three instances the dynamics of the neurosis are the same. A dammed-up libido which cannot be satisfied in reality succeeds, with the help of a regression to old fixations, in finding discharge through the repressed unconscious. The sick man's ego, in so far as it can extract a 'gain from illness'[1] out of this process, countenances the neurosis, although there can be no doubt of its injuriousness in its economic aspect.

Nor would our painter's wretched situation in life have provoked a demonological neurosis in him if his material need had not intensified his longing for his father. After his melancholia and the Devil had been disposed of, however, he still had to face a struggle between his libidinal enjoyment of life and his realization that the interests of self-preservation called imperatively for renunciation and asceticism. It is interesting to see that the painter was very well aware of the unity of the two portions of his illness, for he attributed both to the bonds which he had signed with the Devil. On the one hand, he made no sharp distinction between the operations of the Evil Spirit and those of the Divine Powers. He had only one description for both: they were manifestations of the Devil.

1. [A full discussion of 'gain from illness' will be found in Lecture 24 of the *Introductory Lectures* (1916–17), *P.F.L.*, 1, 429–33, and it is mentioned again in a footnote added in 1923 to the 'Dora' case history (1905e), ibid., 8, 75–6 n., where Freud revised his earlier views on the subject.]

HUMOUR
(1927)

DER HUMOR

(A) GERMAN EDITIONS:

1927   *Almanach 1928*, 9–16.
1948   *Gesammelte Werke*, **14**, 383–9.

(B) ENGLISH TRANSLATIONS:

'Humour'

1928   *International Journal of Psycho-Analysis*, **9** (1), 1–6. (Tr. Joan Riviere.)
1950   *Collected Papers*, **5**, 215–21. (Revised reprint of above.)
1961   *Standard Edition*, **21**, 159–66. (Corrected version of above.)

The present edition is a reprint of the *Standard Edition* version.

Freud wrote this paper in five days during the second week of August 1927 (Jones, 1957, 146), and it was read on his behalf by Anna Freud on 1 September before the Tenth International Psycho-Analytical Congress at Innsbruck. It was first published in the autumn of the same year.

The paper returns, after an interval of more than twenty years, to the subject discussed in the last section of the book on *Jokes* (1905*c*), *P.F.L.*, **6**, 293–302. Freud now considers it in the light of his new structural picture of the human mind. Some interesting metapsychological points emerge in the later pages of the paper, and for the first time we find the super-ego presented in an amiable mood.

HUMOUR

IN my volume on *Jokes and their Relation to the Unconscious* (1905c), I in fact considered humour only from the economic point of view. My object was to discover the source of the pleasure obtained from humour, and I think I was able to show that the yield of humorous pleasure arises from an economy in expenditure upon feeling. [*P.F.L.*, **6**, 302.]

There are two ways in which the humorous process can take place. It may take place in regard to a single person, who himself adopts the humorous attitude, while a second person plays the part of the spectator who derives enjoyment from it; or it may take place between two persons, of whom one takes no part at all in the humorous process, but is made the object of humorous contemplation by the other. When, to take the crudest example [ibid., 294], a criminal who was being led out to the gallows on a Monday remarked: 'Well, the week's beginning nicely', he was producing the humour himself; the humorous process is completed in his own person and obviously affords him a certain sense of satisfaction. I, the non-participating listener, am affected as it were at long-range by this humorous production of the criminal's; I feel, like him, perhaps, the yield of humorous pleasure.

We have an instance of the second way in which humour arises when a writer or a narrator describes the behaviour of real or imaginary people in a humorous manner. There is no need for those people to display any humour themselves; the humorous attitude is solely the business of the person who is taking them as his object; and, as in the former instance, the reader or hearer shares in the enjoyment of the humour. To sum up, then, we can say that the humorous attitude – whatever it may consist in – can be directed either towards the subject's own self or towards other people; it is to be assumed that it brings a yield of pleasure to the person who adopts it, and a similar yield of pleasure falls to the share of the non-participating onlooker.

We shall best understand the genesis of the yield of humorous pleasure if we consider the process in the listener before whom someone else produces humour. He sees this other person in a situation which leads the listener to expect that the other will produce the signs of an affect – that he will get angry, complain, express pain, be frightened or horrified or perhaps even in despair; and the onlooker or listener is prepared to follow his lead and to call up the same emotional impulses in himself. But this emotional expectancy is disappointed; the other person expresses no affect, but makes a jest. The expenditure on feeling that is economized turns into humorous pleasure in the listener.

It is easy to get so far. But we soon tell ourselves that it is the process which takes place in the other person – the 'humorist' – that merits the greater attention. There is no doubt that the essence of humour is that one spares oneself the affects to which the situation would naturally give rise and dismisses the possibility of such expressions of emotion with a jest. As far as this goes, the process in the humorist must tally with the process in the hearer – or, to put it more correctly, the process in the hearer must have copied the one in the humorist. But how does the latter bring about the mental attitude which makes a release of affect superfluous? What are the dynamics of his adoption of the 'humorous attitude'? Clearly, the solution of the problem is to be sought in the humorist; in the hearer we must assume that there is only an echo, a copy, of this unknown process.

It is now time to acquaint ourselves with a few of the characteristics of humour. Like jokes and the comic, humour has something liberating about it; but it also has something of grandeur and elevation, which is lacking in the other two ways of obtaining pleasure from intellectual activity. The grandeur in it clearly lies in the triumph of narcissism, the victorious assertion of the ego's invulnerability. The ego refuses to be distressed by the provocations of reality, to let itself be compelled to suffer. It insists that it cannot be affected by the traumas of the external world; it shows, in fact, that such traumas are no more than occasions for it to gain pleasure. This last feature is a quite essential element of humour. Let us suppose that the criminal who was being led to execution on Monday had said: 'It doesn't worry me. What does it matter, after all, if a fellow like me is hanged? The world won't come to an end because of it.' We should have to admit that such a speech does in fact display the same magnificent superiority over the real situation. It is wise and true; but it does not betray a trace of humour. Indeed, it is based on an appraisal of reality which runs directly counter to the appraisal made by humour. Humour is not resigned; it is rebellious. It signifies not only the triumph of the ego but also of the pleasure principle, which is able here to assert itself against the unkindness of the real circumstances.

These last two features – the rejection of the claims of reality and the putting through of the pleasure principle – bring humour near to the regressive or reactionary processes which engage our attention so extensively in psychopathology. Its fending off of the possibility of suffering places it among the great series of methods which the human mind has constructed in order to evade the compulsion to suffer – a series which begins with neurosis and culminates in madness and which includes intoxication, self-absorption and ecstasy.[1] Thanks to this connection, humour possesses a dignity which is wholly lacking, for instance, in jokes, for jokes either serve simply to obtain a yield of pleasure or place the yield of pleasure that has been obtained in the service of aggression. In what, then, does the humorous attitude consist, an attitude by means of which a person refuses to suffer, emphasizes the invincibility

---

1. [Cf. the subsequent long discussion of these various methods of avoiding pain in *Civilization and its Discontents* (1930*a*), *P.F.L.*, **12**, 264 ff. But Freud had already pointed out the defensive function of humour in *Jokes* (1905*c*), ibid., **6**, 299.]

of his ego by the real world, victoriously maintains the pleasure principle – and all this, in contrast to other methods having the same purposes, without overstepping the bounds of mental health? The two achievements seem incompatible.

If we turn to the situation in which one person adopts a humorous attitude towards others, a view which I have already put forward tentatively in my book on jokes will at once suggest itself. This is that the subject is behaving towards them as an adult does towards a child when he recognizes and smiles at the triviality of interests and sufferings which seem so great to it [ibid., 299]. Thus the humorist would acquire his superiority by assuming the role of the grown-up and identifying himself to some extent with his father, and reducing the other people to being children. This view probably covers the facts, but it hardly seems a conclusive one. One asks oneself what it is that makes the humorist arrogate this role to himself.

But we must recall the other, probably more primary and important, situation of humour, in which a person adopts a humorous attitude towards himself in order to ward off possible suffering. Is there any sense in saying that someone is treating himself like a child and is at the same time playing the part of a superior adult towards that child?

This not very plausible idea receives strong support, I think, if we consider what we have learned from pathological observations on the structure of the ego. This ego is not a simple entity. It harbours within it, as its nucleus, a special agency – the super-ego.[1] Sometimes it is merged with the super-ego so that we cannot distinguish between them, whereas in other circumstances it is sharply differentiated from it. Genetically the super-ego is the heir to the parental agency. It often keeps the ego in strict dependence and still really treats it as the parents, or the father, once treated the child, in its early years. We obtain a dynamic explanation of the humorous attitude, therefore, if we assume that it consists in the humorist's having withdrawn

---

1. [It may be remarked that in *The Ego and the Id* (1923*b*) Freud says that 'the system *Pcpt.-Cs.* alone can be regarded as the nucleus of the ego'; *P.F.L.*, **11**, 367 *n.* 2.]

the psychical accent from his ego and having transposed it on to his super-ego. To the super-ego, thus inflated, the ego can appear tiny and all its interests trivial; and, with this new distribution of energy, it may become an easy matter for the super-ego to suppress the ego's possibilities of reacting.

In order to remain faithful to our customary phraseology, we shall have to speak, not of transposing the psychical accent, but of displacing large amounts of cathexis. The question then is whether we are entitled to picture extensive displacements like this from one agency of the mental apparatus to another. It looks like a new hypothesis constructed *ad hoc*. Yet we may remind ourselves that we have repeatedly (even though not sufficiently often) taken a factor of this kind into account in our attempts at a metapsychological picture of mental events. Thus, for instance, we supposed that the difference between an ordinary erotic object-cathexis and the state of being in love is that in the latter incomparably more cathexis passes over to the object and that the ego empties itself as it were in favour of the object.[1] In studying some cases of paranoia I was able to establish the fact that ideas of persecution are formed early and exist for a long time without any perceptible effect, until, as the result of some particular precipitating event, they receive sufficient amounts of cathexis to cause them to become dominant.[2] The cure, too, of such paranoic attacks would lie not so much in a resolution and correction of the delusional ideas as in a withdrawal from them of the cathexis which has been lent to them. The alternation between melancholia and mania, between a cruel suppression of the ego by the super-ego and a liberation of the ego after that pressure, suggests a shift of cathexis of this kind;[3] such a shift, moreover, would have to be brought in to explain a whole number of phenomena belonging to normal mental life. If this has been done hitherto only to a very limited extent, that is on account of our usual

1. [See Chapter VIII of *Group Psychology* (1921c), P.F.L., **12**, 143.]
2. [See Section B of 'Some Neurotic Mechanisms' (1922b), ibid., **10**, 203–4.]
3. [See 'Mourning and Melancholia' (1917e), ibid., **11**, 262–4.]

caution – something which deserves only praise. The region in which we feel secure is that of the pathology of mental life; it is here that we make our observations and acquire our convictions. For the present we venture to form a judgement on the normal mind only in so far as we can discern what is normal in the isolations and distortions of the pathological material. When once we have overcome this hesitancy we shall recognize what a large contribution is made to the understanding of mental processes by the static conditions as well as by the dynamic changes in the *quantity* of energic cathexis.

I think, therefore, that the possibility I have suggested here, that in a particular situation the subject suddenly hypercathects his super-ego and then, proceeding from it, alters the reactions of the ego, is one which deserves to be retained. Moreover, what I have suggested about humour finds a remarkable analogy in the kindred field of jokes. As regards the origin of jokes I was led to assume that a preconscious thought is given over for a moment to unconscious revision [ibid., 223]. A joke is thus the contribution made to the comic by the unconscious [ibid., 270]. In just the same way, *humour would be the contribution made to the comic through the agency of the super-ego*.

In other connections we knew the super-ego as a severe master. It will be said that it accords ill with such a character that the super-ego should condescend to enabling the ego to obtain a small yield of pleasure. It is true that humorous pleasure never reaches the intensity of the pleasure in the comic or in jokes, that it never finds vent in hearty laughter. It is also true that, in bringing about the humorous attitude, the super-ego is actually repudiating reality and serving an illusion. But (without rightly knowing why) we regard this less intense pleasure as having a character of very high value; we feel it to be especially liberating and elevating. Moreover, the jest made by humour is not the essential thing. It has only the value of a preliminary. The main thing is the intention which humour carries out, whether it is acting in relation to the self or other people. It means: 'Look! here is the world, which seems so dangerous! It is nothing but a game for children – just worth making a jest about!'

If it is really the super-ego which, in humour, speaks such kindly words of comfort to the intimidated ego, this will teach us that we have still a great deal to learn about the nature of the super-ego. Furthermore, not everyone is capable of the humorous attitude. It is a rare and precious gift, and many people are even without the capacity to enjoy humorous pleasure that is presented to them. And finally, if the super-ego tries, by means of humour, to console the ego and protect it from suffering, this does not contradict its origin in the parental agency.

DOSTOEVSKY AND PARRICIDE
(1928 [1927])

EDITOR'S NOTE

DOSTOJEWSKI UND DIE VATERTÖTUNG

(A) GERMAN EDITIONS:

1928   In *Die Urgestalt der Brüder Karamasoff*, ed. R. Fülöp-
        Miller and F. Eckstein, Munich.
1929   *Almanach 1930*, 9–31.
1948   *Gesammelte Werke*, **14**, 399–418.

(B) ENGLISH TRANSLATIONS:

'Dostoevski and Parricide'
1929   *The Realist*, **1** (4), 18–33. (Tr. D. F. Tait.)

'Dostoevsky and Parricide'
1945   *International Journal of Psycho-Analysis*, **26** (1–2), 1–8.
        (Considerably revised version of above.)
1945   *Partisan Review*, **12** (4), 530–44. (Reprint of above.)
1947   In F. M. Dostoevsky, *Stavrogin's Confession*, trans.
        V. Woolf and S. S. Koteliansky, New York: Lear
        Publications, 87–114. (Reprint of above.)
1950   *Collected Papers*, **5**, 222–42. (Further revision of above.)
1961   *Standard Edition*, **21**, 173–94. (Corrected reprint of 1950
        version.)

The present edition is a corrected reprint of the *Standard
Edition* version, with some editorial modifications.

From 1925 onwards, Fülöp-Miller and Eckstein began issuing
a series of volumes supplementary to the great complete
German edition of Dostoevsky which, edited by Moeller van
den Bruck, had been completed a few years earlier. The new
volumes, uniform with the complete edition, contained pos-

DOSTOEVSKY AND PARRICIDE

thumous writings, unfinished drafts and material from various sources throwing light on Dostoevsky's character and works. One of these volumes was to contain a collection of preliminary drafts and sketches relating to *The Brothers Karamazov* and a discussion of the book's sources; and the editors were anxious to persuade Freud to contribute an introduction dealing with the psychology both of the book and of its author. They seem to have approached him early in 1926 and he had begun writing his essay by the end of June of that year. He was deflected from it, however, by more urgent work. Thereafter he seems to have lost interest in the Dostoevsky essay, particularly, as Ernest Jones tells us (1957, 152), after he had come across a book on the same subject by Neufeld (1923), which, as he says in a footnote (p. 460) – with considerable modesty, it must be remarked – contained most of the ideas that he himself was putting forward. It is not clear when he took the essay up again. Jones (loc. cit.) suggests that it was finished early in 1927; but this seems scarcely likely, since Stefan Zweig's story with which the later part of the essay is concerned only appeared in 1927. The volume to which Freud's essay served as an introduction was not published until the autumn of 1928.

The essay falls into two distinct parts. The first deals with Dostoevsky's character in general, with his masochism, his sense of guilt, his 'epileptoid' attacks and his double attitude in the Oedipus complex. The second discusses the special point of his passion for gambling and leads to an account of a short story by Stefan Zweig which throws light on the genesis of that addiction. As will be seen from a subsequent letter of Freud's to Theodor Reik (1930*f*), the two parts of the essay are more closely related than appears on the surface. In that letter Freud excused himself for the structural weakness of the essay, and admitted that he had written it reluctantly, having felt hampered by considerations of the place where the essay was to appear. Without these considerations he would have established more clearly that, in a clinical picture such as Dostoevsky's neurosis, the struggle against masturbation plays a special part, proof of this being Dostoevsky's addiction to gambling. In this way, a link with Zweig's short story would have been made, and it would have been shown that Freud was less concerned with the Dostoevsky–Zweig connection than with the relation between masturbation and neurosis.

The present essay may show signs of being an 'occasional' piece, but it contains much that is of interest – for instance, Freud's first discussion of hysterical attacks since his early paper on the subject written twenty years before (1909a),[1] a restatement of his later views on the Oedipus complex and the sense of guilt, and a sidelight on the problem of masturbation which is not to be found in his earlier account of the question (1912f). But above all, he had an opportunity here for expressing his views on a writer whom he placed in the very front rank of all.

1. *P.F.L.*, **10**, 95 ff.

DOSTOEVSKY AND PARRICIDE

FOUR facets may be distinguished in the rich personality of Dostoevsky: the creative artist, the neurotic, the moralist and the sinner. How is one to find one's way in this bewildering complexity?

The creative artist is the least doubtful: Dostoevsky's place is not far behind Shakespeare. *The Brothers Karamazov* is the most magnificent novel ever written; the episode of the Grand Inquisitor, one of the peaks in the literature of the world, can hardly be valued too highly. Before the problem of the creative artist analysis must, alas, lay down its arms.

The moralist in Dostoevsky is the most readily assailable. If we seek to rank him high as a moralist on the plea that only a man who has gone through the depths of sin can reach the highest summit of morality, we are neglecting a doubt that arises. A moral man is one who reacts to temptation as soon as he feels it in his heart, without yielding to it. A man who alternately sins and then in his remorse erects high moral standards lays himself open to the reproach that he has made things too easy for himself. He has not achieved the essence of morality, renunciation, for the moral conduct of life is a practical human interest. He reminds one of the barbarians of the great migrations, who murdered and did penance for it, till penance became an actual technique for enabling murder to be done. Ivan the Terrible behaved in exactly this way; indeed this compromise with morality is a characteristic Russian trait. Nor was the final outcome of Dostoevsky's moral strivings anything very glorious. After the most violent struggles to reconcile the instinctual demands of the individual with the claims of the community, he landed in the retrograde position of submission both to temporal and spiritual authority, of veneration both for the Tsar and for the God of the Christians, and of a narrow Russian nationalism – a position which lesser minds have reached with smaller effort. This is the weak point in that great personality. Dostoevsky threw away the chance of becoming a teacher and liberator of humanity and made himself one with their gaolers. The future of human civilization will have little to thank him for. It seems probable that he was condemned to this failure by his neurosis. The greatness of his intelligence and the strength of his love for humanity might have opened to him another, an apostolic, way of life.

To consider Dostoevsky as a sinner or a criminal rouses violent opposition, which need not be based upon a philistine assessment of criminals. The real motive for this opposition soon becomes apparent. Two traits are essential in a criminal: boundless egoism and a strong destructive urge. Common to both of these, and a necessary condition for their expression, is absence of love, lack of an emotional appreciation of (human) objects. One at once recalls the contrast to this presented by Dostoevsky – his great need of love and his enormous capacity for love, which is to be seen in manifestations of exaggerated kindness and caused him to love and to help where he had a right to hate and to be revengeful, as, for example, in his relations with his first wife and her lover. That being so, it must be asked why there is any temptation to reckon Dostoevsky among the criminals. The answer is that it comes from his choice of material, which singles out from all others violent, murderous and egoistic characters, thus pointing to the existence of similar tendencies within himself, and also from certain facts in his life, like his passion for gambling and his possible confession to a sexual assault upon a young girl.[1] The

1. See the discussion of this in Fülöp-Miller and Eckstein (1926). Stefan Zweig (1920) writes: 'He was not halted by the barriers of bourgeois morality; and no one can say exactly how far he transgressed the bounds of law in his own life or how much of the criminal instincts of his heroes was realized

contradiction is resolved by the realization that Dostoevsky's very strong destructive instinct, which might easily have made him a criminal, was in his actual life directed mainly against his own person (inward instead of outward) and thus found expression as masochism and a sense of guilt. Nevertheless, his personality retained sadistic traits in plenty, which show themselves in his irritability, his love of tormenting and his intolerance even towards people he loved, and which appear also in the way in which, as an author, he treats his readers. Thus in little things he was a sadist towards others, and in bigger things a sadist towards himself, in fact a masochist — that is to say the mildest, kindliest, most helpful person possible.

We have selected three factors from Dostoevsky's complex personality, one quantitative and two qualitative: the extraordinary intensity of his emotional life, his perverse innate instinctual disposition, which inevitably marked him out to be a sado-masochist or a criminal, and his unanalysable artistic gift. This combination might very well exist without neurosis; there are people who are complete masochists without being neurotic. Nevertheless, the balance of forces between his instinctual demands and the inhibitions opposing them (plus the available methods of sublimation) would even so make it necessary to classify Dostoevsky as what is known as an 'instinctual character'. But the position is obscured by the simultaneous presence of neurosis, which, as we have said, was not in the circumstances inevitable, but which comes into being the more readily, the richer the complication which has to be mastered by the ego. For neurosis is after all only a sign that the ego has not succeeded in making a synthesis, that in attempting to do so it has forfeited its unity.

How then, strictly speaking, does his neurosis show itself?

---

in himself.' For the intimate connection between Dostoevsky's characters and his own experiences, see René Fülöp-Miller's remarks in the introductory section of Fülöp-Miller and Eckstein (1925), which are based upon N. Strakhov [1921]. — [The topic of a sexual assault on an immature girl appears several times in Dostoevsky's writings — especially in the posthumous *Stavrogin's Confession* and *The Life of a Great Sinner*.]

Dostoevsky called himself an epileptic, and was regarded as such by other people, on account of his severe attacks, which were accompanied by loss of consciousness, muscular convulsions and subsequent depression. Now it is highly probable that this so-called epilepsy was only a symptom of his neurosis and must accordingly be classified as hystero-epilepsy – that is, as severe hysteria. We cannot be completely certain on this point for two reasons – firstly, because the anamnestic data on Dostoevsky's alleged epilepsy are defective and untrustworthy, and secondly, because our understanding of pathological states combined with epileptiform attacks is imperfect.

To take the second point first. It is unnecessary here to reproduce the whole pathology of epilepsy, for it would throw no decisive light on the problem. But this may be said. The old *morbus sacer* is still in evidence as an ostensible clinical entity, the uncanny disease with its incalculable, apparently unprovoked convulsive attacks, its changing of the character into irritability and aggressiveness, and its progressive lowering of all the mental faculties. But the outlines of this picture are quite lacking in precision. The attacks, so savage in their onset, accompanied by biting of the tongue and incontinence of urine and working up to the dangerous *status epilepticus* with its risk of severe self-injuries, may, nevertheless, be reduced to brief periods of *absence*, or rapidly passing fits of vertigo or may be replaced by short spaces of time during which the patient does something out of character, as though he were under the control of his unconscious. These attacks, though as a rule determined, in a way we do not understand, by purely physical causes, may nevertheless owe their first appearance to some purely mental cause (a fright, for instance) or may react in other respects to mental excitations. However characteristic intellectual impairment may be in the overwhelming majority of cases, at least *one* case is known to us (that of Helmholtz) in which the affliction did not interfere with the highest intellectual achievement. (Other cases of which the same assertion has been made are either disputable or open to the same doubts as the case of Dostoevsky himself.) People who are victims of epilepsy may give an impression of dullness and arrested development just as the disease often accompanies the most palpable idiocy and the grossest cerebral defects, even though not as a necessary component of the clinical picture. But these attacks, with all their variations, also occur in other people who display complete mental development and, if anything, an excessive and as a rule insufficiently controlled emotional life. It is no wonder in these circumstances that it has been found impossible to maintain that 'epilepsy' is a single clinical entity. The similarity that we find in the manifest symptoms seems to call for a functional view of them. It is as though a mechanism for abnormal instinctual discharge had been laid down organically, which could be made use of in quite different circumstances – both in the case of disturbances of cerebral activity due to severe histolytic or toxic affections, and also in the case of inadequate control over the mental economy and at times when the activity of the energy operating in the mind reaches crisis-pitch. Behind this dichotomy we have a glimpse of the identity of the underlying mechanism of instinctual discharge. Nor can that mechanism stand remote from the sexual processes, which are fundamentally of toxic origin: the earliest physicians described coition as a minor epilepsy, and thus recognized in the sexual act a mitigation and adaptation of the epileptic method of discharging stimuli.[1]

The 'epileptic reaction', as this common element may be called, is also undoubtedly at the disposal of the neurosis whose essence it is to get rid by somatic means of amounts of excitation which it cannot deal with psychically. Thus the epileptic attack becomes a symptom of hysteria and is adapted and modified by it just as it is by the normal sexual process of discharge. It is therefore quite right to distinguish between an organic and an 'affective' epilepsy. The practical significance of this is that a person who suffers from the first kind has a disease of the brain, while a person who suffers from the second kind is a neurotic. In the first case his mental life is subjected to

1. [Cf. Freud's earlier paper on hysterical attacks (1909a), P.F.L., 10, 102.]

an alien disturbance from without, in the second case the disturbance is an expression of his mental life itself.

It is extremely probable that Dostoevsky's epilepsy was of the second kind. This cannot, strictly speaking, be proved. To do so we should have to be in a position to insert the first appearance of the attacks and their subsequent fluctuations into the thread of his mental life; and for that we know too little. The descriptions of the attacks themselves teach us nothing and our information about the relations between them and Dostoevsky's experiences is defective and often contradictory. The most probable assumption is that the attacks went back far into his childhood, that their place was taken to begin with by milder symptoms and that they did not assume an epileptic form until after the shattering experience of his eighteenth year – the murder of his father.[1] It would be very much to the point if it could be established that they ceased completely during his exile in Siberia, but other accounts contradict this.[2]

The unmistakable connection between the murder of the father in *The Brothers Karamazov* and the fate of Dostoevsky's

1. See René Fülöp-Miller (1924). [Cf. also the account given by Aimée Dostoevsky (1921) in her life of her father.] Of especial interest is the information that in the novelist's childhood 'something terrible, unforgettable and agonizing' happened, to which the first signs of his illness were to be traced (from an article by Suvorin in the newspaper *Novoe Vremya*, 1881, quoted in the introduction to Fülöp-Miller and Eckstein, 1925, xlv). See also Orest Miller (1921, 140): 'There is, however, another special piece of evidence about Fyodor Mikhailovich's illness, which relates to his earliest youth and brings the illness into connection with a tragic event in the family life of his parents. But, although this piece of evidence was given to me orally by one who was a close friend of Fyodor Mikhailovich, I cannot bring myself to reproduce it fully and precisely since I have had no confirmation of this rumour from any other quarter.' Biographers and scientific research workers cannot feel grateful for this discretion.

2. Most of the accounts, including Dostoevsky's own, assert on the contrary that the illness only assumed its final, epileptic character during the Siberian exile. Unfortunately there is reason to distrust the autobiographical statements of neurotics. Experience shows that their memories introduce falsifications which are designed to interrupt disagreeable causal connections. Nevertheless, it appears certain that Dostoevsky's detention in the Siberian prison markedly altered his pathological condition. Cf. Fülöp-Miller (1924, 1186).

own father has struck more than one of his biographers, and has led them to refer to 'a certain modern school of psychology'. From the standpoint of psychoanalysis (for that is what is meant), we are tempted to see in that event the severest trauma and to regard Dostoevsky's reaction to it as the turning-point of his neurosis. But if I undertake to substantiate this view psychoanalytically, I shall have to risk the danger of being unintelligible to all those readers who are unfamiliar with the language and theories of psychoanalysis.

We have one certain starting-point. We know the meaning of the first attacks from which Dostoevsky suffered in his early years, long before the incidence of the 'epilepsy'. These attacks had the significance of death: they were heralded by a fear of death and consisted of lethargic, somnolent states. The illness first came over him while he was still a boy, in the form of a sudden, groundless melancholy, a feeling, as he later told his friend Soloviev, as though he were going to die on the spot. And there in fact followed a state exactly similar to real death. His brother Andrey tells us that even when he was quite young Fyodor used to leave little notes about before he went to sleep, saying that he was afraid he might fall into this death-like sleep during the night and therefore begged that his burial should be postponed for five days. (Fülöp–Miller and Eckstein, 1925, lx.)

We know the meaning and intention of such death-like attacks.[1] They signify an identification with a dead person, either with someone who is really dead or with someone who is still alive and whom the subject wishes dead. The latter case is the more significant. The attack then has the value of a punishment. One has wished another person dead, and now one *is* this other person and is dead oneself. At this point psychoanalytical theory brings in the assertion that for a boy this other person is usually his father and that the attack (which is termed hysterical) is thus a self-punishment for a death-wish against a hated father.

1. [The explanation was already given by Freud in a letter to Fliess of 8 February 1897 (Freud, 1950a, Letter 58).]

Parricide, according to a well-known view, is the principal and primal crime of humanity as well as of the individual. (See my *Totem and Taboo*, 1912–13.) It is in any case the main source of the sense of guilt, though we do not know if it is the only one: researches have not yet been able to establish with certainty the mental origin of guilt and the need for expiation. But it is not necessary for it to be the only one. The psychological situation is complicated and requires elucidation. The relation of a boy to his father is, as we say, an 'ambivalent' one. In addition to the hate which seeks to get rid of the father as a rival, a measure of tenderness for him is also habitually present. The two attitudes of mind combine to produce identification with the father; the boy wants to be in his father's place because he admires him and wants to be like him, and also because he wants to put him out of the way. This whole development now comes up against a powerful obstacle. At a certain moment the child comes to understand that an attempt to remove his father as a rival would be punished by him with castration. So from fear of castration – that is, in the interests of preserving his masculinity – he gives up his wish to possess his mother and get rid of his father. In so far as this wish remains in the unconscious it forms the basis of the sense of guilt. We believe that what we have here been describing are normal processes, the normal fate of the so-called 'Oedipus complex'; nevertheless it requires an important amplification.

A further complication arises when the constitutional factor we call bisexuality is comparatively strongly developed in a child. For then, under the threat to the boy's masculinity by castration, his inclination becomes strengthened to diverge in the direction of femininity, to put himself instead in his mother's place and take over her role as object of his father's love. But the fear of castration makes *this* solution impossible as well. The boy understands that he must also submit to castration if he wants to be loved by his father as a woman. Thus both impulses, hatred of the father and being in love with the father, undergo repression. There is a certain psychological distinction in the fact that the hatred of the father is given up on account of fear of an *external* danger (castration), while the being in love with the father is treated as an *internal* instinctual danger, though fundamentally it goes back to the same external danger.

What makes hatred of the father unacceptable is *fear* of the father; castration is terrible, whether as a punishment or as the price of love. Of the two factors which repress hatred of the father, the first, the direct fear of punishment and castration, may be called the normal one; its pathogenic intensification seems to come only with the addition of the second factor, the fear of the feminine attitude. Thus a strong innate bisexual disposition becomes one of the preconditions or reinforcements of neurosis. Such a disposition must certainly be assumed in Dostoevsky, and it shows itself in a viable form (as latent homosexuality) in the important part played by male friendships in his life, in his strangely tender attitude towards rivals in love and in his remarkable understanding of situations which are explicable only by repressed homosexuality, as many examples from his novels show.

I am sorry, though I cannot alter the facts, if this exposition of the attitudes of hatred and love towards the father and their transformations under the influence of the threat of castration seems to readers unfamiliar with psychoanalysis unsavoury and incredible. I should myself expect that it is precisely the castration complex that would be bound to arouse the most general repudiation. But I can only insist that psychoanalytic experience has put these matters in particular beyond the reach of doubt and has taught us to recognize in them the key to every neurosis. This key, then, we must apply to our author's so-called epilepsy. So alien to our consciousness are the things by which our unconscious mental life is governed!

But what has been said so far does not exhaust the consequences of the repression of the hatred of the father in the Oedipus complex. There is something fresh to be added: namely that in spite of everything the identification with the father finally makes a permanent place for itself in the ego. It is received into the ego, but establishes itself there as a separate

DOSTOEVSKY AND PARRICIDE

agency in contrast to the rest of the content of the ego. We
then give it the name of super-ego and ascribe to it, the inheritor
of the parental influence, the most important functions. If the
father was hard, violent and cruel, the super-ego takes over
those attributes from him and, in the relations between the
ego and it, the passivity which was supposed to have been
repressed is re-established. The super-ego has become sadistic,
and the ego becomes masochistic – that is to say, at bottom
passive in a feminine way. A great need for punishment
develops in the ego, which in part offers itself as a victim to
Fate, and in part finds satisfaction in ill-treatment by the super-
ego (that is, in the sense of guilt). For every punishment is
ultimately castration and, as such, a fulfilment of the old passive
attitude towards the father. Even Fate is, in the last resort, only
a later projection of the father.

The normal processes in the formation of conscience must
be similar to the abnormal ones described here. We have not
yet succeeded in fixing the boundary line between them. It
will be observed that here the largest share in the outcome
is ascribed to the passive component of repressed femininity.
In addition, it must be of importance as an accidental factor
whether the father, who is feared in any case, is also especially
violent in reality. This was true in Dostoevsky's case, and we
can trace back the fact of his extraordinary sense of guilt and
of his masochistic conduct of life to a specially strong feminine
component. Thus the formula for Dostoevsky is as follows:
a person with a specially strong innate bisexual disposition, who
can defend himself with special intensity against dependence
on a specially severe father. This characteristic of bisexuality
comes as an addition to the components of his nature that we
have already recognized. His early symptoms of death-like
attacks can thus be understood as a father identification on the
part of his ego, which is permitted by his super-ego as a punishment. 'You wanted to kill your father in order to be your
father yourself. Now you *are* your father, but a dead father'
– the regular mechanism of hysterical symptoms. And further:
'Now your father is killing *you*.' For the ego the death symptom

is a satisfaction in phantasy of the masculine wish and at the same time a masochistic satisfaction; for the super-ego it is a punitive satisfaction – that is, a sadistic satisfaction. Both of them, the ego and the super-ego, carry on the role of father.

To sum up, the relation between the subject and his father-object, while retaining its content, has been transformed into a relation between the ego and the super-ego – a new setting on a fresh stage. Infantile reactions from the Oedipus complex such as these may disappear if reality gives them no further nourishment. But the father's character remained the same, or rather, it deteriorated with the years, and thus Dostoevsky's hatred for his father and his death-wish against that wicked father were maintained. Now it is a dangerous thing if reality fulfils such repressed wishes. The phantasy has become reality and all defensive measures are thereupon reinforced. Dostoevsky's attacks now assumed an epileptic character; they still undoubtedly signified an identification with his father as a punishment, but they had become terrible, like his father's frightful death itself. What further content they had absorbed, particularly what sexual content, escapes conjecture.

One thing is remarkable: in the aura of the epileptic attack, one moment of supreme bliss is experienced. This may very well be a record of the triumph and sense of liberation felt on hearing the news of the death, to be followed immediately by an all the more cruel punishment. We have divined just such a sequence of triumph and mourning, of festive joy and mourning, in the brothers of the primal horde who murdered their father, and we find it repeated in the ceremony of the totem meal.[1] If it proved to be the case that Dostoevsky was free from his attacks in Siberia, that would merely substantiate the view that they were his punishment. He did not need them any longer when he was being punished in another way. But that cannot be proved. Rather does this necessity for punishment on the part of Dostoevsky's mental economy explain the fact that he passed unbroken through these years of misery and

1. See *Totem and Taboo* [(1912–13), *P.F.L.*, **13**, 201–2].

humiliation. Dostoevsky's condemnation as a political prisoner was unjust and he must have known it, but he accepted the undeserved punishment at the hands of the Little Father, the Tsar, as a substitute for the punishment he deserved for his sin against his real father. Instead of punishing himself, he got himself punished by his father's deputy. Here we have a glimpse of the psychological justification of the punishments inflicted by society. It is a fact that large groups of criminals want to be punished. Their super-ego demands it and so saves itself the necessity for inflicting the punishment itself.[1]

Everyone who is familiar with the complicated transformation of meaning undergone by hysterical symptoms will understand that no attempt can be made here to follow out the meaning of Dostoevsky's attacks beyond this beginning.[2] It is enough that we may assume that their original meaning remained unchanged behind all later accretions. We can safely say that Dostoevsky never got free from the feelings of guilt arising from his intention of murdering his father. They also determined his attitude in the two other spheres in which the father-relation is the decisive factor, his attitude towards the authority of the State and towards belief in God. In the first of these he ended up with complete submission to his Little Father, the Tsar, who had once performed with him in *reality* the comedy of killing which his attacks had so often represented in *play*. Here penitence gained the upper hand. In the religious sphere he retained more freedom: according to apparently trustworthy reports he wavered, up to the last moment of his life,

---

1. [Cf. Essay III in Freud's 'Some Character-Types Met with in Psychoanalytic Work' (1916*d*), pp. 317–19 above.]

2. The best account of the meaning and content of his attacks was given by Dostoevsky himself, when he told his friend Strakhov that his irritability and depression after an epileptic attack were due to the fact that he seemed to himself a criminal and could not get rid of the feeling that he had a burden of unknown guilt upon him, that he had committed some great misdeed, which oppressed him. (Fülöp-Miller, 1924, 1188.) In self-accusations like these psychoanalysis sees signs of a recognition of 'psychical reality', and it endeavours to make the unknown guilt known to consciousness.

between faith and atheism. His great intellect made it impossible for him to overlook any of the intellectual difficulties to which faith leads. By an individual recapitulation of a development in world-history he hoped to find a way out and a liberation from guilt in the Christ ideal, and even to make use of his sufferings as a claim to be playing a Christ-like role. If on the whole he did not achieve freedom and became a reactionary, that was because the filial guilt, which is present in human beings generally and on which religious feeling is built, had in him attained a super-individual intensity and remained insurmountable even to his great intelligence. In writing this we are laying ourselves open to the charge of having abandoned the impartiality of analysis and of subjecting Dostoevsky to judgements that can only be justified from the partisan standpoint of a particular *Weltanschauung*. A conservative would take the side of the Grand Inquisitor and would judge Dostoevsky differently. The objection is just; and one can only say in extenuation that Dostoevsky's decision has every appearance of having been determined by an intellectual inhibition due to his neurosis.

It can scarcely be owing to chance that three of the masterpieces of literature of all time – the *Oedipus Rex* of Sophocles, Shakespeare's *Hamlet* and Dostoevsky's *The Brothers Karamazov* – should all deal with the same subject, parricide. In all three, moreover, the motive for the deed, sexual rivalry for a woman, is laid bare.

The most straightforward is certainly the representation in the drama derived from the Greek legend. In this it is still the hero himself who commits the crime. But poetic treatment is impossible without softening and disguise. The naked admission of an intention to commit parricide, as we arrive at it in analysis, seems intolerable without analytic preparation. The Greek drama, while retaining the crime, introduces the indispensable toning-down in a masterly fashion by projecting the hero's unconscious motive into reality in the form of a compulsion by a destiny which is alien to him. The hero commits the deed unintentionally and apparently uninfluenced by the woman; this latter element is however taken into account in the circumstance that the hero can only obtain possession of the queen mother after he has repeated his deed upon the monster who symbolizes the father. After his guilt has been revealed and made conscious, the hero makes no attempt to exculpate himself by appealing to the artificial expedient of the compulsion of destiny. His crime is acknowledged and punished as though it were a full and conscious one – which is bound to appear unjust to our reason, but which psychologically is perfectly correct.

In the English play the presentation is more indirect; the hero does not commit the crime himself; it is carried out by someone else, for whom it is not parricide. The forbidden motive of sexual rivalry for the woman does not need, therefore, to be disguised. Moreover, we see the hero's Oedipus complex, as it were, in a reflected light, by learning the effect upon him of the other's crime. He ought to avenge the crime, but finds himself, strangely enough, incapable of doing so. We know that it is his sense of guilt that is paralysing him; but, in a manner entirely in keeping with neurotic processes, the sense of guilt is displaced on to the perception of his inadequacy for fulfilling his task. There are signs that the hero feels this guilt as a super-individual one. He despises others no less than himself: 'Use every man after his desert, and who should 'scape whipping?'[1]

The Russian novel goes a step further in the same direction. There also the murder is committed by someone else. This other person, however, stands to the murdered man in the same filial relation as the hero, Dmitri, in whom the motive of sexual rivalry is openly admitted; the murderer is a brother of the hero's, and it is a remarkable fact that Dostoevsky has attributed to him his own illness, the alleged epilepsy, as though he were seeking to confess that the epileptic, the neurotic, in himself was a parricide. Then, again, in the speech for the defence at the trial, there is the famous mockery of psychology – it is

1. [*Hamlet*, Act II, Scene 2.]

a 'knife that cuts both ways':[1] a splendid piece of disguise, for we have only to reverse it in order to discover the deepest meaning of Dostoevsky's view of things. It is not psychology that deserves the mockery, but the procedure of judicial inquiry. It is a matter of indifference who actually committed the crime; psychology is only concerned to know who desired it emotionally and who welcomed it when it was done.[2] And for that reason all of the brothers, except the contrasted figure of Alyosha, are equally guilty – the impulsive sensualist, the sceptical cynic and the epileptic criminal. In *The Brothers Karamazov* there is one particularly revealing scene. In the course of his talk with Dmitri, Father Zossima recognizes that Dmitri is prepared to commit parricide, and he bows down at his feet. It is impossible that this can be meant as an expression of admiration; it must mean that the holy man is rejecting the temptation to despise or detest the murderer and for that reason humbles himself before him. Dostoevsky's sympathy for the criminal is, in fact, boundless; it goes far beyond the pity which the unhappy wretch has a right to, and reminds us of the 'holy awe' with which epileptics and lunatics were regarded in the past. A criminal is to him almost a Redeemer, who has taken on himself the guilt which must else have been borne by others. There is no longer any need for one to murder, since *he* has already murdered; and one must be grateful to him, for, except for him, one would have been obliged oneself to murder. That is not kindly pity alone, it is identification on the basis of similar murderous impulses – in fact, a slightly displaced narcissism. (In saying this, we are not disputing the ethical value of this kindliness.) This may perhaps be quite generally the mechanism of kindly sympathy with other people, a mechanism which one can discern with especial ease in this extreme case of a guilt-

1. [In the German (and in the original Russian) the simile is 'a stick with two ends'. The 'knife that cuts both ways' is derived from Constance Garnett's English translation. The phrase occurs in Book XII, Chapter X, of the novel.]

2. [A practical application of this to an actual criminal case is to be found in Freud's comments on the Halsmann Case (1931*d*), *Standard Ed.*, **21**, 251, where *The Brothers Karamazov* is again discussed.]

ridden novelist. There is no doubt that this sympathy by identification was a decisive factor in determining Dostoevsky's choice of material. He dealt first with the common criminal (whose motives are egotistical) and the political and religious criminal; and not until the end of his life did he come back to the primal criminal, the parricide, and use him, in a work of art, for making his confession.

The publication of Dostoevsky's posthumous papers and of his wife's diaries has thrown a glaring light on one episode in his life, namely the period in Germany when he was obsessed with a mania for gambling (cf. Fülöp-Miller and Eckstein, 1925), which no one could regard as anything but an unmistakable fit of pathological passion. There was no lack of rationalizations for this remarkable and unworthy behaviour. As often happens with neurotics, Dostoevsky's sense of guilt had taken a tangible shape as a burden of debt, and he was able to take refuge behind the pretext that he was trying by his winnings at the tables to make it possible for him to return to Russia without being arrested by his creditors. But this was no more than a pretext and Dostoevsky was acute enough to recognize the fact and honest enough to admit it. He knew that the chief thing was gambling for its own sake – *le jeu pour le jeu*.[1] All the details of his impulsively irrational conduct show this and something more besides. He never rested until he had lost everything. For him gambling was a method of self-punishment as well. Time after time he gave his young wife his promise or his word of honour not to play any more or not to play any more on that particular day; and, as she says, he almost always broke it. When his losses had reduced himself and her to the direst need, he derived a second pathological satisfaction from that. He could then scold and humiliate himself before her, invite her to despise him and to feel sorry that she had married such an old sinner; and when he had thus

1. 'The main thing is the play itself,' he writes in one of his letters. 'I swear that greed for money has nothing to do with it, although Heaven knows I am sorely in need of money.'

unburdened his conscience, the whole business would begin again next day. His young wife accustomed herself to this cycle, for she had noticed that the one thing which offered any real hope of salvation – his literary production – never went better than when they had lost everything and pawned their last possessions. Naturally she did not understand the connection. When his sense of guilt was satisfied by the punishments he had inflicted on himself, the inhibition upon his work became less severe and he allowed himself to take a few steps along the road to success.[1]

What part of a gambler's long-buried childhood is it that forces its way to repetition in his obsession for play? The answer may be divined without difficulty from a story by one of our younger writers. Stefan Zweig, who has incidentally devoted a study to Dostoevsky himself (1920), has included in his collection of three stories *Die Verwirrung der Gefühle* [*Confusion of Feelings*] (1927) one which he calls 'Vierundzwanzig Stunden aus dem Leben einer Frau' ['Four-and-Twenty Hours in a Woman's Life']. This little masterpiece ostensibly sets out only to show what an irresponsible creature woman is, and to what excesses, surprising even to herself, an unexpected experience may drive her. But the story tells far more than this. If it is subjected to an analytical interpretation, it will be found to represent (without any apologetic intent) something quite different, something universally human, or rather something masculine. And such an interpretation is so extremely obvious that it cannot be resisted. It is characteristic of the nature of artistic creation that the author, who is a personal friend of mine, was able to assure me, when I asked him, that the interpretation which I put to him had been completely strange to his knowledge and intention, although some of the details woven into the narrative seemed expressly designed to give a clue to the hidden secret.

1. 'He always remained at the gaming tables till he had lost everything and was totally ruined. It was only when the damage was quite complete that the demon at last retired from his soul and made way for the creative genius.' (Fülöp-Miller and Eckstein, 1925, lxxxvi.)

In this story, an elderly lady of distinction tells the author about an experience she has had more than twenty years earlier. She has been left a widow when still young and is the mother of two sons, who no longer need her. In her forty-second year, expecting nothing further of life, she happens, on one of her aimless journeyings, to visit the Rooms at Monte Carlo. There, among all the remarkable impressions which the place produces, she is soon fascinated by the sight of a pair of hands which seem to betray all the feelings of the unlucky gambler with terrifying sincerity and intensity. These hands belong to a handsome young man – the author, as though unintentionally, makes him of the same age as the narrator's elder son – who, after losing everything, leaves the Rooms in the depth of despair, with the evident intention of ending his hopeless life in the Casino gardens. An inexplicable feeling of sympathy compels her to follow him and make every effort to save him. He takes her for one of the importunate women so common there and tries to shake her off; but she stays with him and finds herself obliged, in the most natural way possible, to join him in his apartment at the hotel, and finally to share his bed. After this improvised night of love, she exacts a most solemn vow from the young man, who has now apparently calmed down, that he will never play again, provides him with money for his journey home and promises to meet him at the station before the departure of his train. Now, however, she begins to feel a great tenderness for him, is ready to sacrifice all she has in order to keep him and makes up her mind to go with him instead of saying goodbye. Various mischances delay her, so that she misses the train. In her longing for the lost one she returns once more to the Rooms and there, to her horror, sees once more the hands which had first excited her sympathy: the faithless youth had gone back to his play. She reminds him of his promise, but, obsessed by his passion, he calls her a spoil-sport, tells her to go, and flings back the money with which she has tried to rescue him. She hurries away in deep mortification and learns later that she has not succeeded in saving him from suicide.

The brilliantly told, faultlessly motivated story is of course complete in itself and is certain to make a deep effect upon the reader. But analysis shows us that its invention is based fundamentally upon a wishful phantasy belonging to the period of puberty, which a number of people actually remember consciously. The phantasy embodies a boy's wish that his mother should herself initiate him into sexual life in order to save him from the dreaded injuries caused by masturbation. (The numerous creative works that deal with the theme of redemption have the same origin.) The 'vice' of masturbation is replaced by the addiction to gambling;[1] and the emphasis laid upon the passionate activity of the hands betrays this derivation. Indeed, the passion for play is an equivalent of the old compulsion to masturbate; 'playing' is the actual word used in the nursery to describe the activity of the hands upon the genitals. The irresistible nature of the temptation, the solemn resolutions, which are nevertheless invariably broken, never to do it again, the stupefying pleasure and the bad conscience which tells the subject that he is ruining himself (committing suicide) – all these elements remain unaltered in the process of substitution. It is true that Zweig's story is told by the mother, not by the son. It must flatter the son to think: 'if my mother only knew what dangers masturbation involves me in, she would certainly save me from them by allowing me to lavish all my tenderness on her own body'. The equation of the mother with a prostitute, which is made by the young man in the story, is linked up with the same phantasy. It brings the unattainable woman within easy reach. The bad conscience which accompanies the phantasy brings about the unhappy ending of the story. It is also interesting to notice how the *façade* given to the story by its author seeks to disguise its analytic meaning. For it is extremely questionable whether the erotic life of women is dominated by sudden and mysterious impulses. On the contrary, analysis

1. [In a letter to Fliess of 22 December 1897, Freud suggested that masturbation is the 'primal addiction', for which all later addictions are substitutes (Freud, 1950a, Letter 79).]

reveals an adequate motivation for the surprising behaviour of this woman who had hitherto turned away from love. Faithful to the memory of her dead husband, she had armed herself against all similar attractions; but – and here the son's phantasy is right – she did not, as a mother, escape her quite unconscious transference of love on to her son, and Fate was able to catch her at this undefended spot.

If the addiction to gambling, with the unsuccessful struggles to break the habit and the opportunities it affords for self-punishment, is a repetition of the compulsion to masturbate, we shall not be surprised to find that it occupied such a large space in Dostoevsky's life. After all, we find no cases of severe neurosis in which the auto-erotic satisfaction of early childhood and of puberty has not played a part; and the relation between efforts to suppress it and fear of the father are too well known to need more than a mention.[1]

1. Most of the views which are here expressed are also contained in an excellent book by Jolan Neufeld (1923).

THE GOETHE PRIZE
(1930)

GOETHE-PREIS, 1930

(A) German Editions:

Brief an Dr Alfons Paquet

1930   *Psychoanalytische Bewegung*, **2** (5) (Sept.–Oct.), 419.
1948   *Gesammelte Werke*, **14**, 545–6.

Ansprache im Frankfurter Goethe-Haus

1930   *Psychoanalytische Bewegung*, **2** (5) (Sept.–Oct.), 421–6.
1948   *Gesammelte Werke*, **14**, 547–50.

(B) English Translation:

'The Goethe Prize'

1961   *Standard Edition*, **21**, 205–12. (Tr. Angela Richards.)

The present edition is a reprint of the *Standard Edition* version.

In 1927 the City of Frankfurt founded the 'Goethe Prize', which was to be awarded annually to 'a personality of established achievement whose creative work is worthy of an honour dedicated to Goethe's memory'. The first three awards were made to Stefan George the poet, Albert Schweitzer the musician and medical missionary, and Leopold Ziegler the philosophical writer. The amount of the prize was 10,000 Reichsmark – worth at that time about £500 or $2500.

At the suggestion of Alfons Paquet, a well-known man of letters who was Secretary to the Trustees of the Fund, it was decided to award the 1930 prize to Freud. This was announced to Freud (who was on holiday at the time in the Salzkammergut) in a letter from Paquet dated 26 July 1930 (printed in the

Psychoanalytische Bewegung, **2**, 417–18), to which Freud replied on 3 August. It was the practice, as Paquet explained in his letter, for the prize to be presented each year on 28 August at a ceremony in the house in Frankfurt where Goethe was born, and for the recipient to give an address there, illustrating his own inner relation to Goethe. Owing to his illness, Freud was unable to do this himself, but the address which he prepared was read by Anna Freud at the ceremony in the Goethe House on 28 August.

LETTER TO DR ALFONS PAQUET

Grundlsee, 3.8.1930

My dear Dr Paquet,

I have not been spoilt by public marks of honour and I have so adapted myself to this state of things that I have been able to do without them. I should not like to deny, however, that the award of the Goethe Prize of the City of Frankfurt has given me great pleasure. There is something about it that especially fires the imagination and one of its stipulations dispels the feeling of humiliation which in other cases is a concomitant of such distinctions.

I must particularly thank you for your letter; it moved and astonished me. Apart from your sympathetic penetration into the nature of my work, I have never before found the secret, personal intentions behind it recognized with such clarity as by you, and I should very much like to ask you how you come by such knowledge.

I am sorry to learn from your letter to my daughter that I am not to see you in the near future, and postponement is always a chancy affair at my time of life. Of course I shall be most ready to receive the gentleman (Dr Michel) whose visit you announce.

Unfortunately I shall not be able to attend the ceremony in Frankfurt; I am too frail for such an undertaking. The company there will lose nothing by that: my daughter Anna is certainly pleasanter to look at and to listen to than I am. We propose that she shall read out a few sentences of mine which deal with Goethe's connections with psychoanalysis and defend the analysts themselves against the reproach of having offended against the respect due to the great man by the analytic attempts they have made on him. I hope it will be acceptable if I thus adapt the theme that has been proposed to me – my 'inner relations as a man and a scientist to Goethe' – or else that you will be kind enough to let me know.

Yours very sincerely,
Freud

ADDRESS DELIVERED IN THE
GOETHE HOUSE AT FRANKFURT

My life's work has been directed to a single aim. I have observed the more subtle disturbances of mental function in healthy and sick people and have sought to infer – or, if you prefer it, to guess – from signs of this kind how the apparatus which serves these functions is constructed and what concurrent and mutually opposing forces are at work in it. What we – I, my friends and collaborators – have managed to learn in following this path has seemed to us of importance for the construction of a mental science which makes it possible to understand both normal and pathological processes as parts of the same natural course of events.

I was recalled from such narrow considerations by the astonishing honour which you do me. By evoking the figure of the great universal personality who was born in this house and who spent his childhood in these rooms, your distinction prompts one as it were to justify oneself before him and raises the question of how *he* would have reacted if his glance, attentive to every innovation in science, had fallen on psychoanalysis.

Goethe can be compared in versatility to Leonardo da Vinci, the Renaissance master, who like him was both artist and scientific investigator. But human images can never be repeated, and profound differences between the two great men are not lacking. In Leonardo's nature the scientist did not harmonize with the artist, he interfered with him and perhaps in the end stifled him. In Goethe's life both personalities found room side by side: at different times each allowed the other to predominate. In Leonardo it is plausible to associate his disturbance with that inhibition in his development which withdrew everything erotic, and hence psychology too, from his sphere of interest. In this respect Goethe's character was able to develop more freely.

I think that Goethe would not have rejected psychoanalysis in an unfriendly spirit, as so many of our contemporaries have done. He himself approached it at a number of points, recognized much through his own insight that we have since been able to confirm, and some views, which have brought criticism and mockery down upon us, were expounded by him as self-evident. Thus he was familiar with the incomparable strength of the first affective ties of human creatures. He celebrated them in the Dedication of his *Faust* poem, in words which we could repeat for each of our analyses:

> Ihr naht euch wieder, schwankende Gestalten,
> Die früh sich einst dem trüben Blick gezeigt.
> Versuch' ich wohl, euch diesmal festzuhalten?
>
> .   .   .   .
>
> Gleich einer alten, halbverklungenen Sage
> Kommt erste Lieb' und Freundschaft mit herauf.[1]

He explained to himself the strongest impulse of love that he experienced as a mature man by apostrophizing his beloved: 'Ach, du warst in abgelebten Zeiten meine Schwester oder meine Frau.'[2]

Thus he does not deny that these perennial first inclinations take figures from one's own family circle as their object.

1.
> [Again ye come, ye hovering forms! I find ye,
> As early to my clouded sight ye shone!
> Shall I attempt, this once, to seize and bind ye?
>
> .   .   .   .
>
> And, like an old and half-extinct tradition,
> First love returns, with friendship in his train.

From the opening lines of the Dedication to *Faust*, in Bayard Taylor's translation.]

2. ['Ah, you were, in a past life, my sister or my wife.' From a poem to Charlotte von Stein, 'Warum gabst du uns die tiefen Blicke'.]

Goethe paraphrases the content of dream-life in the evocative words:

> Was von Menschen nicht gewusst
> Oder nicht bedacht,
> Durch das Labyrinth der Brust
> Wandelt in der Nacht.[1]

Behind this magic we recognize the ancient, venerable and incontestably correct pronouncement of Aristotle – that dreaming is the continuation of our mental activity into the state of sleep – combined with the recognition of the unconscious which psychoanalysis first added to it. Only the riddle of dream distortion finds no solution here.

In what is perhaps his most sublime poetical creation, *Iphigenie*, Goethe shows us a striking instance of expiation, of the freeing of a suffering mind from the burden of guilt, and he makes this catharsis come about through a passionate outburst of feeling under the beneficent influence of loving sympathy. Indeed, he himself repeatedly made attempts at giving psychological help – as for example to the unfortunate man who is named as Kraft in the Letters, and to Professor Plessing, of whom he tells in the *Campagne in Frankreich* [*Campaign in France*]; and the procedure which he applied goes beyond the method of the Catholic confessional and approximates in some remarkable details to the technique of our psychoanalysis. There is an example of psychotherapeutic influence which is described by Goethe as a jest, but which I should like to quote in full since it may not be well known and yet is very characteristic. It is from a letter to Frau von Stein (No. 1444, of 5 September 1785):

'Yesterday evening I performed a psychological feat. Frau Herder was still in a state of tension of the most hypochondriacal kind over all the unpleasant things that had happened to her at Carlsbad. Particularly through the woman who was her

1. ['That which, not known or not heeded by men, wanders in the night through the labyrinth of the heart.' From the final version of the poem 'An den Mond', which begins: 'Füllest wieder Busch und Tal'.]

companion in the house. I made her tell and confess everything to me, other people's misdeeds and her own faults with their most minute circumstances and consequences, and at the end I absolved her and made it clear to her, jestingly, in this formula, that these things were now done with and cast into the depths of the sea. She herself made fun of it all and is really cured.'

Goethe always rated Eros high, never tried to belittle its power, followed its primitive and even wanton expressions with no less attentiveness than its highly sublimated ones and has, as it seems to me, expounded its essential unity throughout all its manifestations no less decisively than Plato did in the remote past. Indeed, it is perhaps more than a chance coincidence when in *Die Wahlverwandtschaften* [*The Elective Affinities*] he applies to love an idea taken from the sphere of chemistry – a connection to which the name of psychoanalysis itself bears witness.

I am prepared for the reproach that we analysts have forfeited the right to place ourselves under the patronage of Goethe because we have offended against the respect due to him by trying to apply analysis to him himself: we have degraded the great man to the position of an object of analytic investigation. But I would dispute at once that any degradation is intended or implied by this.

We all, who revere Goethe, put up, without too much protest, with the efforts of his biographers, who try to recreate his life from existing accounts and indications. But what can these biographies achieve for us? Even the best and fullest of them could not answer the two questions which alone seem worth knowing about. It would not throw any light on the riddle of the miraculous gift that makes an artist, and it could not help us to comprehend any better the value and the effect of his works. And yet there is no doubt that such a biography does satisfy a powerful need in us. We feel this very distinctly if the legacy of history unkindly refuses the satisfaction of this need – for example in the case of Shakespeare. It is undeniably painful to all of us that even now we do not know who was the author of the comedies, tragedies and sonnets of Shakespeare; whether it was in fact the untutored son of the provincial citizen of Stratford, who attained a modest position as an actor in London, or whether it was, rather, the nobly-born and highly cultivated, passionately wayward, to some extent *déclassé* aristocrat, Edward de Vere, seventeenth Earl of Oxford, hereditary Lord Great Chamberlain of England.[1] But how can we justify a need of this kind to obtain knowledge of the circumstances of a man's life when his works have become so full of importance to us? People generally say that it is our desire to bring ourselves nearer to such a man in a human way as well. Let us grant this; it is, then, the need to acquire affective relations with such men, to add them to the fathers, teachers, exemplars whom we have known or whose influence we have already experienced, in the expectation that their personalities will be just as fine and admirable as those works of art of theirs which we possess.

All the same, we may admit that there is still another motive force at work. The biographer's justification also contains a confession. It is true that the biographer does not want to depose his hero, but he does want to bring him nearer to us. That means, however, reducing the distance that separates him from us: it still tends in effect towards degradation. And it is unavoidable that if we learn more about a great man's life we shall also hear of occasions on which he has in fact done no better than we, has in fact come near to us as a human being. Nevertheless, I think we may declare the efforts of biography to be legitimate. Our attitude to fathers and teachers is, after all, an ambivalent one since our reverence for them regularly conceals

1. [Freud's first mention of his views on the authorship of Shakespeare's works was in a footnote added in 1930 to Chapter V (D) of *The Interpretation of Dreams* (1900a), *P.F.L.*, **4**, 368 n. 1. In the above text he goes into more detail. He mentioned the point again in a footnote added in 1935 to Chapter VI of his *Autobiographical Study* (1925d), ibid., **15**, and in *Moses and Monotheism* (1939a), ibid., **13**, 307 n. 1. There is a further reference to the point in the posthumously published *Outline* (1940a), ibid., **15**. A letter from Freud arguing in favour of his opinion is included in the third volume of Jones's biography (1957, 487–8).]

a component of hostile rebellion. That is a psychological fatality; it cannot be altered without forcible suppression of the truth and is bound to extend to our relations with the great men whose life histories we wish to investigate.[1]

When psychoanalysis puts itself at the service of biography, it naturally has the right to be treated no more harshly than the latter itself. Psychoanalysis can supply some information which cannot be arrived at by other means, and can thus demonstrate new connecting threads in the 'weaver's masterpiece'[2] spread between the instinctual endowments, the experiences and the works of an artist. Since it is one of the principal functions of our thinking to master the material of the external world psychically, it seems to me that thanks are due to psychoanalysis if, when it is applied to a great man, it contributes to the understanding of his great achievement. But, I admit, in the case of Goethe we have not yet succeeded very far. This is because Goethe was not only, as a poet, a great self-revealer, but also, in spite of the abundance of auto-biographical records, a careful concealer. We cannot help thinking here of the words of Mephistopheles:

> Das Beste, was du wissen kannst,
> Darfst du den Buben doch nicht sagen.[3]

---

1. [Freud had made some remarks on the relation of psychoanalysis to biography in his essay on Leonardo (1910c), p. 228 above.]

2. [A quotation from Mephistopheles's description of the fabric of thought, in *Faust*, Part I, Scene 4. Freud had quoted the whole passage, in connection with the complexity of dream associations, in Chapter VI (A) of *The Interpretation of Dreams* (1900a), *P.F.L.*, 4, 388.]

3. [The best of what you know may not, after all, be told to boys.

(*Faust*, Part I, Scene 4.)]

BIBLIOGRAPHY
AND AUTHOR INDEX

Titles of books and periodicals are in italics, titles of papers are in inverted commas. Abbreviations are in accordance with the *World List of Scientific Periodicals* (London, 1963–5). Further abbreviations used in this volume will be found in the List at the end of this bibliography. Numerals in bold type refer to volumes, ordinary numerals refer to pages. The figures in round brackets at the end of each entry indicate the page or pages of this volume on which the work in question is mentioned.

In the case of the Freud entries, only English translations are given. The initial dates are those of the German original publications. (The date of writing is added in square brackets where it differs from the latter.) The letters attached to the dates of publication are in accordance with the corresponding entries in the complete bibliography of Freud's writings included in Volume 24 of the *Standard Edition*. Details of the original publication, including the original German title, are given in the editorial introduction to each work in the *Penguin Freud Library*.

For non-technical authors, and for technical authors where no specific work is mentioned, see the General Index.

ABRAHAM, K., and FREUD, S. (1965) *See* FREUD, S. (1965*a*)
ADLER, A. (1910) 'Der psychische Hermaphroditismus im Leben und in der Neurose', *Fortschr. Med.*, **28**, 486. (407)
  [*Trans.*: 'Psychical Hermaphroditism and the Masculine Protest', *The Practice and Theory of Individual Psychology*, London, 1923.]
ANDREAS-SALOMÉ, L., and FREUD, S. (1966) *See* FREUD, S. (1966*a*)
BINET, A. (1888) *Études de psychologie expérimentale: le fétichisme dans l'amour*, Paris. (71)
BLEULER, E. (1906) *Affektivität, Suggestibilität, Paranoia*, Halle. (78)
  [*Trans.*: *Affectivity, Suggestibility, Paranoia*, New York, 1912.]
BOITO, C. (1883) *Leonardo, Michelangelo, Andrea Palladio* (2nd ed.), Milan. (257)

BOTTAZZI, F. (1910) 'Leonardo biologico e anatomico', in *Conferenze Fiorentine*, Milan, 181. (157, 163)

BRANDES, G. (1896) *William Shakespeare*, Paris, Leipzig and Munich. (235)

BREUER, J., and FREUD, S. (1893) *See* FREUD, S. (1893*a*)
(1895) *See* FREUD, S. (1895*d*)

BURCKHARDT, J. (1927) *Der Cicerone*, Leipzig. (1st ed., 1855.) (257 f.)
[*Trans.*: *The Cicerone: An Art Guide to Painting in Italy for the Use of Travellers and Students*, New York, 1979.]

CONFERENZE FIORENTINE (1910) *Leonardo da Vinci: Conferenze Fiorentine*, Milan. (163, 166)

CONTI, A. (1910) 'Leonardo pittore', in *Conferenze Fiorentine*, Milan, 81. (201)

DARMESTETER, J. (ed.) (1881) *Macbeth*, Paris. (306, 307)

DOSTOEVSKY, A. (1921) *Fyodor Dostoevsky: A Study*, London. (446)

ECKSTEIN, F., and FÜLÖP-MILLER, R. *See* FÜLÖP-MILLER, R., and ECKSTEIN, F.

ELLIS, HAVELOCK (1910) Review of S. Freud's *Eine Kindheitserinnerung des Leonardo da Vinci*, *J. Ment. Sci.*, **56**, 522. (173)

FEDERN, P. (1914) 'Über zwei typische Traumsensationen', *Jb. Psychoanal.*, **6**, 89. (219)
[*Trans.*: 'On Dreams of Flying', *The Psychoanalytic Reader* (ed. R. Fliess), Vol. 1, New York, 1948, 386; London, 1950.]

FERENCZI, S. (1912) 'Über passagère Symptombildung während der Analyse', *Zentbl. Psychoanal.*, **2**, 588. (329)
[*Trans.*: 'Transitory Symptom-Constructions during the Analysis', *First Contributions to Psycho-Analysis*, London, 1952, Chap. VII.]

FREUD, M. (1957) *Glory Reflected*, London. (22)

FREUD, S. (1886*f*) 'Preface to the Translation of Charcot's *Lectures on the Diseases of the Nervous System*', *Standard Ed.*, **1**, 19. (380)
(1891*b*) *On Aphasia*, London and New York, 1953. (14, 24)
(1892–94) 'Preface and Footnotes to the Translation of Charcot's *Tuesday Lectures*', *Standard Ed.*, **1**, 131. (380)
(1893*a*) With BREUER, J., 'On the Psychical Mechanism of Hysterical Phenomena: Preliminary Communication', in *Studies on Hysteria*, *Standard Ed.*, **2**, 3; *P.F.L.*, **3**, 53. (25)
(1893*f*) 'Charcot', *Standard Ed.*, **3**, 9. (380)
(1895*b* [1894]) 'On the Grounds for Detaching a Particular Syndrome from Neurasthenia under the Description "Anxiety Neurosis"', *Standard Ed.*, **3**, 87; *P.F.L.*, **10**, 31. (85)
(1895*d*) With BREUER, J., *Studies on Hysteria*, London, 1956; *Standard Ed.*, **2**; *P.F.L.*, **3**. (14, 25, 79, 112, 315)
(1896*b*) 'Further Remarks on the Neuro-Psychoses of Defence', *Standard Ed.*, **3**, 159. (78)
(1900*a*) *The Interpretation of Dreams*, London and New York, 1955; *Standard*

Ed., **4–5**; *P.F.L.*, **4**. (25, 29, 33, 59, 80 ff., 85, 97 f., 106, 126, 136, 184, 219, 236, 239, 244, 255, 304, 329, 333, 357, 368, 404, 471 f.)

(1901*b*) *The Psychopathology of Everyday Life*, Standard Ed., **6**; *P.F.L.*, **5**. (25, 76, 103, 175, 325, 358, 414)

(1905*c*) *Jokes and their Relation to the Unconscious*, Standard Ed., **8**; *P.F.L.*, **6**. (131, 141, 426 f., 429)

(1905*d*) *Three Essays on the Theory of Sexuality*, London, 1962; Standard Ed., **7**, 125; *P.F.L.*, **7**, 31. (25, 31, 71, 141, 192 f., 210, 230, 376)

(1905*e* [1901]) 'Fragment of an Analysis of a Case of Hysteria', Standard Ed., **7**, 3; *P.F.L.*, **8**, 29. (30, 79, 177, 423)

(1906*f*) 'Contribution to a Questionnaire on Reading', *Int. J. Psycho-Analysis*, **32** (1951), 319; Standard Ed., **9**, 245. (145)

(1907*a*) *Delusions and Dreams in Jensen's 'Gradiva'*, Standard Ed., **9**, 3; *P.F.L.*, **14**, 27. (130)

(1908*a*) 'Hysterical Phantasies and their Relation to Bisexuality', Standard Ed., **9**, 157; *P.F.L.*, **10**, 83. (130)

(1908*b*) 'Character and Anal Erotism', Standard Ed., **9**, 169; *P.F.L.*, **7**, 205. (198, 380)

(1908*c*) 'On the Sexual Theories of Children', Standard Ed., **9**, 207; *P.F.L.*, **7**, 183. (169, 183, 186)

(1908*e* [1907]) 'Creative Writers and Day-Dreaming', Standard Ed., **9**, 143; *P.F.L.*, **14**, 129. (121)

(1909*a* [1908]) 'Some General Remarks on Hysterical Attacks', Standard Ed., **9**, 229; *P.F.L.*, **10**, 95. (439, 445)

(1909*b*) 'Analysis of a Phobia in a Five-Year-Old Boy', Standard Ed., **10**, 3; *P.F.L.*, **8**, 165. (25, 169, 177, 186 f., 319, 332, 403)

(1909*d*) 'Notes upon a Case of Obsessional Neurosis', Standard Ed., **10**, 155; *P.F.L.*, **9**, 31. (65, 76, 329, 361 f.)

(1910*a* [1909]) *Five Lectures on Psycho-Analysis*, Standard Ed., **11**, 3; in *Two Short Accounts of Psycho-Analysis*, Penguin Books, Harmondsworth, 1962. (16, 25)

(1910*c*) *Leonardo da Vinci and a Memory of his Childhood*, Standard Ed., **11**, 59; *P.F.L.*, **14**, 143. (322, 406)

(1911*c* [1910]) 'Psycho-Analytic Notes on an Autobiographical Account of a Case of Paranoia (Dementia Paranoides)', Standard Ed., **12**, 3; *P.F.L.*, **9**, 129. (25, 380, 403, 406 f.)

(1912*c*) 'Types of Onset of Neurosis', Standard Ed., **12**, 229; *P.F.L.*, **10**, 115. (299)

(1912*f*) 'Contribution to a Discussion on Masturbation', Standard Ed., **12**, 243. (439)

(1912–13) *Totem and Taboo*, London, 1950; New York, 1952; Standard Ed., **13**, 1; *P.F.L.*, **13**, 43. (25, 123, 336, 363, 365, 400, 403, 448, 451)

(1913*f*) 'The Theme of the Three Caskets', Standard Ed., **12**, 291; *P.F.L.*, **14**, 233. (68)

FREUD, S. (*cont.*)

(1914*b*) 'The Moses of Michelangelo', *Standard Ed.*, **13**, 211; *P.F.L.*, **14**, 249.

(1914*c*) 'On Narcissism: an Introduction', *Standard Ed.*, **14**, 69; *P.F.L.*, **11**, 59. (138, 192, 357)

(1914*d*) 'On the History of the Psycho-Analytic Movement', *Standard Ed.*, **14**, 3; *P.F.L.*, **15**, 57. (25)

(1915*b*) 'Thoughts for the Times on War and Death', *Standard Ed.*, **14**, 275; *P.F.L.*, **12**, 57. (137, 364)

(1915*e*) 'The Unconscious', *Standard Ed.*, **14**, 161; *P.F.L.*, **11**, 159. (73, 360)

(1916*a*) 'On Transience', *Standard Ed.*, **14**, 305; *P.F.L.*, **14**, 283.

(1916*d*) 'Some Character-Types Met with in Psycho-Analytic Work', *Standard Ed.*, **14**, 311; *P.F.L.*, **14**, 291. (452)

(1916–17 [1915–17]) *Introductory Lectures on Psycho-Analysis*, New York, 1966; London, 1971; *Standard Ed.*, **15–16**; *P.F.L.*, **1**. (26, 423)

(1917*b*) 'A Childhood Recollection from *Dichtung und Wahrheit*', *Standard Ed.*, **17**, 147; *P.F.L.*, **14**, 321. (175)

(1917*e* [1915]) 'Mourning and Melancholia', *Standard Ed.*, **14**, 239; *P.F.L.*, **11**, 245. (285, 402, 431)

(1918*b* [1914]) 'From the History of an Infantile Neurosis', *Standard Ed.*, **17**, 3; *P.F.L.*, **9**, 225. (26, 82, 319, 367, 401)

(1919*e*) 'A Child is Being Beaten', *Standard Ed.*, **17**, 177; *P.F.L.*, **10**, 159. (408)

(1919*h*) 'The "Uncanny"', *Standard Ed.*, **17**, 219; *P.F.L.*, **14**, 335.

(1920*a*) 'The Psychogenesis of a Case of Homosexuality in a Woman', *Standard Ed.*, **18**, 147; *P.F.L.*, **9**, 367. (193)

(1920*g*) *Beyond the Pleasure Principle*, London, 1961; *Standard Ed.*, **18**, 7; *P.F.L.*, **11**, 269. (26, 121, 159, 336, 356, 360, 364)

(1921*c*) *Group Psychology and the Analysis of the Ego*, London and New York, 1959; *Standard Ed.*, **18**, 69; *P.F.L.*, **12**, 91. (26, 217, 237, 357, 431)

(1922*a*) 'Dreams and Telepathy', *Standard Ed.*, **18**, 197. (239)

(1922*b* [1921]) 'Some Neurotic Mechanisms in Jealousy, Paranoia and Homosexuality', *Standard Ed.*, **18**, 223; *P.F.L.*, **10**, 195. (193, 431)

(1923*b*) *The Ego and the Id*, London and New York, 1962; *Standard Ed.*, **19**, 3; *P.F.L.*, **11**, 339. (26, 357, 430)

(1923*d* [1922]) 'A Seventeenth-Century Demonological Neurosis', *Standard Ed.*, **19**, 69; *P.F.L.*, **14**, 377.

(1925*d* [1924]) *An Autobiographical Study*, *Standard Ed.*, **20**, 3; *P.F.L.*, **15**, 183. (12, 141, 471)

(1925*h*) 'Negation', *Standard Ed.*, **19**, 235; *P.F.L.*, **11**, 435. (368)

(1926*d* [1925]) *Inhibitions, Symptoms and Anxiety*, London, 1960; *Standard Ed.*, **20**, 77; *P.F.L.*, **10**, 227. (26, 85)

(1927*a*) 'Postscript to *The Question of Lay Analysis*', *Standard Ed.*, **20**, 251; *P.F.L.*, **15**, 355. (12)

(1927*b*) 'Postscript to "The Moses of Michelangelo"', *Standard Ed.*, **13**, 237; *P.F.L.*, **14**, 281.

(1927*c*) *The Future of an Illusion*, London, 1962; *Standard Ed.*, **21**, 3; *P.F.L.*, **12**, 179. (217)

(1927*d*) 'Humour', *Standard Ed.*, **21**, 161; *P.F.L.*, **14**, 425.

(1927*e*) 'Fetishism', *Standard Ed.*, **21**, 149; *P.F.L.*, **7**, 345. (71)

(1928*b*) 'Dostoevsky and Parricide', *Standard Ed.*, **21**, 175; *P.F.L.*, **14**, 435.

(1930*a* [1929]) *Civilization and its Discontents*, New York, 1961; London, 1963; *Standard Ed.*, **21**, 59; *P.F.L.*, **12**, 243. (26, 217, 429)

(1930*d*) 'Letter to Dr Alfons Paquet', *Standard Ed.*, **21**, 207; *P.F.L.*, **14**, 465.

(1930*e*) 'Address delivered in the Goethe House at Frankfurt', *Standard Ed.*, **21**, 208; *P.F.L.*, **14**, 467.

(1930*f* [1929]) 'Letter to Theodor Reik', in Reik, *From Thirty Years with Freud*, New York, 1940; London, 1942; *Standard Ed.*, **21**, 195. (438)

(1931*d* [1930]) 'The Expert Opinion in the Halsmann Case', *Standard Ed.*, **21**, 251. (455)

(1935*a*) 'Postscript (1935) to *An Autobiographical Study*', new ed., London and New York; *Standard Ed.*, **20**, 71; *P.F.L.*, **15**, 256. (12)

(1936*a*) 'A Disturbance of Memory on the Acropolis', *Standard Ed.*, **22**, 239; *P.F.L.*, **11**, 443. (316)

(1939*a* [1934–38]) *Moses and Monotheism*, *Standard Ed.*, **23**, 3; *P.F.L.*, **13**, 237. (26, 103, 187, 252, 471)

(1940*a* [1938]) *An Outline of Psycho-Analysis*, New York, 1968; London, 1969; *Standard Ed.*, **23**, 141; *P.F.L.*, **15**, 369. (471)

(1942*a* [1905–6]) 'Psychopathic Characters on the Stage', *Standard Ed.*, **7**, 305; *P.F.L.*, **14**, 119. (69, 130, 141)

(1950*a* [1887–1902]) *The Origins of Psycho-Analysis*, London and New York, 1954. (Partly, including 'A Project for a Scientific Psychology', in *Standard Ed.*, **1**, 175.) (15, 23, 25, 29 f., 139, 145 f., 380, 447, 459)

(1956*a* [1886]) 'Report on my Studies in Paris and Berlin, 1885–86', *Int. J. Psycho-Analysis*, **37**, 2; *Standard Ed.*, **1**, 3. (380)

(1957*a* [1911]) With OPPENHEIM, D. E., *Dreams in Folklore*, New York, 1958, Part I; *Standard Ed.*, **12**, 177. (404)

(1960*a*) *Letters 1873–1939* (ed. E. L. Freud) (trans. T. and J. Stern), New York, 1960; London, 1961. (22, 23, 234, 252)

(1963*a* [1909–39]) *Psycho-Analysis and Faith. The Letters of Sigmund Freud and Oskar Pfister* (ed. H. Meng and E. L. Freud) (trans. E. Mosbacher), London and New York, 1963. (23)

(1965*a* [1907–26]) *A Psycho-Analytic Dialogue. The Letters of Sigmund Freud and Karl Abraham* (ed. H. C. Abraham and E. L. Freud) (trans. B. Marsh and H. C. Abraham), London and New York, 1965. (23)

(1966*a* [1912–36]) *Sigmund Freud and Lou Andreas-Salomé: Letters* (ed. E. Pfeiffer) (trans. W. and E. Robson-Scott), London and New York, 1972. (23)

FREUD, S. (*cont.*)

(1968a [1927–39]) *The Letters of Sigmund Freud and Arnold Zweig* (ed. E. L. Freud) (trans. W. and E. Robson-Scott), London and New York, 1970. (23)

(1970a [1919–35]) *Sigmund Freud as a Consultant. Recollections of a Pioneer in Psychoanalysis* (Letters from Freud to Edoardo Weiss, including a Memoir and Commentaries by Weiss, with Foreword and Introduction by Martin Grotjahn), New York, 1970. (23, 252)

(1974a [1906–23]) *The Freud/Jung Letters* (ed. W. McGuire) (trans. R. Manheim and R. F. C. Hull), London and Princeton, N.J., 1974. (23)

FÜLOP-MILLER, R. (1924) 'Dostojewskis heilige Krankheit', *Wissen und Leben*, Heft 19–20, Zürich. (446, 452)

FÜLÖP-MILLER, R., and ECKSTEIN, F. (eds) (1925) *Dostojewski am Roulette*, Munich. (437, 443, 446 f., 456 f.)

(1926) *Der unbekannte Dostojewski*, Munich. (442)

(1928) *Die Urgestalt der Brüder Karamasoff*, Munich. (437)

GARDINER, SIR A. (1950) *Egyptian Grammar* (2nd ed.), London. (148)

GRAF, M. (1942) 'Reminiscences of Professor Sigmund Freud', *Psychoanal. Quart.*, **11**, 465. (120)

GRIMM, H. (1900) *Leben Michelangelos* (9th ed.), Berlin and Stuttgart. (255 f., 259)

GRIMM, J., and GRIMM, W. (1877) *Deutsches Wörterbuch*, Vol. 4, Leipzig. (346)

(1918) *Die Märchen der Brüder Grimm*, Leipzig. (1st ed., *Kinder- und Hausmärchen*, 1812–22.) (240 f., 245)

GUILLAUME, E. (1876) 'Michel-Ange Sculpteur', *Gazette des Beaux-Arts*, 96. (257)

HARTLEBEN, H. (1906) *Champollion: sein Leben und sein Werk*, Berlin. (178)

HAUSER, F. (1903) 'Disiecta membra neuattischer Reliefs', *Jh. österr. archäol. Inst.*, **6**, 79. (118)

HERZFELD, M. (1906) *Leonardo da Vinci: der Denker, Forscher und Poet* (2nd ed.), Jena. (147, 158 f., 166, 194 f., 203, 218 f., 221, 231)

HUNTER, R. A., and MACALPINE, I. *See* MACALPINE, I., and HUNTER, R. A.

JEKELS, L. (1917) 'Shakespeares *Macbeth*', *Imago*, **5**, 170. (307)

[*Trans.*: 'The Riddle of Shakespeare's *Macbeth*', *Selected Papers*, London and New York, 1952, 105.]

(1926) 'Zur Psychologie der Komödie', *Imago*, **12**, 328. (307)

[*Trans.*: 'On the Psychology of Comedy', *Selected Papers*, London and New York, 1952, 97.]

JENSEN, W. (1903) *Gradiva: ein pompejanisches Phantasiestück*, Dresden and Leipzig. (36 f., 78 f., 115)

JENTSCH, E. (1906) 'Zur Psychologie des Unheimlichen', *Psychiat.-neurol. Wschr.*, **8**, 195. (340, 347 f., 351, 354)

JONES, E. (1912) *Der Alptraum in seiner Beziehung zu gewissen Formen des mittelalterlichen Aberglaubens*, Leipzig and Vienna. (400, 402)
[*English text*: *On the Nightmare*, London and New York, 1931.]
(1953) *Sigmund Freud: Life and Work*, Vol. 1, London and New York. (23, 146)
(1955) *Sigmund Freud: Life and Work*, Vol. 2, London and New York. (Page references are to English edition.) (23, 29, 146, 234, 252)
(1957) *Sigmund Freud: Life and Work*, Vol. 3, London and New York. (Page references are to English edition.) (23, 379 f., 426, 438, 471)

JUNG, C. G. (1906) *Diagnostische Assoziationsstudien* (2 vols), Leipzig. (78)
[*Trans.*: *Studies in Word-Association*, London, 1918; New York, 1919.]
(1910) 'Über Konflikte der kindlichen Seele', *Jb. psychoanalyt. psychopath. Forsch.*, **2**, 33. (169, 186)
(1974) With FREUD, S. *See* FREUD, S. (1974a)

JUSTI, C. (1900) *Michelangelo*, Leipzig. (256 f., 260 f.)

KAMMERER, P. (1919) *Das Gesetz der Serie*, Vienna. (360)

KNACKFUSS, H. (1900) *Michelangelo* (6th ed.), Bielefeld and Leipzig. (264)

KNAPP, F. (1906) *Michelangelo*, Stuttgart and Leipzig. (261)

KNIGHT, R. P. (1883) *Le culte de Priape*, Brussels. (188)
[*English text*: *A Discussion of the Worship of Priapus*, London, 1786. (New ed., 1865.)]

KONSTANTINOVA, A. (1907) *Die Entwicklung des Madonnentypus bei Leonardo da Vinci*, Strasbourg. (151, 202, 205)

KRAFFT-EBING, R. VON (1893) *Psychopathia sexualis* (8th ed.), Stuttgart. (1st ed., 1886.) (177)
[*Trans.*: *Psychopathia sexualis*, New York, 1922.]

LANZONE, R. (1882) *Dizionario di mitologia egizia*, Vol. 2, Turin. (178, 185)

LEEMANS, C. (ed.) (1835) *Horapollonis Niloï Hieroglyphica*, Amsterdam. (179 f.)

LEONARDO DA VINCI *Codex Atlanticus*, Ambrosian Library, Milan. Publ. G. Piumati, Milan, 1894–1904. (172, 180, 215)
Quaderni d'Anatomia, Royal Library, Windsor. Catalogued by Sir Kenneth Clark, Cambridge, 1935. (161, 166)
Trattato della Pittura, Vatican Library. *See* LUDWIG, H.

LLOYD, W. WATKISS (1863) *The Moses of Michael Angelo*, London. (278 f.)

LÜBKE, W. (1863) *Geschichte der Plastik*, Leipzig. (256 ff.)

LUDWIG, H. (1909) *Traktat von der Malerei* (2nd ed.), Jena. (Trans. of da Vinci's *Trattato della Pittura*.) (153, 163)

MACALPINE, I., and HUNTER, R. A. (1956) *Schizophrenia 1677*, London. (380 f., 387)

MACH, E. (1900) *Die Analyse der Empfindung* (2nd ed.), Jena. (371)

MEREZHKOVSKY, D. S. (1903) *Leonardo da Vinci*, Leipzig. (Russian original, 1902.) (146 f., 162, 194–7, 204, 215)
[*Trans.*: *The Forerunner*, London, 1902; *The Romance of Leonardo da Vinci*, London, 1903.]

MILLER, O. (1921) 'Zur Lebensgeschichte Dostojewskis', in F. M. Dostojewski, *Autobiographische Schriften*, Munich. (Russian original, 1883.) (446)

MITCHELL, H. P. (1921) 'Two Bronzes of the Twelfth Century', *Burlington Magazine*, 38, No. 217 (April), 157–66. (281)

MÜNTZ, E. (1895) *Histoire de l'Art pendant la Renaissance: Italie*, Paris. (256 f.)
(1899) *Léonard de Vinci*, Paris. (157, 180, 200, 212, 217, 221 f.)

MUTHER, R. (1909) *Geschichte der Malerei* (3 vols), Leipzig. (200, 204, 210, 218)

NEUFELD, J. (1923) *Dostojewski: Skizze zu seiner Psychoanalyse*, Vienna. (438, 460)

OPPENHEIM, D. E., and FREUD, S. *See* FREUD, S. (1957a)

PATER, W. (1873) *Studies in the History of the Renaissance*, London. (156, 202)

PAYER-THURN, R. (1924) 'Faust in Mariazell', *Chronik des Wiener Goethe-Vereins*, 34, 1. (381, 385)

PFISTER, O. (1913) 'Kryptolalie, Kryptographie und unbewusstes Vexierbild bei Normalen', *Jb. psychoanalyt. psychopath. Forsch.*, 5, 115. (208)
(1963) With FREUD, S. *See* FREUD, S. (1963a)

POPHAM, A. E. (1953) *The Drawings of Parmigianino*, London. (276)

PRELLER, L. (1894) *Griechische Mythologie* (4th ed.), ed. C. Robert, Berlin. (1st ed., Leipzig, 1854.) (243)

RANK, O. (1909) *Der Mythus von der Geburt des Helden*, Leipzig and Vienna. (236)
[*Trans.*: *The Myth of the Birth of the Hero*, New York, 1914.]
(1912) *Das Inzest-Motiv in Dichtung und Sage*, Leipzig and Vienna. (316)
(1914) 'Der Doppelgänger', *Imago*, 3, 97. (356, 358)
[*Trans.*: *The Double: A Psychoanalytic Study*, Chapel Hill, N.C., 1971.]

REIK, T. (1919) *Probleme der Religionspsychologie*, Vienna. (400)
[*Trans.*: *Ritual: Psycho-Analytic Studies*, London and New York, 1931.]
(1923) *Der eigene und der fremde Gott*, Leipzig, Vienna and Zürich. (400)

REITLER, R. (1917) 'Eine anatomisch-künstlerische Fehlleistung Leonardos da Vinci', *Int. Z. ärztl. Psychoanal.*, 4, 205. (146, 159, 161)

RICHTER, I. A. (1952) *Selections from the Notebooks of Leonardo da Vinci*, London. (147, 153)

RICHTER, J. P. (1939) *The Literary Works of Leonardo da Vinci* (2nd ed.), Oxford. (1st ed., London, 1883.) (157, 163, 181, 196, 222)

RÖMER, L. VON (1903) 'Über die androgynische Idee des Lebens', *Jb. sex. Zwischenst.*, 5, 732. (179, 185)

ROSCHER, W. H. (ed.) (1884–97) *Ausführliches Lexikon der griechischen und römischen Mythologie*, Leipzig. (178, 184, 241, 243)

ROSENBERG, A. (1898) *Leonardo da Vinci*, Leipzig. (207)

SADGER, I. (1908) *Conrad Ferdinand Meyer: eine pathographisch-psychologische Studie*, Wiesbaden. (146)

(1909a) *Aus dem Liebesleben Nicolaus Lenaus*, Leipzig and Vienna. (146)

(1909b) *Heinrich von Kleist: eine pathographisch-psychologische Studie*, Wiesbaden. (146)

SANCTIS, SANTE DE (1899) *I sogni*, Turin. (80)

[*German trans*.: *Die Träume* (trans. O. Schmidt), Halle, 1901.]

SANDERS, D. (1860) *Wörterbuch der Deutschen Sprache*, Leipzig. (342 ff.)

SCHREBER, D. P. (1903) *Denkwürdigkeiten eines Nervenkranken*, Leipzig. (406)

[*Trans*.: *Memoirs of My Nervous Illness* (trans. I. Macalpine and R. A. Hunter), London, 1955.]

SCOGNAMIGLIO, N. *See* SMIRAGLIA SCOGNAMIGLIO, N.

SEIDLITZ, W. VON (1909) *Leonardo da Vinci, der Wendepunkt der Renaissance* (2 vols), Berlin. (156 f., 200, 206, 215, 227)

SELIGMANN, S. (1910–11) *Der böse Blick und Verwandtes*, Berlin. (362)

SMIRAGLIA SCOGNAMIGLIO, N. (1900) *Ricerche e Documenti sulla Giovinezza di Leonardo da Vinci (1452–1482)*, Naples. (146, 155, 162, 171 f., 203)

SOLMI, E. (1908) *Leonardo da Vinci* (trans. E. Hirschberg), Berlin. (158, 194, 196)

(1910) 'La resurrezione dell' opera di Leonardo', in *Conferenze Fiorentine*, Milan, 1. (155, 165, 215)

SPRINGER, A. (1895) *Raffael und Michelangelo*, Vol. 2, Leipzig. (207, 256, 259)

STEINMANN, E. (1899) *Rom in der Renaissance*, Leipzig. (257)

STEKEL, W. (1911) *Die Sprache des Traumes*, Wiesbaden. (2nd ed., 1922.) (239 f.)

STRAKHOV, N. (1921) 'Über Dostojewskis Leben und literarische Tätigkeit', in F. M. Dostojewski, *Literarische Schriften*, Munich. (Russian original, 1883.) (443)

STUCKEN, E. (1907) *Astralmythen der Hebräer, Babylonier und Ägypter*, Leipzig. (236)

THODE, H. (1908) *Michelangelo: kritische Untersuchungen über seine Werke*, Vol. 1, Berlin. (255 ff., 262 ff.)

VANDENDRIESSCHE, G. (1965) *The Parapraxis in the Haizmann Case of Sigmund Freud*, Louvain and Paris. (381, 387)

VASARI, G. (1550) *Le Vite de' più eccellenti Architetti, Pittori et Scultori Italiani*, Florence. (2nd ed., 1568; ed. Poggi, Florence, 1919.) (152, 203, 217, 221 f., 226)

[*German trans*.: *Leben der ausgezeichnetsten Maler, Bildhauer und Baumeister* (trans. L. Schorn), Stuttgart, 1843.]

VOLD, J. MOURLY (1910–12) *Über den Traum* (2 vols), Leipzig. (219)

WEISS, E., and FREUD, S. (1970) *See* FREUD, S. (1970a)

WILSON, C. HEATH (1876) *Life and Works of Michelangelo Buonarroti*, London. (259)

WÖLFFLIN, H. (1899) *Die klassische Kunst: eine Einführung in die italienische Renaissance*, Munich. (260)

ZINZOW, A. (1881) *Psyche und Eros*, Halle. (245)

ZWEIG, A., and FREUD, S. (1968) *See* FREUD, S. (1968a)

ZWEIG, S. (1920) *Drei Meister*, Leipzig. (442)
    [*Trans.: Three Masters*, London and New York, 1938.]
    (1927) *Die Verwirrung der Gefühle*, Leipzig. (457)
    [*Trans.: Conflicts*, London and New York, 1939.]

LIST OF ILLUSTRATIONS

PHOTO ACKNOWLEDGEMENTS

Ashmolean Museum: Plate 6; Bulloz: Plates 2, 3; Lichtbildwerkstätte Alpenland: Plates 7, 8; Mansell Collection: Plates 1, 4, 5

LIST OF ABBREVIATIONS

Gesammelte Werke	=	Freud, *Gesammelte Werke* (18 vols), Vols 1–17 London, 1940–52, Vol. 18 Frankfurt am Main, 1968. From 1960 the whole edition published by S. Fischer Verlag, Frankfurt am Main.
S.K.S.N.	=	Freud, *Sammlung kleiner Schriften zur Neurosenlehre* (5 vols), Vienna, 1906–22.
Almanach 1927	=	*Almanach für das Jahr 1927*, Internationaler Psychoanalytischer Verlag, Vienna, 1926.
Almanach 1928	=	*Almanach für das Jahr 1928*, Internationaler Psychoanalytischer Verlag, Vienna, 1927.
Almanach 1930	=	*Almanach der Psychoanalyse 1930*, Internationaler Psychoanalytischer Verlag, Vienna, 1929.
Dichtung und Kunst	=	Freud, *Psychoanalytische Studien an Werken der Dichtung und Kunst*, Vienna, 1924.
Studienausgabe	=	Freud, *Studienausgabe* (10 vols), S. Fischer Verlag, Frankfurt am Main, from 1969.
Collected Papers	=	Freud, *Collected Papers* (5 vols), London, 1924–50.
Standard Edition	=	*The Standard Edition of the Complete Psychological Works of Sigmund Freud* (24 vols), Hogarth Press and The Institute of Psycho-Analysis, London, 1953–74.
P.F.L.	=	*Penguin Freud Library* (15 vols), Penguin Books, Harmondsworth, from 1973.

GENERAL INDEX

This index includes the names of non-technical authors as well as those of technical authors where no reference is made in the text to specific works. For references to specific technical works, the Bibliography should be consulted.